Management for Professionals

The Springer series "Management for Professionals" comprises high-level business and management books for executives, MBA students, and practice-oriented business researchers. The topics cover all themes relevant to businesses and the business ecosystem. The authors are experienced business professionals and renowned professors who combine scientific backgrounds, best practices, and entrepreneurial vision to provide powerful insights into achieving business excellence.
The Series is SCOPUS-indexed.

Susanne Durst • Thomas Henschel
Editors

Small and Medium-Sized Enterprise (SME) Resilience

Strategies for Risk and Crisis Management

Springer

Editors
Susanne Durst
Business and Economics
Reykjavík University
Reykjavik, Iceland

Thomas Henschel
Faculty of Business and Law
HTW Berlin – University of Applied Science
Berlin, Berlin, Germany

ISSN 2192-8096 ISSN 2192-810X (electronic)
Management for Professionals
ISBN 978-3-031-50835-6 ISBN 978-3-031-50836-3 (eBook)
https://doi.org/10.1007/978-3-031-50836-3

This Springer imprint is published by the registered company Springer Nature Switzerland AG
The registered company address is: Gewerbestrasse 11, 6330 Cham, Switzerland

Paper in this product is recyclable.

To Guido
Susanne Durst
To Ilka
Thomas Henschel

Preface

Recent years have provided further examples of how crises have become an inescapable reality of the modern economy. As a result of the recent crises, interest in the topic of resilience has grown even more in the literature and in practice. Until very recently, systematic research into organizational resilience has been very fragmented. This book addresses some of the shortcomings found in the existing literature and provides a detailed analysis of resilience in and for small and medium-sized enterprises (SMEs). This book consists of 16 chapters, identifies the major elements for resilience in SMEs, and provides researchers and practitioners with insights on how to develop more resilient smaller firms.

The study of resilience in and for SMEs is still a relatively new area of research. This book is unique in that it focuses specifically on SMEs and presents approaches and solutions aimed at increasing the number of resilient smaller businesses.

We hope you will enjoy reading the book as much as we have enjoyed reading the individual chapters of this book.

We like to thank our universities – Reykjavik University and Hochschule für Technik und Wirtschaft Berlin – that made possible this project. In particular, we would like to thank the research assistant Maria Stellmacher for her technical support in this project.

Reykjavik, Iceland — Susanne Durst
Berlin, Germany — Thomas Henschel

Introduction to the Book, Its Aim, and Content

Outline

The main motivation for the book is that small and medium-sized enterprises (SMEs) are considered particularly vulnerable to the consequences of crises regardless of its origin. Empirical evidence suggests that SMEs are less resilient in crisis situations due to their often more limited assets and resources as well as their greater dependence on local customers; a situation that seems to be exacerbated by lower risk and crisis management capabilities (Altman et al., 2010; Sauser et al., 2018). Consequently, holistic risk management is critical to developing resilience in organizations. According to McShane (2018), a company needs to develop the ability to adapt to changing circumstances in order to be resilient in the face of associated uncertainty. A company's dynamic capabilities are thus critical to building resilience and reflect a company's ability to continuously adapt and expand its resources (Eisenhardt & Martin, 2000; Helfat, 2007).

This book is an attempt to respond to the aforementioned situation. In the book, risk management is addressed holistically, i.e., viewed from different business functions and combined with a clear focus on continuous learning and the development of dynamic and other capabilities to help improve resilience in SMEs. Thereby, the book is not only intended to facilitate rapid recovery of SMEs but to also help them to look to the future in a sustainable way.

Bringing together carefully selected experts, the book provides an in-depth introduction to resilience in and for SMEs. The book looks at different types of small businesses and sectors to map the diversity and complexity of small business resilience practices. These contextual insights provide interested readers with a unique opportunity for comparative research and learning.

The book is also a stringent continuation of the two editors' earlier books on risk management and crisis management knowledge in SMEs, which were also published by Springer.

Structure of the Book

In the course of the book, the reader gets a broad overview of crisis/risk situations and their possible treatment in theory and practice discussed from different resilience perspectives. Recent research insights are presented by international researchers and practitioners in the field, which will help readers develop and/or expand their understanding of this relevant and topical phenomenon. The broad approach taken in this book can also support in broadening, even changing, the mindset regarding the topic under investigation and its application. Thereby, this book places a focus on crisis management applications dedicated to organizational resilience in SMEs and for SMEs.

In order to achieve the above-mentioned goals, the book consists of 16 chapters that are divided into 3 parts. The idea behind Part I is to introduce the main concept of resilience in general and with regard to SMEs. This is followed by Part II, which provides empirical and theoretical research insights into small business resilience. The book concludes with Part III, which addresses promising future avenues regarding the study of resilience in and for SMEs.

In the following, the content of the individual chapters is briefly highlighted.

Part I: Resilience in and for SMEs – State of Research

In Chap. 1, "Introduction to the Research Topic and Its Domains," Susanne Durst and Thomas Henschel set the overall framework of the book. This chapter provides the necessary conceptual basis on the topic, which is required to get the most out of the book.

It follows with Chap. 2, "Digital Transformation as a Means of Achieving SME Resilience During COVID-19 – A Systematic Review and Future Research Agenda," by A.F.M. Jalal Ahamed on the basis of 37 articles, which proposes a consolidated conceptual mode that could be relevant for informing future research on SME resilience with a particular emphasis on digital transformation enablers.

Maik Störmer and Martin R.W. Hiebl offer in Chap. 3, "How Management Control Systems Can Help Small and Medium-Sized Enterprises Develop Resilience," an integrative review of research linking management control systems and resilience development in SMEs to provide interested fellow researchers ideas for future research avenues in this area.

Part II: Resilience Practice in SMEs from Different Perspectives

In Chap. 4, "Enhancing SMEs Resilience by the Implementation of Business Interruption Insurance: Relevance of ERM and Corporate Governance – A Comparative Study," Monika Wieczorek-Kosmala, Thomas Henschel, and Grzegorz Strupczewski provide the outcomes of a survey involving SMEs from Germany and Poland that explores the relationship between enterprise risk management and corporate governance sophistication.

Börje Boers, Thomas Henschel, and Maria Stellmacher explore in Chap. 5, "The Resilience of Family Firms During Crisis," how family firms manage a crisis from a processual perspective. These authors draw on case studies from German and Swedish family firms.

Chapter 6, "Leveraging Knowledge Management and Entrepreneurial Orientation to Enhance Resilience in Small- and Medium-Sized Enterprises," written by Thomas Henschel, Susanne Durst, and Johanna Salzmann, uses data collected from 284 German SMEs to demonstrate the value of crisis management for SMEs. The study shows the role knowledge management plays in enhancing this value.

Chapter 7, "Conceptual Development of a Resilience Maturity Models for SMEs," by Nadine Otter and Mark Uschkurat, proposes a quantitative maturity model for organizational resilience in SMEs based on a review of the existing literature. The model supports the understanding of organizational resilience in SMEs.

Anke Haag discusses in Chap. 8, "A Perspective on Resilient and Sustainable Financial Strategies for SMEs," relevant regulations that could have an impact on SMEs on developing sustainable financial resilience. A checklist is offered to better deal with this.

Ilka Heinze introduces in Chap. 9, "Playing to Win: Enhancing Resilience in SMEs with Gamifaction," a conceptual framework that includes multiple layers of resilience and is based on gamification to develop and strengthen resilience capabilities in SMEs.

Chapter 10, "Organisational Resilience in German Leasing Companies," by Christian Glaser sheds more light into how organizational resilience might be increased in SMEs operating in more regulated industries such as leasing. The findings are translated into a framework for organizational resilience for leasing companies.

Karin Reinhold in Chap. 11, "Building Resilience: Pillars of Workforce Agility at Organizational and Individual Level in SMEs," provides a list of key messages for owners/owner-managers of SMEs interested in developing an agile workforce.

Chapter 12, "Enterprise Risk Management and Resilience in SMEs During COVID-19 Pandemic: The Case of Italian Dealerships," contributed by Cristina Florio and Laura Brotto, provides some empirical evidence on the usefulness and evolution of enterprise risk management to help small Italian dealerships respond to COVID-19.

Raffaele Testorelli, Anna Tiso, and Chiara Verbano present in Chap. 13, "Increasing Value and Resilience Through Project Risk Management: A Case Study in the IT Consulting Sector," the outcome of a case study that explores how a project risk management system could contribute to value generation and resilience of project members.

Chapter 14, "Unlocking Resource Efficiency: Pathways for Microenterprises in Estonia to Offer Green Products and Services," contributed by Samuel Foli, investigates the enablers of resource efficiency that can serve as pathways for microenterprises in Estonia to offer sustainable products and services.

Part II concludes with a position Chap. 15 by Aive Pevkur, "Position Paper: Resilience in SMEs—What Philosophy and Ethics Got to Do With It?," highlighting that to become a resilient organization the philosophical and ethical dimensions of the concept might be considered as well.

Part III: Conclusions and Outlook

In the final and concluding Chap. 16, "Conclusions & Outlook," Susanne Durst and Thomas Henschel present several promising future research directions for the study of resilience in and for SMEs.

Conclusion

All in all, we are very proud to have created another joint book aimed at readers of different levels, from students to professors, from employees to managers. We are convinced that this book will be a useful tool for these readers to promote and develop more resilient SMEs and thus stronger societies. In addition, we hope that this book will also encourage researchers to conduct more thorough research projects on resilience in general and with regard to resilience in and for SMEs.

References

Altman, E. I., Sabato, G., & Wilson, N. (2010). The value of non-financial information in the risk management of small and medium-sized enterprises. *Journal of Credit Risk, 6*(2), 95–127.

Eisenhardt, K. M., & Martin, J. A. (2000). Dynamic capabilities: What are they? *Strategic Management Journal, 21*(10–11), 1105–1121.

Helfat, C. E. (2007). Stylized facts, empirical research and theory development in management. *Strategic Organization, 5*(2), 185–192.

McShane, M. (2018). Enterprise risk management: History and a design science proposal. *The Journal of Risk Finance, 19*(2), 137–153.

Sauser, B., Baldwin, C., Pourreza, S., Randall, W., & Nowicki, D. (2018). Resilience of small-and medium-sized enterprises as a correlation to community impact: An agent-based modeling approach. *Natural Hazards, 90*, 79–99.

Contents

About the Contributors

A. F. M. Jalal Ahamed is an Associate Professor of Business Administration at the University of Skövde, Sweden. He is the author of several academic and professional articles. He serves on the editorial boards of several international marketing journals, including the *International Journal of Business and Applied Sciences* and *Business Perspective Review*. Research interests include digital marketing, digital consumer behavior, relationship marketing, export-import relationships, and transaction cost theories.

Börje Boers is an Associate Professor in Business Administration at the University of Skövde, School of Business, Sweden. His research interests cover family business, organizational identity, entrepreneurship, governance, and ownership issues. His work has been published in, for instance, *Journal of Enterprising Communities*, *Journal of Family Business Strategy*, *Journal of Family Business Management*, *Management Revue*, and *Journal of Small Business and Entrepreneurship*.

Laura Brotto works as Junior Accountant at Quintegia S.p.A. (Treviso, Italy), a strategic and operational partner for automotive industry players. She is in charge of the business relationships with the automotive industry companies. She has recently graduated in the Master's degree in International Economics and Business at the University of Verona (Italy). Combining her studies with the working activity, she had the opportunity to study risk management in practice.

Susanne Durst is a Full Professor of Management at the Department of Business and Economics at Reykjavik University (Iceland) and an Adjunct Professor at Tallinn University of Technology (Estonia). She is also a Visiting Professor at LUT Business School, LUT University (Finland). Her research interests include knowledge (risk) management, innovation management, responsible digitalization, and sustainable business development in the context of small entrepreneurial companies. She has been conducting several national and international research projects. Her work has been awarded different awards and has been published in international peer-reviewed journals. Before joining academia, she worked with private enterprises of different size and industry.

Cristina Florio is Associate Professor of Accounting at the University of Verona, Italy. Her research interests focus on financial and non-financial disclosure, auditing, and enterprise risk management. She is a member of the Committee of the European Risk Research Network. She was guest editor for *Journal of Management and Governance* and has published in top ranked international journals. She won the best paper award assigned by the Institute of Risk Management at the 6th European risk conference.

Samuel Foli holds a master's degree in Business Administration (MBA) at the American University of Malta (AUM), and B.Sc. in Actuarial Science from University of Ghana. He is currently writing his doctoral thesis. He has published in several internationally recognized peer-reviewed journals such as *Journal of Knowledge Management*, *Technology in Society*, and *Management Review Quarterly*. His research interests include knowledge (risk) management, business sustainability, supply chain risk management, and statistical/mathematical modelling.

Christian Glaser graduated from the University of Portsmouth (UK) and received his doctoral degree for researching risk management practices in the German leasing industry. He worked as the chief risk officer of a medium-sized financial servicing firm for more than 10 years and is a lecturer on risk management at two German universities. Furthermore, he is a book author for Springer and a speaker on risk management and financial services-related topics.

Anke Haag is Professor of Business Administration especially Corporate Banking at Technische Hochschule Mittelhessen (Germany). Her specific research interests are in the areas of financing issues of small and medium-sized enterprises (SMEs), credit guarantee schemes, and sustainable finance. Her work has been published in international peer-reviewed journals. She has around 15 years working experience in banking and finance.

Ilka Heinze studied Business Administration and Psychology, earning her Ph.D. with a focus on the learning strategies of failed entrepreneurs. After working as Assistant Director leading one of the HR teams at EY, she started her own business as independent consultant and trainer, leveraging her extensive expertise to assist both medium-sized and international companies in matters of personnel and organizational management, as well as diagnosing and shaping organizational processes. Furthermore, in 2021 she has been appointed to a professorship for Business Psychology and Management at Hochschule Fresenius.

Thomas Henschel is Professor of Management Accounting at the Business School of Hochschule für Technik und Wirtschaft Berlin (Germany). He has held visiting positions at universities in Denmark, Sweden, the United Kingdom, and Italy. His research interests are risk management and crisis management in small and medium-sized enterprises (SMEs). He has published widely in academic journals and serves on the *Journal of International Business and Economic Affairs* editorial board. He is co-editor of the books *Knowledge Risk Management* and *Crisis Management* in Springer's Management for Professionals series.

Martin R. W. Hiebl is Professor of Management Accounting and Control at the University of Siegen, Germany, and Visiting Professor at Johannes Kepler University Linz, Austria. His research focuses on management accounting, management control, and risk management, with an emphasis on small and family-owned businesses. He is co-editor of the German practitioner journal *Controlling – Zeitschrift für erfolgsorientierte Unternehmenssteuerung*, editor of the *European Management Review*, and associate editor of the *Review of Managerial Science* and *the Journal of Accounting and Organizational Change.*

Nadine Otter is a research assistant at the Chair of Business Administration, in particular Accounting and Auditing, at Helmut Schmidt University/University of the Federal Armed Forces Hamburg.In addition, she is a lecturer and examiner at the Euro-FH for the modules "Methodical Problems of External Accounting, Corporate Governance and Company Evaluation" and "Cost and Activity Accounting & Controlling as well as Organization and Corporate Management" from the field of applied business administration within the framework of the §8a WPO Master's program.Within the scope of her previous work as an officer in the logistic system of the air force, she was employed in various areas, which include Logistics, Controlling and Process Management, Cost and Performance Accounting, and Quality Management.The focus of her dissertation was on risk management in public administration, conducting a maturity analysis in the ministry of defense. Her recent publications focus on sustainability reporting.

Aive Pevkur practical philosophy, is a senior lecturer in Tallinn University of Technology and national and international expert in professional and public ethics, and integrity. Dr Pevkur has more than 25 years of experience in teaching philosophy and ethics-related courses in different educational level and designing and conducting ethics research projects in Estonia and internationally. She is an author and co-author of articles and books on ethics and values in public sphere and professional life.

Karin Reinhold has been employed as an Associate Professor in Organization and Management Research Group by Tallinn University of Technology since 2009. She has been active in academic research over 20 years. Her main research interests in recent years are related to risk management in working environments, employees' well-being and health, artificial intelligence-based worker management systems and health and safety practices in SMEs. She has published over 70 scientific articles and has been involved in several EU scientific projects as a project leader, main coordinator, investigator or national expert. She has been advising and consulting in risk and safety field the following industries: manufacturing, energy, aviation, public transport, education, private services etc. She has worked as an advisor for governmental bodies in health and safety issues. In her current position in the university, she is also supervising the master level students as well as a number of PhD students.

Johanna Salzmann is an alumni of the Business School, Hochschule für Technik und Wirtschaft Berlin. In 2022, she graduated with a degree in Business Administration, specializing in investment and financing as well as digital business. Besides her studies, she completed a research internship on crisis management. She supported Prof. Dr. Thomas Henschel in forming a structural equation model from a statistical perspective. Today, she is an IT project manager and supports the expansion of the digital infrastructure in the energy sector.

Maria Stellmacher is a student of Business Administration at the Business School Hochschule für Technik und Wirtschaft in Berlin. Since 2020, she has been working there as a research assistant in the field of risk management in small and medium-sized enterprises, supporting Thomas Henschel in his research work in this area. In addition, she participated in surveys on failure learning and its statistical evaluation.

Maik Störmer is currently a financial controller for a globally active group of businesses in the waste management sector. He studied Controlling and Risk Management at the University of Siegen and graduated with a Master of Science in 2023. During his studies, he specialized in operational and strategic control systems as well as performance management. His research interests focus on small and medium-sized enterprises and their resilience.

Grzegorz Strupczewski is a professional researcher, analyst, and university teacher in insurance and cyber security. He has 20 years of research experience in insurance market, risk management, risk modelling, reinsurance, cyber security, and information security systems based on ISO/IEC 27001. He is a certified insurance broker and auditor of ISO/IEC 27001 compliance and contractor of research projects, business consulting, and cyber-awareness training. He is a member of ERRN and other risk management-related scientific associations.

Raffaele Testorelli is an expert manager, advisor, and educator. He helps executives, government officials, entrepreneurs, and students understand the fast-changing competitive landscape, design future-proof strategies, and effectively lead future-ready organizations, seizing the opportunities and challenges of turbulent environments increasingly dominated by digital business. His major interests include business strategy and management, entrepreneurship and innovation, digital transformation, program and project management, and risk management in industrial contexts. In these fields, he has gained 25+ years of senior management experience in national and international industrial projects, across multiple business sectors, with leadership roles. He is author and co-author of scientific publications on the topics.

Anna Tiso is a third-year Ph.D. student at the Department of Management and Engineering of the University of Padova, Italy. Her research interests center around healthcare operations management, with a focus on health lean management, but also project management, and risk management in industrial and clinical contexts. She has contributed to this research fields with publications as author and co-author.

Mark Uschkurat is a Ph.D. candidate at the Department of General Business Administration, in particular Accounting and Auditing, at Helmut Schmidt University/University of the Federal Armed Forces Hamburg. His research is in the area of organizational resilience. He is particularly interested in answering the question of how accounting and financial reporting helps Stakeholder to assess the resilience of small- and medium-sized enterprises. Mark has over 8 years' experience in auditing small- and medium-sized as well as listed enterprises and is a German Certified Tax Advisor (Steuerberater) and German Public Auditor (Wirtschaftsprüfer).

Chiara Verbano is an Associate Professor of Innovation and Project Management at the Department of Management and Engineering of the University of Padova (Italy) and Programme Coordinator of the 1^cycle Degree in Engineering and Management. Her major research interests include risk management both in industrial and clinical context and healthcare operations management. In these fields, she participated to various national and international research projects, funded by public and private organizations. She has regularly contributed to scientific journals as a reviewer, and she is author and co-author of more than 100 scientific publications.

Monika Wieczorek-Kosmala has a post-Ph.D. in Finance. She is currently Associate Professor at the College of Finance, University of Economics in Katowice, Poland. Her research interests and expertise merge risk management and financial management, with a special interest in the financial outcomes of business interruptions. She is a member of the Committee of the European Risk Research Network. She also has professional experience in risk management and property insurance.

Part I

Resilience in and for SMEs – State of Research

Introduction to the Research Topic and Its Domains

1

Susanne Durst and Thomas Henschel

1.1 Definition and Concept of Resilience

The first chapter of this book is a general introduction to the topic of resilience, thus developing the necessary background to the book. This chapter overviews the relevant terms and explores resilience's meaning, concept, and scope. It is essential to understand that there is no single definition of resilience or one right way to pursue it. The chapter is designed to help readers think strategically rather than provide specific solutions to suit particular situations. The chapter considers, in a concise way, the whole concept of resilience and its importance for SMEs and the economy/ society in general.

Resilience is a concept that has been studied in many fields, including psychology, ecology, engineering, and economics. Despite differences in specific applications, there seems to be agreement that resilience generally refers to the ability of a system or person to cope with and recover from adversity. The following sections explore different definitions and conceptualizations of resilience in different disciplines.

Psychological Resilience

Psychological resilience refers to the ability of an individual to cope with and adapt to adversity or stress. One of the most widely used definitions of psychological

S. Durst (✉)
Reykjavik University, Reykjavik, Iceland
e-mail: susanned@ru.is

T. Henschel (✉)
Hochschule für Technik und Wirtschaft Berlin, University of Applied Sciences, Berlin, Germany
e-mail: henschel@htw-berlin.de

S. Durst, T. Henschel (eds.), *Small and Medium-Sized Enterprise (SME) Resilience*, Management for Professionals, https://doi.org/10.1007/978-3-031-50836-3_1

resilience comes from Masten and Reed (2002), who define resilience as "the capacity of a dynamic system to withstand or recover from significant disturbance or adversity that threatens its survival, function, or development" (p. 72). This definition highlights the dynamic nature of resilience and its relevance across different levels of analysis. Resilience in psychology is conceptualized as a set of skills or characteristics that enable individuals to cope with and overcome adversity. Luthar et al. (2020), for example, identified three key factors that contribute to resilience in children: (1) a positive attitude and sense of humor, (2) the ability to regulate emotions and cope with stress, and (3) a supportive social network.

However, resilience is not solely a product of individual characteristics or skills. It is also influenced by the environment in which an individual operates. For example, Rutter (1987) proposed that resilience is the result of a so-called protective triad of factors: (1) individual characteristics (e.g., intelligence, temperament), (2) supportive relationships (e.g., with parents, peers, or teachers), and (3) external resources (e.g., access to healthcare, education, or employment opportunities).

Ecological Resilience

Ecological resilience refers to the ability of an ecosystem to maintain its structure and function in the face of disturbance or change. Ecological resilience emerged from ecology, where it was initially used to describe the ability of ecosystems to resist or recover from disturbance (Holling, 1973). There are multiple definitions of ecological resilience in the literature. However, one commonly used definition comes from Folke et al. (2004), who define ecological resilience as "the capacity of a social-ecological system to absorb disturbance and reorganize while undergoing change to retain essentially still the same function, structure, identity, and feedback" (p. 557). This definition emphasizes the interdependence between ecological and social systems and the importance of maintaining essential functions and feedback within an ecosystem. Ecological resilience can be influenced by a range of factors, including biodiversity, resource availability, and the presence of keystone species (Holling, 1996).

Engineering Resilience

In engineering, resilience refers to the ability of a system to withstand and recover from shock or failure (Bodin & Wiman, 2004; Hollnagel et al., 2006). Engineering resilience has been applied to various systems, including buildings, transportation networks, and power grids. One commonly used definition of engineering resilience comes from Bruneau et al. (2003), who define resilience as "the ability of a system to resist or recover from damage or disruption and to continue to function" (p. 733). This definition highlights the importance of resistance to initial damage and the ability to recover from that damage. Engineering resilience can be enhanced through a range of strategies, including redundancy (i.e., having multiple components that can perform the same function), diversity (i.e., having different types of components that can perform different functions), and modularity (i.e., having components that can be easily replaced or reconfigured) (Holling, 1973; Walker et al., 2004).

Economic Resilience
Economic resilience refers to the ability of an economy to withstand and recover from shocks or disruptions. Economic resilience is influenced by various factors, including the diversity of industries and the availability of financial resources and government support facilities (Rose, 2004; Martin & Sunley, 2015).

To summarize, resilience has become crucial in various fields, including organizational management, engineering, and disaster management. The ability to withstand and recover from disruptions is essential to building and maintaining sustainable organizations, systems, and communities (Williams et al., 2017).

1.2 Individual Versus Organizational Resilience

The concept of resilience is further divided into individual and organizational resilience; these forms are presented in the following.

Individual Resilience
Individual resilience refers to the ability of an individual to cope with and recover from adversity or stress (psychological resilience). It is often studied in psychology and can be influenced by various individual and environmental factors. Individual resilience is not a fixed trait but a dynamic process that can change over time (Luthans et al., 2006; Bonanno & Mancini, 2012; Masten, 2013). It can be enhanced through various strategies, including developing coping skills, social support, and cultivating positive emotions and attitudes (Coutu, 2002). Research on individual resilience has identified several factors that can contribute to resilience. These include:

- Positive attitude: Individuals with a positive attitude tend to be more resilient and better able to cope with stress. This may be because a positive attitude can help individuals see challenges as opportunities for growth and learning (Weick & Sutcliffe, 2006).
- Emotional regulation: Individuals who can regulate their emotions effectively tend to be more resilient. Emotional regulation involves recognizing and managing one's emotions in an adaptive, not disruptive way (Avey et al., 2009).
- Social support: A supportive social network can help individuals cope with stress and adversity. Social support can come from family, friends, or other sources and can provide emotional and practical assistance during difficult times (Richtnér & Löfsten, 2014).
- Self-efficacy: Individuals with a sense of self-efficacy (i.e., the belief in one's ability to accomplish tasks and goals) tend to be more resilient. Self-efficacy can help individuals feel more in control of their lives and better cope with challenges (Akgün & Keskin, 2014).
- Flexibility: Adapting to changing circumstances is an essential aspect of resilience. Individuals who are flexible and able to adjust their goals and expectations as needed tend to be more resilient.

- A sense of purpose: Having a sense of purpose or meaning in life can help individuals cope with adversity. This may be because a sense of purpose can provide motivation and a sense of direction during difficult times.

Environmental factors, such as access to resources and social support, can also influence individual resilience. For example, individuals who live in poverty or communities with limited resources may have fewer opportunities to develop resilience. Similarly, individuals who lack social support may have a more challenging time coping with adversity.

Organizational Resilience

Organizational resilience refers to an organization's ability to withstand and recover from a crisis (Välikangas & Hamel, 2003). Resilient organizations can adapt to changing circumstances, maintain business continuity, and operate effectively in the face of adversity (Weick & Sutcliffe, 2015).

As with individual resilience, research on organizational resilience has also identified several key factors that can contribute to resilience at the organizational level (Conz & Magnani, 2020; Williams et al., 2017; Bhamra & Dani, 2011; Henschel & Lantzsch, 2022; Durst et al., 2022). These include the following:

- Risk management: Effective risk management is essential for building resilience. Organizations must identify potential risks and vulnerabilities, assess their impact and likelihood, and develop strategies to mitigate or manage them.
- Resource management: The effective management of resources, including financial, technological, and human resources, can also contribute to organizational resilience. Organizations need to allocate resources strategically and adaptively to meet the changing demands of the business environment.
- Adaptability: Adaptable and flexible organizations can better respond to changes in the business environment and to unexpected disruptions. This may involve changing strategies, products, or services, learning from past experiences, and adapting to new circumstances.
- Collaboration: Collaboration and cooperation among different parts of the organization, as well as with external stakeholders, can help build resilience. Effective communication and coordination can ensure that resources are used effectively and that responses to disruptions are coordinated and efficient.
- Leadership: Effective leadership is essential for building resilience. Leaders must inspire and motivate employees, make tough decisions, and create a culture supporting resilience.
- Business continuity planning: Organizations with effective business continuity plans can better maintain essential functions and services during disruptions. These plans should include contingency plans, backup systems, and alternative work arrangements.
- Crisis management: Effective crisis management is essential for responding to unexpected disruptions. Organizations should have clear protocols and proce-

dures for responding to different types of crises and trained personnel who can implement these procedures effectively.

1.3 The Current State of Research on Resilience

This section provides a short overview of the current state of research on resilience. Thereby, the focus is put on research on organizational resilience.

Organizational resilience has gained increasing attention recently as a critical capability for firms to navigate turbulent environments (Williams et al., 2017). A review of prior literature reveals several key findings that shed light on the importance of organizational resilience.

- Firstly, research has highlighted the role of leadership in fostering resilience within organizations. For example, Linnenluecke and Griffiths (2010) found that proactive leadership is crucial for building resilience and enabling organizations to respond effectively to shocks. Similarly, Hong and Liao emphasized the importance of transformational leadership in promoting organizational resilience and adapting to changing circumstances.
- Secondly, scholars have emphasized the importance of organizational culture in developing resilience. This view is supported by research by Shi et al. (2018), who found that a supportive and adaptable culture positively relates to organizational resilience.
- Finally, prior research has explored the relationship between resilience and other vital organizational capabilities. For example, Lacity and Willcocks (2013) found that more agile and responsive firms are more resilient to external shocks. Not surprisingly, resilience has become a popular concept in the field of management, particularly in the context of organizations responding to adversity. Research has shown that resilient organizations are better equipped to cope with challenges, adapt to changing circumstances, and recover from setbacks (Chrisman et al., 2011; Pal et al., 2014).

Several studies have been conducted to understand the concept of organizational resilience, including systematic reviews and meta-analyses. For example, Conz and Magnani (2020) conducted a systematic review of the literature on the resilience of firms and developed a framework for future research in this area. They argued that resilience should be viewed as a dynamic process involving both proactive and reactive strategies and that resilience can be influenced by various factors, including organizational culture, leadership, and strategy. Similarly, Bhamra and Dani (2011) conducted a comprehensive literature review on organizational resilience and proposed a framework for understanding the concept. They defined resilience as an organization's ability to cope with unexpected events and disruptions. Bhamra and Dani (2011) identified several crucial factors contributing to organizational resilience, including flexibility, redundancy, and collaboration.

For instance, Williams et al. (2017) built on these earlier studies by examining the relationship between crisis management and resilience research streams. They argued that while these two streams of research are often studied separately, they are inherently linked and should be considered together to understand better how organizations can effectively respond to adversity.

Furthermore, prior research has highlighted the role of leadership and organizational culture in building resilience and improving financial performance. For instance, Conz and Magnani (2020) found that transformational leadership and a supportive organizational culture were positively associated with organizational resilience and financial performance. Korhonen et al. studied Finnish SMEs and found that resilient firms had higher sales growth and profitability than non-resilient firms.

In addition to these empirical studies, several conceptual frameworks have been proposed to explain the relationship between organizational resilience and financial performance. For instance, Liu et al. (2018) proposed a framework based on the dynamic capability theory, which suggests that firms with higher levels of dynamic capabilities are better equipped to respond to environmental changes and thus have better financial performance.

On the other hand, organizations also require practical and actionable frameworks for managing risk and responding to adversity. Williams et al.'s (2017) model, for instance, offers a practical approach to crisis management by breaking down the response process into four stages: prevention, preparation, response, and recovery. Such an approach is critical in the fast-paced and unpredictable business environment, where organizations must quickly adapt to changes and respond to unexpected challenges.

The study of resilience in small firms has also increased recently; heavily triggered by the pandemic and its consequences. This research is vital, considering that small firms are often subject to various external shocks, including changes in economic conditions, competition, technological advances, and natural disasters (Eggers, 2020).

A growing body of literature has focused on the factors contributing to small firms' resilience. One key factor is the entrepreneurial orientation of the firm. This concept refers to the degree to which the firm is focused on innovation, risk-taking, and proactivity. Studies have shown that firms with a high entrepreneurial orientation are more likely to be resilient in the face of external shocks (Herbane, 2013; Morrish & Jones, 2020; Boers & Henschel, 2022a).

Another critical factor is the firm's social capital. This refers to the firm's relationships with other firms, organizations, and individuals in its network. Studies have shown that firms with substantial social capital are more likely to be resilient in the face of external shocks. Again, this is because they can better access resources, knowledge, and support from their network.

The leadership style of the firm is also crucial in building resilience. Research has shown that transformational leadership, which emphasizes inspiring and empowering employees, is associated with greater resilience in small firms.

Transformational leaders can better motivate employees to work toward the firm's goals and adapt to changing circumstances (Williams et al., 2017).

The empirical evidence on what resilience strategies SMEs apply and are successful is scarce. The few identified literature sources mostly use qualitative research methods such as focus groups (Branicki et al., 2018), in-depth research interviews, single case studies (Hong et al., 2012), and longitudinal case studies (Pathak et al., 2023).

For example, the papers by Conz (2016), Hong et al. (2012), and Zutshi et al. (2022) discuss the resilience strategies of small- and medium-sized enterprises (SMEs) operating in various industrial clusters. The authors aimed to identify the different resilience strategies SMEs use to cope with external shocks, such as economic crises, changes in customer preferences, and technological disruptions.

- The first resilience strategy identified was diversification. SMEs diversified their product and service offerings, customer base, and geographic reach to mitigate the impact of external shocks. For example, SMEs expanded their product lines or entered new markets to reduce dependence on a single product or market.
- The second resilience strategy identified was collaboration. SMEs in the studies collaborated with other firms in their cluster, suppliers, customers, and research institutions to share knowledge and resources, access new markets, and develop new products and services. The collaboration helped SMEs reduce costs, increase efficiency, and improve their competitive position.
- The third resilience strategy identified was innovation. SMEs invest in research and development (R&D) to develop new products and services, adopt new technologies, and improve their production processes. Innovation helped SMEs differentiate themselves from competitors, increase efficiency, and reduce costs.
- The fourth resilience strategy identified was responsiveness. SMEs quickly adapted to changes in the business environment, such as changes in customer preferences, new regulations, and economic crises. SMEs that were responsive to changes were better equipped to survive and thrive in turbulent times.

The literature highlighted the importance of a supportive institutional environment, such as the presence of industry associations, research institutions, and government policies, in enabling SMEs to adopt resilience strategies (Boers & Henschel, 2022b). As Hong et al. (2012) point out, relationship building and network strength are essential levers to enhance SMEs' resilience and success further.

Overall, the literature suggests that resilience in small firms is a complex phenomenon influenced by a range of factors, including the entrepreneurial orientation of the firm, its social capital, leadership style, and organizational learning and adaptation (Branicki et al., 2018). By understanding these factors, policymakers and practitioners can develop strategies to support the resilience of small firms, which is critical for economic development and growth (Fasth et al., 2022).

1.4 Fusion of the Concepts of Crisis Management and Resilience

In today's rapidly changing and unpredictable business environment, organizations face a range of crises that can threaten their operations and survival (Durst & Henschel, 2022). Organizations must be prepared to respond quickly and effectively to unexpected disruptions, from natural disasters to cyberattacks and pandemics. At the same time, building resilience has become increasingly important to ensure organizations' long-term sustainability and success. In this context, integrating crisis management and resilience has emerged as a critical strategy for organizations to better prepare for and respond to disruptions (Williams et al., 2017).

Crisis management is a set of processes and strategies designed to help organizations respond to unexpected events that threaten their operations or reputation. Effective crisis management involves various activities, including risk assessment, planning, communication, and response. It is a critical component of organizational resilience, as it helps organizations to better prepare for and respond to unexpected disruptions (Durst & Henschel, 2021).

Resilience, on the other hand, refers to the ability of organizations to adapt and recover from disruptions. It involves building the capacity to withstand and respond to adversity, to learn from past experiences, and to anticipate and prepare for future challenges. Building resilience requires a range of activities, including risk management, resource management, adaptability, collaboration, leadership, business continuity planning, and crisis management (Brewton et al., 2010).

Integrating crisis management and resilience involves aligning these two approaches to build a more comprehensive and effective response to disruptions. This integration can take several forms, including incorporating resilience-building activities into crisis management planning, leveraging crisis management activities to build resilience, and using resilience-building strategies to enhance crisis response (Williams et al., 2017).

One approach to integrating crisis management and resilience is incorporating resilience-building activities into crisis management planning. This may involve conducting a risk assessment to identify potential disruptions and vulnerabilities, developing business continuity plans to maintain essential functions and services during disruptions, and building relationships with external stakeholders to enhance collaboration and communication during crises. By incorporating resilience-building activities into crisis management planning, organizations can ensure that they are better prepared to respond to disruptions and recover quickly (Hong et al., 2012).

Another approach to integrating crisis management and resilience is to leverage crisis management activities to build resilience. This may involve using crises to learn from past experiences and identify improvement areas. For example, organizations may review their response after a crisis to identify strengths and weaknesses and opportunities to enhance their resilience. By leveraging crises to build resilience, organizations can learn from their experiences and develop the capacity to withstand future disruptions better (Heinze, 2013).

A third approach to integrating crisis management and resilience is to use resilience-building strategies to enhance crisis response. This may involve building the capacity to adapt quickly to changing circumstances, leveraging social networks and partnerships to enhance collaboration and communication, and fostering a culture of resilience that encourages innovation and learning (Boers & Henschel, 2022a). Organizations can better respond to disruptions and maintain essential functions and services by using resilience-building strategies to enhance crisis response.

Research has highlighted several key benefits of integrating crisis management and resilience. For example, integrating crisis management and resilience can help organizations to better prepare for and respond to disruptions, reduce the risk of reputational damage and financial losses, and enhance organizational agility and innovation (Conz & Magnani, 2020). Additionally, integrating crisis management and resilience can help foster a culture of resilience within the organization, enhancing employee engagement and retention and improving overall organizational performance (Williams et al., 2017).

From a research perspective, Williams et al. (2017) explore the integration of crisis management and resilience research streams. They argue that both approaches are essential for effective organizational response to adversity. Crisis management research focuses on responding to disruptions and minimizing their impact, while resilience research focuses on the ability to adapt and recover from disruptions. They argue that these themes overlap in both research streams and that a fusion can lead to a more comprehensive understanding of organizational response to adversity. Williams et al. (2017) propose a conceptual model for integrating crisis management and resilience research that includes four stages: proactive preparedness, reactive response, adaptive recovery, and reflective learning. They argue that each stage builds on the previous one and that a comprehensive approach to organizational response to adversity should incorporate all four stages.

Finally, Pathak et al. (2023) and Conz and Magnani (2020) stress that integrating crisis management and resilience research streams can lead to a more comprehensive understanding of organizational response to adversity. They suggest that future research should focus on the practical implications of the integrated approach, such as developing tools and frameworks that SMEs can use to enhance their resilience and crisis management capabilities.

1.5 The Dark Side of the Resilience Concept

Resilience research in the context of small firms focuses on understanding how these organizations can adapt, survive, and thrive in the face of adversity. While resilience is generally seen as a positive concept, certain aspects can be considered potential dark sides or limitations in the research and its application to small firms. Researchers and practitioners should be aware of these potential dark sides and work toward a more nuanced and comprehensive understanding of resilience in the context of small firms. The authors of this chapter consider it essential that not only the good side of resilience is presented but also any downsides to enabling a more holistic view of the concept.

Resilience is often regarded as a desirable trait for organizations, enabling them to cope with adverse situations and bounce back from crises (Bhamra & Dani, 2011). However, growing evidence shows that excessive resilience can negatively affect firms in the long run (Williams et al., 2017).

One negative effect of resilience is that it can lead to complacency and overconfidence. When organizations are highly resilient, they may become less vigilant about potential threats and fail to take proactive measures to address them. This can leave them vulnerable to unexpected shocks and disruptions (Vogus & Sutcliffe, 2007; Shepherd, 2003). Another adverse effect of resilience is that it can stifle innovation and change. Firms that are too focused on maintaining their existing operations and systems may be less inclined to explore new ideas and technologies (Williams & Shepherd, 2016). This can leave them at a disadvantage in a rapidly changing business environment.

Furthermore, excessive resilience can lead to organizational rigidity and inflexibility. When firms become too focused on maintaining their current processes and structures, they may be less able to adapt to changing market conditions or customer needs. It can limit their ability to innovate and grow over time. In addition, excessive resilience can lead to a lack of diversity and overreliance on a narrow range of products or markets. When firms are highly resilient, they may be less inclined to explore new business areas or diversify their product offerings. This can leave them vulnerable to shifts in consumer preferences or changes in the competitive landscape (Durst & Henschel, 2021). Finally, excessive resilience can lead to a lack of accountability and a reluctance to take risks (Tinsley et al., 2012). When SMEs become too focused on avoiding failure and maintaining the status quo, they may be less willing to take calculated risks and pursue new opportunities (Durst & Henschel, 2021). This can limit their ability to grow and innovate over time.

Resilience research primarily focuses on short-term outcomes, such as survival or recovery from a crisis (Pathak et al., 2023). While these outcomes are essential, they may not capture the complete picture of small firm resilience. Neglecting long-term outcomes, such as growth, innovation, or sustained success, may result in an incomplete understanding of resilience and hinder the development of strategies that promote long-term viability (Branicki et al., 2018).

Furthermore, resilience research may not sufficiently address systemic issues that impact small firms. These can include structural inequalities, regulatory barriers, or broader economic and social factors disproportionately affecting small businesses (Dejardin et al., 2023). Focusing solely on individual-level factors and internal strategies might overlook small firms' more significant systemic challenges and limit the effectiveness of resilience interventions (Conz & Magnani, 2020; Conz et al., 2017). In summary, while resilience can be valuable for firms, excessive resilience can negatively affect their long-term success. Organizations must balance resilience and flexibility, innovation and stability, and risk taking and caution to thrive in today's business environment (Eggers, 2020).

1.6 Conclusion

This introductory chapter has concisely introduced the concept of resilience, its different types, and recent research. It could be underlined that research in this area is done from different perspectives and is somewhat fragmented particularly when SMEs are addressed. The present book addresses the latter by emphasizing the relevance of the concept for SMEs and offers different ideas and approaches, to develop more resilient smaller firms.

In this book, the concept of resilience is addressed holistically, i.e., viewed from different business functions and combined with a clear focus on continuous learning and the development of dynamic capabilities to help improve resilience in SMEs. The book is intended to facilitate the rapid recovery of SMEs and help them look to the future with success. These contextual differences will give interested readers a unique learning opportunity.

References

Akgün, A. E., & Keskin, H. (2014). Organisational resilience capacity and firm product innovativeness and performance. *International Journal of Production Research, 52*(23), 6918–6937. https://doi.org/10.1080/00207543.2014.910624

Avey, J. B., Luthans, F., & Jensen, S. M. (2009). Psychological capital: A positive resource for combating employee stress and turnover. *Human Resource Management, 48*(5), 677–693. https://doi.org/10.1002/hrm.20294

Bhamra, R., & Dani, S. (2011). Creating resilient SMEs. *International Journal of Production Research, 49*(18), 5373–5374. https://doi.org/10.1080/00207543.2011.563999

Bodin, P., & Wiman, B. (2004). Resilience and other stability concepts in ecology: Notes on their origin, validity, and usefulness. *ESS Bulletin, 2*(2), 33–43.

Boers, B., & Henschel, T. (2022a). Different crises in family SMEs and how to prepare for them. In S. Durst & T. Henschel (Eds.), *Springer eBook collection. Crisis management for small and medium-sized enterprises (SMEs): Strategies for external crises* (pp. 101–117). Springer International Publishing; Imprint Springer. https://doi.org/10.1007/978-3-030-91727-2_8

Boers, B., & Henschel, T. (2022b). The role of entrepreneurial orientation in crisis management: Evidence from family firms in enterprising communities. *Journal of Enterprising Communities: People and Places in the Global Economy, 16*(5), 756–780. https://doi.org/10.1108/JEC-12-2020-0210

Bonanno, G. A., & Mancini, A. D. (2012). Beyond resilience and PTSD: Mapping the heterogeneity of responses to potential trauma. *Psychological Trauma: Theory, Research, Practice, and Policy, 4*(1), 74–83. https://doi.org/10.1037/a0017829

Branicki, L. J., Sullivan-Taylor, B., & Livschitz, S. R. (2018). How entrepreneurial resilience generates resilient SMEs. *International Journal of Entrepreneurial Behavior & Research, 24*(7), 1244–1263. https://doi.org/10.1108/IJEBR-11-2016-0396

Brewton, K. E., Danes, S. M., Stafford, K., & Haynes, G. W. (2010). Determinants of rural and urban family firm resilience. *Journal of Family Business Strategy, 1*(3), 155–166. https://doi.org/10.1016/j.jfbs.2010.08.003

Bruneau, M., Chang, S. E., Eguchi, R. T., Lee, G. C., O'Rourke, T. D., Reinhorn, A. M., Shinozuka, M., Tierney, K., Wallace, W. A., & von Winterfeldt, D. (2003). A framework to quantitatively assess and enhance the seismic resilience of communities. *Earthquake Spectra, 19*(4), 733–752. https://doi.org/10.1193/1.1623497

Chrisman, J. J., Chua, J. H., & Steier, L. P. (2011). Resilience of family firms: An introduction. *Entrepreneurship Theory and Practice, 35*(6), 1107–1119. https://doi.org/10.1111/j.1540-6520.2011.00493.x

Conz, E. (2016, September 6). The resilience of firms: A conceptualization through inductive content analysis. In *BAM 2016. Thriving in turbulent times*. Newcastle University.

Conz, E., & Magnani, G. (2020). A dynamic perspective on the resilience of firms: A systematic literature review and a framework for future research. *European Management Journal, 38*(3), 400–412. https://doi.org/10.1016/j.emj.2019.12.004

Conz, E., Denicolai, S., & Zucchella, A. (2017). The resilience strategies of SMEs in mature clusters. *Journal of Enterprising Communities: People and Places in the Global Economy, 11*(1), 186–210. https://doi.org/10.1108/JEC-02-2015-0015

Coutu, D. (2002). How resilience works. *Harvard Business Review, 80*(5), 46–56.

Dejardin, M., Raposo, M. L., Ferreira, J. J., Fernandes, C. I., Veiga, P. M., & Farinha, L. (2023). The impact of dynamic capabilities on SME performance during COVID-19. *Review of Managerial Science, 17*(5), 1703–1729. https://doi.org/10.1007/s11846-022-00569-x

Durst, S., & Henschel, T. (2021). COVID-19 as an accelerator for developing strong(er) businesses? Insights from Estonian small firms. *Journal of the International Council for Small Business, 2*(1), 1–29. https://doi.org/10.1080/26437015.2020.1859935

Durst, S., & Henschel, T. (2022). Crisis management: From a theoretical point of view. In S. Durst & T. Henschel (Eds.), *Springer eBook collection. Crisis management for small and medium-sized enterprises (SMEs): Strategies for external crises* (pp. 9–14). Springer International Publishing; Imprint Springer. https://doi.org/10.1007/978-3-030-91727-2_2

Durst, S., Henschel, T., & Salzmann, J. (2022). Crisis management practices in small- and medium-sized firms. In S. Durst & T. Henschel (Eds.), *Springer eBook collection. Crisis management for small and medium-sized enterprises (SMEs): Strategies for external crises* (pp. 15–27). Springer International Publishing; Imprint Springer. https://doi.org/10.1007/978-3-030-91727-2_3

Eggers, F. (2020). Masters of disasters? Challenges and opportunities for SMEs in times of crisis. *Journal of Business Research, 116*, 199–208. https://doi.org/10.1016/j.jbusres.2020.05.025

Fasth, J., Åkerman, N., Elliot, V., & Hilmersson, M. (2022). Small and medium-sized enterprises response to Covid-19: The effect of external openness and procedural management. *International Small Business Journal, 41*, 465–487. https://doi.org/10.1177/02662426221101528

Folke, C., Carpenter, S., Walker, B., Scheffer, M., Elmqvist, T., Gunderson, L., & Holling, C. S. (2004). Regime shifts, resilience, and biodiversity in ecosystem management. *Annual Review of Ecology, Evolution, and Systematics, 35*(1), 557–581. https://doi.org/10.1146/annurev.ecolsys.35.021103.105711

Heinze, I. (2013). Entrepreneur sense-making of business failure. *Small Enterprise Research, 20*(1), 21–39. https://doi.org/10.5172/ser.2013.20.1.21

Henschel, T., & Lantzsch, A. D. (2022). The relationship between ERM and performance revisited: Empirical evidence from SMEs. In C. Florio, M. Wieczorek-Kosmala, P. M. Linsley, & P. Shrives (Eds.), *Risk management* (Vol. 20, pp. 95–113). Springer International Publishing. https://doi.org/10.1007/978-3-030-88374-4_5

Herbane, B. (2013). Exploring crisis management in UK small- and medium-sized enterprises. *Journal of Contingencies and Crisis Management, 21*(2), 82–95. https://doi.org/10.1111/1468-5973.12006

Holling, C. S. (1973). Resilience and stability of ecological systems. *Annual Review of Ecology and Systematics, 4*(1), 1–23. https://doi.org/10.1146/annurev.es.04.110173.000245

Holling, C. S. (1996). Engineering resilience versus ecological resilience. In P. Schulze (Ed.), *Engineering within ecological constraints*. National Academy Press.

Hollnagel, E., Woods, D. D., & Leverson, N. (2006). *Resilience engineering: Concepts and precepts*. Ashgate.

Hong, P., Huang, C., & Li, B. (2012). Crisis management for SMEs: Insights from a multiple-case study. *International Journal of Business Excellence, 5*(5), Article 48802, 535. https://doi.org/10.1504/IJBEX.2012.048802

Lacity, M. C., & Willcocks, L. P. (2013, March 19). Outsourcing business processes for innovation. *MIT Sloan Management Review*.

Linnenluecke, M., & Griffiths, A. (2010). Beyond adaptation: Resilience for business in light of climate change and weather extremes. *Business & Society, 49*(3), 477–511. https://doi.org/10.1177/0007650310368814

Liu, C.-L., Shang, K.-C., Lirn, T.-C., Lai, K.-H., & Lun, Y. V. (2018). Supply chain resilience, firm performance, and management policies in the liner shipping industry. *Transportation Research Part A: Policy and Practice, 110*, 202–219. https://doi.org/10.1016/j.tra.2017.02.004

Luthans, F., Vogelgesang, G. R., & Lester, P. B. (2006). Developing the psychological capital of resiliency. *Human Resource Development Review, 5*(1), 25–44. https://doi.org/10.1177/1534484305285335

Luthar, S. S., Kumar, N. L., & Zillmer, N. (2020). High-achieving schools connote risks for adolescents: Problems documented, processes implicated, and directions for interventions. *The American Psychologist, 75*(7), 983–995. https://doi.org/10.1037/amp0000556

Martin, R., & Sunley, P. (2015). On the notion of regional economic resilience: Conceptualization and explanation. *Journal of Economic Geography, 15*(1), 1–42. https://doi.org/10.1093/jeg/lbu015

Masten, A. S. (2013). Resilience in development: Implications of the study of successful adaptation for developmental psychopathology. In D. Cicchetti (Ed.), *Rochester symposium on developmental psychopathology series. The emergence of a discipline: Rochester symposium on developmental psychopathology* (Vol. 1, pp. 261–295). Taylor and Francis.

Masten, A. S., & Reed, M.-G. J. (2002). Resilience in development. In C. R. Snyder (Ed.), *Handbook of positive psychology* (pp. 74–88). Oxford University Press.

Morrish, S. C., & Jones, R. (2020). Post-disaster business recovery: An entrepreneurial marketing perspective. *Journal of Business Research, 113*, 83–92. https://doi.org/10.1016/j.jbusres.2019.03.041

Pal, R., Torstensson, H., & Mattila, H. (2014). Antecedents of organizational resilience in economic crises—An empirical study of Swedish textile and clothing SMEs. *International Journal of Production Economics, 147*, 410–428. https://doi.org/10.1016/j.ijpe.2013.02.031

Pathak, M. D., Kar, B., Panigrahi, R. R., & Shrivastava, A. K. (2023). Role of entrepreneurial resilience in SMEs to promote marketing and entrepreneurship amid Covid19 challenges. *Journal of Research in Marketing and Entrepreneurship*. Advance online publication. https://doi.org/10.1108/JRME-04-2022-0050

Richtnér, A., & Löfsten, H. (2014). Managing in turbulence: How the capacity for resilience influences creativity. *R&D Management, 44*(2), 137–151. https://doi.org/10.1111/radm.12050

Rose, A. (2004). Defining and measuring economic resilience to disasters. *Disaster Prevention and Management: An International Journal, 13*(4), 307–314. https://doi.org/10.1108/09653560410556528

Rutter, M. (1987). Psychosocial resilience and protective mechanisms. *The American Journal of Orthopsychiatry, 57*(3), 316–331. https://doi.org/10.1111/j.1939-0025.1987.tb03541.x

Shepherd, D. A. (2003). Learning from business failure: Propositions of grief recovery for the self-employed. *The Academy of Management Review, 28*(2), 318. https://doi.org/10.2307/30040715

Shi, M., Liu, L., Sun, X., & Wang, L. (2018). Associations between symptoms of attention-deficit/hyperactivity disorder and life satisfaction in medical students: The mediating effect of resilience. *BMC Medical Education, 18*(1), 164. https://doi.org/10.1186/s12909-018-1261-8

Tinsley, C. H., Dillon, R. L., & Cronin, M. A. (2012). How near-miss events amplify or attenuate risky decision making. *Management Science, 58*(9), 1596–1613. https://doi.org/10.1287/mnsc.1120.1517

Välikangas, L., & Hamel, G. (2003). En busca de la resiliencia. *Harvard Business Review, 81*(9), 40–52.

Vogus, T. J., & Sutcliffe, K. M. (2007). Organizational resilience: Towards a theory and research agenda. In *2007 IEEE international conference on systems, man and cybernetics* (pp. 3418–3422). IEEE. https://doi.org/10.1109/ICSMC.2007.4414160

Walker, B., Holling, C. S., Carpenter, S. R., & Kinzig, A. P. (2004). Resilience, adaptability and transformability in social-ecological systems. *Ecology and Society, 9*(2). https://doi.org/10.5751/ES-00650-090205

Weick, K. E., & Sutcliffe, K. M. (2006). Mindfulness and the quality of organizational attention. *Organization Science, 17*(4), 514–524. https://doi.org/10.1287/orsc.1060.0196

Weick, K. E., & Sutcliffe, K. M. (2015). *Managing the unexpected: Sustained performance in a complex world* (3rd ed.). Wiley.

Williams, T. A., & Shepherd, D. A. (2016). Building resilience or providing sustenance: Different paths of emergent ventures in the aftermath of the Haiti earthquake. *Academy of Management Journal, 59*(6), 2069–2102. https://doi.org/10.5465/amj.2015.0682

Williams, T. A., Gruber, D. A., Sutcliffe, K. M., Shepherd, D. A., & Zhao, E. Y. (2017). Organizational response to adversity: Fusing crisis management and resilience research streams. *Academy of Management Annals, 11*(2), 733–769. https://doi.org/10.5465/annals.2015.0134

Zutshi, A., Creed, A., Bhattacharya, A., Croy, G., & Dahms, S. (2022). Sustainability during the COVID pandemic: Analysis of hotel association communication. *Current Issues in Tourism, 25*(23), 3840–3853. https://doi.org/10.1080/13683500.2022.2057842

Digital Transformation as a Means of Achieving SME Resilience During COVID-19 – A Systematic Review and Future Research Agenda

2

A. F. M. Jalal Ahamed

2.1 Introduction

During the COVID-19 pandemic, businesses suffered from unique and powerful disruptions to their internal and external environments, resulting in many lives lost and a global recession that forced organizations to find new ways to adapt (Eriksson et al., 2022). People, societies, businesses, and governments worldwide were devastated by the sudden outbreak of the unprecedented pandemic (Cugno et al., 2022). Many companies did not have business continuity plans and never practiced operations during adverse economic conditions (Roffia & Dabić, 2023). Small- and medium-sized enterprises (SMEs) were particularly vulnerable to external crises and shocks due to their limited resources and lack of specialized knowledge. SMEs need entrepreneurial decisions, actions, and methods to survive such a catastrophe (Durst & Henschel, 2021; Klein & Todesco, 2021; Maroufkhani et al., 2020; Penco et al., 2022; Roffia & Dabić, 2023). The COVID-19 coronavirus pandemic shows that companies and organizations are unprepared for an adversity of this scale; however, it is also understood that they should review their strategies and plans to become more resilient to future adversities (Miceli et al., 2021). As a result of the COVID-19 pandemic, many SMEs around the world took a number of steps to survive and recover (Hu & Kee, 2022). In the post-pandemic era, business resilience, particularly among SMEs, has become a priority (Rofia & Dabić, 2023).

The concept of resilience has been conceptualized in a variety of ways, although it is a very relevant and current one for SME research. In an organizational context, resilience refers to a company's ability to survive, recover, and grow when a crisis disrupts its operations (Torres et al., 2019). In other words, resilience refers to the characteristics that enable some organizations to respond faster and recover faster than others (Eriksson et al., 2022; González-Serrano et al., 2023). Increasing

A. F. M. J. Ahamed (✉)
School of Business, University of Skövde, Skövde, Sweden
e-mail: jalal.ahamed@his.se

S. Durst, T. Henschel (eds.), *Small and Medium-Sized Enterprise (SME) Resilience*, Management for Professionals, https://doi.org/10.1007/978-3-031-50836-3_2

resilience involves designing, planning, and building flexibility (González-Serrano et al., 2023). When an organization is resilient, it can withstand and recover from shocks, disasters, or traumatic events, either internally or externally, and adapt to changes in the environment. According to Baral et al. (2022), four capabilities contribute to organizational resilience: information availability, collaboration between partners, flexibility, and reaction speed for uncertain situations. Resilience among SMEs is essential in today's turbulent world because it provides a means of renewal and adaptation. The use of digital technologies helps SMEs become more resilient by increasing their ability to deal with business interruptions (Khalil et al., 2022). As described by Guan et al. (2023), organizational resilience in the digital era involves two aspects: the ability to deal with challenges and use digital technology to restore the organization's original state as well as the ability to transcend the organization's original situation. Digitally savvy SMEs outperformed their peers in many instances (Rajagopaul et al., 2020). In addition to helping SMEs to survive business interruptions, digital technologies also enable them to focus on providing the necessary services (Khalil et al., 2022). Researchers have identified digital transformation as a means of achieving organizational resilience in SMEs during the pandemic (Penco et al., 2022). By using digital technology and Internet services, "digital business transformation" transforms an organization's way of managing and conducting business, creating new value; this represents a firm's initiative to leverage its capabilities through the use of digital technologies, transforming its strategies and operations (Al-Omoush et al., 2023a). Several research studies produced during and after the pandemic report different aspects of digitalization and digital transformation related to SME resilience.

However, studies of resilience in SMEs during the pandemic are fragmented and focus on a number of heterogeneous issues. For instance, according to Ojha et al. (2023), despite widespread acknowledgment of the need for digitalization in SMEs, there are fewer frameworks explaining why some firms are more responsive to the environment than others. SMEs in emerging markets face challenges with digital transformation, according to Al-Omoush et al. (2023a, b); prior literature (Khurana et al., 2022) indicated that firms face a variety of challenges to embrace digital technologies, including senior management's unwillingness to adopt new business models. As noted by Isensee et al. (2023), many SME management practices and research still view resilience, sustainability, and digitalization as sub-strategic and nonintegrated. In addition, SME entrepreneurs rarely manage sustainability and digitalization simultaneously, so their resilience is often compromised. As a result, a coherent compilation of existing research on digital transformation with the aim of promoting organizational resilience for small- and medium-sized businesses during the pandemic is required, which will represent the current state of the literature and will provide a stimulating agenda for the development of new literature (Paul et al., 2021a, b). The purpose of this systematic review was to first gain a better understanding of enablers of digital transformation and, second, to gain a better understanding on how the digital transformations affects organizational resilience. According to my knowledge, this is the first systematic presentation of research findings about SMEs' digital transformation during the pandemic. This chapter is organized as follows: Sect. 2.2 describes the methodology for addressing the research aim; Sect. 2.3 presents the results; and Sect. 2.4 discusses future research directions and conclusions.

2.2 Methodology

To identify, select, and synthesize literature related to organizational resilience, digital transformation, and COVID-19, I conducted a systematic literature review (SLR) (Tranfield et al., 2003). It has been shown that systematic literature reviews (SLR) improve the quality, reproducibility, transparency, and validity of the reviews as a research design technique; as a result, it provides unbiased, rigorous, convenient, and reliable searching of the relevant literature with explanatory findings and identifies potential research gaps for further investigation (Durst et al., 2022; Kamboj et al., 2018; Reim et al., 2015; Tranfield et al., 2003; Xiao & Watson, 2019). To conduct the systematic review, I followed the three-step procedure proposed by Tranfield et al. (2003) (Fig. 2.1).

I applied the Preferred Reporting Items for Systematic Reviews and Meta-Analyses (PRISMA) (Liberati et al., 2009) to search and screen potentially relevant literature so that the quality of the evidence, its rigorousness, and consistency can be ensured (Jäger-Roschko & Petersen, 2022). Relevant articles were identified using the following expressions in the title, abstract, or keywords in Scopus (Table 2.1).

The systematic review also used inclusion and exclusion criteria, which are displayed in the Table 2.2 below.

Scopus identified 164 articles after the initial search, but only 122 remained after the exclusion and inclusion criteria were applied. Five articles were further excluded after screening the titles. The screening was conducted on the remaining 117 abstracts. About 38 articles were discarded after screening the abstracts for relevance to the research aim. A total of 79 articles were left for the full-text screening, of which 42 were further removed in the full-text screening, leaving 37 for the final review. The full PRISMA process is shown in Table 2.3.

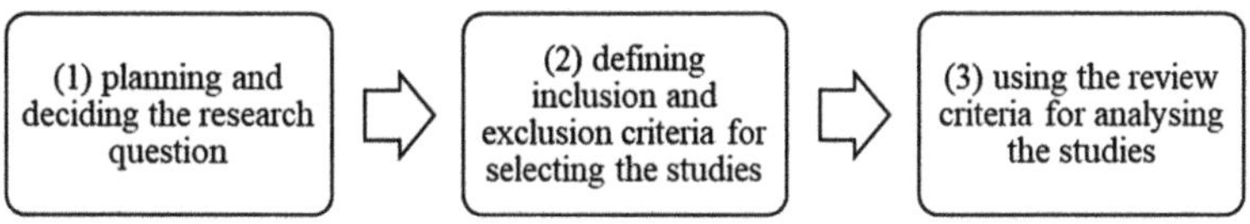

Fig. 2.1 SLR process. (Tranfield et al., 2003)

Table 2.1 Search string (Boolean operators)

"organizational resilience" AND "digital transformation" AND SME AND (LIMIT-TO (SUBJAREA, "SOCI") OR LIMIT-TO (SUBJAREA, "BUSI") OR LIMIT-TO (SUBJAREA, "ECON")) AND (LIMIT-TO (DOCTYPE, "ar")) AND (LIMIT-TO (PUBYEAR, 2023) OR LIMIT-TO (PUBYEAR, 2022) OR LIMIT-TO (PUBYEAR, 2021) OR LIMIT-TO (PUBYEAR, 2020) OR LIMIT-TO (PUBYEAR, 2019)) AND (LIMIT-TO (LANGUAGE, "English"))

Source: Compiled by author

Table 2.2 Summary of inclusion and exclusion criteria

Inclusion criteria	Exclusion criteria
Types of documents: journal articles	Books (textbooks), book chapters, conference papers, dissertations, and gray literature
Written in English	Not written in English
Peer reviewed	Not peer reviewed
Published in business or management journals	Papers without a significant focus on KM
Published between 2019 and 2023	Published before 2019

Source: Compiled by author

Table 2.3 Flow of information through the different phases of the systematic review (PRISMA)

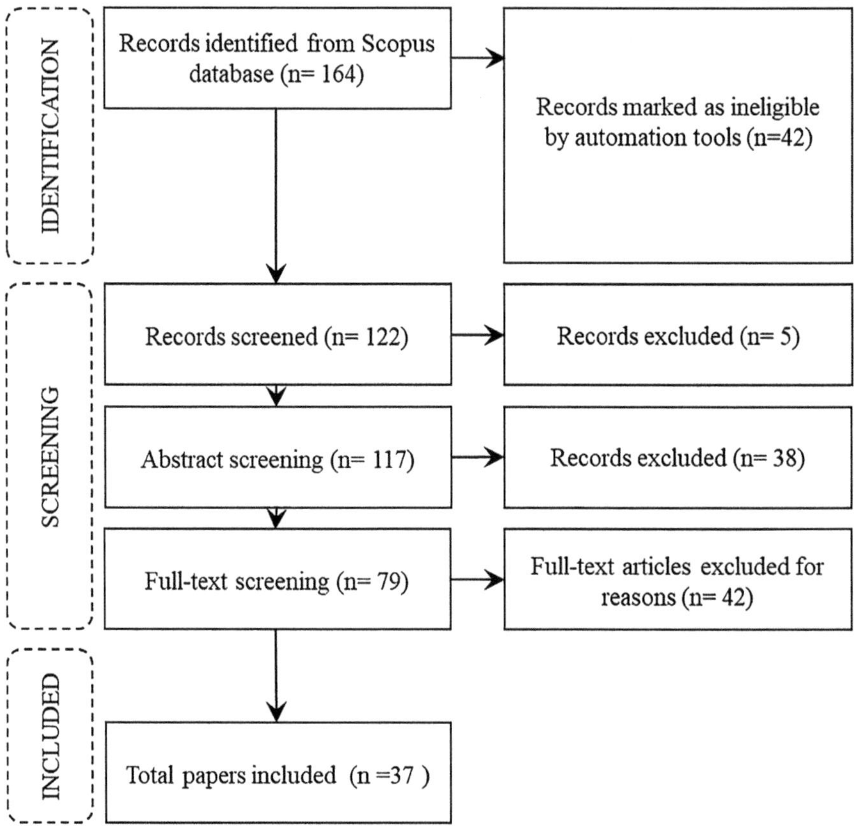

Source: Compiled by author

2.3 Results

2.3.1 Description of Included Studies

This study included 37 articles from 17 countries, of which four from China and India, three from Italy, and two from Finland, Spain, and Jordan.

The Fig. 2.2 above shows a number of research articles published in between 2019 and 2023 (until May). Four studies were published in the Technological Forecasting and Social Change; three in Journal of Open Innovation: Technology, Market, and Complexity; and two on Benchmarking: An International Journal, Journal of Enterprise Information Management, Review of Managerial Science, and Sustainability. Among the 37 articles, eight (about 22%) were either conceptual or review articles. About 19 studies (51%) employed quantitative research design as the methodological choice, while six studies (16%) were conducted using the qualitative research design. Figure 2.3 illustrates the most frequently used keywords, including "COVID-19," "SMEs," "organizational resilience," "digital technologies," and "innovation," which indicate the need for resilience and digital transformation during the pandemic. The co-occurrence of keywords indicates how a field of study has evolved over time. Co-occurrences are indicated by lines connecting large nodes; a large node indicates a frequent occurrence (Van Nunen et al., 2018).

In Table 2.4, I listed the studied papers with author names, year of publication, methodological choices, country of research, key findings, and future research directions based on the limitations sought on the papers. Based on the literature reviewed, I presented a consolidated conceptual model in Fig. 2.4. According to the model, several enablers facilitate SMEs' digital transformation during the pandemic. There are various forms and levels of digital transformation. Digital transformation forms can directly affect SME resilience, or they can affect it through other strategic options.

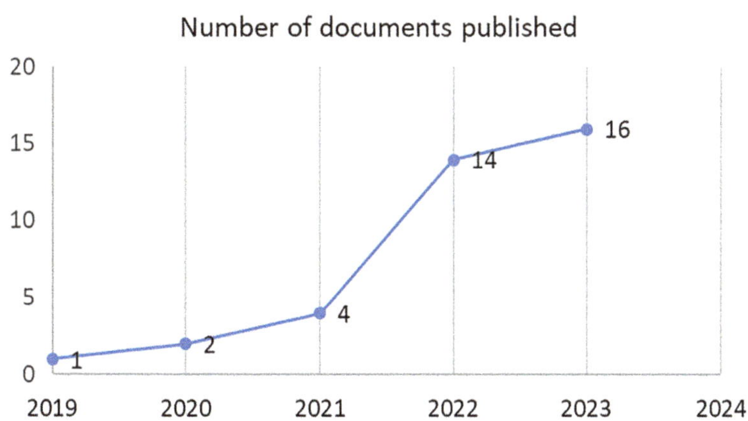

Fig. 2.2 Number of studies by year. (Source: Compiled by author)

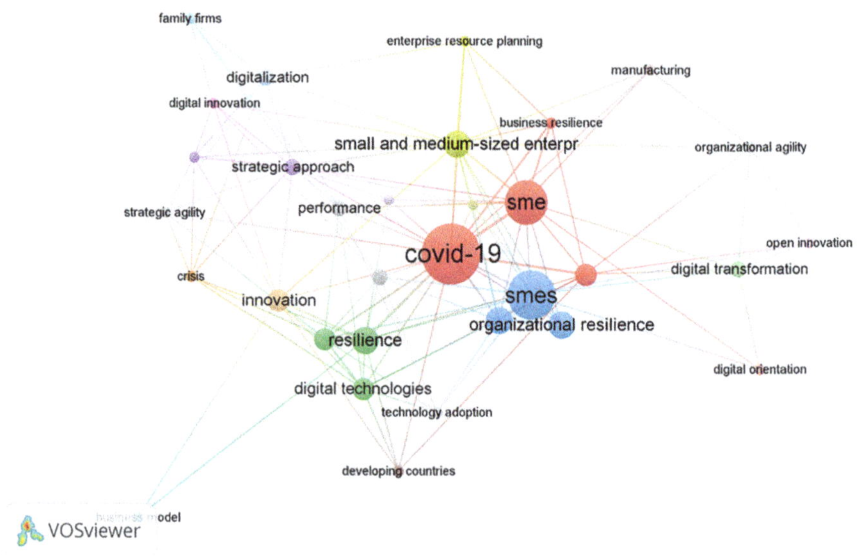

Fig. 2.3 The keyword network visualization of the surveyed literature. (Source: Compiled by author)

Table 2.4 The distribution of reviewed papers among methodology, country of research with the key findings, and research gaps

Author(s)	Year	Methodology	Country of research	Key findings
Ahmed et al.	2022	Quantitative, SEM	Pakistan	1. The capability of SMEs to use digital platforms positively correlates with their agility
Al-Omoush et al.	2023	Quantitative, SEM	Jordan	2. Digital business transformation significantly impacts frugal innovation and SMEs' resilience in emerging markets
Al-Omoush et al.	2023	Quantitative, SEM	Jordan	3. Digital CSR has a significant impact on social entrepreneurship and organizational resilience. Social entrepreneurship and competitive intelligence significantly impact organizational resilience
Baral et al.	2022	Quantitative, SEM	India	4. Organizational resilience mediates the effects of all four latent variables (flexibility, digitalization, risk management culture, and collaboration) on the firm performance of MSMEs
Chatterjee et al.	2022	Quantitative, SEM	India	5. Internationalization and performance are moderated by digitalization and international networking capabilities

Table 2.4 (continued)

Author(s)	Year	Methodology	Country of research	Key findings
Cugno et al.	2022	Quantitative, KHB	Italy	6. Industry 4.0 has a significant direct impact on short-term and medium-term production recovery perceptions. Digital reorganization accelerated the effect in the short term
Eriksson et al.	2022	Qualitative, case study	Finland	7. Digitalization, strategic collaboration, customer intimacy, agile resource/expertise usage, and improved revenue models constituted the critical sources of resilience.
Ganotakis et al.	2023	Quantitative, Tobit model	Caribbean	8. Introducing specific digital tools alongside certain types of innovations further enhances sales growth and inhibits it in other instances
von Garrel and Jahn	2022	Conceptual	N/A	9. In light of the implications abstracted by artificial intelligence for (1) business models, (2) process development, and (3) service-based business model development by SMEs – a design framework can be developed based on research activities related to digital transformation for SMEs to create AI-based business models (services)
González-Serrano et al.	2023	FsQCA	Spain	10. To maintain the performance of the sports industry during the pandemic, increased use of technologies (sports services digitization) was critical.
Guan et al.	2023	Quantitative, SEM	China	11. A firm's prior R&D investment is indicative of its digital technology level, which makes it more resilient to the pandemic. Digital transformation is easier for small-scale firms because they are more flexible in responding to technological changes.
Hu and Kee	2022	Conceptual	Malaysia	12. A company that fails to embrace digital transformation will eventually fail
Huang and Farboudi Jahromi	2021	Conceptual	N/A	13. SME resilience is affected by five resilience-building strategies (market orientation, supply chain orientation, strategic corporate reorganization, innovation, and business model transformation)

(continued)

Table 2.4 (continued)

Author(s)	Year	Methodology	Country of research	Key findings
Kala Kamdjoug	2023	Quantitative, SEM	DR Congo	14. Recipe for successful digital transformation (DT) projects. DT is essential for enhancing SMEs' performance and resilience in the DRC
Khalil et al.	2022	Quantitative	Bahrain, Egypt, Pakistan, Saudi Arabia, Tunisia, UAE	15. Digital technology has helped SMEs survive the pandemic, becoming more robust and ensuring their survival
Khurana et al.	2022	Qualitative, case study	India	16. There are three levels of resilience capability (entrepreneurial, organizational, and ecosystem resilience), and digitalization fosters these levels
Klein and Todesco	2021	Literature review	N/A	17. Digitalization can foster "new normal organizations," which will enable SMEs to adapt and respond to exogenous shocks and create value
Kumar et al.	2023	Literature review and Delphi method	India	18. SME digital transformation can be enhanced in four ways. "Management competencies," "knowledge management," and "monitoring and controlling" are the most crucial enablers of SME digital resilience.
Le-Dain et al.	2023	Literature review and focus group	France	19. Barriers and opportunities share four core themes: digital strategy, ecosystem network, internal and operational organization, and human capabilities. SMEs' digital strategies benefited most from digital servitization
Li et al.	2022	FsQCA	China	20. Multiple factors interact to determine the success of a firm's digital innovation practice
Maroufkhani et al.	2020	Quantitative	Iran	21. Big data analytics (BDA) mediates the relationship between technological, organizational, and environmental contexts, and SMEs' performance, which could further enhance SMEs' financial and market performance

(continued)

Table 2.4 (continued)

Author(s)	Year	Methodology	Country of research	Key findings
Martín-Rojas et al.	2023	Quantitative, SEM	Spain	22. Social media tools positively impact entrepreneurial capabilities. Organizational resilience mediates the impact on firm performance
Miceli et al.	2021	Conceptual		23. Organizational sustainability requires understanding strategic resilience as a multi-domain concept, similar to the holistic view of sustainability
Ojha et al.	2023	Quantitative, SEM	USA	24. Through fluid partnering, business continuity planning, and market acuity, digitalization is manifested in dynamic strategic planning (DSP). The benefits of digitalization cascade through DSP through virtual integration
Raut et al.	2019	Literature review and expert opinion, DEMATEL	N/A	25. Five factors (hardware scalability and standardization, cost, innovation, installation, upgradation, and quality of service) are the most significant factors influencing cloud computing adoption (CCA)
Robertson et al.	2022	Mixed method	South Africa	26. Organizational resilience was higher in digitally mature SMEs. Organizational resilience is driven more by digital leadership than by digital capabilities
Roffia and Dabić	2023	Quantitative, regression	Italy	27. COVID-19 resilience and organizational resilience are positively affected by budgeting, business continuity tools, and supplementary financial resources. SMEs that intended to use ERP systems had a high level of resilience as well.
Rupeika-Apoga et al.	2022	Quantitative, regression	Latvia	28. Both digital orientation and digital capability have direct positive effects on digital transformation
Soluk	2022	Qualitative, semi-structured interview	Germany	29. Entrepreneurial action led to digital innovation (digital process innovation, digital product innovation, and digital business model innovation)
Thekkoote	2023	Quantitative, SEM	India	30. Individual characteristics of entrepreneurs, technology utilization, government support, and pro-social leadership and impact business resilience

(continued)

Table 2.4 (continued)

Author(s)	Year	Methodology	Country of research	Key findings
Trieu et al.	2023	Quantitative, SEM	Vietnam	31. Organizational resilience, and SME performance are stimulated by information technology capabilities and government supports
Valdez-Juárez et al.	2022	Quantitative, SEM	Mexico	32. SME performance and economic indicators are positively impacted by innovation management
Wang and Bai	2021	Mixed method	China	33. By connecting firms to different stakeholder groups, firms can gain knowledge about how to respond to diverse situations
Zahoor et al.	2022	Qualitative, case study	Finland	34. By enacting different processes and utilizing resources and capabilities creatively, SMEs mitigated the impact of the pandemic. The digital capability of B2B SMEs enhanced their strategic agility
Zhang et al.	2022	Quantitative	China	35. Strategic orientations positively influence innovation. Responsible innovation is more likely to be promoted by environmental orientation than by digital orientation.
Penco et al.	2022	Qualitative, case study	Italy	36. How entrepreneurial orientation (EO) deals with the changing environment and helps address the market opportunities related to digitalization
Priyono et al.	2020	Qualitative, case study	Indonesia	37. SMEs adopt a different degree of digital transformations

Source: Compiled by author
Note: *SEM* structural equation modelling, *FsQCA* fuzzy-set qualitative comparative analysis

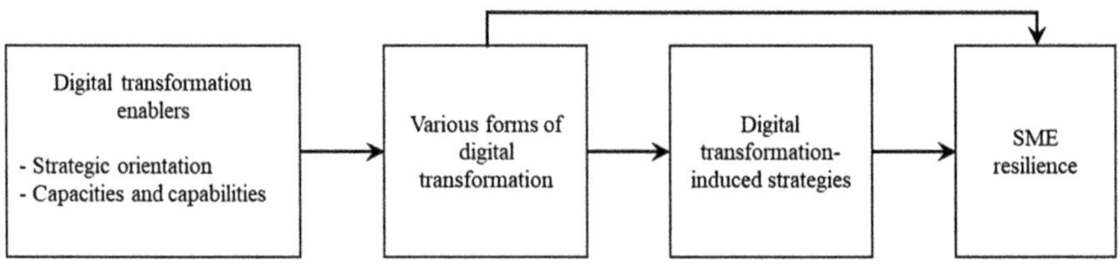

Fig. 2.4 The consolidated conceptual model based on the surveyed studies. (Source: Compiled by author)

2.3.2 Enablers of Digital Transformation of SMEs During COVID-19

The compilation of the surveyed literature indicates two clusters of enablers of digital transformation – strategic orientations and competencies and capabilities. The first cluster of enablers is the "strategic orientations" of the SMEs. Gatignon and Xuereb (1997) defined strategic orientation as "reflects the firm's philosophy of how to conduct business through a deeply rooted set of values and beliefs that guides the firm's attempt to achieve superior performance" (pp. 44–45). In line with this definition, I found several strategic orientations as discussed below:

An organization's digital orientation, which focuses on the changes brought by digital tools and technologies, is one of the latest varieties of strategic orientation (Kindermann et al., 2021). According to several authors during the pandemic, digital orientation is a significant driver of digital transformation. In the case of Latvian SMEs, Rupeika-Apoga et al. (2022) found that digital orientation positively impacted digital transformation. According to Zhang et al. (2022), digital orientation facilitates responsible innovation among Chinese SMEs. In addition to digital orientation, Zhang et al. (2022) found that environmental orientation promotes responsible innovation. As most SMEs are run by entrepreneurs, entrepreneurs are also the chief executive officers (CEOs), and their entrepreneurial orientation is crucial to implementing digital transformation. This statement is attested by Penco et al. (2022) for Italian SMEs. Cugno et al. (2022) found that Italian manufacturing SMEs' openness to Industry 4.0 has also contributed to the faster pandemic recovery. It is an entrepreneurial orientation, as far as I am concerned. Companies are more likely to adopt digital transformation as they become more open to industry 4.0. Roffia and Dabić (2023) found that SMEs with a high intention to use ERP systems also displayed high-resilience levels. This signals an entrepreneurial or organizational orientation toward digital transformation.

The second cluster of enablers is the capabilities and competencies for various forms of digital transformation. Raut et al. (2019) found that hardware scalability and standardization, cost, innovation, installation and upgrade, and quality of service are the most significant factors influencing cloud computing adoption for SMEs. Martín-Rojas et al. (2023) found that the use of social media tools increases entrepreneurial capabilities during the pandemic. Zahoor et al. (2022) found that in case of Finnish SMEs digital capability fosters digital transformation. Trieu et al. (2023) found that information technology capabilities of Vietnamese SMEs play a crucial role in stimulating organizational resilience during the pandemic. In a study published in 2022, Rupeika-Apoga et al. found that digital capability has a direct positive effect on digital transformation. According to Robertson et al. (2022) and Priyono et al. (2020), digital maturity is defined as a capability that enables organizations to align their "people, culture, structure and tasks to compete effectively by taking advantage of opportunities enabled by technological infrastructure," and digital maturity is seen as facilitating business resilience through digital transformation. Also, Robertson et al. (2022) highlighted the importance of digital leadership as a digital transformation competency. In their study, Kumar et al. (2023) found that "management competencies," "knowledge management," and "monitoring and controlling" are the most crucial enablers of digital transformation of SMEs. Le-Dain et al. (2023) articulated that for French service SMEs, the digital strategies benefited most from digital servitization.

2.3.3 Various Forms of Digital Transformation

Scholars conceptualize digital transformation differently. As such, understanding digital transformation as a single monolithic construct will be like "blind men feeling elephants." Several understandings of digital transformation have been used in this review, and some authors (Baral et al., 2022; Chatterjee et al., 2022; Eriksson et al., 2022) used the holistic term "digitalization," while others (Wang & Bai, 2021) divided digitalization into internal and external categories. Cugno et al. (2022) referred to it as digital reorganization, while Al-Omoush et al. (2023a, b) called it digital business transformation. Authors have also used domain-specific terms, such as big data analytics (BDA) adoption (Maroufkhani et al., 2020), cloud computing adoption (CCA) (Raut et al., 2019), digital virtual integration (Ojha et al., 2023), digital platform capability (Ahmed et al., 2022), social media usages (Martín-Rojas et al., 2023), adoption of digital technologies (Khurana et al., 2022), and ERP-type information systems (Roffia & Dabić, 2023). However, most authors (Guan et al., 2023; Hu & Kee, 2022; Khurana et al., 2022; Kumar et al., 2023; Penco et al., 2022; Priyono et al., 2020; Rupeika-Apoga et al., 2022; von Garrel & Jahn, 2022; Zahoor et al., 2022) tend to use "digital transformation" to denote a significant and more complete digital change in the organization. These digital transformation initiatives affect SME resilience directly or through other strategic options.

2.3.4 Digital Transformation to SME Resilience Direct and Indirect Paths (Though Another Strategic Option)

According to several authors, digitalization (Baral et al., 2022; González-Serrano et al., 2023) and digital transformation (Guan et al., 2023; Khalil et al., 2022; Klein & Todesco, 2021) directly increases the organization's resilience. Al-Omoush et al. (2023a, b) found that digital business transformation fosters SEM's resilience in Jordan. Further, in another study, Al-Omoush et al. (2023a, b) found that digital CSR enhances SME resilience directly. Cugno et al. (2022) found that digital business reorganization fosters SME resilience. Eriksson et al. (2022) found that business model innovation fosters resilient international growth. Raut et al. (2019) found that cloud computing adoption affects organizational resilience. Thekkoote (2023) found that technology utilization increases organizational resilience for SMEs. Huang and Farboudi Jahromi (2021) found that business model transformation positively affects organizational resilience building.

There were six mediating strategic options bypassing the effect of digital transformation of organizational resilience. Al-Omoush et al. (2023a, b) found that digital business transformation nurtures frugal innovation in Jordan, and frugal innovation accelerates SME resilience during the pandemic. Al-Omoush et al. (2023a, b) in another research found that digital CSR affects organizational resilience through social entrepreneurship and competitive intelligence. Ahmed et al. (2022) found that digital platform capability enhances organization agility, which interns assumed to excel resilience. Miceli et al. (2021) found that digitalization increases the strategic agile process in the SMEs, which makes firms more strategically resilient. Ojha et al. (2023) found that virtual integration enhances the possibility of dynamic strategic planning that fosters financial performance (i.e., make SMEs resilient in front of external shocks). Hu and Kee (2022) found digital transformation positively affects sustainable business practices, which interns will be more resilient to external shocks.

2.4 Conclusion

The shock caused by COVID-19 was unprecedented for SMEs. In spite of this, SMEs from around the world have rebounded like a phoenix from the ashes as one of the major engines of the global economy. Small- and medium-sized businesses have taken several measures for resilience, and digital transformation is perhaps the most common and effective technique. This systematic review compiles the enablers of digital transformation and summarizes how digital transformation affects organizational resilience for SMEs. The main findings are summarized in Table 2.4 and Fig. 2.4. Further, a rapid recommendation checklist is provided in Table 2.5.

Despite the theoretical and practical contributions described above, some limitations remain. It will be possible to empirically investigate, especially after the pandemic, the enablers of digital transformation and the effects of digital transformation on SME resilience. Additionally, I collected relevant literature from one source (Scopus). Other databases, such as the Web of Science, should be surveyed in future research. Future research should also consider more complex and dynamic aspects of digitalization, such as virtual reality and open AI (artificial intelligence) and their impacts, since digital transformation is a continuous process. Future research also should include other dimensions of strategic orientations such as learning and market orientation.

Table 2.5 Rapid recommendations for SME professionals

1. A key component of organizational resilience is digital transformation
2. The meanings and scope of organizational resilience vary. Managing resilience requires managers to identify their goals and areas of focus
3. Digital transformation relies heavily on strategic orientation as well as organizational capacity and capabilities
4. The organization's resilience is strengthened by several in-between strategic options
5. Organizational resilience is a constantly evolving concept. Therefore, SME managers must be aware of technological changes, such as artificial intelligence, OpenAI, and human-computer interactions

Source: Compiled by author

References

Ahmed, A., Bhatti, S. H., Gölgeci, I., & Arslan, A. (2022). Digital platform capability and organizational agility of emerging market manufacturing SMEs: The mediating role of intellectual capital and the moderating role of environmental dynamism. *Technological Forecasting and Social Change, 177*, 121513.

Al-Omoush, K., Lassala, C., & Ribeiro-Navarrete, S. (2023a). The role of digital business transformation in frugal innovation and SMEs' resilience in emerging markets. *International Journal of Emerging Markets*. Ahead of print. https://doi.org/10.1108/IJOEM-12-2022-1937

Al-Omoush, K., Ribeiro-Navarrete, B., & McDowell, W. C. (2023b). The impact of digital corporate social responsibility on social entrepreneurship and organizational resilience. *Management Decision*. Ahead of print. https://doi.org/10.1108/MD-11-2022-1613

Baral, M. M., Mukherjee, S., Nagariya, R., Singh Patel, B., Pathak, A., & Chittipaka, V. (2022). Analysis of factors impacting firm performance of MSMEs: Lessons learnt from COVID-19. *Benchmarking: An International Journal*. Ahead of print, *30*, 1942. https://doi.org/10.1108/BIJ-11-2021-0660

Chatterjee, S., Chaudhuri, R., Vrontis, D., & Maalaoui, A. (2022). Internationalization of family business and its performance: Examining the moderating role of digitalization and international networking capability. *Review of Managerial Science*, 1–28.

Cugno, M., Castagnoli, R., Büchi, G., & Pini, M. (2022). Industry 4.0 and production recovery in the covid era. *Technovation, 114*, 102443.

Durst, S., & Henschel, T. (2021). COVID-19 as an accelerator for developing strong (er) businesses? Insights from Estonian small firms. *Journal of the International Council for Small Business, 2*(1), 1–29.

Durst, S., Foli, S., & Edvardsson, I. R. (2022). A systematic literature review on knowledge management in SMEs: Current trends and future directions. *Management Review Quarterly*, 1–26.

Eriksson, T., Heikkilä, M., & Nummela, N. (2022). Business model innovation for resilient international growth. *Small Enterprise Research, 29*(3), 205–226.

Ganotakis, P., Angelidou, S., Saridakis, C., Piperopoulos, P., & Dindial, M. (2023). Innovation, digital technologies, and sales growth during exogenous shocks. *Technological Forecasting and Social Change, 193*, 122656.

Gatignon, H., & Xuereb, J.-M. (1997). Strategic orientation of the firm and new product performance. *Journal of Marketing Research, 34*(1), 77–90.

González-Serrano, M. H., Dos Santos, M. A., Sendra-Garcia, J., & Calabuig, F. (2023). Sports entrepreneurship during COVID-19: Technology as an ally to maintain the competitiveness of small businesses. *Technological Forecasting and Social Change, 187*, 122256.

Guan, F., Tienan, W., & Tang, L. (2023). Organizational resilience under COVID-19: The role of digital technology in R&D investment and performance. *Industrial Management & Data Systems, 123*(1), 41–63.

Hu, M. K., & Kee, D. M. H. (2022). Fostering sustainability: Reinventing SME strategy in the new normal. *Foresight, 24*(3/4), 301–318.

Huang, A., & Farboudi Jahromi, M. (2021). Resilience building in service firms during and post COVID-19. *The Service Industries Journal, 41*(1–2), 138–167.

Isensee, C., Teuteberg, F., & Griese, K. M. (2023). Success factors of organizational resilience: A qualitative investigation of four types of sustainable digital entrepreneurs. *Management Decision, 61*(5), 1244–1273.

Jäger-Roschko, M., & Petersen, M. (2022). Advancing the circular economy through information sharing: A systematic literature review. *Journal of Cleaner Production, 133210*, 133210.

Kala Kamdjoug, J. R. (2023). Change management and digital transformation project success in SMEs located in the Democratic Republic of the Congo. *Journal of Enterprise Information Management*. Ahead of print. https://doi.org/10.1108/JEIM-09-2022-0340

Kamboj, S., Sarmah, B., Gupta, S., & Dwivedi, Y. (2018). Examining branding co-creation in brand communities on social media: Applying the paradigm of Stimulus-Organism-Response. *International Journal of Information Management, 39*, 169–185.

Khalil, A., Abdelli, M. E. A., & Mogaji, E. (2022). Do digital technologies influence the relationship between the COVID-19 crisis and SMEs' resilience in developing countries? *Journal of Open Innovation: Technology, Market, and Complexity, 8*(2), 100.

Khurana, I., Dutta, D. K., & Ghura, A. S. (2022). SMEs and digital transformation during a crisis: The emergence of resilience as a second-order dynamic capability in an entrepreneurial ecosystem. *Journal of Business Research, 150*, 623–641.

Kindermann, B., Beutel, S., de Lomana, G. G., Strese, S., Bendig, D., & Brettel, M. (2021). Digital orientation: Conceptualization and operationalization of a new strategic orientation. *European Management Journal, 39*(5), 645–657.

Klein, V. B., & Todesco, J. L. (2021). COVID-19 crisis and SMEs responses: The role of digital transformation. *Knowledge and Process Management, 28*(2), 117–133.

Kumar, V., Sindhwani, R., Behl, A., Kaur, A., & Pereira, V. (2023). Modelling and analysing the enablers of digital resilience for small and medium enterprises. *Journal of Enterprise Information Management*. Ahead of print. https://doi.org/10.1108/JEIM-01-2023-0002

Le-Dain, M.-A., Benhayoun, L., Matthews, J., & Liard, M. (2023). Barriers and opportunities of digital servitization for SMEs: The effect of smart Product-Service System business models. *Service Business, 17*(1), 359–393.

Li, F., Long, J., & Zhao, W. (2022). Mining braces of innovation linking to digital transformation grounded in TOE framework. *Sustainability, 15*(1), 301.

Liberati, A., Altman, D. G., Tetzlaff, J., Mulrow, C., Gøtzsche, P. C., Ioannidis, J. P., Clarke, M., Devereaux, P. J., Kleijnen, J., & Moher, D. (2009). The PRISMA statement for reporting systematic reviews and meta-analyses of studies that evaluate health care interventions: Explanation and elaboration. *Annals of Internal Medicine, 151*(4), W-65-W-94.

Maroufkhani, P., Wan Ismail, W. K., & Ghobakhloo, M. (2020). Big data analytics adoption model for small and medium enterprises. *Journal of Science and Technology Policy Management, 11*(4), 483–513.

Martín-Rojas, R., Garrido-Moreno, A., & García-Morales, V. J. (2023). Social media use, corporate entrepreneurship and organizational resilience: A recipe for SMEs success in a post-Covid scenario. *Technological Forecasting and Social Change, 190*, 122421.

Miceli, A., Hagen, B., Riccardi, M. P., Sotti, F., & Settembre-Blundo, D. (2021). Thriving, not just surviving in changing times: How sustainability, agility and digitalization intertwine with organizational resilience. *Sustainability, 13*(4), 2052.

Ojha, D., Patel, P. C., & Parida, V. (2023). Virtual integration in SMEs: The digitalization circuitry of dynamic strategic planning for SMEs. *International Journal of Information Management*, 102657. https://doi.org/10.1016/j.ijinfomgt.2023.102657

Paul, J., Lim, W. M., O'Cass, A., Hao, A. W., & Bresciani, S. (2021a). Scientific procedures and rationales for systematic literature reviews (SPAR-4-SLR). *International Journal of Consumer Studies, 45*(4), O1–O16.

Paul, J., Merchant, A., Dwivedi, Y. K., & Rose, G. (2021b). Writing an impactful review article: What do we know and what do we need to know? *Journal of Business Research, 133*, 337–340.

Penco, L., Profumo, G., Serravalle, F., & Viassone, M. (2022). Has COVID-19 pushed digitalisation in SMEs? The role of entrepreneurial orientation. *Journal of Small Business and Enterprise Development, 30*(2), 311–341.

Priyono, A., Moin, A., & Putri, V. N. A. O. (2020). Identifying digital transformation paths in the business model of SMEs during the COVID-19 pandemic. *Journal of Open Innovation: Technology, Market, and Complexity, 6*(4), 104.

Rajagopaul, A., Magwentshu, N., & Kalidas, S. (2020). How South African SMEs can survive and thrive post COVID-19. Providing the right support to enable SME growth now and beyond the crisis, McKinsey & Company, Johannesburg.

Raut, R. D., Gardas, B. B., Narkhede, B. E., & Narwane, V. S. (2019). To investigate the determinants of cloud computing adoption in the manufacturing micro, small and medium enterprises: A DEMATEL-based approach. *Benchmarking: An International Journal, 26*(3), 990–1019.
Reim, W., Parida, V., & Örtqvist, D. (2015). Product–Service Systems (PSS) business models and tactics – A systematic literature review. *Journal of Cleaner Production, 97*, 61–75.
Robertson, J., Botha, E., Walker, B., Wordsworth, R., & Balzarova, M. (2022). Fortune favours the digitally mature: the impact of digital maturity on the organisational resilience of SME retailers during COVID-19. *International Journal of Retail & Distribution Management, 50*(8/9), 1182–1204. https://doi.org/10.1108/IJRDM-10-2021-0514
Roffia, P., & Dabić, M. (2023). The role of management control and integrated information systems for the resilience of SMEs. *Review of Managerial Science*, 1–23. https://doi.org/10.1007/s11846-023-00657-6
Rupeika-Apoga, R., Petrovska, K., & Bule, L. (2022). The effect of digital orientation and digital capability on digital transformation of SMEs during the COVID-19 pandemic. *Journal of Theoretical and Applied Electronic Commerce Research, 17*(2), 669–685.
Soluk, J. (2022). Organisations' resources and external shocks: Exploring digital innovation in family firms. *Industry and Innovation, 29*(6), 792–824.
Thekkoote, R. (2023). Factors influencing small and medium-sized enterprise (SME) resilience during the COVID-19 outbreak. *The TQM Journal*. Ahead-of-print. https://doi.org/10.1108/TQM-08-2022-0266
Torres, A. P., Marshall, M. I., & Sydnor, S. (2019). Does social capital pay off? The case of small business resilience after Hurricane Katrina. *Journal of Contingencies and Crisis Management, 27*(2), 168–181. https://doi.org/10.1111/1468-5973.12248
Tranfield, D., Denyer, D., & Smart, P. (2003). Towards a methodology for developing evidence-informed management knowledge by means of systematic review. *British Journal of Management, 14*(3), 207–222.
Trieu, H. D., Van Nguyen, P., Nguyen, T. T., Vu, H. M., & Tran, K. (2023). Information technology capabilities and organizational ambidexterity facilitating organizational resilience and firm performance of SMEs. *Asia Pacific Management Review*. https://doi.org/10.1016/j.apmrv.2023.03.004
Valdez-Juárez, L. E., Castillo-Vergara, M., & Ramos-Escobar, E. A. (2022). Innovative business strategies in the face of COVID-19: An approach to open innovation of SMEs in the Sonora Region of Mexico. *Journal of Open Innovation: Technology, Market, and Complexity, 8*(1), 47. https://doi.org/10.3390/joitmc8010047
Van Nunen, K., Li, J., Reniers, G., & Ponnet, K. (2018). Bibliometric analysis of safety culture research. *Safety Science, 108*, 248–258.
von Garrel, J., & Jahn, C. (2022). Design framework for the implementation of AI-based (service) business models for small and medium-sized manufacturing enterprises. *Journal of the Knowledge Economy, 1–19*, 3551. https://doi.org/10.1007/s13132-022-01003-z
Wang, J., & Bai, T. (2021). How digitalization affects the effectiveness of turnaround actions for firms in decline. *Long Range Planning*, 102140. https://doi.org/10.1016/j.lrp.2021.102140
Xiao, Y., & Watson, M. (2019). Guidance on conducting a systematic literature review. *Journal of Planning Education and Research, 39*(1), 93–112.
Zahoor, N., Golgeci, I., Haapanen, L., Ali, I., & Arslan, A. (2022). The role of dynamic capabilities and strategic agility of B2B high-tech small and medium-sized enterprises during COVID-19 pandemic: Exploratory case studies from Finland. *Industrial Marketing Management, 105*, 502–514.
Zhang, X. E., Teng, X., Le, Y., & Li, Y. (2022). Strategic orientations and responsible innovation in SMEs: The moderating effects of environmental turbulence. *Business Strategy and the Environment, 32*(4), 2522–2539.

3 How Management Control Systems Can Help Small and Medium-Sized Enterprises Develop Resilience

Maik Störmer and Martin R. W. Hiebl

3.1 Introduction

In today's rapidly changing business environment, companies face a variety of challenges. Natural disasters, political instability, and pandemics can disrupt supply chains, the public sector, and financial markets, resulting in significant economic consequences (e.g., Bürgel et al., 2023; Huang et al., 2022a, b). It is difficult to predict the impact and duration of such unexpected events on individual companies and the economy as a whole. As a result, organizations must be equipped with change management and adaptation capabilities to remain competitive and survive (Ruiz-Martin et al., 2018; Zhang et al., 2022).

Small- and medium-sized enterprises (SMEs) comprise a large portion of all organizations and thus form an integral part of the economy.[1] They generate a significant share of gross domestic product in most countries and have a significant impact on wealth and economic growth (Alberti et al., 2018; Mitchell & Reid, 2000; Williams et al., 2013). As a result, SMEs are considered crucial in the fight against unemployment and poverty (Page & Söderbom, 2015). At the same time, policymakers are increasingly recognizing the importance of resilience in SMEs and the need to support their ability to adapt to unexpected events (Alberti et al., 2018; Marcazzan et al., 2022). SMEs' resilience is thus becoming increasingly important from a societal and general business perspective, especially when combined with

[1] The understanding of SMEs underlying this chapter is discussed in Sect. 2.1.

M. Störmer
University of Siegen, Siegen, Germany

M. R. W. Hiebl (✉)
University of Siegen, Siegen, Germany

Johannes Kepler University Linz, Linz, Austria
e-mail: martin.hiebl@uni-siegen.de

S. Durst, T. Henschel (eds.), *Small and Medium-Sized Enterprise (SME) Resilience*, Management for Professionals, https://doi.org/10.1007/978-3-031-50836-3_3

the growing awareness of unexpected events, such as natural disasters or political unrest and the resulting difficulties in managing markets (Gianiodis et al., 2022; Tukamuhabwa et al., 2015; Zhou et al., 2022).

Although SMEs are considered more flexible than larger companies due to their smaller size and flat hierarchies, in practice they are often less resilient and take longer to recover from unexpected events (Ingirige et al., 2008; Juergensen et al., 2020). It has been shown that despite their greater flexibility, SMEs are often less prepared for unexpected events, in part due to the greater external uncertainty in the SME environment (Storey, 1994). As a result, they often have great difficulty not only recovering from such events but also coping with them (Ingirige et al., 2008). In this context, the resilience of SMEs, like that of their larger competitors, is influenced by a variety of different organizational characteristics and behaviors (Moore & Manring, 2009), as well as scarcer resources (Bürgel et al., 2023; Van Gils, 2005). Although some findings from resilience research on large firms can be directly applied to SMEs (Ates & Bititci, 2011), the importance of organizational resilience has been shown to vary with firm size (Sullivan-Taylor & Branicki, 2011), and even SMEs have varying degrees of success in responding to unexpected events under similar circumstances (Fiksel et al., 2015). Despite the potentially greater challenges in building organizational resilience in SMEs than their larger counterparts (Tognazzo et al., 2016), organizational resilience appears achievable and desirable, as it can help not only sustain operations but also improve organizational performance during difficult times (Lee et al., 2013).

Broadly, organizational resilience can be described as the ability to avoid, absorb, respond to, and recover from unexpected situations such as natural disasters or political turmoil (Chrisman et al., 2011; Ingirige et al., 2008). Despite strong interest in the development of resilient organizations, it has been shown that the approach and understanding of unexpected events varies due to a variety of factors and definitions of organizational resilience (Linnenluecke, 2017; Sullivan-Taylor & Wilson, 2009). The development of a universal approach to creating a resilient organization therefore seems unrealistic. At the same time, the traditional challenges of SMEs including resource scarcity and cash flow limitations are also relevant to the concept of resilience (Storey, 1994; Sullivan-Taylor & Branicki, 2011). In addition, in some cases, the resilience of organizations can be attributed to their size and, by extension, the way they operate with these resources compared with their larger competitors (Sullivan-Taylor & Branicki, 2011).

Although research on organizational resilience is a relatively young field, there are already several approaches to the understanding of organizational resilience that have been influenced by different research streams including supply chain management, safety and reliability management, and the adaptability of entire business models (Linnenluecke, 2017). Recently, many studies have looked into how various organizations have handled the COVID-19 crisis to learn more about organizational resilience against or in response to such extreme external shocks (e.g., Ali et al., 2022; Bürgel et al., 2023; Durst & Henschel, 2021; Guan et al., 2023; Xie et al., 2022).

In summary, studies on organizational resilience have long focused on defensive responses, but the perspective has increasingly broadened to include offensive or anticipatory responses, examining different types of resilience (e.g., Boin & van Eeten, 2013; Duchek, 2020). Duchek (2020) notes that there are few studies that have examined resilience capabilities and therefore draws on related topics (e.g., crisis management) or insights from other sectors (e.g., the public sector) to explain resilience capabilities. According to Duchek's (2020) approach, organizational resilience can be divided into three phases: anticipation, coping, and adaptation. Each of the three phases is associated with important organizational capabilities, and there are possible interrelationships between organizational capabilities and these resilience phases (Duchek, 2020). Various authors mention and emphasize different organizational capabilities and show their complex contribution to organizational resilience (e.g., Duchek, 2020; Tognazzo et al., 2016; Van Gils, 2005). According to Duchek (2020), such capabilities are the drivers and the basis for the three defined resilience phases. These drivers of organizational resilience include an organization's knowledge and information base, resource availability, and accountability.

In many organizations, an important part of the knowledge and information base for managers are management accounting and control systems (Burns et al., 2013; Merchant & Van der Stede, 2017). It can thus be followed that one of the drivers of organizational resilience may be management control systems (e.g., Beuren & Santos, 2019; Roffia & Dabić, 2023). However, although organizational resilience is increasingly researched in the general management and business literature (Duchek, 2020; Hillmann & Guenther, 2021; Linnenluecke, 2017), the available studies that focus on management control systems as a driver of resilience are small in their numbers and have largely argued that relatively little is known about its relationship to accounting and management control or how it can be used to form a holistic management control system (Beuren & Santos, 2019; Roffia & Dabić, 2023).

However, a management control system might be very useful in developing organizational resilience as it can include and monitor the drivers of organizational resilience, capabilities, factors, and indicators, some of which can have a significant impact on organizational resilience. Just like resilience, management control systems are defined quite differently. Although there is no single definition of management control systems, it can be said that a management control system is basically a collection of practices, tools, and systems that managers use to ensure that employee behaviors and decisions are consistent with organizational goals (Malmi & Brown, 2008).

While relatively little is known about management control systems' exact effects on resilience, there is some evidence that management control systems can promote resilient behaviors and capabilities and support management coping with adverse effects (Bracci & Tallaki, 2021). However, most research in this domain has focused on large firms (Alberti et al., 2018; Sullivan-Taylor & Branicki, 2011), where management control systems are long established and help to implement corporate strategy (Langfield-Smith, 1997). Since the literature shows that SMEs face different challenges than their larger competitors, the different perception of challenges and unexpected events may be reflected in the understanding of SME resilience (Sullivan-Taylor & Branicki, 2011) and their reliance on management control systems to cope with resilience. However, the specific impact of management control systems on SME resilience remains poorly understood, despite growing interest in organizational resilience and management control systems. In particular, a synthesized and holistic understanding of how management control systems can help SMEs in developing resilience has not yet emerged from the literature. Based on a traditional integrative review (cf. Cronin & George, 2023; Jesson et al., 2011) of the literature on management control systems and organizational resilience in SMEs, the present study addresses this void. In particular, it seeks to provide answers to the following research question: How can management control systems affect SMEs' resilience to unexpected events?

We take an integrative approach because we found evidence of the role of management control systems as potential drivers of SME organizational resilience in several strands of literature (management control, SME management, organizational resilience). However, in our reading, these literatures have remained largely disconnected, hence our integrative approach (see Cronin & George, 2023). The purpose of this integrative review is thus to establish a link between the development and use of management accounting and management control systems in SMEs and resilience research by examining the contribution of management control systems in use to SME resilience, their mechanisms, and key considerations. For this purpose, Sect. 2 provides an overview of the current understanding of SMEs, as well as a review of different conceptualizations of organizational resilience, and Malmi and Brown's (2008) conceptualization of management control systems. Section 3 focuses on individual management control systems and their potential benefits to organizations, particularly SMEs. Section 4 relates Duchek's (2020) three dimensions of resilience (anticipation, coping, adaptation) and resilience-building capabilities to Malmi and Brown's (2008) five types of management control systems in the context of their application in SMEs. These relationships are then discussed in detail and possible interrelationships are identified. Finally, the most important implications from this literature review, its limitations, and future research needs are identified in Sect. 5.

3.2 Understanding SMEs, Organizational Resilience, and Management Control Systems

3.2.1 Definition of SMEs

SMEs generate a significant share of the gross domestic product of most countries, making them a fundamental component of the global economy (Alberti et al., 2018). In the European Union alone, SMEs represent over 99% of all businesses and employ well over 50% of the working population (European Commission, 2023). Despite representing such a large proportion of businesses, there is no generally accepted definition of SMEs. So, different authors have defined SMEs in different ways, including by the number of employees, assets, or sales (Abor & Quartey, 2010). It has also been found that it can be difficult to categorize firms based on their size, for instance, when taking into account the analyzed industry or country. This can lead to a situation in which no companies are considered to be large, while in other industries, it is the large companies that are predominantly active (Storey, 1994).

Despite these difficulties, research studies usually have to come up with a clear definition, such as those provided by legislation (Lavia López & Hiebl, 2015). For example, while the Bolton Committee defines SMEs differently for different sectors (e.g., retail firms based on turnover), the European Commission has long defined SMEs based on the number of employees (Abor & Quartey, 2010; Storey, 1994). The most recent definition of SMEs recommended by the European Commission combines the number of employees, turnover, and/or total assets. According to this recommendation, companies with up to 250 employees and a turnover of less than 50 million Euros and/or a balance sheet total of no more than 43 million Euros are considered SMEs (European Commission, 2023). While other researchers used their own definitions, most of them were also based on the number of employees and/or turnover (Lavia López & Hiebl, 2015). For example, Hussain et al. (1998) and Shore et al. (2020) defined SMEs as firms with fewer than 500 employees. This definition is consistent with the US Code of Federal Regulations, which also defines SMEs as independent businesses with fewer than 500 employees (Code of Federal Regulations, 1996; U.S. Small Business Administration, 2016). In addition, the United Nations Industrial Development Organization also defines enterprise size for developed and developing countries based on the number of employees. In this context, SMEs in developed countries are also defined as firms with up to 500 employees (see Elaian, 1996). In the following, we therefore also rely on the number of employees as the defining characteristic of SMEs. In particular, for the purpose of this study, SMEs are considered as firms with up to 500 employees, since the latter threshold is broader than the one used by the European Commission (2023) and does not exclude potentially relevant companies with more than 250 employees.

3.2.2 Definitions and Conceptualizations of Organizational Resilience

Although organizational resilience is a relatively new field of research, there are numerous approaches to understanding organizational resilience informed by different research directions (Boin & van Eeten, 2013; Hepfer & Lawrence, 2022; Lengnick-Hall et al., 2011; Linnenluecke, 2017). In consequence, numerous researchers use their own concepts, models, and capabilities to understand organizational resilience. Such resilience is thus defined and conceptualized differently depending on the study. For example, three main conceptualizations (i.e., organizational resilience as an outcome, process, or capability) can be distinguished in the literature (Duchek, 2020; Ruiz-Martin et al., 2018) and can lead to ambiguities or even contradictions between the different conceptualizations and capabilities used.

Organizational resilience is therefore a multidimensional concept that has been extensively studied in the literature. Earlier studies often consider only single aspects of organizational resilience in this context, while more recent studies increasingly consider multiple aspects of organizational resilience (e.g., Boin & van Eeten, 2013; Ortiz-de-Mandojana & Bansal, 2016) and combine them as shown in Fig. 3.1. According to the most recent views of several different authors, organizational resilience can be divided into two or more dimensions, but these dimensions may additionally differ in their naming and overlap. For example, some authors use the terms operational and strategic resilience (Välikangas & Romme, 2012), while others use the terms precursor and/or recovery resilience (e.g., Boin & van Eeten, 2013; Lengnick-Hall et al., 2011; Välikangas & Romme, 2012). Still other authors focus on additional dimensions and capabilities of organizational resilience, such as the anticipation of unexpected events (e.g., Boin & van Eeten, 2013), ranging from recovery from such events to post-event adaptation (Välikangas & Romme, 2012). Thus, resilience is not a static trait but rather a set of capabilities that enable organizations to respond appropriately to unexpected events (Ortiz-de-Mandojana & Bansal, 2016). Despite differences in terminology and capabilities, there is some agreement in the literature that organizational resilience encompasses an organization's ability to adapt to, recover from, and learn from unexpected events (Boin & van Eeten, 2013; Chrisman et al., 2011; Ingirige et al., 2008; Välikangas & Romme, 2012).

In response to this plethora of different approaches to defining organizational resilience, Duchek (2020) provides an overview of the most important definitions from 1998 to 2015. According to her analysis, the definitions of resilience can be divided into three groups: anticipation, recovery, and adaptation. While previous research on organizational resilience tends to interpret resilience as defensive behavior in terms of resistance and recovery, more recent research also attributes resilience to more proactive behavior in terms of adaptation (e.g., Lengnick-Hall et al., 2011) and anticipation of unexpected events (e.g., Ortiz-de-Mandojana &

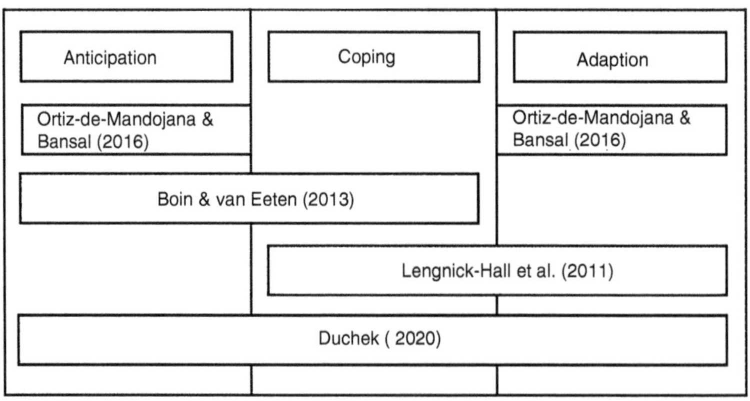

Fig. 3.1 Different dimensions of organizational resilience

Bansal, 2016). To combine all dimensions, Duchek's (2020) conceptualization relies on a process-oriented approach and proposes a consideration of the three dimensions of anticipation, coping, and adaptation resilience. In this chapter, we follow Duchek's (2020) conceptualization.

In the following, we briefly discuss all three dimensions and the key organizational capabilities that contribute to organizational resilience.

The first dimension of organizational resilience refers to the time before an unexpected event occurs. This approach envisages an offensive response to unexpected events in the form of anticipation (e.g., Boin & van Eeten, 2013) through the focused observation of the organizational environment. In this context of anticipation resilience, organizational resilience is defined as the ability to anticipate unexpected events and undesirable developments early and before they occur, thus enabling the organization to withstand them better. This form of resilience is therefore also referred to as antecedent resilience (Ortiz-de-Mandojana & Bansal, 2016; Boin & van Eeten, 2013). Duchek (2020) proposes three specific capabilities to help anticipate unexpected events. The first two are observing and recognizing risks and are intended to help identify and avert unexpected events at an early stage. This includes perceiving and interpreting internal and external information (e.g., Ortiz-de-Mandojana & Bansal, 2016). In addition, anticipation also enables people to make preparations (Lengnick-Hall et al., 2011). For this purpose, it can be helpful to develop future enhancements in scenario planning and to develop measures such as emergency response systems (Duchek, 2020; Hillmann & Guenther, 2021; Hillmann et al., 2018; Kendra & Wachtendorf, 2003). Anticipation can thus form the basis of an effective coping response, but it can only provide a limited scope for action. It is also emphasized that anticipation cannot avert all negative consequences (Duchek, 2020).

The second dimension concerns coping, also referred to as recovery resilience (Boin & van Eeten, 2013) or operational resilience (Välikangas & Romme, 2012). Coping represents an organization's ability to deal with and recover from unexpected events in order to return to a state of normalcy or pre-crisis levels (Boin & van Eeten, 2013). Therefore, organizations should adopt a coping strategy to adapt quickly to unexpected events. The goal of this view on organizational resilience is that unexpected events, such as natural disasters, may not have a significant impact on the resilient organization because they can be managed by the organization or if they exceed the coping capacity, the organization can at least easily recover from the impact (Duchek, 2020; Linnenluecke et al., 2012). Other authors describe the necessary coping level as the maximum achievable level of unexpected events that can be managed by an organization (e.g., Ortiz-de-Mandojana & Bansal, 2016; Ruiz-Martin et al., 2018). Coping capacities describe the organization's actions as the unexpected event occurs or looms on the horizon. To develop coping resilience, problems must be quickly identified, solutions rapidly developed, and resources speedily targeted to best mitigate the unexpected event that has occurred and its consequences (Duchek, 2020). In order to manage the problems resulting from the unexpected event, acceptance skills are first required before the second skill, the development and implementation of appropriate solutions, can begin. In order to develop viable solutions, it is necessary to regularly review implemented solutions to ensure they are still fit for purpose (Duchek, 2020; Lengnick-Hall et al., 2011).

Finally, the third dimension of organizational resilience goes beyond coping to include the restoration of the pre-crisis state and the development of new capabilities (Lengnick-Hall et al., 2011) and the adaptation of existing processes in a post-crisis manner (Ortiz-de-Mandojana & Bansal, 2016). For this reason, this phase can be considered an adaptation phase and is also referred to as strategic resilience (Välikangas & Romme, 2012). Among other things, this phase is about reflecting on the actions taken during a crisis and learning lessons from them (Duchek, 2020). This approach is intended to help an organization emerge sustainably stronger from an unexpected event (Ortiz-de-Mandojana & Bansal, 2016; Sullivan-Taylor & Wilson, 2009). Thus, adaptation in the context of organizational resilience represents a more proactive approach to dealing with unexpected events and requires a set of organizational adaptation skills and competencies to deal sustainably and effectively with unexpected events (Duchek, 2020; Lengnick-Hall et al., 2011). According to Duchek (2020), the adaptation phase includes the skills of reflection and learning as well as organizational change. To do this, the organization must be able to understand actions and outcomes and to draw conclusions for the future. In addition, to drive organizational change, management skills, and good strategic planning are also required.

As indicated when describing these three dimensions of organizational resilience, the availability of key resources such as capital, labor, and financial resources form the foundation of organizational resilience (Lengnick-Hall & Beck, 2005) and are a critical component (Duchek, 2020; Van Gils, 2005). As Duchek (2020) points out, time and professionalism are particularly needed to monitor the business environment and identify critical developments as well as opportunities. If the organization's employees do not have time, they will not be able to identify critical developments nor create and implement scenarios and training in a timely manner. In addition, financial resources are needed to prepare, develop, and deliver training (Duchek, 2020; Pal et al., 2014). Financial resources can be of particular importance here, as they play a fundamental role not only in anticipation but also in coping and the subsequent adaptation and learning phase. Studies on this topic consistently show that financial resources such as cash serve as buffers and can be used to mitigate the negative consequences of unexpected events (de Carvalho et al., 2016; Pal et al., 2014; Roffia & Dabić, 2023).

To respond to such unexpected events and build organizational resilience, the quality of knowledge and information in general seems to play an important role (e.g., Duchek, 2020; Sullivan-Taylor & Wilson, 2009). The knowledge base can be continuously expanded in all dimensions but especially in the dimension of the adaptation process after coping with the unexpected event. Especially in the context of anticipation, a broad knowledge and information base is considered one of the most important prerequisites for organizational resilience, but it also influences the coping process (Duchek, 2020).

It is important to note here that a broad existing knowledge base can both facilitate and hinder the generation of new knowledge (Cohen & Levinthal, 1990;

Duchek, 2020). In this context, perceived risk will be significantly influenced by the quality and completeness of information. It has been shown that despite attempts to complete information, decisions are often made based on incomplete or outdated information because it was not possible to complete the data (Sullivan-Taylor & Wilson, 2009). As a result of perceived risk and its importance to the industry, some organizations tend to strengthen their resilience proactively in some areas and learn, while others remain reactive and take fewer actions (Durst et al., 2022; Sullivan-Taylor & Wilson, 2009). According to Duchek (2020), an organization's knowledge base contributes significantly to organizational resilience by training anticipatory skills and can contribute to each dimension (anticipation, coping, adaptation).

In addition to resources such as a strong knowledge base, access to sufficient capital, and work time, it can be helpful to draw on social resources to deal with unexpected situations as quickly and effectively as possible (Duchek, 2020). Social capital can increase an organization's resilience in several ways. For example, multiple organizations can support each other by sharing free resources such as work time and information or through collaboration (Lengnick-Hall & Beck, 2016). Mutual support can lead social resources to promote resilience by helping to implement actions and contributing to recovery after an unexpected event (Duchek, 2020). To some extent, social resources also include a trusting organizational culture with a willingness to learn and open communication (Pal et al., 2014). Moreover, social resources do not emerge ad hoc but often require a long-term, respectful relationship between organizations and employees, as well as with external corporate partners (Lengnick-Hall et al., 2011).

The final driver of organizational resilience according to Duchek (2020) is power and responsibility, and she points out that organizations are often unable to translate generated knowledge into action. However, generated knowledge can only be effective if the respective employees have the appropriate responsibility and power to implement it. Organizational resilience comes from power based on expertise and experience rather than the hereditary position of potential decision-makers (Duchek, 2020; Lengnick-Hall et al., 2011). In this context, it is emphasized that decentralized organized firms benefit from shared decision-making among units because of the concentrated expertise. The more an organization is decentralized, the more likely that individual employees and departments will act on their own discretion and expertise, contributing to the achievement of the organization's goals (Duchek, 2020; Lengnick-Hall et al., 2011). In summary, the drivers and capabilities of organizational resilience, with the help of implementation through appropriate accountability, enable an organization to withstand unexpected events and make continuous progress. Thus, they can provide an important competitive advantage in dealing with unexpected events.

At the same time, previous research has found that different types of organizations differ in how they can achieve organizational resilience and what resources are most likely to help them do so (e.g., Duchek et al., 2020; Hepfer & Lawrence, 2022). Most importantly for this chapter, SMEs have specific characteristics and challenges when it comes to building resilience (e.g., Gianiodis et al., 2022; Tukamuhabwa et al., 2015; Zhou et al., 2022). In the following sections – particularly Sects. 3 and 4 – we will therefore focus on the specific challenges that SMEs face when trying to develop resilience and use management control systems for this purpose. Before doing so, however, we need to discuss our underlying understanding of these control systems.

3.2.3 Management Control Systems as a Package

While there are several approaches to defining management control systems, most authors agree that a central feature of these systems is to align employee behavior with organizational goals (e.g., Chenhall, 2003; Malmi & Brown, 2008; Merchant & Van der Stede, 2017). At the same time, there are several specific control systems that can support this general effort. To this end, Malmi and Brown (2008) define a conceptual framework with five types of management control, which include planning, cybernetic controls, reward and compensation, administrative controls, and cultural controls, which are discussed in more detail below. These controls can be formal, such as budgets that follow a fixed framework, or more informal, such as organizational culture. According to the package idea proposed by Malmi and Brown (2008), an individual organization can freely choose which specific management control systems to include in the organizational control package, and the included controls do not necessarily have to be related to each other.

Planning, for example, is an upstream control and is divided within the control type into long-term planning, which is more strategic, and short-term action planning. The latter's horizon defines a period of up to 12 months and is used for operational or tactical decisions, while long-term planning reflects the corporate strategy. In this context, planning can be used to coordinate the internal goals of individual departments and to allocate available resources in a targeted manner. It can also be used to coordinate the activities of individuals and groups to align them with corporate goals. In this regard, planning does not always require a financial background (Malmi & Brown, 2008). In addition, cybernetic control establishes quantitative, measurable performance indicators. By comparing them to budget targets, they can provide feedback as part of reporting, identify opportunities for improvement, and support decision-making. Cybernetic systems can include both financial and nonfinancial components. In the context of cybernetic systems, variance analysis is considered a particularly important tool because it is used in almost all organizations on the basis of budgeting and can serve as a performance measure (Bunce et al., 1995). Performance in the form of financial and nonfinancial measures can also be assigned to individual groups and employees in the context of cybernetic management to hold them accountable for specific actions (Malmi & Brown, 2008). Rewards can be given when employees or departments achieve their internal goals. The purpose is to motivate individuals or groups to act in the best interest of the organization. In the context of management control systems, according to Malmi and Brown (2008), reward and compensation systems are separate but usually linked to cybernetic controls and include external rewards. Another goal of rewards is to retain employees and their knowledge. Administrative control systems manage employees or groups through organizational design, task assignment, and policy implementation. In addition, the system ensures that the major bodies of the organization come together to coordinate their activities, set boundaries, and manage behavior (Malmi & Brown, 2008). Thus, administrative control represents a bureaucratic approach that can be understood as extended action control (Merchant & Van der Stede, 2017). The last type of control according to Malmi and Brown (2008) is cultural control. This is expressed in the beliefs, values, and social norms lived by individual members of the organization. Malmi and Brown (2008) consider three components of cultural control, which include values control, symbol control, and clan control. Values-based control is actively reinforced by leaders through open communication or by hiring employees who share the organization's values. Symbol-based control involves visible features that indicate a particular culture, such as interior decor or work attire. In third place are clan controls, which describe selection and design, as well as training and job design (Merchant & Van der Stede, 2017). However, there can be overlap in this area. For example, training can be classified as either administrative control or cultural control, depending on its purpose (Malmi & Brown, 2008).

Malmi and Brown's (2008) conceptualization of management control systems focuses on controlling the behavior of employees to align them with organizational goals. Management control systems are not seen as purely information or decision support systems but as a more comprehensive system. This system is not necessarily based on purely cybernetic ideas but includes them as an important component of a management control system. In addition, at a higher level, the system includes cultural controls, which are a more comprehensive and lengthy process than planning, cybernetic, or reward and compensation controls. The latter represent more flexible approaches and are generally more closely linked within the organizational control framework. These packages are believed to be in place at a very early stage in an organization and are more actively managed than, for example, cultural controls. It is emphasized that management control systems are not purely cybernetic, but cybernetic controls can be an important function within an organization and the system (Malmi & Brown, 2008).

3.3 Management Control Systems in SMEs

Since the 2000s, the use of management control systems in SMEs has gained an importance. While research in the field of management control systems initially focused only on large companies and their effects, it is becoming increasingly clear that SMEs can also benefit from the use of management control systems. However, although the use of management control practices can have a positive impact on firm performance, SMEs tend to increase their use of management control practices only as firm size and complexity increase, and no clear threshold for increased use has yet been identified (Davila & Foster, 2005; Lavia López & Hiebl, 2015).

Due to their smaller size and scarcer resources, SMEs are generally not comparable with larger companies when it comes to implementing management control systems and facing particular difficulties. In this regard, research has identified numerous variables that influence the adoption of management control systems, such as ownership (e.g., Pelz, 2019; Schachner et al., 2006). In addition, SMEs are more likely to experience difficulties in implementing management control systems due to a lack of information systems or financial and human resources. SME managers are often very involved in operations, and unexpected events and incidents therefore compete with the main business activity (Sullivan-Taylor & Branicki, 2011; Tognazzo et al., 2016), which ultimately results in fewer resources available for the implementation and use of management control systems and ultimately fewer benefits (Davila, 2005). In addition, many SMEs are family firms (e.g., Hiebl et al., 2012; Steiger et al., 2015) and the family owners often maintain a management style characterized by close and personal interaction (El Masri et al., 2017; Pagliarussi & Leme, 2020).

It has been shown that SMEs, like larger companies, can use a variety of management control systems. In his review study, Pelz (2019) summarizes the findings of the literature on six types of management controls, including management control activities that focus on accounting, planning, and organizing; management control systems that focus on internal decision-making but go beyond familiar accounting techniques, human resource management activities and controls, external stakeholder reporting, and liquidity planning. In this context, the review study by Pelz (2019) showed that accounting-related management control activities are among the most effective tools of management control practices and offer several benefits, such as reducing information asymmetries and coping with increasing complexity in SMEs. For this reason, the use of management control systems in SMEs is also considered a helpful tool to overcome growth difficulties (Cosenz & Noto, 2015; Palazzi et al., 2023).

Moreover, ownership and length of service have been shown to have a significant impact on the adoption and implementation of management control procedures, as well as on the hiring of financial accounting staff and the professionalization of accounting systems (Davila & Foster, 2007; Hiebl, 2017; Weigel & Hiebl, 2022). In line with this notion, the use of management control systems has been shown to increase in growing SMEs. While SMEs that remain family owned, regardless of size, often use management control systems later or not at all, SMEs that transition from a family-owned business to one run by external managers tend to use management control systems more (Hiebl & Li, 2020; Hiebl et al., 2015; Schachner et al., 2006). In addition, it has been shown that managers who have experience with implementing management control systems and are aware of the benefits stay with the company longer and can accelerate the implementation of the systems (Davila, 2005; Davila & Foster, 2007). Here, it is emphasized that venture capitalists bring not only financial support but often also an extensive knowledge base. This enables the SME to learn from the insights of other growth companies, to drive the efficient selection and implementation of conducive management control systems, and to inform and motivate relevant stakeholders through participation in the venture (Granlund & Taipaleenmäki, 2005; Hiebl, 2013).

In addition to the use of external managers and external risk capital, other variables impact the use of management control systems due to increasing complexity, such as international operations, duration of implementation, and return on investment (Lavia López & Hiebl, 2015). Due to such increasing complexity of SMEs, the adoption of management control systems is increasingly due to the need for coordination and cost monitoring (Davila & Foster, 2005; Lavia López & Hiebl, 2015; Pelz, 2019). Here, the implementation of management control systems is of great importance due to the increasing complexity caused by growth and international operations, so the implementation of management control systems positively supports growth in SMEs (Cosenz & Noto, 2015; Davila & Foster, 2007; Palazzi et al., 2023).

Financial and human resource planning have been shown to be not only among the earliest and most rapidly adopted management control systems (Davila & Foster, 2005; Davila & Foster, 2007) but also among the most widely used ones in general (Broccardo et al., 2017). Meanwhile, management control systems such as business planning are less well understood than financial and human resource planning (Pelz, 2019). Here, traditional management control systems such as budgets, financial statement analyses, and cost center analyses were most commonly used, while more advanced approaches such as balanced scorecards or benchmarking were less commonly used. The main drivers for the use of management control systems in SMEs identified in the Broccardo et al. (2017) study are the production of accurate and correct information, as well as the separation of costs and vulnerabilities, and the better management of employees and improvement of products (Broccardo et al., 2017).

3.4 Relationship Between Management Control Packages and Organizational Resilience in SMEs

Management control systems have not only proven to be an effective tool to overcome various difficulties in SMEs, such as business growth (Pelz, 2019), but have also been able to contribute to overall organizational resilience (Bracci & Tallaki, 2021). For this reason, this section discusses the impact of different management control systems, which can be classified into five different types according to Malmi and Brown (2008), and their influence on the different levels of organizational resilience according to Duchek (2020) in SMEs. To this end, the five control types (planning, cybernetic control, reward and compensation, administrative, and cultural control) are structured and examined for their contribution to Duchek's (2020) anticipation, coping, and adaptation stages, highlighting SME-specific characteristics. Moreover, it has been shown that management control systems can help reduce information asymmetries within the SME itself and with its external partners or prevent resource scarcity through planning by improving information capabilities (Pelz, 2019). For this reason, the contributions of each control type to the four drivers of organizational resilience identified by Duchek (2020) (knowledge base, resource availability, social resources, power, and accountability) are also examined. In addition, management control systems have been found to operate in multiple dimensions of organizational resilience, rather than just one, and thus can contribute to the development of organizational resilience in multiple dimensions (Bracci & Tallaki, 2021).

3.4.1 Management Control Systems and Anticipatory Forms of Organizational Resilience

According to Duchek (2020), the first dimension of organizational resilience is to identify unexpected events early on and avoid them as best as possible, although not every unexpected event can be prevented. To this end, Duchek (2020) emphasizes the business skills of observation and identification, as well as preparation and building organizational resilience. To do this, management control systems can foster the development of resilient behaviors and capabilities. In the context of anticipating, observing, and identifying unexpected events, some management control systems have been shown to be more effective overall than others (Bracci & Tallaki, 2021).

The study by Roffia and Dabić (2023) examined the resilience of Italian SMEs with limited liability during the COVID-19 pandemic and the impact of management control systems through a survey conducted in spring 2020. The results of the study revealed that the resilience of SMEs in different sectors can benefit from the use of budgets, business continuity tools, and contingency plans in the anticipation phase. The empirical study demonstrated the usefulness of budgets as cybernetic controls and planning controls according to Malmi and Brown (2008) for organizational resilience of SMEs. SMEs that use monthly budgets as a cybernetic control package were found to be more capable of anticipating unexpected events due to deviations earlier and better, and thus, the organizations respond to them more effectively (Roffia & Dabić, 2023). Moreover, the use of various crisis management practices in the anticipation phase proved to be an effective means of increasing organizational resilience in SMEs. As the study by Hong et al. (2012) shows, these include techniques such as scanning the business environment or an inclusive corporate culture, especially at the management level, to withstand better the unexpected events from the anticipation phase. The resulting strengthening of anticipatory knowledge also helps to reduce in advance the negative consequences of unexpected events in SMEs. This advantage, and furthermore the growing awareness of the importance of anticipatory knowledge information, therefore increasingly leads to the implementation of information systems and thus to the strengthening of organizational resilience (Roffia & Dabić, 2023).

In addition, preparation before the unexpected event (e.g., through the development of short-term action and contingency plans or the use of business continuity tools and enterprise resource management systems as part of planning controls, according to Malmi and Brown (2008)) has been shown to have a positive impact on organizational resilience (Roffia & Dabić, 2023). One of the purposes of planning control systems is to enable the creation of additional resources, such as a financial buffer (Pal et al., 2014), which can be drawn upon in the event of an unexpected event. In addition, the findings of Roffia and Dabić (2023) confirm the importance of management control systems in SMEs to expand the knowledge base and the relevance for the development of contingency plans, which are within the framework of anticipatory organizational resilience according to Duchek (2020). Furthermore, it was shown that the development of contingency plans requires sufficient financial resources and trained personnel to prepare the organization for targeted coping activities. Financial and, at the same time, liquid resources and human capital represent, on the one hand, one of the most important and effective components of resilience-building activities in SMEs, but, on the other hand, one of the main vulnerabilities (Pal et al., 2014; de Carvalho et al., 2016). Similarly, Roffia and Dabić (2023) were able to highlight the importance of resource availability in relation to unexpected events as a driving force and antecedent of organizational resilience in companies (Duchek, 2020). Further complicating the issue, SMEs have been shown to have more difficulties accessing financial resources due to their smaller size, greater vulnerability, and less room to maneuver. This presents the more vulnerable SMEs with even greater challenges than their larger counterparts (Sullivan-Taylor & Branicki, 2011; Tognazzo et al., 2016).

Although this is only the case in the broader context of anticipation as defined by Duchek (2020), some flexibility in strategic planning, as another important management control type (Malmi & Brown, 2008), can be an essential part of preparing for unexpected events. Flexible but long-term strategic planning can prevent resource scarcity, which is considered a significant risk in SMEs (Pal et al., 2014), through some variability and broad positioning, such as the formation of different resource sourcing paths. Thus, the possibility of different sourcing channels makes the SME less vulnerable to resource scarcity, contributing to organizational performance and resilience (Pal et al., 2014; Roffia & Dabić, 2023). This form of planning, however, often does not receive sufficient attention due to the heavy workload and involvement of SME managers in operations (Van Gils, 2005). Moreover, a study on change management in SMEs recommends proactive, long-term, and strategic planning based on the finding that well-communicated plans lead to better handling of unexpected events (Ates & Bititci, 2011; Seville et al., 2006). To bring about the proactive change and development of a resilient enterprise, human factors such as training and management skills can support the implementation of long-term strategic planning (Ates & Bititci, 2011; Moore & Manring, 2009; Seville et al., 2006) and bring about better business performance (Page & Söderbom, 2015). For this reason, human capacity building, such as effective communication and relationship building with stakeholders, is important for SMEs' resilience (Seville et al., 2006) and is a component that should emerge in advance of a crisis.

In addition, according to Malmi and Brown (2008), administrative control structures can help create organizational structure. Administrative controls are the bureaucratic approach to establishing and controlling certain behaviors and workflows within an organization (Malmi & Brown, 2008). While large companies can rely on established structures, work processes in SMEs are comparatively less routinized. The impact of routinization on organizational resilience has been studied. In this context, many authors see the creation of routines and their action orientation as an important aspect for building organizational resilience in companies (e.g., Lengnick-Hall & Beck, 2005; Lengnick-Hall et al., 2011; Weick & Sutcliffe, 2011). The study by Haase and Eberl (2019) shows that founders have come to appreciate the value of routines for organizational resilience in SMEs due to bad experiences in the past. According to Duchek (2020), the development of routines causes a strengthening of organizational resilience in the run-up to a crisis or the anticipation phase. Haase and Eberl (2019) emphasize that routines can prevent crises, especially those caused or reinforced internally by a lack of reflection and information flow, and help safeguard important processes by codifying procedures for the entire workforce and making them concrete instructions for action. In addition, routinization can lead to time savings through fixed structures.

The results showed that SMEs can improve their resilience by using budgets, business continuity tools, and contingency plans in the anticipation phase. Monthly budgets as a cybernetic control package help SMEs effectively anticipate and respond to unexpected events (Roffia & Dabić, 2023). Crisis management practices such as scanning the business environment and fostering an inclusive corporate culture were effective in increasing organizational resilience. The findings highlight the importance of financial resources and trained personnel in developing contingency plans (Hong et al., 2012). In addition, flexible strategic planning and creating multiple ways to obtain resources can help avoid resource shortages and improve resilience (Pal et al., 2014; Roffia & Dabić, 2023). Training on human factors in the context of Malmi and Brown's (2008) Cultural Controls, such as effective communication with stakeholders, is important for strengthening SME resilience (Ates & Bititci, 2011; Seville et al., 2006). In addition, administrative control structures and the development of routines contribute to organizational resilience by safeguarding processes during crises (Haase & Eberl, 2019).

3.4.2 Management Control Systems and Coping Forms of Organizational Resilience

The second phase of organizational resilience is the phase in which the unexpected event inevitably occurs (Duchek, 2020) and must be managed by the SME. To this end, Duchek (2020) describes two elementary entrepreneurial capabilities that can be used to cope with unexpected events. The first capability describes the ability of the company to accept unexpected events and thus to face them straight away and not to flee. The second essential capability is the development and implementation of short-term solutions, as implementing short-term and creative planning can help prevent disasters (Duchek, 2020; Kendra & Wachtendorf, 2003).

In order to accept the uncertain environment as well as the occurrence of unexpected events according to Duchek (2020), it is necessary to develop an understanding of the environment and to identify critical developments over time. For this purpose, it is necessary to characterize disruptive events, i.e., the occurrence of an unexpected event by thresholds. For this reason, it may be useful to compare actual states with an acceptable level of target states (Catalan & Robert, 2011). At this point, for example, budgets as the best-known cybernetic management control systems according to Malmi and Brown can be used in the context of a variance analysis or balanced scorecard with financial and nonfinancial metrics to compare target and actual states.

Management control systems in the form of long-term and short-term flexible planning (Malmi & Brown, 2008) in SMEs can help to maintain high employee motivation through the formation of perspectives and action plans. When an unexpected event occurs, it becomes apparent whether the long-term strategic planning and short-term implementation prove their worth by demonstrating, for example, whether the risk of resource shortages in the SME can be avoided through the substitute supply channels developed in advance of a crisis (Pal et al., 2014). In addition, short-term planning (i.e., operational management including inventory management based on internal and external information, such as accounting information) can respond to current events at short notice. Based on this information, many companies focus on cost reduction as a first step (Hong et al., 2012) or even a new consideration of the make-or-buy decision (Pal et al., 2014). This short-term action planning allows the SME to address a lack of flexibility (e.g., in the supply chain) in the long-term planning despite alternative sourcing paths, thus improving crisis management in case of unexpected events. The study by Thun et al. (2011) highlighted the impact of risk management systems on supply chain resilience in SMEs. The empirical study of small- and medium-sized automotive suppliers in Germany showed that SMEs and their larger competitors are almost equally affected by supply chain uncertainty, but SMEs are often more dependent on other companies and, for this reason, more vulnerable to unexpected events. However, SMEs tend to rely less on cybernetic risk measurement systems and controls than their larger competitors, and they tend to react reactively rather than proactively by incorporating supply chain risks and replacement procurement routes already incorporated in the long-term planning process (Thun et al., 2011).

This reactive behavior of SMEs often leads to the creation of redundancies and overcapacities that can be relied upon to cope with unexpected events. In turn, the creation of excess capacity represents a higher cost burden for SMEs than a lean production, inventory, and risk management structure (Shingo, 1989; Thun et al., 2011). Nevertheless, several authors emphasize the positive impact of resources such as human capital and access to sufficient financial resources on organizational resilience (Duchek, 2020; Tognazzo et al., 2016; Van Gils, 2005). At the same time, the lack of resources and the resulting dwindling flexibility in SMEs is often referred to in this context (Tognazzo et al., 2016; Van Gils, 2005). In particular, financial resources play a special role in coping with unexpected events for SMEs (de Carvalho et al., 2016; Pal et al., 2014). While larger companies can use their resources strategically, resource constraints in SMEs often compete for strategic priority with core business. This often leads to actions that the SME can still afford at the time of the crisis, but not to those that would have the best impact (Tognazzo et al., 2016). For this reason, the empirical study by Pal et al. (2014) points out the importance of resource efficiency in SMEs. The authors show that although overcapacity costs a lot, its use, for example, as a financial buffer contributes positively to the preservation of the SME in case of an unexpected event. In the study, the SMEs interviewed considered system information on the status of resources as a cybernetic measurement tool according to Malmi and Brown (2008), combined with proper and strict budgetary control as one of the most important management control systems for organizational resilience. Using information from these management control systems, some of the SMEs surveyed generated additional resources for crisis management by, for example, retaining profits or reducing costs. Moreover, despite the high cost of excess capacity such as the financial buffer, SMEs were found to not only cope better with unexpected events but also to have better overall performance, indicating a significant relationship between resource availability and organizational resilience (Pal et al., 2014).

The coping phase can also be closely linked to the anticipation phase, for example by drawing on previously developed contingency plans (Roffia & Dabić, 2023). As mentioned, SME managers tend not to pay enough attention to planning and control activities (Van Gils, 2005) and are too busy with day-to-day operations and solving short-term problems (Ates & Bititci, 2011). Thus, if an unexpected event occurs, managers can fall back on the previously developed contingency plans without investing additional resources. Such prior active management involvement in business planning can have a positive impact on business performance through the optimal use of resources and production capacity (Finkelstein & Hambrick, 1996) while also having the positive effect that companies with active planning are more likely to pursue and implement their plans (Malmi & Brown, 2008). When implementing plans, management control systems adapted to each company can help to perform monitoring activities and take corrective actions when needed (Merchant & Van der Stede, 2017). Through this preparation, management control systems can relieve entrepreneurs and help to plan further, make decisions, and monitor cash flow. For planning further, financial accounting practices in particular and management control systems based on them can help improve the financial situation, ensuring access to credit and favorable borrowing costs in general (Pelz, 2019; Vander Bauwhede et al., 2015).

3.4.3 Management Control Systems and Adoption Forms of Organizational Resilience

According to Duchek (2020), the third dimension of organizational resilience is the adaptation phase. In this phase, the unexpected event that has occurred is considered to have been managed and focus is on reflecting upon the event and the actions implemented. The goal of this phase is to draw lessons and actions from the situation and to optimize and harness them for organizational needs. The dimension is thus associated with a kind of long-term learning in dealing with new situations and thus with a constant expansion of the knowledge base, which is fundamental for the ability to anticipate future unexpected events. According to Duchek (2020), this dimension requires two organizational capabilities in particular: the ability to reflect and learn and the ability to change.

Duchek (2020) emphasizes that reflection and learning require certain behaviors in order to gain information for future challenges from an unexpected event. To this end, according to Malmi and Brown (2008), management control systems that target culture can significantly influence employee learning. Cultural management control systems can include, for example, behaviors and belief systems conducive to organizational goals but also training (Merchant & Van der Stede, 2017). Pal et al. (2014) emphasized in their study of Swedish SMEs in the textile industry that learning and culture-related aspects play an important role in the development of organizational resilience in SMEs. While SMEs can learn faster due to their smaller size and easier decision-making ability (Pal et al., 2014), previous studies show that learning in groups increases motivation and effectiveness in coping with and reflecting on new situations, and thus is also beneficial to organizational resilience (Sutcliffe & Vogus, 2003). In order to enable effective learning in general, the SMEs interviewed mainly considered responsibility, respect and trust, and sense making as elementary components to initiate learning. In addition, it is emphasized that organizational resilience results from the learned expertise of all employees and their response to unexpected events (Pal et al., 2014). However, the authors add that learning as a cultural aspect is not an immediate remedy during an unexpected event but needs to be established in the long term and not crisis-dependent, thus also promoting anticipatory knowledge. The effectiveness of cultural learning in this regard is based on several reasons, such as the sense of belonging that can be created when learning together in groups and developing solutions. In addition, it became clear that the SMEs interviewed considered that one of the barriers to organizational resilience was the lack of cross-functional training, as part of the cultural and organizational management control system (Pal et al., 2014). Here, group learning could help to provide cross-functional knowledge and overcome barriers. This long-term and not necessarily crisis-dependent culture management can also help create a shared corporate vision (Ates & Bititci, 2011). However, building resilient SMEs is not only about developing values and a long-term vision but also about identifying the strengths and weaknesses of groups or individuals and eliminating them. The authors explain that organizational circumstances should be taken into account through targeted actions in the context of culture and organizational control to establish new behaviors and strengths that prevent, for example, the continuous learning mentioned above (Ates & Bititci, 2011) and promote organizational resilience.

With regard to the second resilience-enhancing capability, the ability to change (Duchek, 2020), the literature shows that organizational resilience and change management go hand in hand. For example, the ability to adapt to new market events and unexpected events represents an important contribution to resilience (Ates & Bititci, 2011; Fiksel, 2006). In their study on the importance of change processes, Ates and Bititci (2011) identify several characteristics, behaviors, and resources that influence both change management and the adaptation phase after an unexpected event and are therefore considered important influencing variables in this phase of organizational resilience. In the context of the adaptation phase as well as change management, resource availability and long- and short-term planning in particular play an important role (Alberti et al., 2018; Duchek, 2020; Pal et al., 2014; Sullivan-Taylor & Branicki, 2011). In addition, management control systems such as variance analysis contribute to the availability of knowledge and information and support managers in pursuing entrepreneurial goals, the change process, and thus to adapt as a result of a crisis (Ates & Bititci, 2011). In this context, Ates and Bititci (2011) emphasize that SMEs pay special attention to core operational tasks while often neglecting human aspects (i.e., cultural and communication), which may lead to change resistance and thus adaptation resistance within resilience (Seville et al., 2006). However, this can be avoided by promoting cultural controls through effective internal communication of shared values and goals, as well as reward systems. To this end, it can be beneficial to establish continuous internal communication, e.g., through interim reports on important decisions, and to involve stakeholders in order to minimize resistance to change. Furthermore, the type of decision-making and leadership culture in SMEs is also questioned here, with a centralized decision-making process being a potential barrier to necessary change (Ates & Bititci, 2011). Instead, a leadership style that conveys to employees the importance of being an essential part of and responsible for the SME through the use of cultural controls should be used to increase resilience (Ates & Bititci, 2011; Malmi & Brown, 2008).

3.5 Summary and Implications

The objective of this study was to clarify the use of management control systems and their contribution to the degree of SME resilience to unexpected events. For this purpose, the existing literature was reviewed, including the state of research on the use of management control systems in SMEs according to Malmi and Brown's (2008) categorization of control types in times of unexpected events. The available findings were classified into the three phases of organizational resilience (anticipation, coping, adoption) according to Duchek (2020). Here, it is clear that SMEs have several levers to increase their organizational resilience through the use of different management control systems. In addition, it was highlighted that some resources and management control systems (e.g., planning controls including short-term or strategic planning) as well as cultural control systems can have cross-phase effects in SMEs. At the same time, and consistent with the idea that management control systems can be individually combined (Malmi & Brown, 2008), the available literature suggests that any combination of such controls and other resources must be tailored to the individual needs of the specific small- or medium-sized enterprise. This is reflected in Fig. 3.2, which shows that across all three dimensions of resilience (Duchek, 2020), various management control systems and other resources can be combined to achieve resilience. Thus, the dots and lines reflecting a particular combination of control systems and other resources in Fig. 3.2 are illustrative only. Nevertheless, Fig. 3.2 illustrates the possible choices that SMEs can make when seeking to equip themselves with the three forms of resilience and primarily using management control systems for this purpose.

In addition, and similar to the orientation of a holistic management control system, it is emphasized here that a high level of organizational resilience can only be achieved if all three phases of the organizational resilience model are taken into account (Duchek, 2020). Management control systems in the different dimensions of resilience can help SMEs to identify, manage, and/or learn from negative

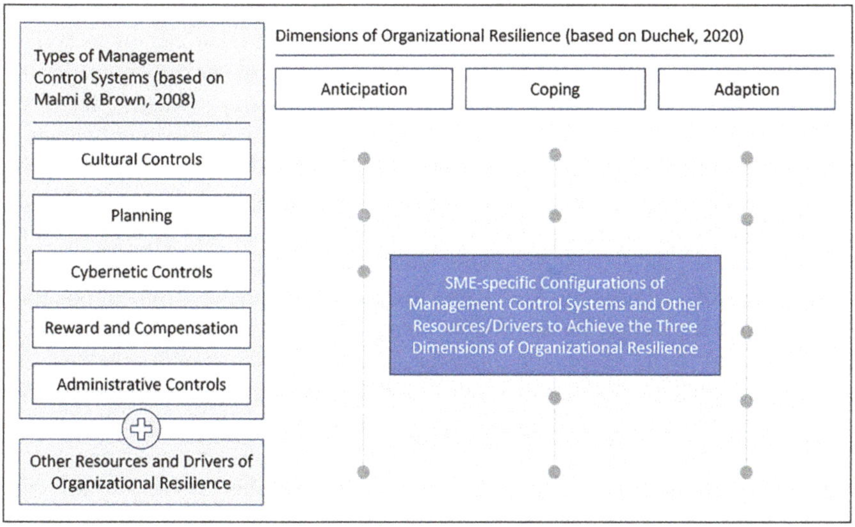

Fig. 3.2 Individual combinations of management control systems and other resources to achieve organizational resilience in SMEs

developments at an early stage. However, this requires a holistic focus of control packages in order to achieve effective benefits in all phases. SMEs also need to be aware of the organizational capabilities and resources required to implement the measures to achieve effective benefits. The present chapter shows that the organizational capabilities associated with each dimension of resilience according to Duchek (2020) are also of particular importance for SMEs to increase organizational resilience (Pal et al., 2014; de Carvalho et al., 2016). Some of these resilience-building capabilities are more difficult and challenging to implement in SMEs than others. This is particularly related to drivers of organizational resilience, such as access to human resources or capital, the availability of which is often lower or more difficult to obtain in SMEs than in larger firms (Sullivan-Taylor & Branicki, 2011; Tognazzo et al., 2016; Van Gils, 2005).

In particular, the knowledge base appears to be of great importance for organizational resilience (Duchek, 2020). Due to the lower use of formal management control systems, internal information processing in individual SMEs is often less sophisticated than in larger companies, which in turn creates new difficulties in the use of management control systems (Lavia López & Hiebl, 2015; Sullivan-Taylor & Branicki, 2011). Although it has been shown that the adoption of management control practices in areas such as the environment, human resources, and organizational factors could have positive effects on firm performance and resilience, SMEs tend to adopt more management control practices only as their firm size increases (Lavia López & Hiebl, 2015). To counteract lower information processing in SMEs, social resources as a cultural control type in the form of relationships and business collaborations could contribute to business performance and resilience through knowledge sharing by enabling SMEs to benefit from the insights and developments of other SMEs. This, in turn, requires fostering trusting relationships as well as adopting comprehensive management control practices of their own so that the SME can also contribute to the entrepreneurial relationship (Duchek, 2020; Pal et al., 2014). Interorganizational relationships help not only in sharing or gathering information but also in implementing decisions quickly and maintaining an ongoing business relationship through mutual support (Sullivan-Taylor & Branicki, 2011).

Duchek (2020) also emphasized in her study that the phases of organizational resilience cannot be clearly delineated and may overlap. Similarly, the different types of controls according to Malmi and Brown (2008) and the drivers of organizational resilience can operate in multiple phases. The coping phase, for example, is closely related to the adaptation phase because the former provides the basis for learning from the previous unexpected event. That is, the phases of organizational resilience build on each other and learning can occur from bad coping as well as good coping. The sequence of organizational resilience phases can influence each other both positively and negatively (Duchek, 2020). For this reason, it is advisable not to underestimate the impact of interaction effects of individual resilience phases, especially in SMEs that are already more vulnerable. Furthermore, there is the possibility that the individual management control types according to Malmi and Brown (2008) also influence each other and thus also reinforce or cancel out their effect with regard to organizational resilience (cf. Grabner & Moers, 2013). For example, it has been shown that the implementation of efficiency controls in SMEs can reciprocally influence or even cancel out the influence of cultural controls. When developing holistic management control systems with the aim of strengthening organizational resilience, attention should therefore be paid to possible interactions between different management control systems, such as cybernetic and cultural control packages, in order to avoid negative effects (Nguyen et al., 2023; Voss & Brettel, 2014).

In this context, resource alignment and key strategy formation emerged as important components of organizational resilience and are closely linked. The study by Alberti et al. (2018) examined the resilience of Italian SMEs in terms of profitability and competitiveness. While resource availability emerged as an important attribute of organizational resilience, the less mentioned investment activity and diversification of products and distribution channels also contribute to organizational resilience and to ensuring profitability but could not be attributed to any specific phase of building organizational resilience (Alberti et al., 2018). However, the study by Alberti et al. (2018) showed that SMEs that, for example, strengthen the core business and invest in machinery by means of targeted investment planning can improve product and supply quality and often reduce costs, which thus contribute to organizational resilience and maintaining competitiveness (Alberti et al., 2018). Investments that thus achieve the unique selling proposition of products, as well as the broadening of offerings, represent an effective way for SMEs to differentiate themselves from competitors and build resilience (Alberti et al., 2018; Ibrahim, 1993).

In order to make decisions such as those on investments, management control systems can effectively support decision-making in the stages of coping and adjustment. However, Malmi and Brown (2008) suggest that implementing plans requires the management structure within administrative controls to not only equip the relevant staff with the information provided by management control systems but also to ensure that they have the appropriate authority and responsibilities for the area in question (Bracci & Tallaki, 2021). In addition, management control systems can help focus individual behavior on core tasks to support organizational resilience and coping with uncertain times (Simons, 1994). In addition to the impact of appropriate governance structures at the management level in SMEs, it has been shown that the adoption of management control systems can depend on both firm size (Lavia López & Hiebl, 2015; Sullivan-Taylor & Branicki, 2011) and ownership (Akroyd & Kober, 2020). For example, in Akroyd and Kober's (2020) study, it was shown that both owners and managers can have a major impact on the practices and extent of management control packages used. In addition, managers who use more management control systems have been shown to stay in management longer (Davila & Forster, 2007). However, they must be careful not to over-bureaucratize management control systems, which can be detrimental to organizational culture (Akroyd & Kober, 2020) and could strain SMEs' already scarce resources (Bürgel et al., 2023). In addition, managers face the challenge of changing requirements for management control systems, especially in times of high uncertainty. In this context, it has been found that the more uncertain the business environment becomes due to unexpected events, the more the management control system is affected by change, and the need for flexibility and complementarity of the control system increases (Chenhall, 2003).

This and other work have therefore underscored that management control systems can support organizational resilience in SMEs and that owners have a strong influence on the management control practices used and are involved in their professionalization (Hiebl & Mayrleitner, 2019; Weigel & Hiebl, 2022). In addition to influencing the adoption and use of management control systems, a manager's personal resilience has also been shown to influence organizational resilience (e.g., Branicki et al., 2017; Roffia & Dabić, 2023). However, the entrepreneur's personal resilience could not be attributed to any specific dimension of resilience in Duchek's (2020) conceptualization. Nevertheless, the entrepreneur's personal resilience showed a positive relationship with the SME's organizational resilience due to the high influence of this personal resilience on strategic decisions (Roffia & Dabić, 2023), and so it can be taken into account in the selection process and implementation of cultural controls training. Therefore, the authors deliberately recommend training the personal resilience of decision makers so that they can contribute to the organizational resilience of the SME (Roffia & Dabić, 2023). However, one of the criticisms is the learning experience during training, as theory often teaches outdated concepts that do not correspond to the new challenges, especially those of SMEs (Hillmann et al., 2018). For this reason, specific skills should be targeted in the selection process and training of managers within the framework of cultural controls according to Malmi and Brown (2008). While managers directly influence resilience through their decisions, especially in small SMEs, an indirect effect can be seen through the influence of managers on the corporate culture and climate

(Branicki et al., 2017), so that, for example, uncertainties in management are transmitted to employees.

3.6 Concluding Remarks

The rapidly changing business environment and the occurrence of unexpected events increasingly pose new challenges to enterprises, especially the more vulnerable SMEs. In order to protect these SMEs and save them from lasting consequences, it is necessary to anticipate unexpected events in a timely manner and provide for efficient and effective coping management and adaptation. Against the backdrop of a growing awareness of the dangers of unexpected events (Tukamuhabwa et al., 2015), organizational resilience is becoming increasingly important and, as a result, is increasingly the focus of decision-makers and researchers. This chapter contributes to the literature on the use of management control systems in SMEs and their entry points for building organizational resilience. It identifies which control systems and drivers can have a significant impact on organizational resilience in SMEs. The above discussion highlights various relationships and interactions as well as the influence of other factors that do not fall within the dimensions of organizational resilience. The main contribution of this chapter to the available literature is that it is the first to provide an overview of currently established and potential further relationships between management control systems and organizational resilience in SMEs. Also, our summary framework depicted in Fig. 3.2 may be used as a map by fellow researchers who want to dig deeper into the combinations of control systems and further resources to achieve the three discussed dimensions of resilience.

Our above integrative review was able to demonstrate a positive contribution of different types of controls. It showed that management control systems can support the management at each stage of resilience in different ways. Here, the planning, cybernetic, cultural, and organizational controls mentioned by Malmi and Brown (2008) were found by available research to be helpful control types, while little is known about the effect of reward and compensation controls on organizational resilience in SMEs. In particular, the planning and cybernetic control types seem to be effective through the use of variance analysis and the development of contingency plans, especially in the anticipation and coping phases. Meanwhile, cultural and organizational controls were thus far found to be more effective in the coping phase and subsequent adaptation phase. At the same time, as mentioned above, we found various indications of highly individual combinations of control systems and other resources for achieving resilience in SMEs. We therefore generally call for further empirical research before we can provide more general advice for SME practice on which types of controls seem particularly promising for developing resilience.

Many studies, including ours, have limitations and provide suggestions for future research. The results of this integrative review are based on studies from the qualitative or quantitative empirical literature. While these studies reflect the influence of management control types according to Malmi and Brown (2008), they generally do not provide specific recommendations for action or design guidance for control systems to support individual resilience measures, nor do they provide guidance on developing overall organizational resilience. Therefore, this integrative review serves to fill existing gaps in the literature on organizational resilience in SMEs through the use of management control systems according to Malmi and Brown (2008). The results of the study contribute to the understanding of the relationship between organizational resilience and the supporting effect of management control systems in SMEs and may help companies to set new organizational resilience goals or to use control systems for this purpose or to optimize existing ones.

A limitation of this study is the selection of literature, which was elective, as is typical of integrative reviews (Cronin & George, 2023). Although we searched extensively for relevant literature, potentially relevant works may not have been included in the study. In addition, this study focused on Malmi and Brown's (2008) conceptualization of management control packages and Duchek's (2020) understanding of organizational resilience and its drivers, so further research could explore the interplay and interaction of other conceptualizations of management control systems such as that of Simons (1994) and other forms of classifying organizational resilience. In any case, the findings need to be examined critically for their applicability to individual SMEs in question. For example, SMEs have different understandings and resource availabilities, organizational resilience, and/or management control systems. Moreover, small SMEs with less than 50 employees have been declared a special case in some studies because their management is often structured differently than that of larger SMEs (e.g., Ates & Bititci, 2011). Although the studies reviewed here do not allow us to identify specific differences between small- and medium-sized firms, we call for further research that specifically considers heterogeneity among large groups of SMEs worldwide. In addition, further empirical studies are needed that examine management control systems in the context of organizational resilience in SMEs, and research would be useful on the importance and influence of rewards and compensation as a control system. In addition, future research could be conducted on an industry-specific basis to provide more specific insights and highlight differences.

References

Abor, J., & Quartey, P. (2010). Issues in SME development in Ghana and South Africa. *International Research Journal of Finance and Economics, 39*(6), 215–228.

Akroyd, C., & Kober, R. (2020). Imprinting founders' blueprints on management control systems. *Management Accounting Research, 46*, 100645.

Alberti, F. G., Ferrario, S., & Pizzurno, E. (2018). Resilience: Resources and strategies of SMEs in a new theoretical framework. *International Journal of Learning and Intellectual Capital, 15*(2), 165–188.

Ali, I., Arslan, A., Chowdhury, M., Khan, Z., & Tarba, S. Y. (2022). Reimagining global food value chains through effective resilience to COVID-19 shocks and similar future events: A dynamic capability perspective. *Journal of Business Research, 141*, 1–12.

Ates, A., & Bititci, U. (2011). Change process: A key enabler for building resilient SMEs. *International Journal of Production Research, 49*(18), 5601–5618.

Beuren, I. M., & Santos, V. D. (2019). Enabling and coercive management control systems and organizational resilience. *Revista Contabilidade & Finanças, 30*, 307–323.

Boin, A., & Van Eeten, M. J. (2013). The resilient organization. *Public Management Review, 15*(3), 429–445.

Bracci, E., & Tallaki, M. (2021). Resilience capacities and management control systems in public sector organisations. *Journal of Accounting & Organizational Change, 17*(3), 332–351.

Branicki, L. J., Sullivan-Taylor, B., & Livschitz, S. R. (2017). How entrepreneurial resilience generates resilient SMEs. *International Journal of Entrepreneurial Behavior & Research, 24*(7), 1244–1263.

Broccardo, L., Giacosa, E., Culasso, F., & Ferraris, A. (2017). Management control in Italian SMEs. *Global Business and Economics Review, 19*(5), 632–647.

Bunce, P., Fraser, R., & Woodcock, L. (1995). Advanced budgeting: A journey to advanced management systems. *Management Accounting Research, 6*(3), 253–265.

Bürgel, T. R., Hiebl, M. R., & Pielsticker, D. I. (2023). Digitalization and entrepreneurial firms' resilience to pandemic crises: Evidence from COVID-19 and the German Mittelstand. *Technological Forecasting and Social Change, 186*, 122135.

Burns, J., Quinn, M., Warren, L., & Oliveira, J. (2013). *Management accounting*. McGraw Hill.

Catalan, C., & Robert, B. (2011). *Evaluation of organizational resilience: Application in Quebec*. Centre Risque & Performance, École Polytechnique de Montréal.

Chenhall, R. H. (2003). Management control systems design within its organizational context: Findings from contingency-based research and directions for the future. *Accounting, Organizations and Society, 28*(2–3), 127–168.

Chrisman, J. J., Chua, J. H., & Steier, L. P. (2011). Resilience of family companies: An introduction. *Entrepreneurship Theory and Practice, 35*(6), 1107–1119.

Code of Federal Regulations. (1996). *PART 121 – Small business size regulations*. Available on: https://www.ecfr.gov/current/title-13/chapter-I/part-121. Last accessed on 19 Apr 2023.

Cohen, W. M., & Levinthal, D. A. (1990). Absorptive capacity: A new perspective on learning and innovation. *Administrative Science Quarterly, 35*(1), 128–152.

Cosenz, F., & Noto, L. (2015). Combining system dynamics modelling and management control systems to support strategic learning processes in SMEs: A dynamic performance management approach. *Journal of Management Control, 26*, 225–248.

Cronin, M. A., & George, E. (2023). The why and how of the integrative review. *Organizational Research Methods, 26*(1), 168–192.

Davila, T. (2005). An exploratory study on the emergence of management control systems: Formalizing human resources in small growing firms. *Accounting, Organizations and Society, 30*(3), 223–248.

Davila, A., & Foster, G. (2005). Management accounting systems adoption decisions: Evidence and performance implications from early-stage/startup companies. *The Accounting Review, 80*(4), 1039–1068.

Davila, A., & Foster, G. (2007). Management control systems in early-stage startup companies. *The Accounting Review, 82*(4), 907–937.

De Carvalho, A. O., Ribeiro, I., Cirani, C. B. S., & Cintra, R. F. (2016). Organizational resilience: A comparative study between innovative and non-innovative companies based on the financial performance analysis. *International Journal of Innovation, 4*(1), 58–69.

Duchek, S. (2020). Organizational resilience: A capability-based conceptualization. *Business Research, 13*(1), 215–246.

Duchek, S., Raetze, S., & Scheuch, I. (2020). The role of diversity in organizational resilience: A theoretical framework. *Business Research, 13*(2), 387–423.

Durst, S., & Henschel, T. (2021). COVID-19 as an accelerator for developing strong (er) businesses? Insights from Estonian small firms. *Journal of the International Council for Small Business, 2*(1), 1–29.

Durst, S., Henschel, T., & Salzmann, J. (2022). Crisis management practices in small- and medium-sized firms. In S. Durst & T. Henschel (Eds.), *Crisis management for small and medium-sized enterprises (SMEs)* (pp. 15–27). Springer International Publishing.

El Masri, T., Tekathen, M., Magnan, M., & Boulianne, E. (2017). Calibrating management control technologies and the dual identity of family firms. *Qualitative Research in Accounting & Management, 14*(2), 157–188.
Elaian, K. (1996). Employment implications of small-scale industries in developing countries: Evidence from Jordan. *Science Technology and Development, 14*, 80–101.
European Commission. (2023). *SME definition*. https://single-market-economy.ec.europa.eu/smes/-sme-definition_en. Last accessed on 19 Apr 2023.
Fiksel, J. (2006). Sustainability and resilience: Toward a systems approach. *Sustainability: Science, Practice and Policy, 2*(2), 14–21.
Fiksel, J., Polyviou, M., Croxton, K. L., & Pettit, T. J. (2015). From risk to resilience: Learning to deal with disruption. *MIT Sloan Management Review, 56*(2), 79–86.
Finkelstein, S., & Hambrick, D. C. (1996). *Strategic leadership: Top executives and their effects on organizations*. West Publishing Company.
Gianiodis, P., Lee, S. H., Zhao, H., Foo, M. D., & Audretsch, D. (2022). Lessons on small business resilience. *Journal of Small Business Management, 60*(5), 1029–1040.
Grabner, I., & Moers, F. (2013). Management control as a system or a package? Conceptual and empirical issues. *Accounting, Organizations and Society, 38*(6–7), 407–419.
Granlund, M., & Taipaleenmäki, J. (2005). Management control and controllership in new economy firms—A life cycle perspective. *Management Accounting Research, 16*(1), 21–57.
Guan, F., Tienan, W., & Tang, L. (2023). Organizational resilience under COVID-19: The role of digital technology in R&D investment and performance. *Industrial Management & Data Systems, 123*(1), 41–63.
Haase, A., & Eberl, P. (2019). The challenges of routinizing for building resilient startups. *Journal of Small Business Management, 57*(S2), 579–597.
Hepfer, M., & Lawrence, T. B. (2022). The heterogeneity of organizational resilience: Exploring functional, operational and strategic resilience. *Organization Theory, 3*(1), 26317877221074701.
Hiebl, M. R. (2013). Management accounting in the family business: Tipping the balance for survival. *Journal of Business Strategy, 34*(6), 19–25.
Hiebl, M. R. (2017). Finance managers in family firms: An upper-echelons view. *Journal of Family Business Management, 7*(2), 207–220.
Hiebl, M. R., & Mayrleitner, B. (2019). Professionalization of management accounting in family firms: the impact of family members. *Review of Managerial Science, 13*, 1037–1068.
Hiebl, M. R. W., & Li, Z. (2020). Non-family managers in family firms: Review, integrative framework and future research agenda. *Review of Managerial Science, 14*(4), 763–807.
Hiebl, M. R. W., Feldbauer-Durstmüller, B., Duller, C., & Neubauer, H. (2012). Institutionalisation of management accounting in family businesses: Empirical evidence from Austria and Germany. *Journal of Enterprising Culture, 20*(4), 405–436.
Hiebl, M. R. W., Duller, C., Feldbauer-Durstmüller, B., & Ulrich, P. (2015). Family influence and management accounting usage: Findings from Germany and Austria. *Schmalenbach Business Review, 67*(3), 368–404.
Hillmann, J., & Guenther, E. (2021). Organizational resilience: A valuable construct for management research? *International Journal of Management Reviews, 23*(1), 7–44.
Hillmann, J., Duchek, S., Meyr, J., & Guenther, E. (2018). Educating future managers for developing resilient organizations: The role of scenario planning. *Journal of Management Education, 42*(4), 461–495.
Hong, P., Huang, C., & Li, B. (2012). Crisis management for SMEs: Insights from a multiple-case study. *International Journal of Business Excellence, 5*(5), 535–553.
Huang, H. H., Kerstein, J., Wang, C., & Wu, F. (2022a). Firm climate risk, risk management, and bank loan financing. *Strategic Management Journal, 43*(13), 2849–2880.
Huang, Q., Li, Y., Lin, M., & McBrayer, G. A. (2022b). Natural disasters, risk salience, and corporate ESG disclosure. *Journal of Corporate Finance, 72*, 102152.
Hussain, M. M., Gunasekaran, A., & Laitinen, E. K. (1998). Management accounting systems in Finnish service firms. *Technovation, 18*(1), 57–67.

Ibrahim, A. B. (1993). Strategy types and small firms' performance: An empirical investigation. *Journal of Small Business Strategy, 4*(1), 13–22.
Ingirige, M. J. B., Jones, K., & Proverbs, D. (2008, February 11–15). Investigating SME resilience and their adaptive capacities to extreme weather events: A literature review and synthesis. In *Proceedings of the Building Resilience BEAR 2008* (pp. 582–593), Kandalama, Sri Lanka.
Jesson, J., Matheson, L., & Lacey, F. M. (2011). *Doing your literature review: Traditional and systematic techniques*. Sage.
Juergensen, J., Guimón, J., & Narula, R. (2020). European SMEs amidst the COVID-19 crisis: Assessing impact and policy responses. *Journal of Industrial and Business Economics, 47*(3), 499–510.
Kendra, J. M., & Wachtendorf, T. (2003). Elements of resilience after the world trade center disaster: Reconstituting New York City's Emergency Operations Centre. *Disasters, 27*(1), 37–53.
Langfield-Smith, K. (1997). Management control systems and strategy: A critical review. *Accounting, Organizations and Society, 22*(2), 207–232.
Lavia López, O., & Hiebl, M. R. (2015). Management accounting in small and medium-sized enterprises: Current knowledge and avenues for further research. *Journal of Management Accounting Research, 27*(1), 81–119.
Lee, A. V., Vargo, J., & Seville, E. (2013). Developing a tool to measure and compare organizations' resilience. *Natural Hazards Review, 14*(1), 29–41.
Lengnick-Hall, C. A., & Beck, T. E. (2005). Adaptive fit versus robust transformation: How organizations respond to environmental change. *Journal of Management, 31*(5), 738–757.
Lengnick-Hall, C. A., & Beck, T. E. (2016). Resilience capacity and strategic agility: Prerequisites for thriving in a dynamic environment. In *Resilience engineering perspectives* (Vol. 2, pp. 61–92). CRC Press.
Lengnick-Hall, C. A., Beck, T. E., & Lengnick-Hall, M. L. (2011). Developing a capacity for organizational resilience through strategic human resource management. *Human Resource Management Review, 21*(3), 243–255.
Linnenluecke, M. K. (2017). Resilience in business and management research: A review of influential publications and a research agenda. *International Journal of Management Reviews, 19*(1), 4–30.
Linnenluecke, M. K., Griffiths, A., & Winn, M. (2012). Extreme weather events and the critical importance of anticipatory adaptation and organizational resilience in responding to impacts. *Business Strategy and the Environment, 21*(1), 17–32.
Malmi, T., & Brown, D. A. (2008). Management control systems as a package—Opportunities, challenges and research directions. *Management Accounting Research, 19*(4), 287–300.
Marcazzan, E., Campagnolo, D., & Gianecchini, M. (2022). Reaction or anticipation? Resilience in small-and medium-sized enterprises. *Journal of Small Business and Enterprise Development, 29*(5), 764–788.
Merchant, K. A., & Van der Stede, W. A. (2017). *Management control systems: Performance measurement, evaluation and incentives* (4th ed.). Pearson.
Mitchell, F., & Reid, G. C. (2000). Problems, challenges and opportunities: The small business as a setting for management accounting research. *Management Accounting Research, 11*(4), 385–390.
Moore, S. B., & Manring, S. L. (2009). Strategy development in small and medium sized enterprises for sustainability and increased value creation. *Journal of Cleaner Production, 17*(2), 276–282.
Nguyen, D. H., Hiebl, M. R., & Quinn, M. (2023). Integrating a new management accounting routine into a routine cluster: The role of interactions between multiple management accounting routines. *Qualitative Research in Accounting & Management*, in press. https://doi.org/10.1108/QRAM-03-2022-0049
Ortiz-de-Mandojana, N., & Bansal, P. (2016). The long-term benefits of organizational resilience through sustainable business practices. *Strategic Management Journal, 37*(8), 1615–1631.
Page, J., & Söderbom, M. (2015). Is small beautiful? Small enterprise, aid and employment in Africa. *African Development Review, 27*(S1), 44–55.

Pagliarussi, M. S., & Leme, M. A. (2020). The institutionalization of management control systems in a family firm. *Qualitative Research in Accounting & Management, 17*(4), 649–673.

Pal, R., Torstensson, H., & Mattila, H. (2014). Antecedents of organizational resilience in economic crises—An empirical study of Swedish textile and clothing SMEs. *International Journal of Production Economics, 147*, 410–428.

Palazzi, F., Sgrò, F., Ciambotti, M., Bontis, N., & Gelsomini, L. (2023). The moderating effect of corporate size on the relationship between prospector strategy and management accounting practices. *Journal of Management Control*, in press. https://doi.org/10.1007/s00187-023-00353-2

Pelz, M. (2019). Can management accounting be helpful for young and small companies? Systematic review of a paradox. *International Journal of Management Reviews, 21*(2), 256–274.

Roffia, P., & Dabić, M. (2023). The role of management control and integrated information systems for the resilience of SMEs. *Review of Managerial Science*, in press. https://doi.org/10.1007/s11846-023-00657-6

Ruiz-Martin, C., López-Paredes, A., & Wainer, G. (2018). What we know and do not know about organizational resilience. *International Journal of Production Management and Engineering, 6*(1), 11–28.

Schachner, M., Speckbacher, G., & Wentges, P. (2006). Steuerung mittelständischer Unternehmen: Größeneffekte und Einfluss der Eigentums- und Führungsstruktur. *Zeitschrift für Betriebswirtschaft, 76*(6), 589–614.

Seville, E., Brunsdon, D., Dantas, A., Le Masurier, J., Wilkinson, S., & Vargo, J. (2006, August). *Building organisational resilience: A summary of key research findings*. Resilient Organizations Research Programme, Christchurch, New Zealand.

Shingo, S. (1989). *A study of the Toyota production system from an industrial viewpoint*. Productivity Press.

Shore, E., Schwatka, N., Dally, M., Brown, C. E., Tenney, L., & Newman, L. S. (2020). Small business employees perceptions of leadership are associated with safety and health climates and their own behaviors. *Journal of Occupational and Environmental Medicine, 62*(2), 156–162.

Simons, R. (1994). *Levers of control: How managers use innovative control systems to drive strategic renewal*. Harvard Business Press.

Steiger, T., Duller, C., & Hiebl, M. R. W. (2015). No consensus in sight: An analysis of ten years of family business definitions in empirical research studies. *Journal of Enterprising Culture, 23*(1), 25–62.

Storey, D. (1994). *Understanding the small business*. Thomson.

Sullivan-Taylor, B., & Branicki, L. (2011). Creating resilient SMEs: Why one size might not fit all. *International Journal of Production Research, 49*(18), 5565–5579.

Sullivan-Taylor, B., & Wilson, D. C. (2009). Managing the threat of terrorism in British travel and leisure organizations. *Organization Studies, 30*(2–3), 251–276.

Sutcliffe, K. M., & Vogus, T. (2003). Organizing for resilience. In K. S. Cameron, J. E. Dutton, & R. E. Quinn (Eds.), *Positive organizational scholarship: Foundations of a new discipline* (pp. 94–110). Berrett-Koehler.

Thun, J. H., Drüke, M., & Hoenig, D. (2011). Managing uncertainty–An empirical analysis of supply chain risk management in small and medium-sized enterprises. *International Journal of Production Research, 49*(18), 5511–5525.

Tognazzo, A., Gubitta, P., & Favaron, S. D. (2016). Does slack always affect resilience? A study of quasi-medium-sized Italian firms. *Entrepreneurship & Regional Development, 28*(9–10), 768–790.

Tukamuhabwa, B. R., Stevenson, M., Busby, J., & Zorzini, M. (2015). Supply chain resilience: Definition, review and theoretical foundations for further study. *International Journal of Production Research, 53*(18), 5592–5623.

U.S. Small Business Administration. (2016). *Size Standards – SBA's size standards determine whether or not your business qualifies as small*. Available on: https://www.sba.gov/federal-contracting/contracting-guide/size-standards#section-header-0. Last accessed on 19 Apr 2023.

Välikangas, L., & Romme, A. G. L. (2012). Building resilience capabilities at "Big Brown Box, Inc.". *Strategy & Leadership, 40*(4), 43–45.
Van Gils, A. (2005). Management and governance in Dutch SMEs. *European Management Journal, 23*(5), 583–589.
Vander Bauwhede, H., De Meyere, M., & Van Cauwenberge, P. (2015). Financial reporting quality and the cost of debt of SMEs. *Small Business Economics, 45*(1), 149–164.
Voss, U., & Brettel, M. (2014). The effectiveness of management control in small firms: Perspectives from resource dependence theory. *Journal of Small Business Management, 52*(3), 569–587.
Weick, K. E., & Sutcliffe, K. M. (2011). *Managing the unexpected: Resilient performance in an age of uncertainty* (Vol. 8). John Wiley & Sons.
Weigel, C., & Hiebl, M. R. (2022). Accountants and small businesses: Toward a resource-based view. *Journal of Accounting & Organizational Change*, in press. https://doi.org/10.1108/JAOC-03-2022-0044
Williams, N., Vorley, T., & Ketikidis, P. H. (2013). Economic resilience and entrepreneurship: A case study of the Thessaloniki City Region. *Local Economy, 28*(4), 399–415.
Xie, X., Wu, Y., Palacios-Marqués, D., & Ribeiro-Navarrete, S. (2022). Business networks and organizational resilience capacity in the digital age during COVID-19: A perspective utilizing organizational information processing theory. *Technological Forecasting and Social Change, 177*, 121548.
Zhang, Y., Wang, W., Mi, L., Huang, C., Xiao, H., Shang, K., Qiao, L., & Wang, L. (2022). Organizational resilience in development: A systematic review based on bibliometric analysis and visualization. *International Journal of Disaster Risk Reduction, 83*, 103408.
Zhou, Q., Edafioghor, T. E., Wu, C. H., & Doherty, B. (2022). Building organisational resilience capability in small and medium-sized enterprises: The role of high-performance work systems. *Human Resource Management Journal*, in press. https://doi.org/10.1111/1748-8583.12479

Part II

Resilience Practice in SMEs from Different Perspectives

4 Enhancing SMEs Resilience by the Implementation of Business Interruption Insurance: Relevance of ERM and Corporate Governance – A Comparative Study

Monika Wieczorek-Kosmala, Thomas Henschel, and Grzegorz Strupczewski

4.1 Introduction

According to Hammond (1999), business interruption insurance (hereafter BI) is designed to insure business against losses arising from its inability to continue normal business operations after a material damage. Thus, this coverage provides a vehicle to recoup earnings lost as a result of an occurrence of a covered risk that interrupts the insured's business operations (Hummer, 2002). The BI has been available since the eighteenth century (McCallum & Knapp, 2016) in the USA, as attachment to fire insurance. Currently, the BI policies cover the indirect (consequential) loss of income or additional costs that follow the major risk event that results in breakdown of firm's operating activity. In this regard, the BI is an example of the insurance product that is straightforwardly addressing the concept of resilience. More specifically, implementation of the BI in firm's insurance strategies helps to be better prepared for the outcomes of unexpected events and their long-term consequences. In this aspect, the BI could be regarded as one of the hallmarks of

M. Wieczorek-Kosmala (✉)
University of Economics in Katowice, Katowice, Poland
e-mail: monika.wieczorek-kosmala@uekat.pl

T. Henschel (✉)
Hochschule für Technik und Wirtschaft Berlin, University of Applied Sciences Berlin, Berlin, Germany
e-mail: henschel@htw-berlin.de

G. Strupczewski
Cracow University of Economics, Kraków, Poland
e-mail: grzegorz.strupczewski@uek.krakow.pl

S. Durst, T. Henschel (eds.), *Small and Medium-Sized Enterprise (SME) Resilience*, Management for Professionals, https://doi.org/10.1007/978-3-031-50836-3_4

resilience-oriented strategies. There is some prior empirical evidence to confirm the importance of the BI insurance for firm's risk resilience strategies (Kao et al., 2020). Indirect losses could reach 25% or even more of the total loss (McCallum & Knapp, 2016; Hoppe et al., 2017) but often remain unnoticed while designing resilience strategies. This evidence suggests that SMEs need to consider the impact of indirect losses and implement adequate tools that help to manage these losses.

In the context of business, organizational resilience refers to the ability of an organization to withstand and recover from significant disruptions, such as natural disasters, cyber-attacks, economic crises, or other unexpected events that can threaten the functioning and survival of the organization (Williams et al., 2017). It involves the ability to adapt, respond, and learn from these disruptions in order to maintain essential functions, services, and operations. Organizational resilience is increasingly recognized as a critical factor in ensuring organizations' long-term success and sustainability in today's complex and uncertain business environment. It can help organizations to maintain customer trust and loyalty, prevent reputational damage, and reduce financial losses during disruptions. One important vehicle to build effective resilience is the application of enterprise risk management for this purpose (Conz & Magnani, 2020). Organizations need to identify potential risks and vulnerabilities, assess their impact and likelihood, and develop strategies to mitigate or manage these risks.

The major motivation behind our study is that small- and medium-sized enterprises (SMEs) are particularly vulnerable to external shocks' consequences. Prior empirical evidence suggests that SMEs are less resilient due to the limited tangible assets, dependence on neighbourhood customers and limited slack resources, and these constraints seem amplified by their lower risk management capabilities (Altman et al., 2010; Sauser et al., 2018). For these reasons, SMEs are perceived as target customers for the BI cover, and there is a need for studies that help to understand of what drives their interest in BI cover. On the other hand, there is some empirical evidence that shed some light on the possible relevant barriers of wider implementation of the BI in the SMEs. Hoppe et al., 2017; Cervellati et al., 2019; and Krummaker, 2019, have revised whether the SMEs implement insurance or not, and what drives these decisions. They found evidence that SMEs demonstrate low interest in insurance, and it is driven by their price sensitivity, risk management constraints, and limited insurance literacy. Thus, the purpose of our study is to contribute to this debate by covering one specific type of insurance (the BI) and exploring the possible relevance of two unsearched determinants: the SMEs risk management and corporate governance maturity. In particular, we are interested if the SMEs are somehow constrained in the wider implementation of the BI by misunderstanding the relevance of this insurance, its complexity, or cost.

4.2 Relevance, Cost, and Complexity of BI Implementation in SMEs

The SMEs decision on the implementation of the BI is typically covering the evaluation of the BI relevance, then the cost, and finally – its complexity. These three decisive aspects emerge as important in prior empirical investigations, as far as the SMEs decision on the purchase of insurance (of any type) is considered (Hoppe et al., 2017; Cervellati et al., 2019; Krummaker, 2019). Overall, the evidence on the SMEs insurance purchases is relatively limited, and the survey-based investigations are prevalent. Strong evidence on the overall importance of insurance implementation in the SMEs risk management strategies was provided by Petroni (1999), on the sample of 95 Italian SMEs. Similar evidence was provided by Cioccio and Michael (2007), based on their study of 11 Australian SMEs. The recent studies consider some mediating factors that could explain the SMEs demand for insurance, such as business demography characteristics (Chodokufa, 2016 on 203 South African SMEs), managerial risk aversion (Krummaker, 2019 interviewed 9 managers of German SMEs) or behavioural biases (Carvellatti et al. 2019 on 2295 Italian SMEs).

However, studies that refer to the practical implementation of the BI in the SMEs are very rare. Hoppe et al. (2017) report the results of the survey on 1802 German SMEs with up to 100 employees. It was showed that larger SMEs (number of employees as proxy of size) and SMEs operating in manufacturing or trade are more interested in the purchase of BI policy. Hoppe et al. (2017) findings are relevant for our work, as they also confirmed the existence and importance of 'insurance mentality' defined by risk aversion, price sensitivity, and insurance know-how in insurance-related decision-making.

The consideration of Hoppe's et al. (2017) risk aversion context reflects our understanding of the BI relevance and is simply covering the predominant context of prior empirical works, asking the question on whether the SMEs is interested in this kind of cover and finds it important for their performance. The price-sensitivity context is also relatively intuitive and reflects in our study the SMEs perceptions of the cost of the BI.

Finally, in our study, we associate the importance of the SMEs' insurance know-how with the complexity of the BI. This problem is linked with the more general issue of low financial literacy of the SMEs, as confirmed by Mashizha et al. (2019). Financial literacy is defined as a combination of awareness, knowledge, skill, attitude, and behaviour necessary to make sound financial decisions and ultimately achieve individual financial wellbeing (Atkinson & Messy, 2012). Financial literacy of the SME managers' influences their risk management practices (Shanahan & McParlane, 2005) and thus undoubtedly affects their insurance decision-making. The BI cover is regarded as one of the most complex, due to the specifics of terms and conditions, as well as the calculations of the loss of income. Crichton (2009) highlights the need to provide the SME managers with professional advice by insurers and intermediaries (e.g. banks, insurance brokers) on the importance of BI

Table 4.1 Decisive dimensions of practical implementation of the BI

Relevance	Is our business vulnerable to the lock-down? In the case of the break of operating activity, are we able to return on the market quickly? Do we have strong competitors on the market?
	Is it easy for our competitors to replace us in supply chains?
	Is our financial position strong, so that we can survive for 2–3 months without operating incomes?
Cost	What is the price of BI cover for our business?
	Is this cost a relevant part of operating costs of our activity?
Complexity	Have we ever purchased the BI cover? Are we familiar with terms and conditions of this kind of insurance? Are we able to compute the consequences of break in operating activity? Are we aware of the fixed costs that we would have to cover in that period? Are we aware of how many incomes we could potentially loose?

insurance purchase, how the adequate sum insured should be set up, and how to prepare a business continuity plan in case of emergency situation. While searching SMEs claim experience, the British Financial Conduct Authority (FCA, 2015) found that lack of clarity and poor channels of communication were the most common reasons of SMEs dissatisfaction. Due to its perceived complexity, particularly regarding the lost income calculation, BI insurance has become recently a source of growing number of lawsuits filed by business owners in state and federal US courts (McCallum & Knapp, 2016). Finally, as French (2020) notices in his study on BI insurance losses in the USA, the policy language in BI insurance policies is not standardized, so it can vary from insurer to insurer. The BI policies are sold on a 'take-it-or-leave-it' basis, with little room for negotiation. The above examples of practical difficulties illuminate the complexity of the BI, which could be highly influential on their interest in the purchase of the BI cover, given the of overall lower financial literacy among the SMEs.

In Table 4.1, we provide decisive dimensions of practical implementation of the BI, as far as the practical implementation of this insurance is considered. We suggest a list of questions that a manager shall ask, to cover the relevance, cost, and complexity of the BI, from the perspective of the given SMEs.

4.3 Sophistication of the ERM (Enterprise Risk Management) in the SMEs

Enterprise risk management is critical in building firm's resilience strategy (Wieczorek-Kosmala & Henschel, 2022). As noted by McShane (2018), a firm to be resilient while facing uncertainty must develop capability to adopt to changing circumstances. This is, in fact, the essence of the concept of organizational resilience and the related dynamic capabilities. The concept of organizational resilience emphasizes firm's ability to absorb, recover, and adapt after a shock has occurred (Bonß, 2016; Lorenz & Dittmer, 2016; McManus et al., 2008; Mallak, 1998). Firm's dynamic capabilities are regarded as critical in building resilience and reflect firm's capacity to create, extent, or modify its resources in the adaptation to changing and turbulent environment (Eisenhardt & Martin, 2000; Helfat et al., 2007). Bogodistov and Wohlgemuth (2017) have pointed on the interplay between the enterprise risk management and dynamic capabilities – the ERM concept is strengthened if considered from dynamic capabilities perspective, as it clarifies the priorities in ERJ implementation in the context of firm's resilience.

In our study, we link the ERM sophistication in the SMEs with their BI implementation strategies. To capture ERM sophistication, we follow the approach proposed by Brustbauer (2016). He revised simple SMEs practices that are informative in the context of risk identification, risk assessment, and risk monitoring. Based on this information, he evaluated the sophistication of the ERM practices – the SMEs that implement more activities in these critical ERM areas are regarded as those of more sophisticated ERM practices. Overall, we expect that the SMEs with greater degree of ERM sophistication find the BI as more relevant, less costly, and less complex.

4.4 Sophistication of Corporate Governance Mechanisms in the SMEs

There is much less focus on corporate governance issues that affect SMEs. Nevertheless, as pointed by Abor and Adjasi (2007), the corporate governance mechanisms observed in large firms are applicable in the SMEs and beneficial to their performance. It is very tempting, given the importance of SMEs to all economies and their central role in the economic development of the EU.

Many researchers point out that smaller firms depend on their owners who are frequently also a manager (Brunninge et al., 2007; Charas & Perelli, 2013; Calabrò & Mussolino, 2013; Coulson-Thomas, 2007; Durst & Henschel, 2014). There seems to be a common understanding that the success of the SME is dependent on the owner-manager's commitment and behaviour (Brunninge et al., 2007; Cortes & Kiss, 2023). However, Banham and He (2010) mention that 'the organizational size and the overlap of management and ownership add complexity to governance in the SME context. On the other hand, SMEs are highly flexible in adapting to change. There is no typical principal-agency issue that often occurs when the governance theories are applied to PLCs' (Charas & Perelli, 2013).

In this study, we consider corporate governance mechanisms as potentially supportive in responding to external shocks and thus relevant for SMEs resilience strategies (Wieczorek-Kosmala & Henschel, 2022). The corporate governance is perceived as a first line of defence to meet risk-related challenges (Kirkpatrick, 2009), and in this context, Stein and Wiedemann (2016) highlight the interplay of risk governance and risk management, given the holistic perspective featuring the ERM concept. For large firms, there is empirical evidence that confirms the relevance of boards in strengthening risk management (Beasley et al., 2021), as well as in preventing the failures in managing risk (in this – in recognizing its negative consequences) (Ellul, 2015). In the SMEs context, there is some evidence to supports a view that stronger corporate governance mechanisms add complexity to governance of the SMEs (Bahnam and He 2010). Thus, it seems that corporate governance mechanisms are influential on the perceptions of and response to a risk, which is no longer dependent on a single-person (the owner) perspective. In other words, the stronger corporate governance mechanisms may potentially limit the biased view at the impact of the external shocks (such as COVID-19) and prevent the chaotic risk response.

In this regard, in our study we link corporate governance sophistication of the SMEs with their BI strategies. Overall, we expect that the SMEs with greater degree of corporate governance sophistication find the BI as more relevant, less costly, and less complex.

4.5 Research Design

We present the results of a survey which we designed to learn on the implementation of the BI in the SMEs and possible relevance of ERM and corporate governance sophistication on the decisions within. The survey was conducted simultaneously on the sample of German and Polish SMEs, in 2021. We selected these two country settings, based on the differences in the scale of implementing insurance in these countries. According to the Insurance Europe (IE, 2023) database, as on 2020, the contribution of property and casualty insurance to GDP (referred to as insurance penetration ratio) for Germany was of c.a. 2.25%, while for Poland, only 1.66%. This discrepancy is observed in long-term perspective and is one of the features of the less mature insurance markets. In the case of Poland, this trend is regarded as the one echoing the consequences of the performance of insurance market under the centrally planned economy, which is influential on the SMEs decisions to implement insurance.

The online questionnaire was initially pilot-tested on 10 SMEs, to obtain an impression of how the questions were perceived and to clarify any ambiguity.

All survey responses were anonymous, and all data used in this study, including the demographic data such as organization size (number of employees) and industry sector classification, were self-reported by the survey respondents.

In Poland, the survey was carried out by a professional survey agency that used their own database on the SMEs across the whole Poland (random sample). In Germany, we drew a random sample of 4460 firms from the Firmenwissen database. All enterprises with the number of employees below 250 were selected from the relevant database, which is in line with the EU definition of the SMEs.

The SMEs were invited to participate anonymously in the survey via an established online survey system. No extrinsic incentive was used. We did one reminder. In Poland, the response rate was 12.5%. After the consistency checks, we received 526 complete questionnaires. In Germany, the response rate was 9.9% (453 firms). After consistency checks, 238 out of the responses were removed, due to incompleteness. A total of 215 were valid with an effective questionnaire response rate of 4.8%.

Table 4.2 The definitions of business demographic variables in the survey

Variables	Definition
	Size – The number of employees:
Micro	Up to 9 persons
Small	10–49 persons
Medium	50–249 persons
	Age – The number of years the company actively performs on the market:
Infant	Up to 5 years
Young	6–10 years
Intermediate	11–20 years
Mature	21 years or more
	The legal form of business performance
SP	Sole proprietor
P-personal	Partnership – Personal (owners bear whole responsibility for the business)
P-capital	Partnership – Capital (owners bear limited liability for the business)
	Do you consider your business as a family firm? (the members of the family / the relatives are engaged in the business)
Fam	YES – Family firm
N-fam	NO – Non-family firm
	Sector
T	Trade
P	Production
S	Services

In Table 4.2, we present the definitions of demographic variables considered in our study. We considered several SMEs' features that are commonly revised in the survey-based works (e.g., Semrau et al., 2016). As a measure of SMEs' size, we controlled for firm's employment, to distinguish between micro-, small- and medium-sized ones. Further, we have considered SME's age, by considering the number of years the firms actively perform on the market. In this regard, we have distinguished between the infant, young, immediate, and mature SMEs. Further, we have considered two characteristics that could be associated with firm's corporate governance policies. First of all, we controlled for the legal form of SMEs' performance. The considered businesses characteristics distinguish between sole proprietors and the type of partnership (in the context of the SMEs liability for the partnership performance). We have also asked our respondents whether they find their business to be a family firm or not. Finally, we considered the general sector belonging, by asking whether the SMEs is a producer, trader, or services provider. In Table 4.3, we provide the data that specify the business demographic variables for the surveyed SMEs, separately for Poland and for Germany.

Table 4.3 Sample characteristics (business demographics)

Variables		Germany (*N*)	%	Poland (*N*)	%
In total		215	100.00	526	100.00
Size	Micro	41	19.07	181	34.41
	Small	147	68.37	206	39.16
	Medium	27	12.56	139	26.43
Age	Infant	15	6.98	86	16.35
	Young	32	14.88	137	26.05
	Intermediate	53	24.65	185	35.17
	Mature	115	53.49	118	22.43
Legal form	SP	23	10.70	195	37.07
	P-personal	67	31.16	77	14.64
	P-capital	125	58.14	254	48.29
Family business	Fam	125	58.14	167	31.75
	N-fam	90	41.86	359	68.25
Sector	Trade	36	16.74	95	18.06
	Production	45	20.93	198	37.64
	Services	134	62.33	233	44.30
In total		215	100.00	526	100.00

4.6 Selection of Variables

In Table 4.4, we provide detailed list of questions included in our survey, and the related definitions of the empirical variables we further examine. Apart from the business demographic variables, our survey covered the three aspects of the BI implementation (relevance, complexity and cost), the ERM sophistication, and the corporate governance sophistication.

To address the three aspects of the BI implementation of our interest, we asked the surveyed SMEs on how far they agree with the given assertations. To address the relevance of the BI, we asked how far the respondents agree that BI is a relevant component of their insurance program (Table 4.3). To address the cost of the BI, we asked how far the respondents agree that BI is expensive, as the premiums are hight. Finally, to address the complexity of the BI, we have asked our respondents on how far they agree that terms and conditions of the BI are difficult and complicated. These assertations were evaluated on 7-points Likert scale, ranging from 1 (strongly disagree) to 7 (strongly agree).

To address the ERM sophistication of the SMEs, we followed the approach proposed by Brustbauer (2016). In his survey, Brustbauer's covered a set of 12 simple questions that enable to scale SME's activities within risk identification, risk assessment, and risk monitoring. In our work, we have modified slightly this methodical approach, by defining two sets of questions, covering 10 items in total. More specifically, our survey covered (i) risk analysis (identification and evaluation) and (ii) risk monitoring and response. The detailed list of our variables and the related survey questions are presented in Table 4.4. Out of 10 questions, in 3, we replicate

Table 4.4 List of examined variables and their definitions

Variables	Definition
Implementation of the business interruption insurance (BI)	
Assertations, on 7-point Likert scale, ranging from 1 (strongly disagree) to 7 (strongly agree)	
BI_Rel	Business interruption insurance is a relevant component of our insurance program
BI_Cost	Business interruption insurance is expensive (insurance premiums are high)
BI_Complex	Terms and conditions of business interruption insurance are difficult and complicated
ERM sophistication	
Assertations, on 7-point Likert scale, ranging from 1 (strongly disagree) to 7 (strongly agree)	
	Risk analysis (identification and evaluation)
ERM.exp	Our company employs external experts to identify risks*
ERM.report	Our company writes reports on intensified risks*
ERM.ident	Our risk identification considers all aspects of our performance
ERM.list	We regularly review our list of identified risks
ERM.eval	We always evaluate risk impact from the perspective of our business objectives**
	Risk monitoring and response
ERM.cust	Our company regularly surveys customers' satisfaction**
ERM.prev	To prevent errors, we always follow the predefined procedures/plans**
ERM.cont	We have contingency plans for emergencies*
ERM.owners	Our company defined 'risk owners', that is key persons who are responsible for monitoring and handling particular exposures
ERM.metrics	We have implemented risk measures/metrics that are helpful in monitoring the first symptoms of risk
Corporate governance sophistication	
	CG strategic thinking
CG.succ	Does the company have any plan of succession? (Who will run the business in the case the owner is retired or ill?)
	1 – No, 2 – Yes, but informal; 3 – Yes, formal
CG.strat	Does a company have a formal business strategy plan?
	1 – No, 2 – Yes, with 1-year horizon; 3 – Yes, with a horizon up to 3 years
	CG internal organizational structure
	How important is each of the below listed elements of the internal organizational structure? (all questions evaluated on 3-point Likert scale: 1 minor importance, 2 moderately important, 3 very important)
CG.rules	Clearly defined rules of decision-making
CG.com	Control of internal and external communication
CG.confl	Handling of conflicts of interests
CG.r&o	Defined rights and obligations of the management team
CG.dcr	Qualifications and competences of the management team
CG.size	Size and composition of the management team

Notes: In ERM sophistication section: *are questions directly repeated from Brustbauer's (2016) survey and **are modified questions from Brustbauer's survey. The remaining questions are author's questions

Brustbauer's wording; then in further 3, we slightly modified the context; and we added 4 additional questions that reflect Brustbauer's intentions but are formulated in a different way, to better address the attributes of ERM sophistication (this applies to integration and continuity of risk identification, presence of risk owners, and monitoring of key risk indicators). Following Brustbauer (2016), we applied 7-point Likert scale, ranging from 1 (strongly disagree) to 7 (strongly agree).

To capture the sophistication of corporate governance mechanisms, we have followed the evidence stemming from prior literature, as there is some evidence that SMEs have a completely different understanding of corporate governance in comparison to large and public companies. In methodical context, our intention was to be convergent with the approach to capturing EMR sophistication. Thus, we defined the set of questions that reflect (a) corporate governance strategic thinking and (b) internal organization structure of corporate governance. Each item is measured on qualitative scale, ranging from 1 to 3. For corporate governance strategic thinking, we adhered the scale to sophistication of succession plans and business strategy in such a way that 1 reflects low sophistication and 3 high sophistication. Further, for internal CG organizational structure items, we applied a 3-point Likert scale, to capture SMEs assertations on how important is each of the CG organization hallmark in their organizational structure.

In methodical context, our study relies on application of non-parametric methods that allow to capture the differences in the BI items of our interest between the groups of companies of low or high ERM and CG sophistication. As our variables are measured on qualitative scales, we apply non-parametric ANOVA. Following Brustbauer's (2016) approach, we first identify the groups of companies that distinguish with low or high ERM or CG sophistication, by applying k-means algorithm. Further, we compare between the groups of low and high sophistication, to identify whether there are statistically significant differences between the perceptions of relevance, cost, or complexity of the BI.

4.7 Findings

Based on survey results, we compared the responses of German and Polish SMEs, for each aspect of our variables of interest (BI implementation, ERM sophistication, and corporate governance sophistication). These comparisons are provided in figures. Further, we applied statistical tests to address the significance of the observed similarities or differences, at country level.

In Fig. 4.1, we report the results of our survey, as regards the assertations concerning relevance, cost, and complexity of the BI. On average, the surveyed German SMEs regard the BI as more relevant, less costly, and more complex, in comparison to the surveyed Polish SMEs. However, the results of Mann-Whitney U test indicate that only in the case of cost and complexity, the observed differences between German and Polish SMEs are statistically significant (Table 4.5).

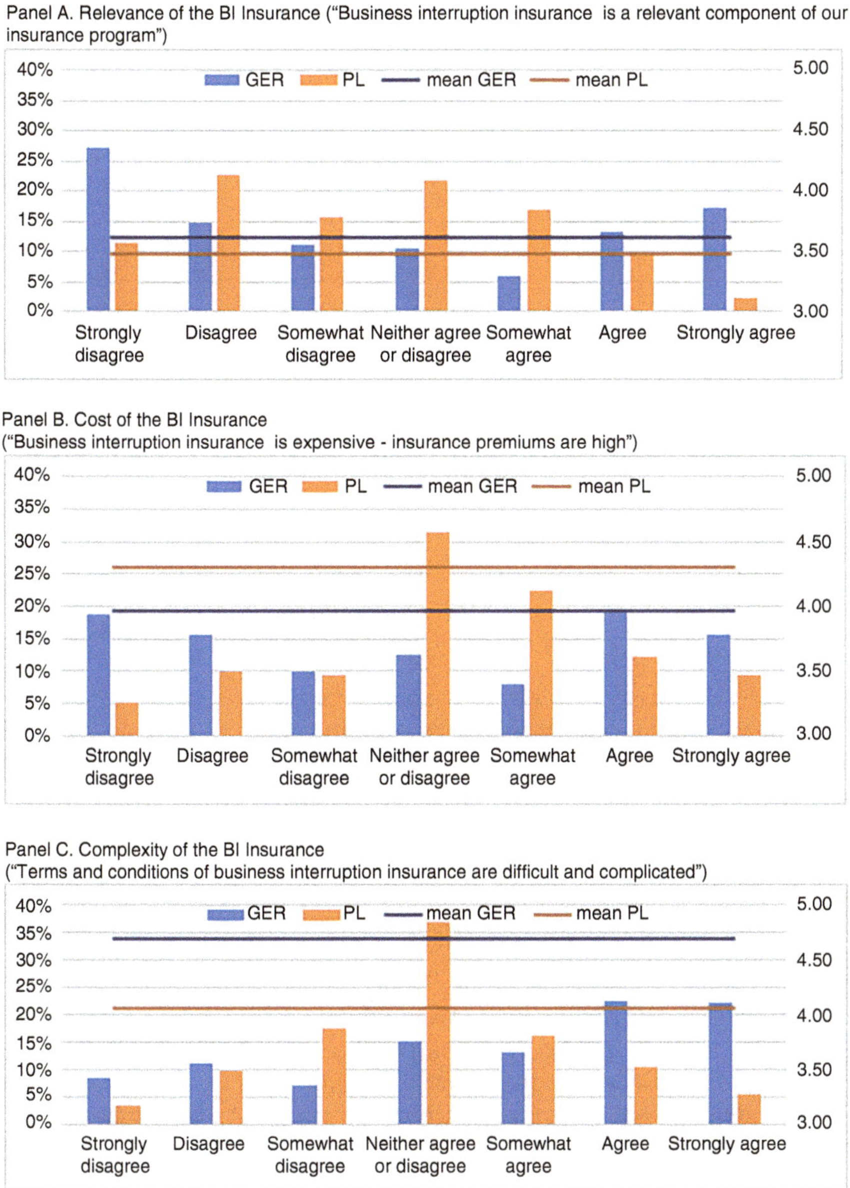

Fig. 4.1 Comparison of the BI implementation – Germany vs Poland (distributions of scores assigned by the responding firms and the mean values of the scores)

On the further stage of our analysis, we have verified whether the BI relevance, cost, and complexity differ at statistically significant level between the SMEs of low or hight ERM and corporate governance sophistication. For that purpose, we have first grouped our respondents into clusters of low and high sophistication of ERM

Table 4.5 Significance of the differences between German and Polish respondents' BI implementation

	Relevance	Cost		Complexity	
Mann-Whitney U	52,001,500	47,655,000		39,625,500	
W Wilcoxon	71,702,500	67,356,000		178,226,500	
Z	−0.029	−1.790		−5.068	
p-value	0.977	0.073	*	0.000	***
Mean ranks of Mann-Whitney U					
Poland	36,213	34,018		42,537	
Germany	36,264	37,090		33,883	

Table 4.6 Low vs high RM sophistication and BI perceptions

	Relevance		Cost		Complexity
Mann-Whitney U	4,860,550		5,429,400		6,252,700
W Wilcoxon	11,724,050		12,292,900		12,118,000
Z	−5.421		−3.327		−0.277
p-value	0.000	***	0.001	***	0.782
Mean ranks of Mann-Whitney U					
Low	31,687		33,224		35,851
High	39,938		38,275		35,433

or corporate governance mechanisms. We have implemented k-mean clustering, for each country separately (as we observed some statistically significant country-level differences). In the process of clustering, we have excluded the SMEs with missing assertations for ERM and CG sophistication, which applied to German sample. In Appendix, we provide the detailed results of clustering, with the mean values obtained for German and Polish SMEs, for ERM and CG clusters. We have then applied the Mann-Whitney U test to verify whether the groups of low or high ERM or CG sophistication differ with their perceptions of the BI relevance, cost, and complexity.

ERM Sophistication The results of Mann-Whitney U test presented in Table 4.6 indicate that there are statistically significant differences between the SMEs of low or high ERM sophistication if the relevance and cost of the BI are considered. The mean ranks of post hoc tests uncover that firms of low ERM sophistication find the BI of lower relevance. In this aspect, the difference between firms in the cluster of low and high ERM sophistication is statistically significant at 0.1%. Further, the post hoc tests indicate that firms of low ERM sophistication find the BI as less costly than the firms in the cluster of high ERM sophistication (significant at 1%). This observation suggests that firms of higher ERM sophistication are more aware of the costs related to the implementation of risk management tools, in this – implementa-

Table 4.7 Low vs high CG sophistication and BI perceptions

	Relevance		Cost	Complexity
Mann-Whitney U	5,058,250		5,698,650	5,808,800
W Wilcoxon	9,277,750		9,918,150	10,028,300
Z	−3.557		−1.112	−0.693
p-value	0.000	***	0.266	0.488
Mean ranks of Mann-Whitney U				
Low	31,992		34,201	34,580
High	37,452		35,902	35,635

tion of the insurance protection. There were no statistically significant differences between the firms of low or high ERM sophistication, if the complexity of the BI is considered.

Corporate Governance Sophistication The results of Mann-Whitney U test presented in Table 4.7 show that there are statistically significant differences between SMEs of low and high corporate governance sophistication only if the relevance of the BI is considered (sig. at 0.1%). The ranks of post hoc indicate that the SMEs of lower corporate governance sophistication perceived the BI as less relevant. The perceptions of the cost of the BI, as well as its complexity, were comparable for the SMEs of both low and high corporate governance sophistication.

4.8 Conclusions and Practical Implications

The results of our survey on German and Polish SMEs indicate that the greater sophistication of ERM and corporate governance was related to the assertations on higher relevance of the BI. The SMEs of higher ERM sophistication perceived also the BI as more costly. Interestingly, there was no statistically significant difference between SMEs of low and high ERM or corporate governance sophistication and the perceived complexity of the BI. Further studies are targeted at uncovering which particular ERM practices and corporate governance features are linked to the perceptions of the relevance, cost, and complexity of the BI in the surveyed sample of the German and Polish SMEs.

Our study has some practical managerial implications. First of all, it provides some advice for managers, as regards major decisive areas on the implementation of the BI. The proper analysis of BI relevance is critical. Managers shall be aware that smaller firms are more vulnerable to business interruptions than larger firms because they often have limited resources and a smaller customer base. They are also less likely to have access to credit and other sources of financing that can help them recover from a loss of income. BII can help small firms by providing them with the financial resources they need to continue operating after a disaster or other event that interrupts their business. Managers shall also take into account that BI can help

Table 4.8 Practitioner checklist to successful BI implementation

This checklist intends to provide SMEs with a basic advice on how to use Business Interruption Insurance properly to become more resilient:
***
1. Assess your risks: Identify the risks that are most likely to cause a business interruption and determine the potential financial impact of those risks
2. Purchase adequate coverage: Work with an insurance broker or agent to ensure that your policy provides adequate coverage to fully cover your potential losses
3. Maintain accurate records: Maintain accurate financial records and other documentation that can be used to support an insurance claim in the event of a business interruption
4. Develop a business continuity plan: Develop a plan that outlines the steps you will take to minimize the impact of a business interruption and ensure that you can resume operations as quietly as possible
5. Review and update your policy: Regularly review and update your BII policy to ensure that it continues to meet your needs as your business grows and changes
6. Notify your insurer: In the event of a business interruption, notify your insurer as soon as possible and provide them with all necessary documentation to support your claim
7. Work with your insurer: Work closely with your insurer throughout the claims process to ensure that you receive the full benefits of your policy
***
By following this checklist. SMEs can maximize the benefits of Business interruption Insurance and become more resilient in the face of unexpected events that can impact their operations and financial stability

their firms to provide them with the sense of security. Knowing that they have insurance coverage in the event of a business interruption can help small business owners feel more confident about taking risks and investing in their businesses. This can lead to increased innovation and growth, which can help small firms become more resilient over time. To maximize the benefits of the BI, small firms should take the steps outlined in Table 4.8 (checklist).

Taking this into account, here are some more specific ways that BII can be used for SMEs to be more resilient:

1. Maintaining Cash Flow: Business Interruption Insurance can help small businesses maintain their cash flow during a period of interruption. By covering the lost income and extra expenses incurred during the interruption, BII can provide financial stability to SMEs, allowing them to pay their bills, salaries, and other expenses even when their operations are halted.
2. Faster Recovery: BII can help small businesses recover faster from a business interruption. With the funds received from BII, SMEs can invest in repairs, replacement of damaged equipment or inventory, and other expenses to get back on track quickly. This can help them to resume their operations faster and avoid losing customers or market share to competitors.
3. Business Continuity Planning: In order to get the most out of their BII policies, SMEs should have a business continuity plan in place. This plan should detail how the business will continue operating during an interruption and how it will recover after the event. With a plan in place, SMEs can maximize their BII benefits and ensure a faster recovery.

4. Enhanced Creditworthiness: By having BII, small businesses can enhance their creditworthiness in the eyes of lenders. With BII, small businesses can show lenders that they are better prepared for unexpected events, and as a result, lenders may be more willing to provide them with financing when they need it.
5. Peace of Mind: Lastly, BII can provide peace of mind to small business owners. Knowing that they are covered by insurance can give small business owners the confidence to take risks, invest in their businesses, and pursue growth opportunities without fear of catastrophic losses that could otherwise put them out of business.

Overall, Business interruption insurance can be a valuable tool for SMEs to become more resilient by providing them with the financial resources they need to withstand unexpected events and continue operating with minimal disruption.

Appendix (Tables 4.9 and 4.10)

Table 4.9 Clusters of firms of low vs high ERM sophistication

	Germany				Poland			
	Low ($N = 61$)		High ($N = 125$)		Low ($N = 249$)		High ($N = 277$)	
	Mean	St.D.	Mean	St.D.	Mean	St.D.	Mean	St.D.
ERM.exp	1.49	0.994	2.34	1.601	1.72	0.867	3.13	1.574
ERM.report	1.61	1.053	4.05	1.887	2.22	1.093	4.34	1.373
ERM.ident	2.28	1.427	5.36	1.291	3.38	1.541	5.22	1.030
ERM.list	2.93	1.652	5.72	0.964	2.77	1.274	4.86	1.108
ERM.eval	3.00	1.612	5.19	1.452	3.85	1.544	5.30	1.012
ERM.cust	2.33	1.805	3.10	1.911	3.72	1.723	5.01	1.305
ERM.prev	2.85	1.721	4.85	1.632	3.81	1.446	5.23	1.003
ERM.cont	2.67	1.375	5.34	1.338	3.51	1.473	5.16	0.998
ERM.owners	2.39	1.563	5.26	1.487	3.73	1.471	5.14	1.091
ERM.metrics	2.15	1.195	4.83	1.528	3.22	1.262	4.86	1.051

Table 4.10 Clusters of firms of low vs high CG sophistication

	Germany				Poland			
	Low ($N = 61$)		High ($N = 125$)		Low ($N = 249$)		High ($N = 277$)	
	Mean	St.D.	Mean	St.D.	Mean	St.D.	Mean	St.D.
ERM.exp	1.49	0.994	2.34	1.601	1.72	0.867	3.13	1.574
ERM.report	1.61	1.053	4.05	1.887	2.22	1.093	4.34	1.373
ERM.ident	2.28	1.427	5.36	1.291	3.38	1.541	5.22	1.030
ERM.list	2.93	1.652	5.72	0.964	2.77	1.274	4.86	1.108
ERM.eval	3.00	1.612	5.19	1.452	3.85	1.544	5.30	1.012
ERM.cust	2.33	1.805	3.10	1.911	3.72	1.723	5.01	1.305
ERM.prev	2.85	1.721	4.85	1.632	3.81	1.446	5.23	1.003
ERM.cont	2.67	1.375	5.34	1.338	3.51	1.473	5.16	0.998
ERM.owners	2.39	1.563	5.26	1.487	3.73	1.471	5.14	1.091
ERM.metrics	2.15	1.195	4.83	1.528	3.22	1.262	4.86	1.051

References

Abor, J., & Adjasi, C. K. (2007). Corporate governance and the small and medium enterprises sector: Theory and implications. *Corporate Governance: The International Journal of Business in Society, 7*(2), 111–122. https://doi.org/10.1108/14720700710739769

Altman, E. I., Sabato, G., & Wilson, N. (2010). The value of non-financial information in small and medium-sized enterprise risk management. *The Journal of Credit Risk, 6*(2), 95.

Atkinson, A., & Messy, F.-A. (2012). Measuring financial literacy: Results of the OECD/International Network on Financial Education (INFE) Pilot Study. *OECD Working Papers on Finance, Insurance and Private, 15*. https://doi.org/10.1787/5k9csfs90fr4-en

Banham, H., & He, Y. (2010). SME governance: Converging definitions and expanding expectations. *International Business & Economics Research Journal (IBER), 9*(2), 77–82. https://doi.org/10.19030/iber.v9i2.524

Beasley, M., Branson, B., Pagach, D., & Panfilo, S. (2021). Are required SEC proxy disclosures about the board's role in risk oversight substantive? *Journal of Accounting and Public Policy, 40*(1), 106816. https://doi.org/10.1016/j.jaccpubpol.2020.106816

Bogodistov, Y., & Wohlgemuth, V. (2017). Enterprise risk management: A capability-based perspective. *The Journal of Risk Finance, 18*(3), 234–251. https://doi.org/10.1108/JRF-10-2016-0131

Bonß, W. (2016). The notion of resilience: Trajectories and social science perspective. In A. Maurer (Ed.), *New perspectives on resilience in socio-economic spheres* (pp. 9–24). Springer. https://doi.org/10.1007/978-3-658-13328-3_2

Brunninge, O., Nordqvist, M., & Wiklund, J. (2007). Corporate governance and strategic change in SMEs: The effects of ownership, board composition and top management teams. *Small Business Economics, 29*(3), 295–308. https://doi.org/10.1007/s11187-006-9021-2

Brustbauer, J. (2016). Enterprise risk management in SMEs: Towards a structural model. *International Small Business Journal: Researching Entrepreneurship, 34*(1), 70–85. https://doi.org/10.1177/0266242614542853

Calabrò, A., & Mussolino, D. (2013). How do boards of directors contribute to family SME export intensity? The role of formal and informal governance mechanisms. *Journal of Management & Governance, 17*(2), 363–403. https://doi.org/10.1007/s10997-011-9180-7

Cervellati, E. M., Corea, F., & Zanghieri, P. (2019). Entrepreneurs' behavioural biases, risk misperception and company underinsurance. *Risk Governance and Control: Financial Markets and Institutions, 9*(4), 49–66. https://doi.org/10.22495/rgcv9i4p5

Charas, S., & Perelli, S. (2013). Threats to board stability: Understanding SME director behavior. *International Journal of Disclosure and Governance, 10*(2), 175–191. https://doi.org/10.1057/jdg.2013.10

Chodokufa, K. (2016). Risk management practices and the purchase of insurance by SMES. *Risk Governance and Control: Financial Markets and Institutions, 6*(3), 100–104. https://doi.org/10.22495/rcgv6i3c2art13

Cioccio, L., & Michael, E. J. (2007). Hazard or disaster: Tourism management for the inevitable in Northeast Victoria. *Tourism Management, 28*(1), 1–11. https://doi.org/10.1016/j.tourman.2005.07.015

Conz, E., & Magnani, G. (2020). A dynamic perspective on the resilience of firms: A systematic literature review and a framework for future research. *European Management Journal, 38*(3), 400–412. https://doi.org/10.1016/j.emj.2019.12.004

Cortes, A. F., & Kiss, A. N. (2023). Is managerial discretion high in small firms? A theoretical framework. *Small Business Economics, 60*(1), 157–172.

Coulson-Thomas, C. (2007). SME directors and boards: The contribution of directors and boards to the growth and development of Small and Medium-sized Enterprises (SMEs). *International Journal of Business Governance and Ethics, 3*(3), 250–261. https://doi.org/10.1504/IJBGE.2007.014316

Crichton, D. (2009). Small and medium-sized enterprises. In A. Dlugolecki (Ed.), *Coping with climate change: Risks and opportunities for insurers*. Chartered Insurance Institute.

Durst, S., & Henschel, T. (2014). Governance in small firms – A country comparison of current practices. *International Journal of Entrepreneurship and Small Business, 3, 21(1)*, 16–32.

Eisenhardt, K. M., & Martin, J. A. (2000). Dynamic capabilities: What are they? *Strategic Management Journal, 21*(10–11), 1105–1121. https://doi.org/10.1002/1097-0266(200010/11)21:10/11<1105::AID-SMJ133>3.0.CO;2-E

Ellul, A. (2015). The role of risk management in corporate governance. *Annual Review of Financial Economics, 7*(1), 279–299. https://doi.org/10.1146/annurev-financial-111414-125820

FCA. (2015). *Handling of insurance claims for Small and Medium-sized Enterprises (SMEs)*. https://www.fca.org.uk/publication/thematic-reviews/tr15-06.pdf

French, C. C. (2020). COVID-19 business interruption insurance losses: The cases for and against coverage. *Penn State Law Research Paper, 14*. https://ssrn.com/abstract=3639589

Hammond, R. (1999). *Underlying principles of business interruption insurance*. Retrieved from http://library.findlaw.com/1999/Jun/1/127909.html

Helfat, C. E., Finkelstein, S., Mitchell, W., Peteraf, M., Singh, H., Teece, D. J., & Winter, S. G. (2007). *Dynamic capabilities: Understanding strategic change in organizations*. Blackwell. https://ebookcentral.proquest.com/lib/kxp/detail.action?docID=4957031

Hoppe, F., Gatzert, N., & Gruner, P. (2017). Betriebsunterbrechungsversicherung bei kleinen und mittleren Unternehmen. *Zeitschrift Für Die Gesamte Versicherungswissenschaft, 106*(5), 555–590. https://doi.org/10.1007/s12297-017-0391-0

Hummer, P. M. (2002). Basics of business interruption insurance: The ins and outs of tricky coverage. *Defense Counsel Journal, 69*(3), 307–315.

IE. (2023). *Insurance Europe Statistics database*. Available at: https://www.insuranceeurope.eu/statistics. Accessed 03.08.2023.

Kao, Y. M., Keskin, N. B., & Shang, K. (2020). *Impact of information asymmetry and limited production capacity on business interruption insurance*. https://ssrn.com/abstract=3184530. https://doi.org/10.2139/ssrn.3184530. Accessed 26 Aug 2020.

Kirkpatrick, G. (2009). The corporate governance lessons from the financial crisis. *Financial Market Trends, 1*. http://citeseerx.ist.psu.edu/viewdoc/download?doi=10.1.1.444.6047&rep=rep1&type=pdf

Krummaker, S. (2019). Firm's demand for insurance: An explorative approach. *Risk Management and Insurance Review, 22*(3), 279–301. https://doi.org/10.1111/rmir.12128

Lorenz, D. F., & Dittmer, C. (2016). Resilience in catastrophes, disasters and emergencies. In A. Maurer (Ed.), *New perspectives on resilience in socio-economic spheres* (pp. 25–59). Springer. https://doi.org/10.1007/978-3-658-13328-3_3

Mallak, L. (1998). Putting organizational resilience to work. *Industrial Management, 40*(6), 8–13.

Mashizha, M., Sibanda, M., & Maumbe, B. (2019). Financial literacy among small and medium enterprises in Zimbabwe. *The Southern African Journal of Entrepreneurship and Small Business Management, 11*(1), 208–217. https://doi.org/10.4102/sajesbm.v11i1.241

McCallum, B. T., & Knapp, M. C. (2016). Coping with catastrophes. Business interruption insurance claims. *The CPA Journal*, 54–59.

McManus, S., Seville, E., Vargo, J., & Brunsdon, D. (2008). Facilitated process for improving organizational resilience. *Natural Hazards Review, 9*(2), 81–90. https://doi.org/10.1061/(ASCE)1527-6988(2008)9:2(81)

McShane, M. (2018). Enterprise risk management: History and a design science proposal. *The Journal of Risk Finance, 19*(2), 137–153. https://doi.org/10.1108/JRF-03-2017-0048

Petroni, A. (1999). Mapping the diffusion of advanced risk management practices among Italian small- and medium-sized firms. *Risk Management and Insurance Review, 2*(3), 125–140. https://doi.org/10.1111/j.1540-6296.1999.tb00007.x

Sauser, B., Baldwin, C., Pourreza, S., Randall, W., & Nowicki, D. (2018). Resilience of small- and medium-sized enterprises as a correlation to community impact: An agent-based modeling approach. *Natural Hazards, 90*(1), 79–99. https://doi.org/10.1007/s11069-017-3034-9

Semrau, T., Ambos, T., & Kraus, S. (2016). Entrepreneurial orientation and SME performance across societal cultures: An international study. *Journal of Business Research, 69*(5), 1928–1932. https://doi.org/10.1016/j.jbusres.2015.10.082

Shanahan, P., & McParlane, J. (2005). Serendipity or strategy? An investigation into entrepreneurial transnational higher education and risk management. *On the Horizon, 13*(4), 220–228. https://doi.org/10.1108/10748120510627349

Stein, V., & Wiedemann, A. (2016). Risk governance: Conceptualization, tasks, and research agenda. *Journal of Business Economics, 86*(8), 813–836. https://doi.org/10.1007/s11573-016-0826-4

Wieczorek-Kosmala, M., & Henschel, T. (2022). The role of ERM and corporate governance in managing COVID-19 impacts: SMEs perspective. *Journal of Risk and Financial Management, 15*(12), 587.

Williams, T. A., Gruber, D. A., Sutcliffe, K. M., Shepherd, D. A., & Zhao, E. Y. (2017). Organizational response to adversity: Fusing crisis management and resilience research streams. *Academy of Management Annals, 11*(2), 733–769. https://doi.org/10.5465/annals.2015.0134

The Resilience of Family Firms During Crisis

5

Börje Boers, Thomas Henschel, and Maria Stellmacher

5.1 Introduction

The recent Corona pandemic has caused multiple problems in many places around the world (Boers & Henschel, 2021; Durst & Henschel, 2021; Durst et al., 2021). Small- and medium-sized enterprises are especially challenged due to their resource constraints (Durst et al., 2021; Falkner & Hiebl, 2015; Mayr & Lixl, 2019). A crisis, irrespective of its cause, comes suddenly and questions the regular way of conducting business. Therefore, family SMEs have to react and in the best of all cases they are prepared, yet prior research points into another direction, i.e. many lack formal crisis planning (Faghfouri et al., 2015). Recently, the demands on SMEs have increased considerably (Boers & Henschel, 2022b) due to the multitude of crises following another, such as Corona pandemic, followed by the war in Ukraine, leading to increased energy prices and increased inflation rates. However, small firms (Doern, 2016) and family firms have been exposed to crises before (Amann & Jaussaud, 2012; Cater III & Beal, 2014; Salvato et al., 2020). Currently, it seems that crises affect firms more frequently, due to the war in Ukraine, disturbances in supply chains, and increasing inflation, which call for a new perspective of handling these. It is not only necessary to manage the acute crisis but also to prepare the business to be able to sustain the crisis and its consequences. In other words, there is a need for firms, and in particular family firms, to become resilient.

B. Boers (✉)
University of Skövde, Skövde, Sweden
e-mail: borje.boers@his.se

T. Henschel (✉) · M. Stellmacher
Hochschule für Technik und Wirtschaft Berlin, University of Applied Sciences Berlin, Berlin, Germany
e-mail: henschel@htw-berlin.de

S. Durst, T. Henschel (eds.), *Small and Medium-Sized Enterprise (SME) Resilience*, Management for Professionals, https://doi.org/10.1007/978-3-031-50836-3_5

Resilience is a term used in different literatures such as ecology, engineering, and psychology (Korber & McNaughton, 2018; Linnenluecke, 2017). This has resulted in different perspectives (Andersson et al., 2019). Also, Linnenluecke, in a review, noted five different streams of literature in the business management literature (Linnenluecke, 2017). Consequently, this has led to a lack of clarity and multiple debates and conceptualizations, which need to be acknowledged when investigating the topic of resilience in family firms. Nonetheless, it can be argued that it could be useful to focus on, e.g. traits or competencies, instead of planning (Andersson et al., 2019). In this chapter, we define resilience as "the process by which an actor (individual, organization, or community) builds and uses its capability endowments to interact with the environment in a way that positively adjusts and maintains functioning prior to, during, and following adversity" (Williams et al., 2017, p. 742).

A crisis could be seen as a process (Boers & Henschel, 2022a; Hong et al., 2012; Roux-Dufort, 2007), whose consequences may not be visible at first sight. A crisis is not only the triggering event but also a process unfolding both before and after the crisis event has taken place (Roux-Dufort, 2007). Therefore, we argue for a processual perspective, which is able to account for the respective circumstances, to be able to account for the complexities of family businesses. Accordingly, a crisis can be related to several family-specific characteristics, which determine how a family firm is able to turn around in a crisis situation (Boers & Henschel, 2021; Cater III & Beal, 2014; Cater & Schwab, 2008). Varying circumstances of an owning family and its owning firm will influence how it reacts in a crisis situation. Accordingly, an owning family can both hinder and promote crisis management in family firms (Boers & Henschel, 2022b; Cater III & Beal, 2014). Therefore, owning families are decisive for handling crises.

The purpose of this chapter is to understand how small- and medium-sized family firms manage a crisis from a processual perspective. The chapter contributes with empirical illustrations of family firms that faced a crisis situation, which threatened the existence of the business as a family business. We draw on case studies from two different countries, i.e. Germany and Sweden. Both countries are signified by a great share of family firms (Andersson et al., 2018; Lehrer & Schmid, 2015) and are two advanced economies in Europe. By selecting cases from two different countries, we contribute to the ongoing debate and multiplicity of family businesses (Nordqvist et al., 2014; Prügl, 2019).

The concept of entrepreneurial orientation (EO) can significantly contribute to enhancing the crisis resilience of family firms. EO refers to the proactive and risk-taking mindset that entrepreneurs possess, characterized by innovation, proactiveness, and risk-taking. In the context of family firms, adopting an EO can lead to several benefits during times of crisis. Firstly, the innovative dimension of EO encourages family firms to continually explore new opportunities and adapt their business models, allowing them to identify and seize potential avenues for growth even amidst uncertainty. Secondly, the proactive dimension prompts family firms to anticipate and respond swiftly to emerging challenges, enabling them to mitigate risks and minimize the impact of crises. Finally, the EO concept drives family firms to be assertive and resilient, enabling them to withstand competitive pressures and navigate through turbulent market conditions. By embracing EO, family firms can foster a culture of resilience, adaptability, and resourcefulness, ultimately enhancing their ability to withstand and overcome crises (Boers & Henschel, 2021).

The main focus of this chapter is to develop a resilience recovery model, using the concept of EO as a means to become more resilient and by accounting for the peculiarities of family firms. The chapter proceeds with presenting our theoretical framework and methods, before we give empirical illustrations, which settle the ground for our discussion and conclusions.

5.2 Family Firm and Entrepreneurial Orientation

There is still no agreement on how to define a family business (Steiger et al., 2015; Zahra & Sharma, 2004; Roffia et al., 2021). Therefore, it is important to state an operational definition. We follow other researchers (Chua et al., 1999) to define a family business, which is owned by an individual or a family and is involved in the firm. There is prior research looking at family firms and how they act and behave in a crisis situation (Cater III & Beal, 2014; Cater & Schwab, 2008). Issues related to crisis management have gained momentum, but there are still many open questions (Trahms et al., 2013; Ventura et al., 2020). For instance, family firms are known for caring for their socioemotional wealth (Gómez-Mejía et al., 2007), which is in danger in a crisis situation, and it becomes relevant to ask how and what owning families are willing and able to do in order to protect their socioemotional endowment they are receiving from owning their firm (Boers & Henschel, 2021; Boers et al., 2017; Gomez-Mejia et al., 2011).

Entrepreneurial orientation (EO) is a concept which has gained much attention in the entrepreneurship literature (Randerson, 2016). There are different ways of conceptualizing EO, and one prominent stream includes five dimensions (Lumpkin & Dess, 1996), whereas another stream includes three dimensions (Miller, 1983). In this study, we follow the three-dimension approach, including the dimensions of risk-taking, innovativeness and proactiveness (Miller, 1983, 2011).

Rauch et al. argue that "EO refers to the strategy-making processes that provide organizations with a basis for entrepreneurial decisions and actions" (Rauch et al., 2009, p. 762). This definition highlights the dynamic character of the concept. However, Zellweger and Sieger (2012) specifically investigated how the subdimensions of EO change over time in long-lived family firms. They argued that family firms must continuously adapt their EO profile and that generational change significantly impacts the EO's sub-dimensions.

There is some recent research, arguing that EO leads to resilience, such as supply chain resilience (Al-Hakimi & Borade, 2020). Other research argues that firms' EO can affect the individual resilience of entrepreneurs (Gottschalck et al., 2021).

5.3 Family Firm Resilience

More and more research addresses resilience in family firms (Chrisman et al., 2011). Whereas some researchers suggested the disappearance of family firms for the sake of publicly listed firms, which are said to be more professional than family firms (Chandler, 1990), other argue for family firms continued success (Daily & Dollinger, 1992). Thus, there is doubt whether distinguishing between different types of firms and their professionalization is at all meaningful (Watson, 1995). There is a literature suggesting that family firms could be a particular type of hybrid identity organizations (Boers & Andersson, 2023; Börje & Nordqvist, 2020), contributing to their continued resilience (Ljungkvist & Boers, 2016).

Resilience can be defined as "the ability of organizations to avoid, absorb, respond to, and recover from situations that could threaten their existence (Lengnick-Hall & Beck, 2005)" (Chrisman et al., 2011, p. 1107).

Chrisman et al. took this definition from (Lengnick-Hall & Beck, 2005), who refer to organizations in general. For family businesses, it is important to note that there are two important dimensions, i.e. the family and the firm (Boers & Henschel, 2022a) forming a unique type of organization, the family business.

In other words, an organization's existence can be threatened internally and externally. External threats can be single events, such as catastrophes, e.g. floods. Thus, family firm resilience has to encompass both parts, the family and the firm, in order to become resilient. Thus, being able to achieve resilience in this specific type of firms is even more complex than in "ordinary" organizations (Carney, 2005; Chua et al., 1999).

Prior literature stresses the need and ability of firms to being flexible to respond to disruptions and disasters (Alonso, 2015) quickly, requiring also flexibility (De Vries & Shields, 2006). In addition, flexibility requires a certain availability of resources, which are, however, limited in SMEs (Bhamra & Dani, 2011; Branicki et al., 2018; Kraus et al., 2013) in comparison to larger organizations.

5.3.1 The Pandemic as Crisis

According to Doern et al. (2019), most definitions describe a crisis as an extreme, unexpected, or unpredictable event that requires an urgent response from organizations and creates challenges for them – by interfering with its operations, creating ambiguity in its decision-making processes, threatening its goals and values, damaging its public image and bottom line.

The Corona pandemic is a crisis, which however differs significantly from other crises due to its global nature and impact on almost all areas of life. If one compares COVID-19 with previous crises, e.g. the financial crisis 2008–2009, one can see that the current pandemic has many consequences (external and internal) that require multiple actions from the organization on both the strategic (e.g. development of new skills and competences and repositioning) as well as the operational level (e.g. organizational reorganization and cost retrenchment). Thus, COVID-19 is different from past crises and requires new solutions (Boers & Henschel, 2022a, b). The pandemic has also hit industries differently. Whereas, for instance, the tourism industry has been affected tremendously by it (Brozović & Saito, 2022), or industries such as hotels (Lai & Wong, 2020) and restaurants (Byrd et al., 2021) suffered severely, other industries such as supermarkets and convenience stores had an upswing of demand (Anastasiadou et al., 2020; El Fikri et al., 2020).

According to Doern et al. (2019), a process-based definition of a crisis has not yet been adopted in SME research. Nevertheless, it is argued that it has the potential to capture more fully the kinds of crises entrepreneurs face from the unexpected to every day, and how they come into being, and the opportunities or challenges they bring. Within the area of SMEs specifically, crisis-based research has typically centred around external, extreme major crises, particularly the economically-oriented (Kottika et al., 2020; Williams & Vorley, 2015; Smallbone, 2012). While there has been some research on economic crises and its effects on SMEs, little or no attention has been brought to personal, emotional, and psychological effects of crises on entrepreneurs and SMEs (Doern et al., 2019; Stephan, 2018).

5.3.2 Development of Resilience Framework

In order to become resilient, we develop a framework, which can help SMEs in this endeavour. Resilience in family firms need to include both the family and the firm. Accordingly, family firm resilience is a multilevel construct, as it spans the individual, family, and firm level. EO is a firm-level construct. However, concerning resilience, the individual and the family level contribute to firm level resilience. Therefore, we combine organizational resilience with crisis management. Whereas crisis management initially was event- or crisis-driven, resilience research adopted a processual perspective. In this chapter, we combine the literatures of crisis and resilience management to with that on EO. We argue that EO gives a more activity-based perspective.

As the context of this chapter concerns and deals with family firms, they form another ingredient in this framework.

First, the proactive crisis management process based on Krystek (1981) begins with anticipating or preparing for a crisis. Accordingly, potential crises and their consequences are identified and corresponding scenarios of a crisis are developed. Alternative plans can then be derived on this basis. In the subsequent sub-phase of preventive crisis management, measures to identify and avoid crises are therefore defined, and appropriate strategies are planned in order to define how to deal with a crisis and make it the most efficient.

After a crisis has been recognized and occurred, an initial damage limitation is carried out as part of the acute or reactive crisis management, so that initial damage and direct negative effects can be kept as low as possible.

In principle, the crisis can either lead to the collapse of the company or be overcome through restructuring measures. A wide variety of measures can contribute to crisis management. These can be carried out at the organizational or liquidity-securing level or include measures to reduce costs and increase revenue (Rüsen, 2009).

The effect of the crisis measures should then be checked and evaluated so that conclusions can be drawn from them and thus learned from experience. The results and findings are consequently fed back into crisis prevention as part of a proactive crisis management. If necessary, crisis plans should be adjusted here.

The foundation of the crisis process model is built on the earlier work by Hong et al. (2012), which was originally developed for SMEs. It shows that the different dimensions of crisis management as suggested by (Hong et al., 2012) need to be extended for family firms. First, the family dimension influences potentially all modes. The degree of influence in part depends on the level of involvement of the owner family in each firm (Chrisman et al., 2012; Chua et al., 1999).

The study by Faghfouri et al. (2015) reveals small- and medium-sized family firms with higher levels of family ownership are less professionalized and formalized in terms of their crisis procedures. Due to ownership control and identification of the owning families, the families could contribute to a resolution of the crisis. This is very evident in the family leadership, involving several family members and generations (e.g. Boers & Henschel, 2022b). Further, the ambition for renewal through generational succession gives the owner families incentives to proactively contributing to the crisis resolution.

In this regard, family ownership and control can become prerequisites for continued learning from crises. Crisis situations should trigger learning to avoid repetition (Hong et al., 2012). As family firms represent a specific context, a situated learning approach (Konopaski et al., 2015) can be advisable, where knowledge about the crisis, and its handling, is shared among and across the owning family. Such an approach will be supported by binding social ties as well as identification of family members with the business. This will be supported by continued family leadership. Notwithstanding, there could also be obstacles to learning, such as individual and structural barriers to learning (Schilling & Kluge, 2009). Both can be relevant for family firms, in particular when the crisis is family induced. Further, due to dynastic motive, an owning family may become split into different branches (Tagiuri & Davis, 1996) with different ambitions and intentions, which can hinder learning processes from crises.

5.4 Method

The authors specifically targeted owners and senior managers, who had direct involvement in the decision-making processes within their family firms. This approach allowed for the gathering of rich and relevant data from individuals with first-hand knowledge and experience in running family firms. The sample size consisted of ten participants, which ensured a diverse range of perspectives and experiences. The researchers have conducted ten semi-structured interviews in family firms based throughout Germany and Sweden (see Table 5.1).

Semi-structured interviews were conducted with the participants as the primary method of data collection. This interview format allowed for flexibility in questioning while ensuring consistency across interviews. The interviews were carried out

Table 5.1 Demographic profile of the interviewed firms

Firm	Firm type	Legal status	Company age (years)	Family generations involved	Industry sector	Directors All	Directors Man	No employees
GER A	Small	Ltd	50	2nd generation	Logistics	2	1	20
GER B	Micro	Sole trader	10	1st generation	Restaurant	1	1	3
GER C	Small	Ltd	30	1st and 2nd generation	Printing	2	2	11
GER D	Medium	Ltd	90	3rd and 4th generation	Engineering	3	3	130
SWE A	Micro	Ltd	40	2nd generation	Camp site	1	1	6
SWE B	Micro	Ltd	10	1st generation	Restaurant	2	1	3
SWE C	Small	Ltd	30	1st and 2nd generation	Construction and service	1	1	17
SWE D	Micro	Ltd	50	3rd generation	Garage	1	1	7

between April and October 2022, with the majority of them taking place during this period. The interviews were conducted in a face-to-face or virtual setting, depending on the preference of the participants.

To capture detailed responses and ensure accuracy, the interviews were audio-recorded. This approach enabled the authors to transcribe the interviews accurately and analyse the data thoroughly. In addition to audio recordings, field notes were taken during the interviews to supplement the recorded data. These field notes included observations, nonverbal cues, and any other contextual information that could contribute to the understanding of the participants' responses.

To enhance the understanding of the industry or sector in which each family firm operated, data from databases and press clippings were also analysed. This approach allowed the researchers to gather additional information about the specific businesses and gain a broader perspective on the consequences of the crisis. Analysing external sources of data helped to triangulate the findings and provide a more comprehensive understanding of the research topic (Denzin, 2007).

To ensure the reliability of the study, the authors maintained consistency in the interview process. The use of semi-structured interviews allowed for a standardized approach, with a predetermined set of core questions, while allowing for follow-up and probing to explore specific areas in more depth. The interview questions are presented in Appendix. The audio recordings and field notes provided additional sources of data that could be referred to for verification and clarification.

Regarding validity, the purposive sampling technique (Guest et al., 2006) was employed to select participants who had direct involvement in the decision-making processes within their family firms. This sampling strategy aimed to ensure that the chosen participants were knowledgeable and had the relevant experiences to provide valuable insights into the research topic. By conducting interviews in both Germany and Sweden, the researchers sought to capture a diverse range of perspectives and experiences, increasing the external validity of the study.

Overall, the combination of semi-structured interviews, audio recordings, field notes, and analysis of external data sources helped to ensure the reliability and validity of the study, providing a robust foundation for analysing and interpreting the findings.

Thematic analysis was employed to analyse the interview data. Both authors have a family business background and first-hand crisis experience. This combination indicated that they would have sufficient expertise and objectivity for the study's data collection and data interpretation (Cater & Schwab, 2008). We performed an in-depth data analysis using content analysis and pattern identification. As Eisenhardt (1989) recommends, we selected a theme and looked for within-group similarities coupled with differences. Then, we developed theoretical points (so-called secondary codes) that are contextually grounded in the interview data and choose the most expressive comments to bring theoretical points to life (aggregated dimensions) (McCarthy, 2000). The code system in Fig. 5.1 provides information about how we arrived at the theoretical dimensions and about the drivers of resilience in family firms. It also shows the contextual issues informing resilience strategies under which decisions were made.

The transcripts were carefully reviewed and coded to identify recurring themes and patterns. The researchers conducted an iterative process of coding and theme development to ensure the reliability and validity of the analysis. Data from databases and press clippings complemented and triangulated the interview findings.

To establish reliability, several measures were taken. Firstly, a detailed interview guide was developed to ensure consistency in the questions asked across all interviews. Secondly, the two authors independently coded and analysed the interview data to minimize bias and increase intercoder reliability. Finally, meetings and discussions were held to ensure agreement and consensus on the emerging themes. The themes relevant for this chapter were related to how the firms managed the pandemic initially, while it evolved and in particular influence of the owning family on their firm.

To enhance the validity of the findings, various strategies were employed. Firstly, member checking was conducted, where participants were allowed to review and confirm the accuracy of their interview transcripts. This process ensured the alignment between the participants' perspectives and the findings presented.

When researching family businesses, the industry and size of the companies become less critical factors in the sampling process. The primary reason for this is that the common element that binds these businesses together is the functioning and actions of the entrepreneurial family.

Regardless of industry or size, family businesses share distinctive characteristics that set them apart from non-family enterprises (Chua et al., 1999). These characteristics include the family's influence on decision-making, the impact of family dynamics on business operations, and the long-term orientation inherent in family-owned firms. Therefore, when studying family businesses, it is crucial to focus on

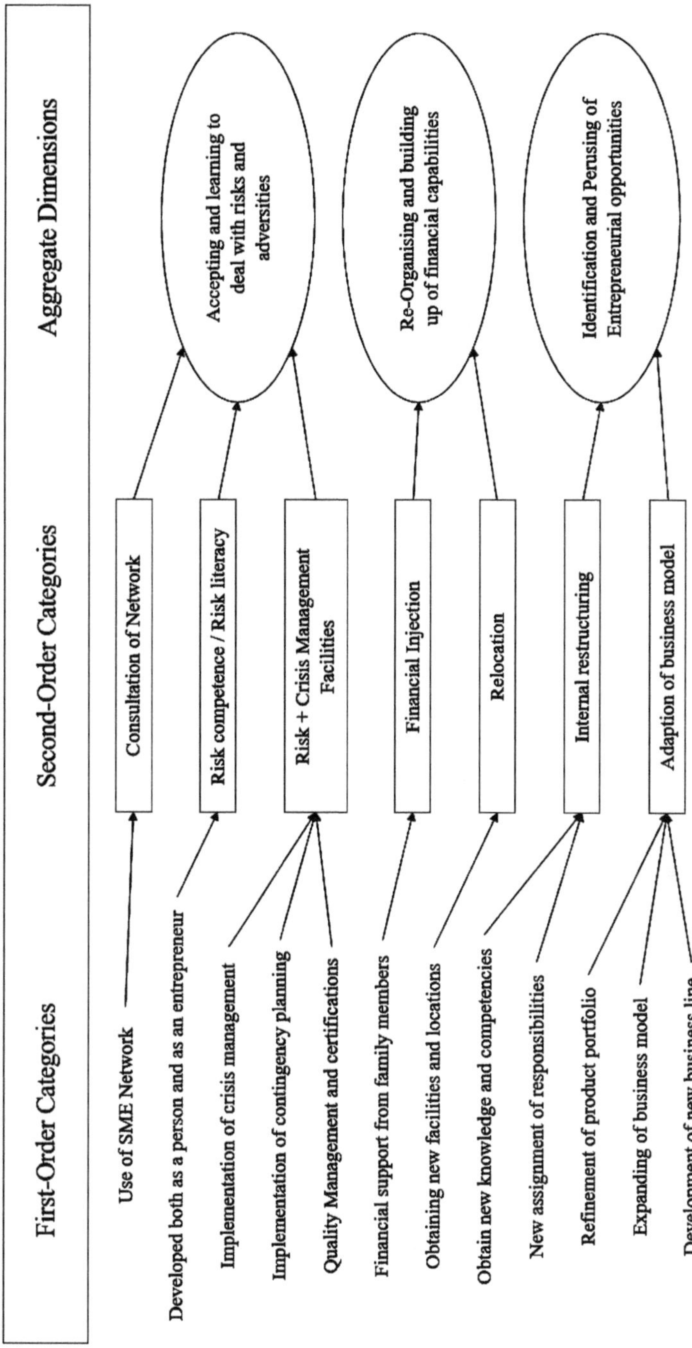

Fig. 5.1 Data structure of semi-structured interview process

the dynamics within the entrepreneurial family rather than external factors such as industry or size.

The entrepreneurial family's behaviour, values, and goals shape the business's operations. Their unique governance structures, succession planning, communication styles, and intergenerational relationships heavily influence decision-making processes and the overall direction of the company. Therefore, our selected companies cover inter-generational family firms accounting for the diversity family generations involved and years of foundation.

Moreover, the three dimensions of EO, that is, risk-taking, innovativeness, and proactiveness, are used when analysing the answers of the respondents on how, when, and why they reacted to the crisis.

Table 5.1 shows the demographic profile of our interview firms.

5.5 Empirical Findings and Results

The empirical results presented below showcase the findings of a qualitative study investigating the resilience of family firms. This research focuses specifically on eight family-owned businesses from Germany and Sweden, aiming to uncover the factors and strategies that contribute to their resilience in the face of challenges and disruptions. By delving into the experiences and practices of these family firms, this study provides valuable insights into how resilience is nurtured and maintained within the context of family-owned businesses.

Quotes span from the beginning of the pandemic until the end of 2022.

The empirical results presented in this section offer insights into the key findings derived from the qualitative analysis. The findings are organized around several thematic areas that emerged from the data, allowing for a structured exploration of the resilience mechanisms observed within the sample. By presenting the empirical results, this section aims to contribute to the existing knowledge base on family business resilience and offer practical implications for family firm owners, practitioners, and policymakers.

In the beginning, there was a general concern among family SMEs both in Germany and Sweden due to the uncertainty.

> Several employees were worried about getting infected. Especially in March [2020]. (SWE B, owner manager)

A store owner recalls (SWEA):

> It was March 12th, on that very day somehow it became clear to everyone that it was serious when the news that it was a pandemic aired. It was as if it came to all of us then. It was absolutely stunning. Since then it has only gone downhill and April brought everything crashing down.
>
> Our whole business model was deteriorating, the cancellation fairs in Germany and Europe posed a big challenge for us and we had to think of new ways to do our business. (GER A, owner manager)

In the company GER D, the son had to take over the leadership of the business, as his father and the managing director had to take 2 weeks of self-isolation after returning from ski trips in Austria. "After their [father and managing director] return they had to take two weeks of self-isolation and for the first time I was responsible for running the firm" (GER D, son owner manager).

5.5.1 The Development During Summer and Autumn

During the summer, the general feeling was more relaxed and the Corona pandemic from spring seemed far away. This is confirmed by one interviewee who says: "It is important to see things positively. Both privately and at the company" (SWE A, owner manager).

Some interviewees were looking for ways to cover their fixed costs in different ways. One owner manager (GER B) explains that he took another job:

> …[I] was really happy to see, even after more than 10 years as a self-employed I'm able to fit in a salary based job and to cope with this routine. Thanks to God I did this early move and was successful. Later in the crisis I wouldn't had have this luck as more people were thinking of that.

Another owner manager (GER A) says:

> I'm working from 8 to 8 at night. I must say I'm getting really frustrated by now. I look permanently on our bank account; talk to customers, employees and so on… What really helps me is my family. My mother is now in her 70s and tells me we had to overcome the financial crisis in 2009/10, the loss of a subsidiary in East Germany, we will pass this crisis as well. I do a lot of sport, spent more time with my wife and the children.

5.5.2 Entrepreneurial Orientation in a Crisis Situation

We were surprised how fast our interview firms adjusted their business model to cope with the new situation. A good example is GER A:

> "Overall in the transport sector we saw a huge decline in orders due to the cancelation of fairs, delays in the value chain by our customers and so on…". Then, the owner-manager of GER A created very quickly a new business idea. The firm owns a large warehouse, which was nearly empty right now. As some major customers in their area had problems with storing the delivery of goods as some ordered more than usual to cover the longer delivery time, GER A was renting out that space in the warehouse and organized the deliveries from and to customers. Furthermore, he also offered value-added services for his clients, such as cleaning and re-packing of warehouse items. This clearly shows how entrepreneurial orientation can be helpful in a crisis.

As owner-manager of GER A commented:

> Expanding our business model in terms of offering value added services for logistic orders to get a new sales stream to account for the loss of orders from trade fairs was a good idea

> and we are planning to carry on with such services in the future which can be a route to escape from the high margin pressure in bread and butter business of logistic services. (Second generation Owner-manager GER A).

A further example is GER D, as they opened up a new business line just in the beginning of the Corona crisis. Due to the deferral of the larger automotive projects by their current customers, GER D set up a new business line. They are now taking part in the biding process for public sector projects, which they did not before. According to the managing director, this business line provides promising results so far.

The firm GER C did also a quick refinement of their product portfolio in April 2020 as the owner-manager reported:

> We expanded our product portfolio and concentrating more on sophisticated print jobs which provide a better margin which the majority print firms can't offer. We also use our SME Network to generate new orders from partner firms in that network which proved to be successful in the current pandemic.

Also, the Swedish entrepreneurs have gained a lot of experience from the Corona pandemic in spring 2020. As he recalls:

> It was a very tough spring, but after that we felt a slight brightening during the summer and the beginning of autumn…Then it became as if some reputation escaped the carpet with the second wave and new restrictions. (Owner manager, SWE C).

> Once you have got through it [the pandemic in spring], you have learned a lot from it as well and developed both as a person and as an entrepreneur … we try to find other solutions and packaging.

Here, the owner-manager (SWE C) addresses explicitly the need to become entrepreneurial.

5.5.3 Crisis Management Procedures

Our interviews revealed that no firm had implement a comprehensive crisis management system so far. There are some replacement regulations for key personnel; however, there are no succession or replacement regulations for the managing board. Here, many firms would be in a difficult situation if the owner-manager fell ill. In terms of contingency planning, the IT recovery planning is the most advanced area in the crisis management of the family firms. Initiated through the current pandemic the interviewees did some efforts in formalizing contingency regulations to provide some guidance to stakeholders, such as customers or employees as exemplified through the following quote:

> .... Yes, it was well received by the employees and the big customers from the automotive industry. It provides further assurance that the company is well equipped for handling the crisis. (GER D, fourth generation owner-manager)

The firm SWE B holds ISO certifications for the quality management system (ISO 9000) and the environmental management system (ISO 14000) and sees a further need for risk analysis, especially in terms of a crisis as the owner-manager stated:

> .... the current crisis is not covered in ISO standards. (SWE B, first generation owner-manager).

This shows a clear need for the development of a crisis management standard, which is applicable for small firms. All new ISO standards follow the so-called high-level structure that will allow a better integration of the different management standards for developing a holistic crisis management system in family firms.

5.6 Discussion

The following discussion of the research results is guided by Fig. 5.2, which represents our proposed resilience model for family firms. The resilience model being presented herein is a product of our research findings obtained through interviews, complemented by the pattern matching technique explained in the methodological section of this chapter. It further accounts for the theoretical literature, presented in this chapter. The model concentrates on the post disaster environment of a crisis. Obviously, in this phase, there is opportunity for being entrepreneurial. There is also a need for adapting the different dimensions continuously, which has been described as a factor contributing to the longevity of family firms (Ljungkvist et al., 2020; Zellweger & Sieger, 2012). This adaptability becomes even more relevant in post

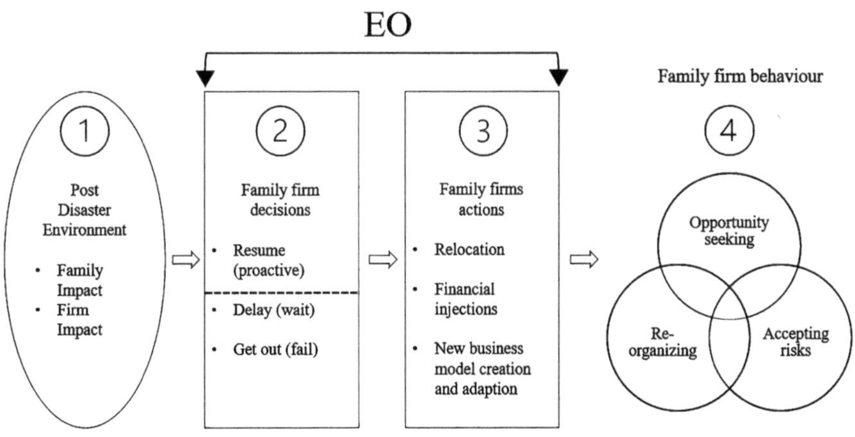

Fig. 5.2 Resilience framework. (Adopted from Morrish and Jones 2020)

crises situations. Drawn from this chapter is that companies should develop leaders' core competencies in advance to survive and ensure competitive advantages for the future.

The framework focuses on the behaviour and decision-making of family firms in post-disaster (crisis) environments. The framework emphasizes the impact of disasters on both the family and the firm, and it identifies three key categories of family firm behaviour to become resilient: opportunity seeking, reorganizing, and accepting risks. It recognizes the interplay between family dynamics, firm operations, and the need for strategic choices to foster resilience and recovery from a crisis. In turn, we discuss how the different elements in the resilience recovery framework interact and will work together.

Family Impact: This element focuses on how the disaster affects the family involved in the family firm. The decisions made by the family members can significantly impact the firm's recovery. They can choose to resume proactive actions, where they actively engage in rebuilding and adapting the business. Alternatively, they may opt for a delay strategy, where they wait and assess the situation before taking further action. In extreme cases, the family may decide to exit the business entirely, acknowledging that recovery might not be feasible.

Firm Impact: The firm impact component considers the direct consequences of the disaster on the business itself. It recognizes the need for reorganization to address the challenges brought about by the disaster. This involves making structural changes, realigning processes, and adapting to new circumstances. Additionally, it involves accepting risks associated with the post-disaster environment, such as changes in market conditions or resource availability.

Family Firm Decisions and Actions: This element focuses on the choices made by family firms in response to the post-disaster environment. Three primary decisions are highlighted: relocation, financial injections, and new business model creation and adaptation. Relocation involves moving the business to a different area, potentially seeking a more favourable location or better market conditions. Financial injections refer to injecting additional resources into the business to support recovery efforts. Lastly, creating and adapting new business models enables the family firm to address the evolving needs and opportunities emerging after the disaster.

The concept of entrepreneurial orientation (EO) can have a significant influence on the resilience recovery framework for family firms in post-disaster environments. EO refers to a firm's strategic orientation towards entrepreneurial activities, such as innovation, risk-taking, proactiveness. The EO concept can influence the framework in the following ways:

Proactiveness: EO emphasizes the proactive identification and pursuit of opportunities. In the resilience recovery framework context, family firms with a higher EO are more likely to exhibit proactive behaviour in response to a disaster. They may quickly identify new opportunities emerging from the post-disaster environment, such as gaps in the market or changing customer needs. This proactive approach can influence their decision-making, such as choosing to resume proactive actions rather than adopting a more passive or reactive stance. An important dimension of EO is proactiveness (Ljungkvist et al., 2020; Miller, 2011), which is also important for crises management (Boers & Henschel, 2021). Especially in a crisis situation, proactiveness can give advantages when the crisis is over. GER A and GER D will have a better position on their markets for introducing new lines of business. During the crises, they will have the human resources available to prepare and launch the new business lines. Also, prior research has pointed to being proactive as an import element for overcoming a crisis (e.g. Rüsen, 2009; Krystek, 1981). This proactiveness is also shown by following the different routines and recommendations which came by the authorities in Germany and Sweden.

Risk-Taking: EO emphasizes a willingness to take calculated risks. Family firms with a higher EO may be more inclined to accept and manage risks associated with the post-disaster environment. They may be willing to explore new markets, invest in innovative solutions, or make bold decisions to adapt their business models. This risk-taking propensity can influence the firm's impact component of the framework, encouraging family firms to be more open to reorganizing and embracing new strategies despite the uncertainties and challenges posed by the disaster. Risk-taking is a debated topic in family business research (Berrone et al., 2012; Boers et al., 2017; Gómez-Mejía et al., 2007; Naldi et al., 2013). The case companies GER A, GER D, and SWE C showed relatively high risk-taking by introducing new lines of business during the crisis. It should be noted that the risk-taking relates to financial risk-taking mostly of the owners (Ljungkvist et al., 2020). Even though the companies were affected differently by the restrictions and recommendations, the companies still had to carry a higher financial risk, as the crisis affected the business climate negatively. Nonetheless, some businesses were affected more than others. Eventually, in small family SMEs, it is the owning family who has to cover the financial risk, which is of course easier, when the business manages their finances conservatively, which is common in family SMEs (e.g. Brundin et al., 2014). This attitude towards risks and risk management is sometimes portrayed as a paradox, since family owners are often aware of certain risks but do not use formal risk management techniques (Mitter et al., 2022).

Innovativeness: EO emphasizes the importance of innovation and adaptation to stay competitive. Family firms with a higher EO are more likely to actively seek innovative solutions and adapt their business models to the post-disaster environment. They may be more open to creating new business models or adapting existing ones to align with the changing circumstances. This entrepreneurial mindset can influence the family firm decisions component of the framework, encouraging family firms to explore and implement new approaches, products, or services that can drive recovery and growth. Of course, the pandemic caused some worries among the employees of the case companies. However, it also opened up for new opportunities. There is a need for adapting to the conditions based on the Corona pandemic. For example, GER A and GER D adapted their business model and started new business lines, thereby showing high degrees of innovativeness (Ljungkvist et al., 2020; Zellweger & Sieger, 2012). Being innovative during a crisis is combined with higher risk-taking because it remains unclear if and how the new lines of business will be received from customers. However, it can also be a better situation to introduce no products or services in a crisis, because competitors are exposed to the same crisis, meaning that they also have to manage the crisis in their companies. Hence, a crisis offers opportunities to adapt to new situations, where the companies obtain new knowledge and competencies making them more competitive (Osiyevskyy et al., 2020). Thereby, a crisis opens up for new ways, leading to potentially radical innovations, such as shortening the working hours while paying the same salary (Boers, 2023). During the pandemic, many supply changes were disturbed, leading to shortage of certain goods and supplies (Pujawan & Bah, 2022). Hence, companies had to develop new ways of handling their customers, considering the restrictions (all companies).

To conclude, entrepreneurial orientation can influence the resilience recovery framework by promoting proactive behaviour, encouraging risk-taking, fostering innovation, and influencing resource allocation decisions. Family firms with a higher EO are likely to exhibit these characteristics, which can shape their responses and decisions within the framework, ultimately influencing their recovery and resilience in post-disaster environments.

One should bear in mind that the resilience recovery framework primarily focuses on internal factors within the family firm, such as family dynamics and firm operations. While it acknowledges the need to accept risks and adapt to the post-disaster environment, it may not sufficiently consider external factors like government policies, community support, or market conditions. These external factors can play a significant role in shaping the recovery trajectory of family firms.

There are also other contextual factors influencing family firm recovery. Different industries, geographic locations, and cultural contexts can significantly impact family firms‘available options and outcomes. The framework's general nature may not adequately address these specificities, requiring additional customization and adaptation for practical implementation.

Overall, the resilience recovery framework illustrates how the family impact, firm impact, and family firm decisions are interconnected and influence each other in recovering from a disaster. It emphasizes the importance of understanding these interactions and making strategic choices to foster resilience and successful recovery for family firms.

5.7 Conclusion and Outlook

In conclusion, this chapter examined the management of the Corona pandemic crisis by family firms and highlighted the importance of resilience in navigating through challenging times. The study revealed that the entrepreneurial characteristics of family firms, such as risk-taking, innovativeness, and proactiveness, played a significant role in their ability to overcome the crisis. While the pandemic is ongoing, the findings suggest that these entrepreneurial qualities have been instrumental in the firms' resilience thus far.

The theoretical framework employed in this study integrated crisis management and entrepreneurial orientation (EO) within a resilience perspective, focusing specifically on family firms. This novel approach holds promise and provides a valuable context for further exploration by researchers in different settings. Investigating the crisis management strategies of family SMEs in various contexts and exploring different types of crises would contribute to a more comprehensive understanding of effective crisis response.

One significant contribution of this study is the recognition of the owning family as a reservoir of resources that can be mobilized during times of need, a unique advantage typically not available to non-family firms. The familial attachment and familiarity with the business demonstrated by family members, even in the absence of a formal connection, facilitate their involvement in the business, making it easier to harness their expertise and support.

Additionally, this research underscores the importance of crisis preparedness in family firms. The study emphasizes the value of implementing crisis planning not only within the business but also within the owning family. Such preparedness enables firms to better handle crisis situations when they arise, mitigating potential adverse effects.

To further advance our knowledge in this area, future studies should examine crisis management approaches in family SMEs across diverse contexts, considering different types of crises. By expanding the scope of research, we can gain deeper insights into the strategies and mechanisms that contribute to the resilience of family firms facing unexpected challenges. Ultimately, this knowledge will enable practitioners and policymakers to develop effective support systems tailored to the unique needs of family businesses, fostering their long-term success and sustainability.

Appendix: Interview Questions

Dimensions	Questions
Crisis management	*Detection phase*:
	Did you experience any crisis in the past? What happened?
	When and how did you detect the crisis?
	What were the first warning signs of the crisis; how did they appear?
	What specific contingency plans did your firm have to prevent the crisis or minimise the negative impacts?
	Occurrence phase:
	How did the crisis affect you, your family, your business in general, the ownership of the firm?
	How are you handling the crises internally and externally (e.g. communication with internal and external stakeholders)?
	What were the major actions implemented?
	How did your firm respond to the crisis events?
	Did your firm find that crisis planning measures were actually useful in crisis events? If not, why not?
	What could have been better crisis managing measures in your opinion?
	Recovery phase:
	What were the major risks and challenges the company was facing during the recovery process?
	What were the major restructuring actions implemented?
	How long did it take to turn round your company?
	During the course of the restructuring, how would you describe the company's position in its field of business?
	After the crisis, what did your firm actually do to recover from the crisis or even convert the crisis into new development opportunities?
	Resolution phase:
	Once the firm recovered from the crisis event, did your firm make any modification in their product, process, market position, or even business paradigm to prevent a similar crisis in the future?
	What have you learned from the crisis, e.g. with regard to ownership and family issues?
	What specific contingency plans does your firm have to prevent the crisis or minimize the negative impacts?
	What is the future outlook about the possible crisis events for your firm and the industry as a whole?
Entrepreneurial orientation	*Innovativeness*
	5 questions
	Proactiveness
	5 questions
	Risk-taking
	4 questions

Dimensions	Questions	
Contingency factors	*Firm size*:	
	Fewer than 10 employees	150–250 employees
	10–50 employees	250–500 employees
	50–150 employees	More than 500 employees
	Educational background:	
	(a) No formal education.	
	(b) Non-university.	
	(c) University degree.	
	Family generations involved:	
	(a) How many family members are involved in the managing board of the firm?	
	(b) How many family members are involved in the supervisory board or other monitoring boards?	
	Gender	
	(a) Male	
	(b) Female	
	Company age	
	Industry sector	
	(a) Low-technology firms.	
	(b) High-technology firms.	
	Uncertainty in the business environment	
	What is your view concerning the predictability of the following changes in your business environment (multiple selection allowed)?	
	(a) Buying patterns of customers.	
	(b) Technological development in your business' primary industry.	
	(c) Competitors.	
	(d) Change in government's regulations.	
	(e) Obtaining resources (labour, raw materials).	

References

Al-Hakimi, M. A., & Borade, D. B. (2020). The impact of entrepreneurial orientation on the supply chain resilience. *Cogent Business & Management, 7*(1), 1847990. https://doi.org/10.1080/23311975.2020.1847990

Alonso, D. A. (2015), Resilience in the context of two traditional Spanish rural sectors: an exploratory study, Journal of Enterprising Communities: *People and Places in the Global Economy, 9*(2), pp. 182–203. https://doi.org/10.1108/JEC-11-2014-0026

Amann, B., & Jaussaud, J. (2012). Family and non-family business resilience in an economic downturn. *Asia Pacific Business Review, 18*(2), 203–223. https://doi.org/10.1080/13602381.2010.537057

Anastasiadou, E., Chrissos Anestis, M., Karantza, I., & Vlachakis, S. (2020). The coronavirus' effects on consumer behavior and supermarket activities: Insights from Greece and

Sweden. *International Journal of Sociology and Social Policy, 40*(9/10), 893–907. https://doi.org/10.1108/IJSSP-07-2020-0275

Andersson, F. W., Johansson, D., Karlsson, J., Lodefalk, M., & Poldahl, A. (2018). The characteristics of family firms: Exploiting information on ownership, kinship, and governance using total population data. *Small Business Economics, 51*(3), 539–556. https://doi.org/10.1007/s11187-017-9947-6

Andersson, T., Cäker, M., Tengblad, S., & Wickelgren, M. (2019). Building traits for organizational resilience through balancing organizational structures. *Scandinavian Journal of Management, 35*(1), 36–45. https://doi.org/10.1016/j.scaman.2019.01.001

Berrone, P., Cruz, C., & Gomez-Mejia, L. R. (2012). Socioemotional wealth in family firms. *Family Business Review, 25*(3), 258–279. https://doi.org/10.1177/0894486511435355

Bhamra, R., & Dani, S. (2011). Creating resilient SMEs. *International Journal of Production Research, 49*(18), 5373–5374. https://doi.org/10.1080/00207543.2011.563999

Boers, B. (2023). (Social) innovation as a way out of a crisis? How small family firms become innovative. In S. Kraus, T. Clauß, & A. Kallmünzer (Eds.), *Research handbooks in business and management series. Research handbook on entrepreneurship and innovation in family firms* (pp. 279–297). Edward Elgar Publishing. https://doi.org/10.4337/9781800889248.00020

Boers, B. & Andersson, T. (2023), Family members as hybrid owner-managers in family-owned newspaper companies: handling multiple institutional logics, *Journal of Family Business Management, 13*(2), pp. 523–543. https://doi.org/10.1108/JFBM-06-2021-0065

Boers, B., & Henschel, T. (2021). Entrepreneurial orientation and crisis: How family firms manage the COVID-19-pandemic. *RethinkingFinance, 1*), REF1357499, 65–72.

Boers, B., & Henschel, T. (2022a). Different crises in family SMEs and how to prepare for them. In S. Durst & T. Henschel (Eds.), *Crisis management for Small and Medium-Sized Enterprises (SMEs)* (pp. 101–117). Springer. https://doi.org/10.1007/978-3-030-91727-2_8

Boers, B., & Henschel, T. (2022b). The role of entrepreneurial orientation in crisis management: Evidence from family firms in enterprising communities. *Journal of Enterprising Communities: People and Places in the Global Economy, 16*(5), 756–780. https://doi.org/10.1108/Jec-12-2020-0210

Boers, B., Ljungkvist, T., Brunninge, O., & Nordqvist, M. (2017). Going private: A socioemotional wealth perspective on why family controlled companies decide to leave the stock-exchange. *Journal of Family Business Strategy, 8*(2), 74–86. https://doi.org/10.1016/j.jfbs.2017.01.005

Börje, B., & Nordqvist, M. (2020). Family businesses as hybrid organisations. In D. Billis & C. Rochester (Eds.), *Handbook on hybrid organisations* (pp. 507–521). Edward Elgar Publishing. https://doi.org/10.4337/9781785366116.00039

Branicki, L. J., Sullivan-Taylor, B., & Livschitz, S. R. (2018). How entrepreneurial resilience generates resilient SMEs. *International Journal of Entrepreneurial Behavior & Research, 24*(7), 1244–1263. https://doi.org/10.1108/IJEBR-11-2016-0396

Brozović, D., & Saito, H. (2022). The impacts of Covid-19 on the tourism sector: Changes, adaptations and challenges. *Tourism: An International Interdisciplinary Journal, 70*(3), 465–479. https://doi.org/10.37741/t.70.3.9

Brundin, E., Samuelsson, E. F., & Melin, L. (2014). Family ownership logic: Framing the core characteristics of family businesses. *Journal of Management & Organization, 20*(1), 6–37. https://doi.org/10.1017/jmo.2014.15

Byrd, K., Her, E., Fan, A., Almanza, B., Liu, Y., & Leitch, S. (2021). Restaurants and COVID-19: What are consumers' risk perceptions about restaurant food and its packaging during the pandemic? *International Journal of Hospitality Management, 94*, 102821. https://doi.org/10.1016/j.ijhm.2020.102821

Carney, M. (2005). Corporate governance and competitive advantage in family–controlled firms. *Entrepreneurship Theory and Practice, 29*(3), 249–265. https://doi.org/10.1111/j.1540-6520.2005.00081.x

Cater, J. J., III, & Beal, B. (2014). Ripple effects on family firms from an externally induced crisis. *Journal of Family Business Management, 4*(1), 62–78. https://doi.org/10.1108/JFBM-02-2013-0006

Cater, J., & Schwab, A. (2008). Turnaround strategies in established small family firms. *Family Business Review, 21*(1), 31–50. https://doi.org/10.1111/j.1741-6248.2007.00113.x

Chandler, A. D. (1990). *Strategy and structure: Chapters in the history of the industrial enterprise*. MIT Press.

Chrisman, J. J., Chua, J. H., & Steier, L. P. (2011). Resilience of family firms: An introduction. *Entrepreneurship Theory and Practice, 35*(6), 1107–1119. https://doi.org/10.1111/j.1540-6520.2011.00493.x

Chrisman, J. J., Chua, J. H., Pearson, A. W., & Barnett, T. (2012). Family involvement, family influence, and family–centered non–economic goals in small firms. *Entrepreneurship Theory and Practice, 36*(2), 267–293. https://doi.org/10.1111/j.1540-6520.2010.00407.x

Chua, J. H., Chrisman, J. J., & Sharma, P. (1999). Defining the family business by behavior. *Entrepreneurship Theory and Practice, 23*(4), 19–39. https://doi.org/10.1177/104225879902300402

Daily, C. M., & Dollinger, M. J. (1992). An empirical examination of ownership structure in family and professionally managed firms. *Family Business Review, 5*(2), 117–136. https://doi.org/10.1111/j.1741-6248.1992.00117.x

De Vries, H., & Shields, M. (2006). Towards a theory of entrepreneurial resilience: A case study analysis of New Zealand SME owner operators. *New Zealand Journal of Applied Business Research, 5*(1), 33–43.

Denzin, N. K. (2007). Triangulation. In G. Ritzer (Ed.), *The Blackwell encyclopedia of sociology*. Wiley. https://doi.org/10.1002/9781405165518.wbeost050

Doern, R. (2016). Entrepreneurship and crisis management: The experiences of small businesses during the London 2011 riots. *International Small Business Journal: Researching Entrepreneurship, 34*(3), 276–302. https://doi.org/10.1177/0266242614553863

Doern, R., Williams, N., & Vorley, T. (2019). Special issue on entrepreneurship and crises: Business as usual? An introduction and review of the literature. *Entrepreneurship & Regional Development, 31*(5–6), 400–412. https://doi.org/10.1080/08985626.2018.1541590

Durst, S., & Henschel, T. (2021). COVID-19 as an accelerator for developing strong(er) businesses? Insights from Estonian small firms. *Journal of the International Council for Small Business, 2*(1), 1–29. https://doi.org/10.1080/26437015.2020.1859935

Durst, S., Palacios Acuache, M. M. G., & Bruns, G. (2021). Peruvian small and medium-sized enterprises and COVID-19: Time for a new start! *Journal of Entrepreneurship in Emerging Economies, 13*(4), 648–672. https://doi.org/10.1108/jeee-06-2020-0201

Eisenhardt, K. M. (1989). Making fast strategic decisions in high-velocity environments. *Academy of Management Journal, 32*(3), 543–576. https://doi.org/10.2307/256434

Faghfouri, P., Kraiczy, N. D., Hack, A., & Kellermanns, F. W. (2015). Ready for a crisis? How supervisory boards affect the formalized crisis procedures of small and medium-sized family firms in Germany. *Review of Managerial Science, 9*(2), 317–338. https://doi.org/10.1007/s11846-014-0158-0

Falkner, E. M., & Hiebl, M. R. (2015). Risk management in SMEs: A systematic review of available evidence. *The Journal of Risk Finance, 16*(2), 122–144. https://doi.org/10.1108/Jrf-06-2014-0079

Fikri, M. E., Andika, R., Febrina, T., Pramono, C., & Pane, D. N. (2020). Strategy to enhance purchase decisions through promotions and shopping lifestyles to supermarkets during the coronavirus pandemic: A case study IJT Mart, Deli Serdang Regency, North Sumatera. *Saudi Journal of Business and Management Studies, 5*(11), 530–538. https://doi.org/10.36348/sjbms.2020.v05i11.002

Gómez-Mejía, L. R., Haynes, K. T., Núñez-Nickel, M., Jacobson, K. J. L., & Moyano-Fuentes, J. (2007). Socioemotional wealth and business risks in family-controlled firms: Evidence from Spanish olive oil mills. *Administrative Science Quarterly, 52*(1), 106–137.

Gomez-Mejia, L. R., Cruz, C., Berrone, P., & de Castro, J. (2011). The bind that ties: Socioemotional wealth preservation in family firms. *Academy of Management Annals, 5*(1), 653–707. https://doi.org/10.1080/19416520.2011.593320

Gottschalck, N., Branner, K., Rolan, L., & Kellermanns, F. (2021). Cross-level effects of entrepreneurial orientation and ambidexterity on the resilience of small business owners. *Journal of Small Business Management*, 1–37. https://doi.org/10.1080/00472778.2021.2002878

Guest, G., Bunce, A., & Johnson, L. (2006). How many interviews are enough? *Field Methods, 18*(1), 59–82. https://doi.org/10.1177/1525822x05279903

Hong, P., Huang, C., & Li, B. (2012). Crisis management for SMEs: Insights from a multiple-case study. *International Journal of Business Excellence, 5*(5), 48802, 535. https://doi.org/10.1504/IJBEX.2012.048802

Konopaski, M., Jack, S., & Hamilton, E. (2015). How family business members learn about continuity. *Academy of Management Learning & Education, 14*(3), 347–364. https://doi.org/10.5465/amle.2014.0244

Korber, S., & McNaughton, R. B. (2018). Resilience and entrepreneurship: A systematic literature review. *International Journal of Entrepreneurial Behavior & Research, 24*(7), 1129–1154. https://doi.org/10.1108/IJEBR-10-2016-0356

Kottika, E., Özsomer, A., Rydén, P., Theodorakis, I. G., Kaminakis, K., Kottikas, K. G., & Stathakopoulos, V. (2020). We survived this! What managers could learn from SMEs who successfully navigated the Greek economic crisis. *Industrial Marketing Management, 88*, 352–365. https://doi.org/10.1016/j.indmarman.2020.05.021

Kraus, S., Moog, P., Schlepphorst, S., & Raich, M. (2013). Crisis and turnaround management in SMEs: A qualitative-empirical investigation of 30 companies. *International Journal of Entrepreneurial Venturing, 5*(4), 406–430.

Krystek, U. (1981). *Krisenbewältigungs-Management und Unternehmungsplanung*. Springer.

Lai, I. K. W., & Wong, J. W. C. (2020). Comparing crisis management practices in the hotel industry between initial and pandemic stages of COVID-19. *International Journal of Contemporary Hospitality Management, 32*(10), 3135–3156. https://doi.org/10.1108/IJCHM-04-2020-0325

Lehrer, M., & Schmid, S. (2015). Germany's industrial family firms: Prospering islands of social capital in a financialized world? *Competition & Change, 19*(4), 301–316. https://doi.org/10.1177/1024529415581970

Lengnick-Hall, C. A., & Beck, T. E. (2005). Adaptive fit versus robust transformation: How organizations respond to environmental change. *Journal of Management, 31*(5), 738–757. https://doi.org/10.1177/0149206305279367

Linnenluecke, M. K. (2017). Resilience in business and management research: A review of influential publications and a research agenda. *International Journal of Management Reviews, 19*(1), 4–30. https://doi.org/10.1111/ijmr.12076

Ljungkvist, T., & Boers, B. (2016). Structural crisis? *Journal of Enterprising Communities: People and Places in the Global Economy, 10*(4), 425–446. https://doi.org/10.1108/JEC-05-2015-0030

Ljungkvist, T., Boers, B., & Samuelsson, J. (2020). Three stages of entrepreneurial orientation: The founder's role. *International Journal of Entrepreneurial Behavior & Research, 26*(2), 285–306. https://doi.org/10.1108/IJEBR-10-2018-0630

Lumpkin, G. T., & Dess, G. G. (1996). Clarifying the entrepreneurial orientation construct and linking it to performance. *The Academy of Management Review, 21*(1), 135–172. https://doi.org/10.2307/258632

Mayr, S., & Lixl, D. (2019). Restructuring in SMEs – A multiple case study analysis. *Journal of Small Business Strategy, 29*(1), 78–91.

McCarthy, B. (2000). The cult of risk taking and social learning: A study of Irish entrepreneurs. *Management Decision, 38*(8), 563–575. https://doi.org/10.1108/00251740010378291

Miller, D. (1983). The correlates of entrepreneurship in three types of firms. *Management Science, 29*(7), 770–791.

Miller, D. (2011). Miller (1983) Revisited: A reflection on EO research and some suggestions for the future. *Entrepreneurship Theory and Practice, 35*(5), 873–894. https://doi.org/10.1111/j.1540-6520.2011.00457.x

Mitter, C., Postlmayr, M., & Kuttner, M. (2022). Risk management in small family firms: Insights into a paradox. *Journal of Family Business Management, 12*(2), 237–250. https://doi.org/10.1108/JFBM-06-2020-0051

Morrish, S. C., & Jones, R. (2020). Post-disaster business recovery: An entrepreneurial marketing perspective. *Journal of Business Research, 113*, 83–92. https://doi.org/10.1016/j.jbusres.2019.03.041

Naldi, L., Cennamo, C., Corbetta, G., & Gomez-Mejia, L. (2013). Preserving socioemotional wealth in family firms: Asset or liability? The moderating role of business context. *Entrepreneurship Theory and Practice, 37*(6), 1341–1360. https://doi.org/10.1111/etap.12069

Nordqvist, M., Sharma, P., & Chirico, F. (2014). Family firm heterogeneity and governance: A configuration approach. *Journal of Small Business Management, 52*(2), 192–209. https://doi.org/10.1111/jsbm.12096

Osiyevskyy, O., Shirokova, G., & Ritala, P. (2020). Exploration and exploitation in crisis environment: Implications for level and variability of firm performance. *Journal of Business Research, 114*, 227–239. https://doi.org/10.1016/j.jbusres.2020.04.015

Prügl, R. (2019). Capturing the heterogeneity of family firms: Reviewing scales to directly measure socioemotional wealth. In E. Memili (Ed.), *The Palgrave handbook of heterogeneity among family firms* (pp. 461–484). Palgrave Macmillan US. https://doi.org/10.1007/978-3-319-77676-7_17

Pujawan, I. N., & Bah, A. U. (2022). Supply chains under COVID-19 disruptions: Literature review and research agenda. *Supply Chain Forum: An International Journal, 23*(1), 81–95. https://doi.org/10.1080/16258312.2021.1932568

Randerson, K. (2016). Entrepreneurial orientation: Do we actually know as much as we think we do? *Entrepreneurship & Regional Development, 28*(7–8), 580–600. https://doi.org/10.1080/08985626.2016.1221230

Rauch, A., Wiklund, J., Lumpkin, G. T., & Frese, M. (2009). Entrepreneurial orientation and business performance: An assessment of past research and suggestions for the future. *Entrepreneurship Theory and Practice, 33*(3), 761–787. https://doi.org/10.1111/j.1540-6520.2009.00308.x

Roffia, P., Moracchiato, S., Liguori, E., & Kraus, S. (2021). Operationally defining family SMEs: A critical review. *Journal of Small Business and Enterprise Development, 28*(2), 229–260. https://doi.org/10.1108/JSBED-11-2020-0399

Roux-Dufort, C. (2007). Is crisis management (only) a management of exceptions? *Journal of Contingencies and Crisis Management, 15*(2), 105–114. https://doi.org/10.1111/j.1468-5973.2007.00507.x

Rüsen, T. A. (2009). *Krisen und Krisenmanagement in Familienunternehmen: Schwachstellen erkennen, Lösungen erarbeiten, Existenzbedrohungen meistern*. Gabler.

Salvato, C., Sargiacomo, M., Amore, M. D., & Minichilli, A. (2020). Natural disasters as a source of entrepreneurial opportunity: Family business resilience after an earthquake. *Strategic Entrepreneurship Journal, 14*(4), 594–615. https://doi.org/10.1002/sej.1368

Schilling, J., & Kluge, A. (2009). Barriers to organizational learning: An integration of theory and research. *International Journal of Management Reviews, 11*(3), 337–360. https://doi.org/10.1111/j.1468-2370.2008.00242.x

Smallbone, D. (2012). Vulnerable or resilient? Smes and the economic crisis in the UK. In B. Dallago & C. Guglielmetti (Eds.), *Routledge studies in the European economy: Vol. 27. The consequences of the international crisis for European SMEs: Vulnerability and resilience* (pp. 109–134). Routledge.

Steiger, T., Duller, C., & Hiebl, M. R. W. (2015). No consensus in sight: An analysis of ten years of family business definitions in empirical research studies. *Journal of Enterprising Culture, 23*(1), 25–62. https://doi.org/10.1142/S0218495815500028

Stephan, U. (2018). Entrepreneurs' mental health and well-being: A review and research agenda. *Academy of Management Perspectives, 32*(3), 290–322. https://doi.org/10.5465/amp.2017.0001

Tagiuri, R., & Davis, J. (1996). Bivalent attributes of the family firm. *Family Business Review, 9*(2), 199–208. https://doi.org/10.1111/j.1741-6248.1996.00199.x

Trahms, C. A., Ndofor, H. A., & Sirmon, D. G. (2013). Organizational decline and turnaround. *Journal of Management, 39*(5), 1277–1307. https://doi.org/10.1177/0149206312471390

Ventura, M., Vesperi, W., Melina, A. M., & Reina, R. (2020). Resilience in family firms: a theoretical overview and proposed theory. International *Journal of Management and Enterprise Development, 19*(2), 164–186. https://doi.org/10.1504/IJMED.2020.107403

Watson, T. J. (1995). Entrepreneurship and professional management: A fatal distinction. *International Small Business Journal: Researching Entrepreneurship, 13*(2), 34–46. https://doi.org/10.1177/0266242695132003

Williams, N., & Vorley, T. (2015). The impact of institutional change on entrepreneurship in a crisis-hit economy: The case of Greece. *Entrepreneurship & Regional Development, 27*(1–2), 28–49. https://doi.org/10.1080/08985626.2014.995723

Williams, T. A., Gruber, D. A., Sutcliffe, K. M., Shepherd, D. A., & Zhao, E. Y. (2017). Organizational response to adversity: Fusing crisis management and resilience research streams. *Academy of Management Annals, 11*(2), 733–769. https://doi.org/10.5465/annals.2015.0134

Zahra, S. A., & Sharma, P. (2004). Family business research: A strategic reflection. *Family Business Review, 17*(4), 331–346. https://doi.org/10.1111/j.1741-6248.2004.00022.x

Zellweger, T., & Sieger, P. (2012). Entrepreneurial orientation in long-lived family firms. *Small Business Economics, 38*(1), 67–84. https://doi.org/10.1007/s11187-010-9267-6

Leveraging Knowledge Management and Entrepreneurial Orientation to Enhance Resilience in Small- and Medium-Sized Enterprises

6

Thomas Henschel, Susanne Durst, and Johanna Salzmann

6.1 Introduction

As a result of the global corona pandemic, the issue of crisis management has come strongly to the fore (e.g., Hammerschmidt et al., 2021; Durst & Henschel, 2021). The economic and social impact of the pandemic is immense for society as a whole and thus also for companies. This applies even more to small- and medium-sized enterprises (SMEs) which have important functions as the backbone of economies; in Europe, for example, SMEs represent 99% of all companies (European Commission, 2022).

A dedicated approach to crisis management in the form of a crisis management system (CMS) may help organizations to better cope with internal as well external crises. These systems support in meeting the business objectives and the company's sustainability (Eggers, 2020; Kottika et al., 2020; Osiyevskyy et al., 2020). Consequently, they can contribute to more resilient companies.

The implementation and maintenance of these systems requires time and resources which becomes a challenge, especially in SMEs as other activities that are important to stay competitive also need time and resources. For example, entrepreneurial orientation (EO) is viewed as essential to organizational performance (Rauch et al., 2009). At the same time, the increasing number of challenges all types of organizations are exposed to calls for an even more rigorous approach to knowledge

T. Henschel (✉) · J. Salzmann
Hochschule für Technik und Wirtschaft Berlin, University of Applied Sciences Berlin, Berlin, Germany
e-mail: henschel@htw-berlin.de

S. Durst (✉)
Reykjavik University, Reykjavik, Iceland
e-mail: susanned@ru.is

S. Durst, T. Henschel (eds.), *Small and Medium-Sized Enterprise (SME) Resilience*, Management for Professionals, https://doi.org/10.1007/978-3-031-50836-3_6

management (KM) (Durst & Zieba, 2020). Thus, in companies that are scarce of resources and time such as smaller firms, the question rises whether the cost-benefit ratio warrants the efforts. To put it more simply, does crisis management lead to more success in SMEs?

To answer this question, an empirical investigation of the impact of CMS on the performance of German SMEs was carried out. More precisely, the study aims to develop a comprehensive understanding of KM and EO's impact on CMS and overall company performance. To the authors' knowledge, there is a lack of empirical studies that have studied the effects of crisis management on performance in SMEs in general and with regard to the role of KM and EO in this context in particular.

This chapter is organized as follows. In the following section, the related literature used for the development of the measurement model is briefly presented. This is followed by a presentation of the research design and the research results. After that, a conclusion is given, which also contains recommendations for the further development of the proposed model.

6.2 Literature Review and Conceptual Framework

A crisis management system serves to avoid and prevent crises affecting the company. Therefore, it helps planning and controlling specific measures for dealing with a crisis to secure the company's goals and, in this context, its existence in the long term (Laskovaia et al., 2019). Crisis management process goes through various phases, starting with proactive crisis management anticipating, preventing, and recognizing, through reactive crisis management, in which crises are to be actively fought, to the reflection of a crisis (Eggers, 2020).

A review of the literature that was conducted for this paper, however, revealed that the study of crisis management in SMEs is still at an early stage of development. The review suggested that there are only a few articles that have dedicatedly focused on the implementation of crisis management and the methods used. As far as Germany is concerned, the review indicated that at the time of the study, no empirical studies have been published that had studied the effect of crisis management on SME performance which stressed a considerable need for research given the role of SMEs for Germany and Europe.

In the following sections, we present the relevant constructs and the derived hypotheses thereof.

6.2.1 Knowledge Management

Knowledge management has been described as useful for all kinds of organizations as it supports the systematic identification, creation, application, and dissemination of critical knowledge which in turn can contribute to organizations' efforts toward sustainability (Durst & Zieba, 2020). In SMEs, KM can contribute to both financial and nonfinancial performance (Durst et al., 2023). Recent research on KM has also highlighted the possible downsides of knowledge. This research stream argues that in order to manage knowledge effectively, companies must also acknowledge the possible negative sides of knowledge, i.e., knowledge as a negative risk. Since every organization is exposed to various so-called knowledge risks which can jeopardize the organizational goals, organizations are recommended to extend their existing approach to KM accordingly. Durst and Zieba (2019) proposed a knowledge risk map that divides knowledge risks into human, technological, and operational knowledge risks to raise awareness for these risks and their high interconnectedness. In this context, it should not be forgotten that contemporary crisis management depends on access to up-to-date and relevant knowledge. Thus, the management of knowledge in general and the inherent negative risks in particular can be viewed as essential for a well-functioning crisis management in SMEs. This leads to the following hypothesis:

H1 There is a positive effect of knowledge management on crisis management in SMEs.

As with crisis management, the question of usefulness also arises with knowledge management. As mentioned before, there is empirical evidence demonstrating the impact of KM on financial and nonfinancial performance in SMEs. Regarding the latter, or the so-called soft factors of performance, including innovativeness, sustainability, agility, and resilience, here too an increasing number of empirical studies are available underlining the pivotal impact KM has on these types of performance.

There is evidence about the crucial role KM plays in enhancing profitability. KM can help small firms optimize their decision-making processes, reduce errors, and improve operational efficiency by effectively capturing, storing, and disseminating knowledge within the organization. Access to relevant and timely knowledge enables organization members to make more informed decisions, identify cost-saving opportunities, and enhance productivity, ultimately leading to improved financial performance (Edvardsson & Durst, 2013). Existing literature has also demonstrated the impact of KM to foster innovativeness in SMEs. By promoting knowledge sharing, collaboration, and learning, companies can tap into their employees' collective knowledge and expertise. This knowledge can fuel the generation of new ideas; facilitate the development of innovative products, services, and processes; and support continuous improvement. Small firms that manage their knowledge assets effectively are better positioned to drive innovation and remain competitive in dynamic markets (Alegre et al., 2013; Ul Zia, 2020; Ferraris et al., 2021). Moreover, KM contributes to sustainability by enabling companies to adapt to changing environmental, social, and economic conditions (Permatasari et al., 2023). By systematically capturing and leveraging knowledge about sustainability practices, companies can identify opportunities for reducing resource consumption, managing environmental risks, and embracing sustainable business models (Marino et al. 2008; Morrish & Jones, 2020). Knowledge management also facilitates the dissemination of sustainability-related best practices throughout the organization, promoting a culture of environmental and social responsibility (Broccardo et al., 2023). The links between KM and organizational agility and resilience has been stressed as well (Audretsch and Belitski (2021).

Through knowledge sharing, organizations can quickly access critical information, learn from past experiences, and adapt their strategies and operations accordingly. This agility enables companies to seize emerging opportunities, mitigate risks, and maintain a competitive position in rapidly changing business environments (Dias et al., 2021).

In conclusion, the literature highlights the positive influence of knowledge management on a company's soft performance dimensions, such as profitability, innovativeness, sustainability, and agility (Eggers & Kraus, 2011; Hong et al., 2012; Pal et al., 2013). Effective knowledge management practices contribute to improved decision-making, enhanced innovation capabilities, increased sustainability practices, and greater organizational agility (Vargo & Seville, 2011; Petzold et al., 2019). Organizations that prioritize and invest in knowledge management initiatives are more likely to achieve superior soft performance outcomes, positioning themselves for long-term success in today's dynamic and volatile business landscape (Le Nguyen & Kock, 2011; Lekmat & Chelliah, 2011). On the basis of the empirical evidence, the following hypothesis can be formulated:

H2 There is a positive effect of knowledge management on soft performance in SMEs.

6.2.2 Entrepreneurial Orientation

EO is associated with innovativeness, risk-taking, and proactiveness (Covin & Slevin, 1989). Innovativeness is about a firm's propensity to produce and support new ideas and creativity, resulting in the introduction of new products, services, or technological processes (Rauch et al., 2009; Lumpkin & Dess, 1996). Risk-taking concerns the possibility of a negative outcome or loss from a financial perspective (Boermans & Willebrands, 2017; Brighetti & Lucarelli, 2015). "Venturing into the unknown," "committing a relatively large portion of assets," and "borrowing heavily" form three kinds of strategic risks, according to Baird and Thomas (1985). Finally, proactiveness is about seeking and acting on opportunities (Zellweger & Sieger, 2012). The entrepreneur aims to act in anticipation of future demand by implying a forward-looking perspective (Dess & Lumpkin, 2005). Scholars have argued that entrepreneurial firms, driven by a high level of EO, are more willing to take risks, explore new opportunities, and challenge the status quo, leading to enhanced innovativeness (Wiklund & Shepherd, 2003; Soinien et al., 2012). Given that, one can expect that EO influences crisis management in SMEs (Soininen et al., 2012). Thus, the third hypothesis is as follows:

H3 There is a negative effect of entrepreneurial orientation on crisis management in SMEs.

Entrepreneurial orientation (EO) has emerged as a critical concept over the years (Covin & Wales, 2012; Lee & Peterson, 2000).

Numerous studies have highlighted the positive impact of EO on various dimensions of soft performance (Alegre & Chiva, 2013; Zighan et al., 2022). EO has been associated with greater organizational flexibility and adaptability, which are crucial in today's dynamic and turbulent business environment (Cioppi et al., 2014; Beliaeva et al., 2020). Organizations that emphasize EO are more likely to possess a higher degree of flexibility, enabling them to respond quickly to changing market conditions, seize emerging opportunities, and effectively manage uncertainties (Covin & Lumpkin, 2011; Zahra et al., 2006). Such adaptability allows entrepreneurial firms to shape their environment proactively, fostering competitive advantage and long-term success. Based on previous studies, we propose the following hypothesis:

H4 There is a positive effect of EO on soft performance in SMEs.

6.2.3 Link Between Crisis Management and Softer Measures of Performance in SMEs

The performance of a company forms the basis for its survival and organizational success. Hence, its measuring serves to evaluate actions taken by firms and managers (Asree et al., 2010). Thus, feedback, for example, regarding efficiency and effectiveness of their activities is provided, and as a result, more informed decisions can be made (Neely et al., 2002). There are different types of performance, those typically used in finance and accounting and so-called softer performance measures (Durst et al., 2019); the latter are focused on in this chapter.

Several studies have emphasized the positive impact of effective crisis management on soft performance outcomes (Puumalainen et al., 2023). Proactive crisis management strategies, such as timely and transparent communication, stakeholder engagement, and reputation management, have been associated with the preservation and enhancement of soft performance measures (Coombs, 2007). By effectively managing crises, organizations can demonstrate their ability to address challenges and protect their image, leading to increased stakeholder trust, customer loyalty, and overall brand equity.

Crisis management practices are crucial in maintaining organizational resilience. How crises are handled can significantly impact employee perceptions and attitudes, affecting their job satisfaction, commitment, and engagement (Pearson & Clair, 1998; Seeger et al., 2003). Effective crisis management that includes employee support, clear communication channels, and psychological well-being initiatives can contribute to the preservation of employee morale during turbulent times, ultimately promoting organizational resilience and the ability to recover from crises more effectively (Williams et al., 2017; Schaltegger, 2021; Osiyevskyy et al., 2020). Accordingly, we posit the following hypothesis:

H5 There is a positive effect of crisis management on soft performance in SMEs.

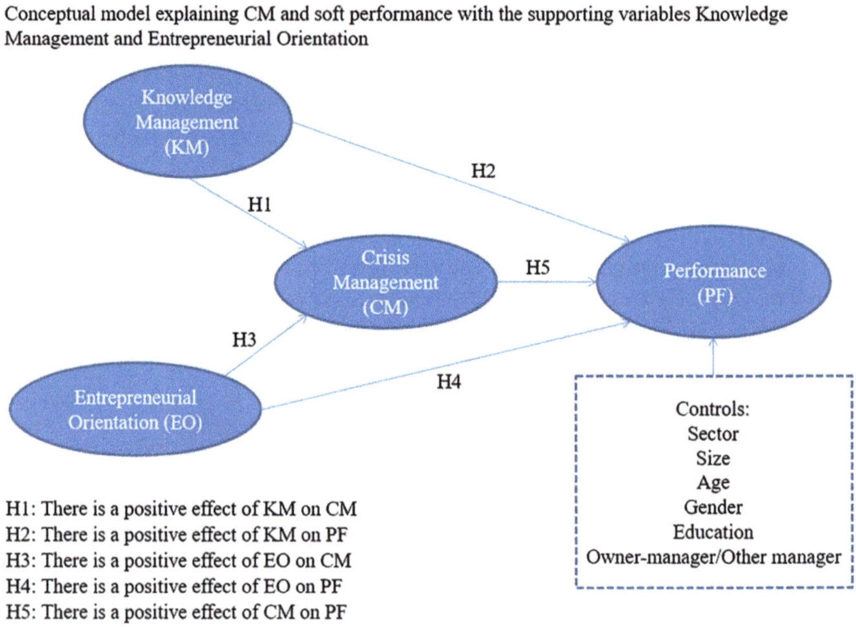

Fig. 6.1 Research model explaining CM and performance with supporting variables knowledge management and entrepreneurial orientation

The proposed research model is presented in Fig. 6.1.

6.3 Method

6.3.1 Data Collection and Sample

Data for the study were collected through a cross-sectional survey. More precisely, the research was carried out using an online questionnaire during the COVID-19 pandemic. The questionnaire contained 21 closed questions. The majority of questions were based on five-point Likert scale. The online questionnaire was initially tested on ten SMEs to obtain an impression of how the questions were perceived and to clarify any ambiguity. The pretest raised no concerns.

A random sample of 16,992 entries from the database Firmenwissen was drawn. This database contains the addresses and financial data from SMEs in Germany and is updated annually. All enterprises with the number of employees covered by the EU definition of SMEs were selected from the relevant database. Suitable companies were invited to participate anonymously in the study via an established online survey system. No extrinsic incentive was offered and one reminder was sent after 2 weeks. Six hundred eighty-one responses were received. After consistency checks,

397 responses were removed due to incompleteness. Thus, a total of 284 responses was left which meant a response rate of 1.67%.

Table 6.1 summarizes the relevant dependent and independent variables, their conceptualizations, and the literature used.

As control variables, typical demographic variables were used in SME research such as firm size, educational background, management type, gender, company age, and the industry sector (Semrau et al., 2016).

6.3.2 Measures

The measures for the relevant variables were derived from the literature. To check for model robustness and background effects, common variables of personal (e.g., gender, age, education) and firm (e.g., firm age, size) characteristics were included in the questionnaire.

6.3.3 Dependent Variable: Soft Performance

SME performance can be measured with archive-based data and self-reported survey data (Semrau et al., 2016). Where financial data are available, researchers usually measure performance with proxies such as ROE, ROI, etc. However, in the case of SMEs, it is difficult to obtain financial performance data from them (Dibrell et al., 2014). Thus, researchers have turned to self-reported approaches to measure SME performance. Prior studies have argued that there is a significant association between archive-based and self-reported performance measures (e.g., Engelen et al., 2015).

In the given study, we built upon Durst et al. (2019) for measuring firm performance, more precisely for measuring so-called soft measures of performance. Hence, the latent construct of soft performance was based on the following five dimensions: profitability, innovativeness, sustainability, responsiveness to changes in the business environment, and agility. These five dimensions were aggregated into a composite measure.

6.3.4 Independent Variables

For the latent construct knowledge management, the study adapted three items from Durst et al. (2019) to develop a measure of knowledge management efforts in SMEs in support of construct reliability and validity; the knowledge management scale has been validated in prior studies.

Entrepreneurial orientation was measured using Eggers et al. (2013) three-item scale, using a five-point Likert scale (1 = strongly disagree, 5 = strongly agree). The scale of entrepreneurial orientation has been validated in prior research and provided a good Cronbach's alpha.

Table 6.1 Dependent and independent variables

Variable	Questions/items	Literature
Performance	Compared with your key competitors, your company	Durst et al. (2019)
Dependent variable	Is more profitable	
	Is more innovative	
	Is more sustainable	
	Has a better responsiveness to changes in the business environment	
	Is more agile	
	Each variable is measured with the following scale:	
	Does not apply (score: 1)	
	Rather does not apply (score: 2)	
	Neutral (score: 3)	
	Rather applies (score: 4)	
	Completely true (score: 5)	
Entrepreneurial orientation	*Innovativeness*	Eggers et al. (2013)
Independent variable	To what extent do the following statements apply?	
	When it comes to problem-solving, we value creative new solutions more than solutions that rely on conventional wisdom	
	We highly value new product lines	
	We consider ourselves as an innovative company	
	Our business is often the first to market with new products and services	
	Competitors in this market recognize us as leaders in innovation	
	Proactiveness	
	To what extent do the following statements apply?	
	We continuously try to discover additional needs of our customers of which they are unaware	
	We consistently look for new business opportunities	
	Our marketing efforts try to lead customers, rather than respond to them	
	We incorporate solutions to unarticulated customer needs in our products and services	
	We work to find new businesses or markets to target	
	Risk-taking	
	To what extent do the following statements apply?	
	We value new strategies/plans even if we are not certain that they will always work	
	To make effective changes to our offering, we are willing to accept at least a moderate level of risk of significant losses	
	We encourage people in our company to take risks with new ideas	
	We engage in risky investments (e.g., new employees, facilities, debt, stock options) to stimulate future growth	
	All categories are measured with a five-point Likert scale with 1 = does not apply at all to 5 = completely true	

(continued)

Table 6.1 (continued)

Variable	Questions/items	Literature
Crisis management	When we are facing a crisis, we normally take/do the following:	Herbane (2019)
Independent variable	Retrenchment activities, i.e., cost-cutting measures	Herbane (2013)
	Trying to preserve the status quo of the firm's business activities	
	Focusing on the strategic renewal of the company's business model(s), its products/services	
	Discontinuation of the firm's business activities, e.g., of some business units	
	Measured with a five-point Likert scale with 1 = never massive to 5 = very often	Wenzel et al. (2020)
	Does your company do risk management?	Brustbauer (2016)
	Yes (score: 3)	Herdmann and Henschel (2018)
	No, but we are planning it (score: 2)	
	No, and we don't plan it (score: 1)	
	The business has certification for business continuity management or risk management	
	Yes (score: 3)	
	No, but we are planning it (score: 2)	
	No, and we don't plan it (score: 1)	
Knowledge management	Does your company do knowledge management?	Durst et al. (2019)
Independent variable	Yes (score: 3)	
	No, but we are planning it (score: 2)	
	No, and we don't plan it (score: 1)	
	If your company does risk management, does this consider knowledge risks as well?	
	Yes (score: 3)	
	To some extent (score: 2)	
	No (score: 1)	
	To what extent do you agree with the statement?	
	The company's knowledge management activities contribute to the overall firm performance practices	
	Measured with a five-point Likert scale with 1 = strongly disagree to 5 = strongly agree	

(continued)

Table 6.1 (continued)

Variable	Questions/items	Literature
Control variables	*Firm size*	Matthews and Scott (1995)
	Less than ten employees (score: 1)	
	10–50 employees (score: 2)	
	50–150 employees (score: 3)	
	150–250 employees (score: 4)	
	250–500 employees (score: 5).	
	Educational background	Barbero et al. (2011)
	Apprenticeship (score: 1)	
	Technician/foreman (score: 2)	
	University degree (score: 3)	
	Management type	Falkner and Hiebl (2015)
	Owner-managed firm (score: 1)	
	Other-managed firm (score: 2)	
	Gender	Brighetti and Lucarelli (2015)
	Male (score: 1)	
	Female (score: 2)	
	Diverse (score: 3)	
	Company age	
	10 years and less (score: 1)	
	11–20 years (score: 2)	
	21 and above years (score: 3)	
	Industry sector	
	Service (score: 1)	
	Industry (score: 2)	
	Trade and logistics (score: 3)	
	Information technology (score: 4)	
	Construction industry (score: 5)	

For the construct of crisis management, we developed a new measure which is based on prior work of Herbane (2013), Herbane (2019), and Wenzel et al. (2020) and consists initially of six items. Two of the items had to be deleted due to low factor loadings. The majority of items were measured on a five-point Likert scale (1 = strongly disagree, 5 = strongly agree).

In establishing our control variables, we considered the main dimensions that previous literature has identified as relevant to the study of crisis management in SMEs (c.f. Herbane, 2013, 2019).

The main scales in this study were adapted from the extant English literature (see Table 6.1). After the scales were translated into German, a professional translated it back into English, then bilinguals compared the original English version with the translated German version, and then the German version for the survey was formed.

6.4 Statistical Analyses

First, descriptive statistical analysis, reliability analysis, and correlation analysis of the valid sample were performed through SPSS 25. Second, using AMOS 26.0 statistical software, confirmed factor analysis and structural equation modeling were analyzed.

The sample of 284 responses is adequate for structural equation model (SEM) analysis as it exceeds the minimum required level of 200 (Loehlin, 1987).

To test for nonresponse bias (Armstrong and Overton, 1977), *t*-tests between the early and late respondents were applied. On average, all pairwise differences between the two groups for all items used to measure the constructs were insignificant. Therefore, a systematic nonresponse bias is highly unlikely.

Table 6.2 summarizes information about the demographic profile of the respondent companies.

Table 6.2 Demographic profile of respondents

	Frequency	Percent
Industry sector		
Service	124	43.7%
Industry	41	14.4%
Trade and logistics	43	15.1%
Information technology	26	9.2%
Construction industry	50	17.6%
Firm size		
Less than ten employees	47	16.5%
10–50 employees	177	62.3%
50–150 employees	52	18.3%
150–250 employees	8	2.8%
Management type		
Owner-managed firms	219	77.1%
Other-managed firms	65	22.9%
Educational background		
Apprenticeship	49	17.3%
Technician/foreman	38	13.4%
University degree	197	69.4%
Gender		
Female	49	17.3%
Male	235	82.7%
Diverse	0	0%
Company age		
10 years and less	65	22.9%
11–20 years	75	26.4%
21 and above years	144	50.7%
N	284	100%

Table 6.3 Summary of means, SD, and normality

Constructs	Mean	SD	Skewness	Kurtosis	VIF	Tolerance
Crisis management	9.469	1.624	0.062	−0.175	1.235	0.810
Entrepreneurial orientation	9.826	1.914	−0.214	−0.053	1.139	0.878
Knowledge management	7.345	2.092	−0.134	−0.911	1.288	0.777
Soft performance	14.708	2.87	−0.735	1.529	–	–

6.4.1 Robustness Checks

We also performed some robustness checks to confirm the results and significance of our models. Certain assumptions have to be tested before the structural equation assessment such as normality and multicollinearity (Hair et al., 2014). Table 6.3 shows mean values, standard deviation (SD), and normality of the variables.

Table 6.3 indicates that all constructs have values in the accepted range for skewness and kurtosis and represent that the data is normal (Hair et al., 2014). To check for multicollinearity, we performed a twofold approach. First, we checked in the correlation matrix that all correlations between items representing different latent variables are well below 0.6, indicating no multicollinearity problems (Hair et al., 2014). The full correlation table and the questionnaire are available from authors upon request. Second, we checked each construct's variance inflation factor (VIF). Hair et al. (2014) suggested that the value of VIF above 10 indicates multicollinearity problems. In the present study, there is no multicollinearity problem as all constructs show values below 3.

Common method bias (CMB) is a potential problem associated with survey studies (Podsakoff et al., 2012). This study also addressed the potential problem of CMB ex ante through the design of the survey instrument and ex post through the use of statistical controls. In line with Podsakoff et al. (2012), we believe that potential biases in responses are countervailed through counterbalancing the order of the measurement of the dependent and independent variables in the questionnaire. Ex post we computed Harman's single-factor test to assess CMB statistically. The solution returned more than one factor with the first factor explaining less than half (23.68%) of the overall variance, implying that single-source bias may not be a significant concern.

6.4.2 Reliability and Validity Checks

Following Gerbing and Anderson (1988), the reliability and the convergent and discriminant validity of constructs were checked via confirmatory factor analysis (CFA) before the framework model was assessed (all estimations were done using AMOS). Table 6.4 provides an overview of the results of these checks. Both exploratory factor analyses and CFA confirmed the dimensionality of the proposed constructs. Some items were removed due to lower factor loadings. Since all constructs

Table 6.4 Factor loadings and scale reliability

Constructs and items	Composite reliability	Loading
Crisis management	0.74	AVE = 0.51
Crisis management measures		0.80
Application of risk management system		0.67
Certification for business continuity management or risk management		0.67
Knowledge management	0.74	AVE = 0.50
Application of knowledge management system (KM)		0.70
Identification and consideration of knowledge risks		0.80
Contribution of KM activities to overall firm performance practices		0.60
Soft performance	0.79	AVE = 0.50
Innovative		0.60
Sustainable		0.60
Responsiveness to changes in the business environment		0.80
Agile		0.80
Entrepreneurial orientation	0.77	AVE = 0.53
Innovativeness		0.73
Risk-taking		0.75
Proactiveness		0.70

Note: $n = 284$, AVE = average variance extracted. Standardized loadings significant at $p < 0.001$

were inherently reflective in nature, the deletion did not endanger the content validity of the constructs' meanings. Consequently, CFA indicated that the given construct structure fit the empirical data reasonably well (chi-square, CFI, RMSEA) following Niemand and Mai (2018).

Further, applying the procedures introduced by Fornell and Larcker (1981), convergent validity (average variance explained >0.5) as well as discriminant validity (>0.7) were also confirmed. The study found acceptable model fits after drawing few covariances among the error terms of the redundant items.

6.5 Results and Discussion

SEM was used to test the proposed research model. Evaluating SEM results involves completing two stages. Stage 1 – assessment of the measurement model – examines the measurement model which specifies the relationships between the observable variables and the theoretical concepts (Pittino et al., 2018). If the results are satisfactory, the researcher moves on to stage 2, which involves evaluating the structural model (Sarstedt et al., 2014). All the constructs were measured with multiple items, thereby increasing construct validity. Internal consistency and reliability were assessed by composite reliability, factor loadings, and AVE for all latent variables, as displayed in Table 6.4. To begin with, the individual item reliability of the measurement model is assessed. Individual item reliability is considered adequate when the factor loading of an item on its respective construct is 0.5 or higher (Hair et al., 2014). Overall, the reliability of individual items is acceptable.

The construct reliability (composite reliability) measures internal consistency and should be 0.7 or higher to indicate adequate convergence or internal consistency (Hair et al., 2014). The results in Table 6.4 show that composite reliability coefficients ranged between 0.7 and 0.8 for all items. The tests for the indicators show satisfactory results. We examined the AVE measure to assess convergent validity, which measures the extent to which a construct converges on its indicators by explaining the item variance. Recommended values for AVE should be greater than 0.50 (Hair et al., 2014; Pittino et al., 2018; Sarstedt et al., 2014). After deleting two individual items (variables, namely, crisis impact and profitability), all latent constructs provide satisfactory AVE values.

To finalize the evaluation of the measurement model, we examined multiple fit indices (Hair et al., 2014). The chi-square test of the measurement model was significant (see Table 6.5); however, its sensitivity to sample size is well-known and criticized (Hair et al., 2014). As Hair et al. (2014) recommended, we used various goodness-of-fit measures. The fit characteristics of the measurement model indicated a fair fitting model (CFI = 0.91) according to Mueller and Hancock (2019). The RMSEA is below the recommended threshold of 0.08.

As the measurement model assessment has shown satisfying results, we can now turn to the second stage in evaluating the structural model. Since SEM does not test for causality and the direction of the effect, the assessed models must be based on theory. Several determinants can be considered to determine the goodness of fit of structural model # 1. In addition to the standard procedure of the normed chi-square test, several comparative goodness-of-fit indicators were analyzed. Firstly, as recommended by Gerbing and Anderson (1992) and Hult et al. (2006), the root mean square error of approximation (RMSEA) was analyzed. The resulting RMSEA of 0.065 indicates a fair model fit. In contrast, the normed fit index (NFI) and the Tucker-Lewis index (TLI) provided mediocre results. All results are presented in detail in Table 6.5. The structural model # 2 including the demographic control variables is depicted in Fig. 6.2.

Path-coefficient levels and the contribution of the exogenous constructs to the amount of variance explained in the endogenous constructs were measured to assess the research hypotheses. Values starting from 0.2 are accepted in the early stages of research, but values higher than 0.3 are preferable (Hair et al., 2017). As a rule of thumb, R^2 values of 0.75 can be considered substantial (Sarstedt et al., 2014).

Table 6.5 Goodness-of-fit statistics

Model	x^2	df	x^2/df	RMSEA	CFI	NFI	TLI
Measurement model	212.3***	97	2.18	0.065	0.91	0.87	0.87
Structural model #1	212.3***	97	2.18	0.065	0.91	0.87	0.87
Structural model #2 with controls	337.1***	175	1.92	0.057	0.92	0.82	0.87
Acceptable range	–	–	1–3	<0.08	>0.90	>0.90	>0.90

Note: significance levels *$p < 0.05$; **$p < 0.01$; ***$p < 0.001$ (two-tailed test)

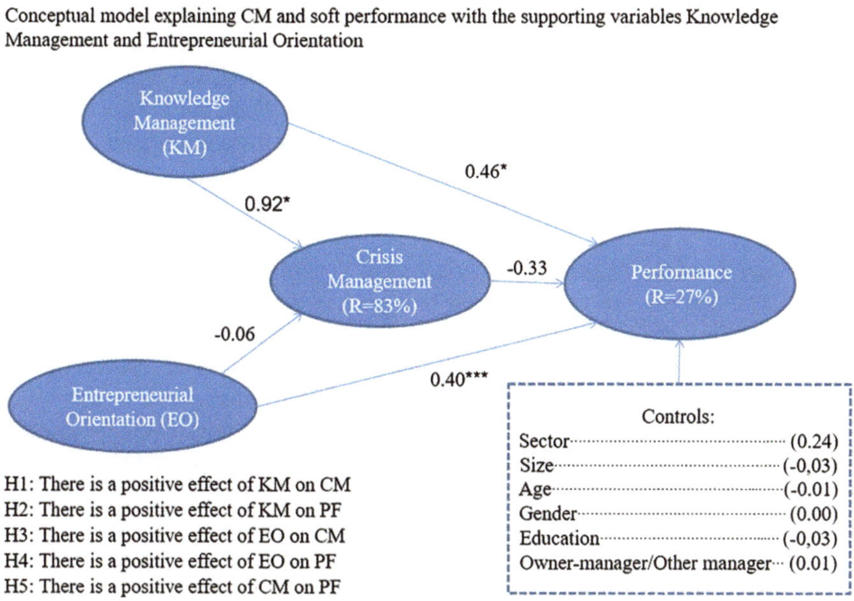

Fig. 6.2 Structural model including the demographic control variables

H1 predicted that a systematic approach to knowledge management has a positive effect on crisis management in SMEs. Looking at the coefficients (see Fig. 6.2), our findings find a significant and positive effect between knowledge management and crisis management ($\beta = 0.92, p < 0.05$). Hence, H1 can be supported. This finding is in line with several studies that have highlighted the potential of KM in enhancing CM (Yew Wong & Aspinwall, 2005).

Furthermore, utilizing knowledge assets and capabilities through KM can enable SMEs to anticipate and mitigate potential crises proactively. Holsapple and Joshi (2000) emphasize the significance of knowledge creation and acquisition in identifying early warning signals, detecting potential vulnerabilities, and implementing preventive measures to avert or minimize the impact of crises. In line with this, Costa and Carvalho (2011) argue that KM can facilitate organizational sensemaking processes, allowing organizations to interpret complex signals and act promptly in response to emerging crises.

With hypothesis H2, we were looking at a possible relationship between KM and performance. Effective KM was associated with positive organizational outcomes, including increased performance ($\beta = 0.46, p < 0.05$). Thus, our result is in line with previous research that suggested as well a positive influence of KM practices in SMEs on organizational performance (here softer measures of performance) (Osiyevskyy et al., 2020; Conz & Magnani, 2020).

H3 predicted that entrepreneurial orientation will enhance the crisis management of small firms; the finding is however negative but not significant ($\beta = -0.06$, $p > 0.1$). Thus, our hypothesis is not supported. As the literature suggested this relationship might be complex and contingent upon various contextual factors, such as industry dynamics, organizational culture needs further investigations (Hitt et al., 2011). In contrast to H3, the conditional correlation between EO and soft performance is positive and significant ($\beta = 0.40$, $p < 0.001$). Thus, our H4 is supported. Therefore, our research hypothesis confirms that SMEs that embrace and cultivate an EO mindset tend to exhibit higher levels of innovation, adaptability, and sustainability which is in line with previous research (Wiklund & Shepherd, 2003; Rauch et al., 2009).

Reviewing the R^2 of the crisis management construct for structural model #2 ($R^2 = 0.83$), one can see that the model's degree of predictive accuracy for crisis management is quite good (Hair et al., 2014). In the structural model #2, the endogenous constructs of knowledge management and entrepreneurial orientation can explain 83% of the variance in the crisis management variable.

When looking at our final hypothesis H5, a negative and nonsignificant association between CM and soft performance was found ($\beta = -0.33$, $p > 0.1$). One explanation might be that for the SMEs, it might be challenging to learn from crises and translate these experiences into improved soft performance in short time. Hence, examining the longitudinal effects of crisis management on soft performance beyond the pandemic period would provide valuable insights into the effect of learning in this regard.

When incorporating the control variables as shown in structural model #2, again 27% of the variance in the company's soft performance can be explained. A closer look at the individual control variables reveals that none of them show a positive and significant effect on SMEs' soft performance. One possible explanation could be that the survey was carried out during the height of the pandemic (in Autumn 2020) and possibly all firms were facing severe financial and performance constraints, which may have influenced the structural equation model.

6.6 Conclusion

The study presented in this chapter investigates the value of crisis management for SMEs – a still rather underdeveloped field of research. Based on extant literature, we take a more comprehensive perspective and investigate to what extent knowledge management supports both crisis management and entrepreneurial orientation and hence the soft performance of SMEs. The results indicate that KM has not only a significant impact on crisis management in SMEs but also on SME performance. Based on these KM-related findings, it can be concluded that KM in SMEs is vital for operating successfully and sustainably in uncertain times. Additionally, the study's findings stressed the impact entrepreneurial orientation has on the soft performance of the surveyed SMEs, yet we did not find the same regarding the link between EO and CM, which suggests that decision-makers need to be aware of these findings and try to find a good balance of how to use EO best so that both CM and performance can be supported.

Even though this study provides interesting novel theoretical and empirical insights into the crisis management and performance relationship in SMEs, the findings must be considered with certain limitations. First, this study focused on a sample of mostly small companies from Germany. To enhance the generalizability of our findings, future research can test our model with samples in different contexts such as emerging markets and larger firms. Furthermore, this research employed self-reported indicators of performance. Future research can extend our findings by including objective measures of performance.

This study used the cross-sectional research method to collect data. Although the study tested common method bias and the reliability and validity of the related constructs, the causal relationship between these variables is still not thoroughly verified. In future research, researchers should collect longitudinal data through lagging points to test the causal relationship between crisis management and firm performance.

Notwithstanding the limitations, the presented research is the first to conceptually test a newly developed scale of crisis management and its impact on firm performance by including knowledge management and entrepreneurial orientation, two relevant concepts of sustainable business development. As crisis management continues to grow in prominence in organizations, economies, and research, our study provides a solid groundwork for additional research on crisis management in SMEs.

References

Alegre, J., & Chiva, R. (2013). Linking entrepreneurial orientation and firm performance: The role of organizational learning capability and innovation performance. *Journal of Small Business Management, 51*(4), 491–507. https://doi.org/10.1111/jsbm.12005

Alegre, J., Sengupta, K., & Lapiedra, R. (2013). Knowledge management and innovation performance in a high-tech SMEs industry. *International Small Business Journal: Researching Entrepreneurship, 31*(4), 454–470. https://doi.org/10.1177/0266242611417472

Armstrong, J. S., & Overton, T. S. (1977). Estimating nonresponse bias in mail surveys. *Journal of Marketing Research, 14*(3), 396. https://doi.org/10.2307/3150783

Asree, S., Zain, M., & Rizal Razalli, M. (2010). Influence of leadership competency and organizational culture on responsiveness and performance of firms. *International Journal of Contemporary Hospitality Management, 22*(4), 500–516. https://doi.org/10.1108/09596111011042712

Audretsch, D. B., & Belitski, M. (2021). Knowledge complexity and firm performance: Evidence from the European SMEs. *Journal of Knowledge Management, 25*(4), 693–713. https://doi.org/10.1108/JKM-03-2020-0178

Baird, I. S., & Thomas, H. (1985). Toward a contingency model of strategic risk taking. *The Academy of Management Review, 10*(2), 230–243. https://doi.org/10.5465/amr.1985.4278108

Barbero, J. L., Casillas, J. C., & Feldman, H. D. (2011). Managerial capabilities and paths to growth as determinants of high-growth small and medium-sized enterprises. *International Small Business Journal: Researching Entrepreneurship, 29*(6), 671–694. https://doi.org/10.1177/0266242610378287

Beliaeva, T., Shirokova, G., Wales, W., & Gafforova, E. (2020). Benefiting from economic crisis? Strategic orientation effects, trade-offs, and configurations with resource availability on

SME performance. *International Entrepreneurship and Management Journal, 16*(1), 165–194. https://doi.org/10.1007/s11365-018-0499-2

Boermans, M. A., & Willebrands, D. (2017). Entrepreneurship, risk perception and firm performance. *International Journal of Entrepreneurship and Small Business, 31*(4), 557–569.

Brighetti, G., & Lucarelli, C. (2015). Gender differences in attitudes towards risk and ambiguity: When psycho-physiological measurements contradict sex-based stereotypes. *International Journal of Entrepreneurship and Small Business, 24*(1), 62–82. https://doi.org/10.1504/IJESB.2015.066153

Broccardo, L., Truant, E., & Dana, L.-P. (2023). The interlink between digitalization, sustainability, and performance: An Italian context. *Journal of Business Research, 158*, 113621. https://doi.org/10.1016/j.jbusres.2022.113621

Brustbauer, J. (2016). Enterprise risk management in SMEs: Towards a structural model. *International Small Business Journal: Researching Entrepreneurship, 34*(1), 70–85. https://doi.org/10.1177/0266242614542853

Cioppi, M., Musso, F., Pencarelli, T., & Savelli, E. (2014). *Economic crisis and SMEs' behavior: An analysis on the furniture sector in Italy.*

Conz, E., & Magnani, G. (2020). A dynamic perspective on the resilience of firms: A systematic literature review and a framework for future research. *European Management Journal, 38*(3), 400–412. https://doi.org/10.1016/j.emj.2019.12.004

Coombs, W. T. (2007). *Crisis management and communications.* Institute for Public Relations Gainesville. University of Florida.

Costa, M. T. G., & Carvalho, L. M. C. (2011). The sustainability of tourism supply chain: A case study research. *Tourismos, 6*(2), 393–404.

Covin, J. G., & Lumpkin, G. T. (2011). Entrepreneurial orientation theory and research: Reflections on a needed construct. *Entrepreneurship Theory and Practice, 35*(5), 855–872. https://doi.org/10.1111/j.1540-6520.2011.00482.x

Covin, J. G., & Slevin, D. P. (1989). Strategic management of small firms in hostile and benign environments. *Strategic Management Journal, 10*(1), 75–87. https://doi.org/10.1002/smj.4250100107

Covin, J. G., & Wales, W. J. (2012). The measurement of entrepreneurial orientation. *Entrepreneurship Theory and Practice, 36*(4), 677–702. https://doi.org/10.1111/j.1540-6520.2010.00432.x

Dess, G. G., & Lumpkin, G. T. (2005). The role of entrepreneurial orientation in stimulating effective corporate entrepreneurship. *Academy of Management Perspectives, 19*(1), 147–156. https://doi.org/10.5465/AME.2005.15841975

Dias, Á. L., Manuel, E. C., Dutschke, G., Pereira, R., & Pereira, L. (2021). Economic crisis effects on SME dynamic capabilities. *International Journal of Learning and Change, 13*(1), 111662, 63. https://doi.org/10.1504/IJLC.2021.111662

Dibrell, C., Craig, J. B., & Neubaum, D. O. (2014). Linking the formal strategic planning process, planning flexibility, and innovativeness to firm performance. *Journal of Business Research, 67*(9), 2000–2007. https://doi.org/10.1016/j.jbusres.2013.10.011

Durst, S., & Henschel, T. (2021). COVID-19 as an accelerator for developing strong(er) businesses? Insights from Estonian small firms. *Journal of the International Council for Small Business, 2*(1), 1–29. https://doi.org/10.1080/26437015.2020.1859935

Durst, S., & Zieba, M. (2019). Mapping knowledge risks: Towards a better understanding of knowledge management. *Knowledge Management Research & Practice, 17*(1), 1–13. https://doi.org/10.1080/14778238.2018.1538603

Durst, S., & Zieba, M. (2020). Knowledge risks inherent in business sustainability. *Journal of Cleaner Production, 251*, 119670. https://doi.org/10.1016/j.jclepro.2019.119670

Durst, S., Hinteregger, C., & Zieba, M. (2019). The linkage between knowledge risk management and organizational performance. *Journal of Business Research, 105*, 1–10. https://doi.org/10.1016/j.jbusres.2019.08.002

Durst, S., Edvardsson, I. R., & Foli, S. (2023). Knowledge management in SMEs: A follow-up literature review. *Journal of Knowledge Management, 27*(11), 25–58. https://doi.org/10.1108/JKM-04-2022-0325

Edvardsson, I. R., & Durst, S. (2013). The benefits of knowledge Management in Small and Medium-sized Enterprises. *Procedia – Social and Behavioral Sciences, 81*, 351–354. https://doi.org/10.1016/j.sbspro.2013.06.441

Eggers, F. (2020). Masters of disasters? Challenges and opportunities for SMEs in times of crisis. *Journal of Business Research, 116*, 199–208. https://doi.org/10.1016/j.jbusres.2020.05.025

Eggers, F., & Kraus, S. (2011). Growing young SMEs in hard economic times: The impact of entrepreneurial and customer orientations – A qualitative study from Silicon Valley. *Journal of Small Business & Entrepreneurship, 24*(1), 99–111. https://doi.org/10.1080/08276331.2011.10593528

Eggers, F., Kraus, S., Hughes, M., Laraway, S., & Snycerski, S. (2013). Implications of customer and entrepreneurial orientations for SME growth. *Management Decision, 51*(3), 524–546. https://doi.org/10.1108/00251741311309643

Engelen, A., Gupta, V., Strenger, L., & Brettel, M. (2015). Entrepreneurial orientation, firm performance, and the moderating role of transformational leadership behaviors. *Journal of Management, 41*(4), 1069–1097. https://doi.org/10.1177/0149206312455244

European Commission. (2022). *Entrepreneurship and small and medium-sized enterprises (SMEs)*. https://ec.europa.eu/growth/smes_en

Falkner, E. M., & Hiebl, M. R. (2015). Risk management in SMEs: A systematic review of available evidence. *The Journal of Risk Finance, 16*(2), 122–144. https://doi.org/10.1108/JRF-06-2014-0079

Ferraris, A., Giachino, C., Ciampi, F., & Couturier, J. (2021). R&D internationalization in medium-sized firms: The moderating role of knowledge management in enhancing innovation performances. *Journal of Business Research, 128*, 711–718. https://doi.org/10.1016/j.jbusres.2019.11.003

Fornell, C., & Larcker, D. F. (1981). Evaluating structural equation models with unobservable variables and measurement error. *Journal of Marketing Research, 18*(1), 39–50. https://doi.org/10.1177/002224378101800104

Gerbing, D. W., & Anderson, J. C. (1988). An updated paradigm for scale development incorporating Unidimensionality and its assessment. *Journal of Marketing Research, 25*(2), 186–192. https://doi.org/10.2307/3172650

Gerbing, D. W., & Anderson, J. C. (1992). Monte Carlo evaluations of goodness of fit indices for structural equation models. *Sociological Methods & Research, 21*(2), 132–160. https://doi.org/10.1177/0049124192021002002

Hair, J. F., Black, W. C., Babin, B. J., & Anderson, R. E. (2014). *Multivariate data analysis (7th)*. Pearson Custom Library. Pearson. https://ebookcentral.proquest.com/lib/kxp/detail.action?docID=5831794

Hair, J. F., Hult, G. T. M., Ringle, C. M., Sarstedt, M., Richter, N. F., & Hauff, S. (2017). Partial Least Squares Strukturgleichungsmodellierung: Eine anwendungsorientierte Einführung. *Franz Vahlen*. https://doi.org/10.15358/9783800653614

Hammerschmidt, J., Durst, S., Kraus, S., & Puumalainen, K. (2021). Professional football clubs and empirical evidence from the COVID-19 crisis: Time for sport entrepreneurship? *Technological Forecasting and Social Change, 165*, 120572. https://doi.org/10.1016/j.techfore.2021.120572

Herbane, B. (2013). Exploring crisis management in UK small- and medium-sized enterprises. *Journal of Contingencies and Crisis Management, 21*(2), 82–95. https://doi.org/10.1111/1468-5973.12006

Herbane, B. (2019). Rethinking organizational resilience and strategic renewal in SMEs. *Entrepreneurship & Regional Development, 31*(5–6), 476–495. https://doi.org/10.1080/08985626.2018.1541594

Herdmann, F., & Henschel, T. (2018). Praktikables Risikomanagement für KMU in Deutschland. *Risk, Fraud & Compliance, 3*, 111–119. https://doi.org/10.37307/j.1867-8394.2018.03.05

Hitt, M. A., Ireland, R. D., Sirmon, D. G., & Trahms, C. A. (2011). Strategic entrepreneurship: Creating value for individuals, organizations, and society. *Academy of Management Perspectives, 25*(2), 57–75. https://doi.org/10.5465/amp.25.2.57

Holsapple, C. W., & Joshi, K. D. (2000). An investigation of factors that influence the management of knowledge in organizations. *The Journal of Strategic Information Systems, 9*(2–3), 235–261. https://doi.org/10.1016/S0963-8687(00)00046-9

Hong, P., Huang, C., & Li, B. (2012). Crisis management for SMEs: Insights from a multiple-case study. *International Journal of Business Excellence, 5*(5), 48802, 535. https://doi.org/10.1504/IJBEX.2012.048802

Hult, G. T. M., Ketchen, D. J., Cui, A. S., Prud'homme, A. M., Seggie, S. H., Stanko, M. A., Xu, A. S., & Cavusgil, S. T. (2006). An assessment of the use of structural equation modeling in international business research. *Research Methodology in Strategy and Management, 3*(4), 385–415. https://doi.org/10.1016/S1479-8387(06)03012-8

Kottika, E., Özsomer, A., Rydén, P., Theodorakis, I. G., Kaminakis, K., Kottikas, K. G., & Stathakopoulos, V. (2020). We survived this! What managers could learn from SMEs who successfully navigated the Greek economic crisis. *Industrial Marketing Management, 88*, 352–365. https://doi.org/10.1016/j.indmarman.2020.05.021

Laskovaia, A., Marino, L., Shirokova, G., & Wales, W. (2019). Expect the unexpected: Examining the shaping role of entrepreneurial orientation on causal and effectual decision-making logic during economic crisis. *Entrepreneurship & Regional Development, 31*(5–6), 456–475. https://doi.org/10.1080/08985626.2018.1541593

Le Nguyen, H., & Kock, S. (2011). Managing SMEs' survival from financial crisis in a transition economy: A chaos theory approach. *Journal of General Management, 37*(1), 31–45. https://doi.org/10.1177/030630701103700103

Lee, S. M., & Peterson, S. J. (2000). Culture, entrepreneurial orientation, and global competitiveness. *Journal of World Business, 35*(4), 401–416. https://doi.org/10.1016/S1090-9516(00)00045-6

Lekmat, L., & Chelliah, J. (2011). Surviving the next economic crisis: Corporate entrepreneurship strategies of Thai automotive SMEs. *Journal of International Management Studies, 6*(3), 18–35.

Loehlin, J. C. (1987). *Latent variable models: An introduction to factor, path and structural analysis*. Erlbaum.

Lumpkin, G. T., & Dess, G. G. (1996). Clarifying the entrepreneurial orientation construct and linking it to performance. *The Academy of Management Review, 21*(1), 135–172. https://doi.org/10.2307/258632

Marino, L. D., Lohrke, F. T., Hill, J. S., Weaver, K. M., & Tambunan, T. (2008). Environmental shocks and SME Alliance formation intentions in an emerging economy: Evidence from the Asian financial crisis in Indonesia. *Entrepreneurship Theory and Practice, 32*(1), 157–183. https://doi.org/10.1111/j.1540-6520.2007.00220.x

Matthews, C. H., & Scott, S. G. (1995). Uncertainty and planning in small and entrepreneurial firms: An empirical assessment. *Journal of Small Business Management, 33*(4), 34–52. https://search.proquest.com/openview/7e03e4d144cc77d10a2f7b44ff705b3c/1?pq-origsite=gscholar&cbl=49244

Morrish, S. C., & Jones, R. (2020). Post-disaster business recovery: An entrepreneurial marketing perspective. *Journal of Business Research, 113*, 83–92. https://doi.org/10.1016/j.jbusres.2019.03.041

Mueller, R. O., & Hancock, G. R. (2019). Structural equation modeling. In G. R. Hancock, L. M. Stapleton, & R. O. Mueller (Eds.), *The reviewer's guide to quantitative methods in the social sciences* (pp. 445–456). Routledge. https://doi.org/10.4324/9781315755649-33

Neely, A. D., Adams, C., & Kennerley, M. (2002). *The performance prism: The scorecard for measuring and managing business success*. Prentice Hall Financial Times.

Niemand, T., & Mai, R. (2018). Flexible cutoff values for fit indices in the evaluation of structural equation models. *Journal of the Academy of Marketing Science, 46*(6), 1148–1172. https://doi.org/10.1007/s11747-018-0602-9

Osiyevskyy, O., Shirokova, G., & Ritala, P. (2020). Exploration and exploitation in crisis environment: Implications for level and variability of firm performance. *Journal of Business Research, 114*, 227–239. https://doi.org/10.1016/j.jbusres.2020.04.015

Pal, R., Westerlind, R., & Torstensson, H. (2013). Exploring the resilience development process by implementing the crisis strategic planning framework: A Swedish textile SME perspective. *International Journal of Decision Sciences, Risk and Management, 5*(1), 57529, 1–57529,34. https://doi.org/10.1504/IJDSRM.2013.057529

Pearson, C. M., & Clair, J. A. (1998). Reframing crisis management. *The Academy of Management Review, 23*(1), 59–76. https://doi.org/10.5465/amr.1998.192960

Permatasari, A., Dhewanto, W., & Dellyana, D. (2023). The role of traditional knowledge-based dynamic capabilities to improve the sustainable performance of weaving craft in Indonesia. *Journal of Enterprising Communities: People and Places in the Global Economy, 17*(3), 664–683. https://doi.org/10.1108/JEC-11-2021-0156

Petzold, S., Barbat, V., Pons, F., & Zins, M. (2019). Impact of responsive and proactive market orientation on SME performance: The moderating role of economic crisis perception. *Canadian Journal of Administrative Sciences/Revue Canadienne Des Sciences De L'administration, 36*(4), 459–472. https://doi.org/10.1002/cjas.1514

Pittino, D., Barroso Martínez, A., Chirico, F., & Sanguino Galván, R. (2018). Psychological ownership, knowledge sharing and entrepreneurial orientation in family firms: The moderating role of governance heterogeneity. *Journal of Business Research, 84*, 312–326. https://doi.org/10.1016/j.jbusres.2017.08.014

Podsakoff, P. M., MacKenzie, S. B., & Podsakoff, N. P. (2012). Sources of method bias in social science research and recommendations on how to control it. *Annual Review of Psychology, 63*, 539–569. https://doi.org/10.1146/annurev-psych-120710-100452

Puumalainen, K., Sjögrén, H., Soininen, J., Syrjä, P., & Kraus, S. (2023). Crisis response strategies and entrepreneurial orientation of SMEs: A configurational analysis on performance impacts. *International Entrepreneurship and Management Journal*. Advance Online Publication. https://doi.org/10.1007/s11365-023-00847-4

Rauch, A., Wiklund, J., Lumpkin, G. T., & Frese, M. (2009). Entrepreneurial orientation and business performance: An assessment of past research and suggestions for the future. *Entrepreneurship Theory and Practice, 33*(3), 761–787. https://doi.org/10.1111/j.1540-6520.2009.00308.x

Sarstedt, M., Ringle, C. M., Smith, D., Reams, R., & Hair, J. F. (2014). Partial least squares structural equation modeling (PLS-SEM): A useful tool for family business researchers. *Journal of Family Business Strategy, 5*(1), 105–115. https://doi.org/10.1016/j.jfbs.2014.01.002

Schaltegger, S. (2021). Sustainability learnings from the COVID-19 crisis. Opportunities for resilient industry and business development. *Sustainability Accounting, Management and Policy Journal, 12*(5), 889–897. https://doi.org/10.1108/SAMPJ-08-2020-0296

Seeger, M. W., Sellnow, T. L., & Ulmer, R. R. (2003). *Communication and organizational crisis*. Praeger.

Semrau, T., Ambos, T., & Kraus, S. (2016). Entrepreneurial orientation and SME performance across societal cultures: An international study. *Journal of Business Research, 69*(5), 1928–1932. https://doi.org/10.1016/j.jbusres.2015.10.082

Soininen, J., Puumalainen, K., Sjögrén, H., & Syrjä, P. (2012). The impact of global economic crisis on SMEs. *Management Research Review, 35*(10), 927–944. https://doi.org/10.1108/01409171211272660

Vargo, J., & Seville, E. (2011). Crisis strategic planning for SMEs: Finding the silver lining. *International Journal of Production Research, 49*(18), 5619–5635. https://doi.org/10.1080/00207543.2011.563902

Wenzel, M., Stanske, S., & Lieberman, M. B. (2020). Strategic responses to crisis. *Strategic Management Journal, 41*, V7–V18. https://doi.org/10.1002/smj.3161

Wiklund, J., & Shepherd, D. (2003). Knowledge-based resources, entrepreneurial orientation, and the performance of small and medium-sized businesses. *Strategic Management Journal, 24*(13), 1307–1314. https://doi.org/10.1002/smj.360

Williams, T. A., Gruber, D. A., Sutcliffe, K. M., Shepherd, D. A., & Zhao, E. Y. (2017). Organizational response to adversity: Fusing crisis management and resilience research streams. *Academy of Management Annals, 11*(2), 733–769. https://doi.org/10.5465/annals.2015.0134

Yew Wong, K., & Aspinwall, E. (2005). An empirical study of the important factors for knowledge-management adoption in the SME sector. *Journal of Knowledge Management, 9*(3), 64–82. https://doi.org/10.1108/13673270510602773

Zahra, S. A., Sapienza, H. J., & Davidsson, P. (2006). Entrepreneurship and dynamic capabilities: A review, model and research agenda. *Journal of Management Studies, 43*(4), 917–955. https://doi.org/10.1111/j.1467-6486.2006.00616.x

Zellweger, T., & Sieger, P. (2012). Entrepreneurial orientation in long-lived family firms. *Small Business Economics, 38*(1), 67–84. https://doi.org/10.1007/s11187-010-9267-6

Zia, N. U. (2020). Knowledge-oriented leadership, knowledge management behaviour and innovation performance in project-based SMEs. The moderating role of goal orientations. *Journal of Knowledge Management, 24*(8), 1819–1839. https://doi.org/10.1108/JKM-02-2020-0127

Zighan, S., Abualqumboz, M., Dwaikat, N., & Alkalha, Z. (2022). The role of entrepreneurial orientation in developing SMEs resilience capabilities throughout COVID-19. *The International Journal of Entrepreneurship and Innovation, 23*(4), 227–239. https://doi.org/10.1177/14657503211046849

7 Conceptual Development of a Resilience Maturity Model for SMEs

Nadine Otter and Mark Uschkurat

7.1 Introduction

In highly volatile and uncertain times, organizations are increasingly facing adversities and unexpected events that threaten their functioning and long-term existence. This holds in particular for small and medium-sized enterprises (SMEs) that are still dominating the business and corporate landscape (Crovini, 2022).

The current energy crisis alongside the Russian invasion of Ukraine and the COVID-19 pandemic are only examples of challenges that modern organizations are confronted with. The frequency of the occurrence of those adversities is increasing rapidly. This urgently calls for organizations to emphasize on their resilience in order to survive uncertain environments and to foster future performance and success.

Therefore, it is necessary to have a solid understanding of the origin of the concept of organizational resilience and how it is defined, by which variables it is determined, and how it can be assessed, maintained, and improved over time (Linnenluecke, 2017).

Although research has been conducted in this area for decades, there is still a lack of a unified practical framework regarding organizational resilience as well as respective assessment tools, which are directly applicable for SMEs (Radic et al., 2022; Herdmann, 2022). The following chapter addresses this identified gap, by developing a maturity model for organizational resilience in SMEs, based on our research findings about organizational resilience.

Supplementary Information The online version contains supplementary material available at https://doi.org/10.1007/978-3-031-50836-3_7.

N. Otter (✉) · M. Uschkurat
Helmut-Schmidt-University/University of the Federal Armed Forces, Hamburg, Germany
e-mail: nadineotter@hsu-hh.de

S. Durst, T. Henschel (eds.), *Small and Medium-Sized Enterprise (SME) Resilience*, Management for Professionals, https://doi.org/10.1007/978-3-031-50836-3_7

Maturity models are assessment tools, which offer an effective possibility to measure and improve the quality of an object of interest. Firstly, they can be used by organizations to assess their strengths and weaknesses, e.g., regarding their organizational resilience, which secondly facilitates to develop targeted roadmaps for improvement. Finally, maturity models provide the opportunity to evaluate the effectiveness of the applied improvement measures.

The organizational resilience maturity model, which will be presented in this chapter, proposes an approach that can be easily adapted by companies. Since SMEs are limited in their financial resources – resulting in a barrier for SMEs to get external support – and often do not have professionals employed (Vargas-Florez et al., 2020; Koppel & Tšernikova, 2022; Yigit Ozkan & Spruit, 2022), the maturity model offers a fast and easy-to-use assessment tool for benchmarking oneself against selected resilience criteria. That will provide an important step towards operationalizing the concept of organizational resilience and making it practical for managers and decision-makers. Thus, the resilience maturity model offers an opportunity for managers and decision-makers to assess and improve the resilience of their organizations. Hence, the resilience maturity model will be an important tool for preparing for unexpected crises. It will ultimately support organizations to resist economic setbacks (Radic et al., 2022).

Since the proposed research is closely related to two research areas – organizational resilience and maturity modeling – the key literature in each of these areas is briefly reviewed. Consequently, Sect. 7.2 outlines a review of the literature on organizational resilience, while Sect. 7.3 addresses the fundamentals of maturity models. Subsequently, the development of the resilience maturity model is presented in Sect. 7.4. This chapter concludes with an appreciation of limitations and recommendations for future research.

7.2 Resilience

The term "resilience" is widely used across research disciplines. However, a unified understanding of the concept has not been reached in research landscape yet (Tognazzo et al., 2016; Amann & Jaussaud, 2012). In order to be a useful concept for SMEs, for assessing and improving their organizational resilience, it is necessary to derive a solid understanding of the definition and concept (Linnenluecke, 2017). Therefore, the following Sect. 7.2.1 will provide an overview of the concept of organizational resilience including a brief historical foundation. Subsequently, Sect. 7.2.2 will illustrate the most important factors that determine organizational resilience.

7.2.1 Definition and Conceptualization of Organizational Resilience

The term "resilience" is etymologically derived from the Latin term *resilire* (meaning "to bounce back" or "to rebound") and has first gained popularity in research disciplines outside business and management research (e.g., engineering, ecology, and psychology). In the early 1980s, the idea of absorbing external threats or bouncing back from them was adopted by business literature for the first time (Staw et al., 1981; Meyer, 1982) and led to the concept of "organizational resilience" as a resistance to negative developments and events. According to Meyer (1982, p. 520), resilience "occurs when responses create negative feedback loops that absorb jolts' impacts and loosen couplings between organizations and their environment." In this understanding, an organization is resilient when it can absorb the impact of an external threat by undergoing some kind of change and learning. When change and learning lead the organization to adopt new configurations or practices in order to deal with the environmental jolt, then it is called retention rather than resilience.

Since then, the literature discussed the definition and conceptualization increasingly (Linnenluecke, 2017), whereat the use of the term organizational resilience is not consistent throughout the business and management literature. After the above-mentioned approach that defines organizational resilience as a capability to react to external threats, there was a profound research stream in the late 1980s and 1990s (Wildavsky, 1988; Weick, 1993; Weick et al., 1999) which led to a focus on the internal reliability of organizations. By focusing on the safety and reliability, Wildavsky (1988, p. 77), defines resilience as "the capacity to cope with unanticipated dangers after they have become manifest, learning to bounce back." With the focus on high reliability organizations (HROs), such as aircrafts, nuclear power plants, hospitals, or space shuttles, many researchers built on Wildavsky's definition by emphasizing resilience as the ability to bounce back (Weick & Sutcliffe, 2001; Weick et al., 1999) and as an outcome of organizational learning (Sitkin, 1992).

Until then, the concept of resilience is widely spread as an outcome-oriented view (resilience as outcome). That is, researchers focused on the question of whether an organization is resilient in the face of negative events after the disturbance has been dealt with. However, since the beginning of the 2000s, researchers were especially interested on what organizations can do in order to deal with adverse events (Sutcliffe & Vogus, 2003; Hamel & Valikangas, 2003; Gittell et al., 2006). This view of resilience as an interactive process became first widespread through Sutcliffe and Vogus (2003), who focused on resilience as the ability to adapt in the face of negative events and changing environments. They define resilience as "maintenance of positive adjustment under challenging conditions" and "capacity to rebound from adversity strengthened and more resourceful" (Sutcliffe & Vogus, 2003, p. 95, 97). Similar to this understanding, Lengnick-Hall et al. (2011, p. 244), define organizational resilience as "a firm's ability to effectively absorb, develop situation-specific responses to, and ultimately engage in transformative activities to capitalize on disruptive surprises that potentially threaten organization survival." Also, Hamel and Valikangas (2003, p. 53), define resilience as "ability to dynamically reinvest business models and strategies as circumstances change." However, as one of the first researchers, they included the anticipatory aspect of resilience in their understanding stating that resilience is "about continuously anticipating and adjusting to deep, secular trends that can permanently impair the earning power of a core business [...] [and] having the capacity to change before the case for change becomes desperately obvious" (Hamel & Valikangas, 2003, p. 53 f). The assumption here is that organizational resilience is characterized not only by adaptive but also by preventive

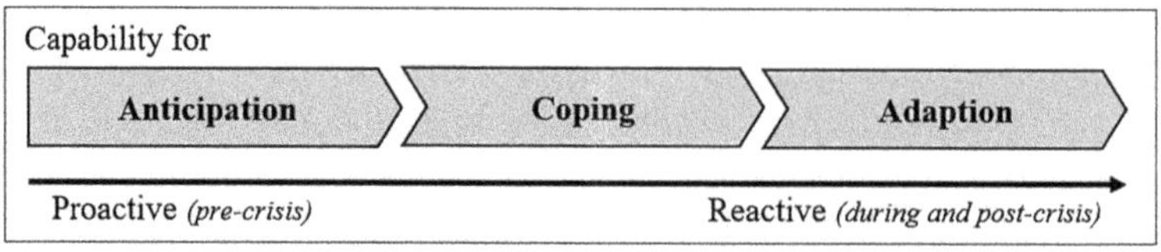

Fig. 7.1 Organizational resilience as an interactive three-step process. (Source: The authors)

(proactive) capacity to act. This enables an organization to adapt in advance and at the earliest possible point in time, even before an adaptation is forced by external circumstances.

Building on this definitions and concepts, we take a process-oriented view and define organizational resilience as the ability of an organization to anticipate, cope, and adapt to challenging conditions (e.g., crisis, disturbance, shock or other adverse events, and environmental developments) with the aim to withstand or bounce back and emerge from them strengthened and more resourceful. Figure 7.1 sums up our understanding of the term organizational resilience.

7.2.2 Determinants

After an understanding of the concept of organizational resilience has been developed, it is important to dive deeper into the question what resilient organizations have in common and which aspects distinguish a resilient organization from a less resilient one. Thus, this section focuses on what exactly determines a resilient organization. However, the literature has not yet been able to develop a systematic overview of all potential factors that enhance and develop organizational resilience (Radic et al., 2022). There is a wide variety of factors mentioned in the literature, whereby these factors can be distinguished between characteristics, capabilities, sources, redundancies, resources, or interpersonal relationships (Hillmann & Guenther, 2021; Duchek, 2020). All these factors can be subsumed under the umbrella term of "determinants."

While the "process-oriented" research stream (Hamel & Valikangas, 2003; Gittell et al., 2006; Somers, 2009) regularly identifies concrete determinants for individual process phases leading the organization to build resilience ex ante, the "outcome-oriented" research stem (e.g. Horne & Orr, 1998; Coutu, 2002; Meyer, 1982) emphasizes on those determinants that characterize resilient organization from an ex post perspective. By looking at a crisis in a retrospective, an analysis of profit or loss figures (e.g., revenue, earnings before interest and taxes, profit or loss) can be used to assess whether and how well a company bounced back from the crisis (Müller & Uschkurat, 2022). Thus, financial statement figures can gain important insights about organizational resilience and enable distinguishing between successful and less successful companies and furthermore inspecting the reasons for that. Therefore, both perspectives provide important insights to the extent to which a resilient organization can be distinguished from a less resilient one. However, it is crucial to examine the research contributions against the background of the specific context (e.g., development or event) and object (e.g., company, supply chain, strategic human resource management) under investigation to determine whether the framework and its situational assumptions allow conclusions to be drawn to reach a general conclusion on organizational resilience.

Following Müller and Uschkurat (2021), we divide the multitude of determinants into three categories, namely, (1) resilience resources, (2) resilience organization, and (3) resilience capabilities. As illustrated in Fig. 7.2, it should be noted that the determinants cannot be viewed in isolation as they are intercorrelated to each other. As an example, the resources (1) form the basic prerequisite of a resilient organization (2). However, the organization and its resources (e.g., employees) on its own do not lead to a resilient organization without adding certain organizational capabilities (3) (e.g., the anticipation ability arises when organizational resources interact with the environment to foresee potential environmental risks). In this context, resilience capabilities are defined as knowledge, skills, and processes (i.e., routines) that enable access to and use of resilience resources. In addition to these interdependencies, it is often not possible to distinguish clearly between the individual determinants (e.g., the provision of redundancies can be regarded as a resource and at the same time as a capability, or a positive corporate culture as a component of the resilience organization is often determined by human resources and their individual values and attitudes). Following the idea of "resilience as a process," the determinants of organizational resilience are characterized by a process-oriented development, so that resilience can also be understood as a continuous, feedback process.

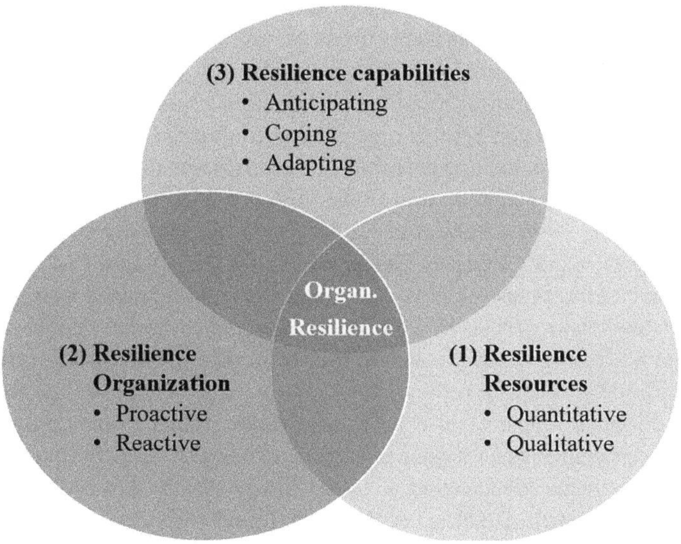

Fig. 7.2 Determinants of organizational resilience. (Based on Müller and Uschkurat (2021))

7.2.2.1 Resilience Resources

Within the resilience research landscape, the availability and accessibility of resources has received an important role (Hillmann & Guenther, 2021). In organizational theory, this aspect is also discussed under the term organizational slack, whereby Scharfenkamp (1987) distinguishes into two approaches of slack. While the first approach focuses on the well-being from an individual perspective, the second approach is of particular importance in the context of organizational resilience, as it assigns a buffer function to the surplus resources. That is, organizational slack can serve as a buffer, and the surplus of resources (e.g., time, money, personnel) helps organizations to absorb external and internal changes, to react to them. This eventually helps organizations to initiate its own strategies and build sustainable competitive advantages (Tognazzo et al., 2016; Schulman, 1993). Accordingly, resilience research sometimes argues that organizational resilience can be the result of a high level of organizational slack (Vogus & Sutcliffe, 2007).

In order to gain more insights in what kind of resources constitute a resilient organization, we focus on those resources that enable organizations to establish and expand their advantages toward their competition. By doing so, we structure the resources into two different categories and distinguish between quantitative (financial) resources and qualitative (nonfinancial) resources.

Quantitative Resources

Various studies examine the role of **financial resources** (also financial capital) as a determinant of organizational resilience (Gittell et al., 2006; Vogus & Sutcliffe, 2007; de Carvalho et al., 2016; Tognazzo et al., 2016). Financial resources are typically prescribed as the level of assets that express the organization's *financial potential* (liquidity) at a certain point in time (e.g., cash on hand, bank deposits) or *financial performance* (e.g., equity ratio, debt ratio). Although an organization's financial capital is essential, because it can be used flexibly (e.g., for investing in new equipment or new technology), their availability is limited. Thus, financial capital is often used as a measure of the organization's financial slack.

Financial resources can help an organization to absorb the negative effects of a crisis or at least reduce them. Accordingly, financial capital can give an answer on what the organization is able to bear in the presence of a crisis until it fails. In this context, the study from Gittell et al. (2006) – on the response of the US airline industry to the terrorist attack of September 11, 2001 – found that airlines with greater financial resources (i.e., low debt, high cash) strengthened their social relationships (relational reserves) by avoiding layoffs and cutbacks. This leads them to better cope with crisis situations and recover from them more quickly compared to airlines with lower financial resources. By taking the terrorist attack as the triggering event for their research, also other researchers found evidence for different industries that companies with extensive financial resources are able to recover from negative events better (Freeman et al., 2003; Burke, 2005). For SMEs, using data from Italian companies, Tognazzo et al. (2016) found empirical evidence for financial slack to be positively correlated to postcrises performance (i.e., growth and profitability). Based on a quantitative analysis, by using longitudinal data from before and after the financial crisis in 2008, the authors conclude that additional resources (i.e., organizational slack) help organizations to become more resilient. Shocks and other negative events can be absorbed, and the organization emerges stronger from them (bouncing forward) by increasing growth and profitability. Researchers also found evidence, by using data before and shortly after the COVID-19 crisis, that financial resources helped organizations to better withstand the shock. For example, by conducting quantitative analyses, different scholars found evidence that greater financial flexibility (i.e., low debt, high liquid assets) leads organizations to suffer lower share price losses (e.g., Fahlenbrach et al., 2021; Ramelli & Wagner, 2020). Despite the fact that these studies lack a link to resilience, these findings show important insights for financial resources as an important driver and determinant of organizational resilience as higher liquid assets and lower liabilities support companies to better withstand and survive a crisis.

Qualitative Resources

The research on qualitative resources takes an important role within the organizational resilience research landscape (Coutu, 2002; Lengnick-Hall et al., 2011). Business and management literature already emphasized human resources (human capital) as one of the most important organizational resources and as a key factor for long-term success through building competitive advantages (Barney, 1991). These insights were used by resilience researchers (Luthans et al., 2007; Luthans et al., 2010) whereby the research on **personnel resources** can be divided into two research stems: individual resilience and team resilience. The individual resilience aims at an individual level (e.g., employee) and is defined as the ability of organizational members to bounce back from distress and even succeed in the face of challenges, problems, and adversity (Shin et al., 2012; Luthans et al., 2007). The individual resilience of employees is of great importance as an organization can only be as resilient as its individuals (Hillmann & Guenther, 2021). However, resilient individuals on its own are not sufficient to make an organization resilient, i.e., organizational resilience cannot be understood as the sum of individual resilience (Lengnick-Hall et al., 2011; Ashmos & Huber, 1987). The term team resilience, however, is used at the team level to describe the ability of a team to bounce back from negative events and developments and succeed (Alliger et al., 2015; Chapman et al., 2020). The same holds for team resilience that neither resilient teams on its own lead to a resilient organization, or is team resilience determined by a sum of resilient individuals but rather as a result of a multifactorial combination of a group (Alliger et al., 2015; Weiss et al., 2015). As a result, an organization cannot be resilient without resilient individuals (e.g., employees, manager) and teams (e.g., working groups, departments). Accordingly, employees manifest a crucial success factor in dealing with negative events and developments, and from an organizational perspective, they represent an important determinant for organizational resilience.

There are different ways in resilience research to express the quality of human capital. On a **cognitive level**, the quality can be determined by various characteristics: *abilities*, *skills*, *experience*, *qualifications*, and *deep knowledge* (know-how) (Luthans et al., 2010; Lengnick-Hall et al., 2011). Those characteristics are typically shown by resilient individuals so that they can be applied in the face of adversities helping them and their organization to maintain and function (Williams et al., 2017). In addition, resilient individuals are typically associated with *strong values*, *optimism*, *hope*, and *a sense of purpose* (Lengnick-Hall et al., 2011). Thus, they are able to make sense of signals, find a purpose and vision, and make appropriate decisions, especially in challenging times of crisis or potential disruptions (Williams et al., 2017; Duchek, 2020). As a result, resilient individuals build and shape a positive corporate culture as a key enhancer for organizational resilience. On a **behavioral level**, personnel resources are "the engine that moves an organization forward" in the face of negative events and developments (Lengnick-Hall & Beck, 2005, p. 751). Research found that a positive behavioral responding to adversities combines behavioral repertoires, rules, rehearsed routines, and patterns on the one hand side with innovative and creative problem-solving and agility on the other hand side (Sutcliffe & Vogus, 2003; Lengnick-Hall & Beck, 2005; Lengnick-Hall et al., 2011). Thus, personnel resources understand (negative) environmental developments, and they ensure through knowledge implementation, improvisation, and experimentation that appropriate actions are taken based on this developments or other negative events (Duchek, 2020). On a **relational level**, personnel resources contribute to the organization's ability to deal with adversity through *social relationships* as they provide access to and exchange of information and other resources (Williams et al., 2017). In this research area, by using the terrorist attack of September 11, 2001, as an event study, Kendra and Wachtendorf (2003) found that social relationships are an important factor in dealing with adversity and crisis. Relationships that already exist prior to a crisis reduce communication challenges during the emergency. They also enable to continue with practiced organizational patterns (e.g., role assignments, well-established procedures, and responsibilities). Also, other authors emphasize the importance of relational reserves as competent and experienced employees can bundle their knowledge to shape a network that can quickly develop in a jointly problem-solving manner (Weick et al., 1999; Shepherd & Williams, 2014). Through *network relationships*, adversities and crisis can be faster and better be coped with. For example, by studying the response to COVID-19, Henschel and Salzmann (2021) found empirical evidence for SMEs that social networks and those networks within the supply chain were crucial to cope with the crisis.

Figure 7.3 sums up the key resources for an organization to be resilient. The qualitative resources can be considered as the fundamental of a sustainable business model, which is needed to avoid layoffs and to generate quantitative resources. The latter is also crucial for keeping the business running without layoffs and cutbacks. In sum, research has shown that organizations that demonstrate these resources are able to cope with crisis and recover from them better as those that do not have these slack resources.

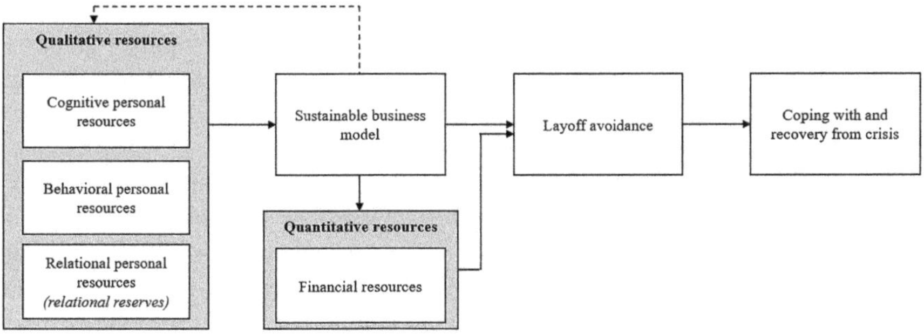

Fig. 7.3 Impact of quantitative and qualitative resources. (Based on Gittell et al. (2006))

7.2.2.2 Resilience Organization

In addition to qualitative and quantitative resources, resilience research often focuses on organizational resources in the form of an appropriate resilience organization (Wildavsky, 1988; Williams et al., 2017). Organization theory typically distinguishes organizational resources into operational (corporate procedures and processes) and organizational structure (e.g., corporate structure) (Bamberger & Wrona, 2013). Depending on the specific resilience phase, there are different organizational resources that are crucial for anticipating or coping with an event or development.

Proactive Resilience Organization (Anticipation Phase)

For an organization to anticipate disruptions (e.g., crisis symptoms), an effective proactive resilience management system is crucial. That means, a resilient organization must implement appropriate measures, processes, and systems (together "systems") for monitoring the internal and external environment to identify and prepare for potential hazards and critical developments within the environment (Williams et al., 2017; Somers, 2009; Duchek, 2020). Thus, a proactive resilience management system must include at least the following four elements (Durst & Henschel, 2021):

1. Systems for environmental observation and scanning
2. Systems for identifying unexpected events and critical developments
3. Systems for preparing for unexpected events and critical developments
4. Corporate culture (esp. risk culture)

The **first element** of an effective proactive resilience organization aims at the implemented **environmental observation and scanning** mechanisms that should be able to detect weak internal and external signals and perceive those identified signals as potentially threatening to the organization (Rerup, 2009; Burnard & Bhamra, 2011; Lewin et al., 2011; Hong et al., 2012). This is based on the theory of weak signals by Ansoff (1975) whose understanding of the term "weak signals" includes information about upcoming problems and challenges without knowing the probability of their occurrence and their potential impact. A systematic approach to identify those weak signals helps organizations to detect potential disruptions or inconsistencies at an early stage, which helps the organization to avoid escalation through an early and quick response (Ortiz-de-Mandojana & Bansal, 2016; Rerup, 2009). However, contributions from crisis research have shown that the growing business complexity makes it more and more complicated to identify and interpret weak signals correctly. That often leads to false response which, in turns, leads to worsening the negative consequences of adversities (i.e., impacts on going concern) (Doubek et al., 2016). Therefore, the growing complexity of a modern corporate environment must be considered by designing and implementing appropriate environmental observation and scanning mechanisms and the other procedures for gathering information (e.g., interview, market research, surveys, gatekeeper) (e.g., Lewin et al., 2011; Aguilar, 1967).

Based on environmental observation and scanning, the second element of an appropriate proactive system aims at the **identification of unexpected negative events and developments**. Although crisis typically do not announce their arrival, some organizations identify the unexpected faster than others and can react faster and better (Duchek, 2020). An effective identification system includes, for example, the use of scenario analyses (e.g., analysis of key performance indicators), simulation methods (e.g., Monte Carlo simulation), and stress tests. Through planning of (unrealistic) scenarios, organizations can simulate and plan a variety of scenarios and derive appropriate remediation measures. Planning also sharpens the organization's awareness for potential danger (Fink et al., 2005).

Additionally, the resilience literature emphasizes the particular importance of **preparing for unexpected events and critical developments** as a **third element** of an effective proactive resilience organization. Therefore, a resilient organization implements measures and precautions to prepare for potential shocks and surprises such as emergency plans, risk handbooks and guidelines (including defining roles and responsibilities), and predefined communication procedures (Lengnick-Hall & Beck, 2009; Duchek, 2020). In the context of HRO, important research contributions were made in answering the question how those organizations are able to prevent failure (Weick et al., 1999; Weick & Sutcliffe, 2001). This is because HROs are technologically complex organizations that act in areas where they cannot learn based on negative experience or experimentation as even small failures and errors can have fatal consequences (Duchek, 2020). Thus, research findings show that HROs are able to pick up on weak signals (e.g., perceiving near-accidents, failed backup routines, or wasted excess resources) in order to continuously improve their organizational structures, processes, and routines with the aim of becoming more effective and creating a culture of high reliability.

Lastly, at the cognitive level, the **organizational culture** takes a crucial role as the **fourth element** of an effective resilience system. Researchers found evidence that the culture of the organization, i.e., the organization's norms, values, behaviors, and underlying assumptions (e.g., about relationships to the environment, about physical and social reality), is an important factor to build resilience through strengthening the organization's anticipation of (latent) dangers and risks (Seville et al., 2008; Teixeira & Werther, 2013). Thereby, a positive organizational culture is significantly shaped by the organization's participants (e.g., employees, management). Management takes a key role in building a positive corporate culture through their behaviors (tone from the top), believes, values, and attitudes (e.g., optimism, mindfulness, trust, respect). This leads to an enhanced awareness for potential danger and risk (Hoitsch et al., 2005) and, thus, helps in building a positive resilience culture. In distinction to risk management, where the risk culture only aims at risk awareness (Ergün, 2014), a resilience culture refers to the willingness of organization's participants to identify, manage, and become sensitive for all kinds of adversities and not only for risks. This also means that a positive culture includes having an open error culture that helps organizations in better and faster detecting failures through encouraging to communicate errors and problems as soon as possible (Weick & Sutcliffe, 2001).

Figure 7.4 sums up our understanding of an effective resilience organization that can be separated into a proactive and reactive resilience organization. The proactive organization aims at those systems that observe and scan the environment, that identify (unexpected) events and developments, and that prepare for handling them. The latter intersects with the reactive organization as those systems were activated when adversities occur to cope with them. While the proactive organization aims essentially at the anticipation phase of the resilience process, the reactive organization is key in the coping phase. The organizational culture, however, gives the framework in which the systems are embedded in.

Reactive Resilience Organization (Coping Phase)

A reactive resilience organization must be able to react quickly to inevitable or unexpected events and developments in order to cope with them and successfully emerge from them. By developing an effective reactive resilience management system, resilience researchers often build on the research findings from other research areas (e.g., crisis management, risk management, business continuity management – BCM) (Duchek, 2020). For example, BCM literature (Kersten & Klett, 2017; Penadés et al., 2017) provides valuable insights into organization's BCM

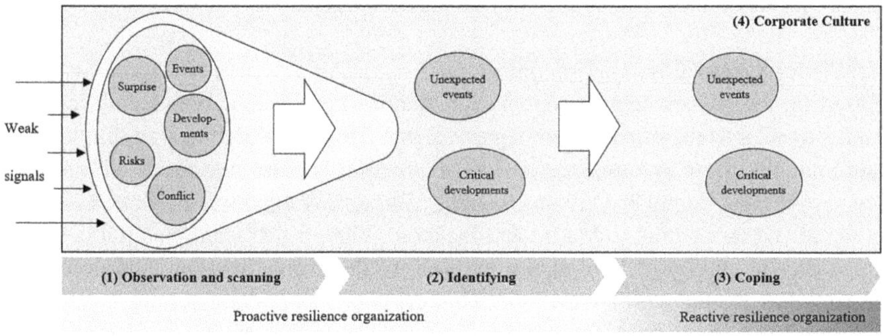

Fig. 7.4 Resilience management system (resilience organization). (Source: Developed by the authors)

systems since BCM plans (also contingency or emergency plans) can be a useful tool for organizations to become resilient. They enable to maintain continuation of important business processes in the face of interruptions and other crisis situations as they define measures, structures, and communication channels for (predefined) specific situations and can be activated when those situations occur. Also, findings from crisis management systems (Boers & Henschel, 2022) can be helpful for organizations in coping with crisis and other phenomena and becoming more resilient.

An important factor in coping with adversities is implementing adequate structures and processes for an effective and timely communication to stakeholders (e.g., communication protocols, international communication to employees via mail, external communication via social media) (Seville et al., 2008; Jacka, 2017). Especially in times of crises, it is crucial to communicate credibility, safety, honesty, and trust in order to reduce reputational risk and strengthen the relationships to stakeholders (e.g., customer, supplier). In this context, different researchers have shown that storytelling is an effective communication tool for promoting organizational resilience (Kampmann & Pedell, 2022; Heinze et al., 2023). By conducting an experimental study, Kampmann and Pedell (2022) found evidence that information presented in stories, rather than in statistical data, promote resilience. Moreover, stories increase awareness and preparedness for risks, leading to a risk communication that supports organizational resilience. Against this backdrop, Heinze et al. (2023) developed a storytelling toolbox that enables organizations to communicate effectively and explain difficult issues in order to enhance organizational resilience.

7.2.2.3 Resilience Capabilities

As mentioned above, slack resources and an effective resilience organization on a standalone basis are not enough to handle adversities. Therefore, resilience capabilities have gained an important focus within resilience research where researchers often consider a capability-based approach of organizational resilience (Williams et al., 2017; Burnard & Bhamra, 2011; Duchek, 2020; Hillmann & Guenther, 2021). Like the resilience organization, resilience capabilities can be structured by looking at the different phases of organizational resilience. Based on that, this section is divided into three subsections: resilience capabilities relevant for the anticipation phase, for the coping phase, and for the adaption phase.

Resilience Capabilities to Anticipate

Based on the processes and systems for identifying negative events and developments as well as the organization's participants (resources) that design, implement, and maintain those systems, the *ability to anticipate* comes into focus within resilience research (Hamel & Valikangas, 2003; Burnard & Bhamra, 2011; de Carvalho et al., 2016). According to Madni and Jackson (2009, p. 187), anticipation is understood as "the ability to 'look down the line' to determine how the environment is expected to change with a view to making decisions and taking actions in the present that promote desirable outcomes and circumvent disruptions in the future." Thus, anticipation focuses on the *ability to identify weak signals* based on the collected and analyzed information (data) and *perceiving those signals as a potential threat*. Whereby in practice, it is not possible to anticipate and prevent all crisis and other disruptions from happening, empirical studies have shown that certain organizations were able to perceive warning signals better as threatening and thereby show a higher level of resilience (Hamel & Valikangas, 2003). Thus, *situation awareness* is an important ability to anticipate unexpected events.

On a cognitive level, resilience researchers discuss increasingly the *ability to interpret* the gathered data correctly and *assign meaning* to them during the course of information gathering and processing (Daft & Weick, 1984; Bamberger & Wrona, 2013). This typically requires experience and knowledge to conclude the correct assumptions about the (expected) cause-effect relationships. In the literature, this is also discussed under the term *mindfulness* (Levinthal & Rerup, 2006; Weick & Sutcliffe, 2006), whereby paradigms such as attention, sensitization, and awareness of internal and external adversities become of special interest. With *sensemaking*, the literature identified a similar paradigm that drives the resilience of an organization (Weick, 1993; Weick et al., 2005). Sensemaking is generally understood as the ability to assign meaning to (negative) events on the basis of a reference frame that consists of individual beliefs (e.g., expectations, values, goals) (Weick et al., 2005; Appelt, 2016; Shepherd et al., 2016). Thereby, a meaning or sense is created through a connection between the reference frame and the (unexpected) event.

Resilience Capabilities to Cope

During the coping phase, it is crucial for an organization to have capabilities that enable an immediate – or at least short-term – reaction to the disturbance (Madni & Jackson, 2009). Thus, after identifying the disruption within the anticipation phase, during the coping phase, the focus shifts to the *acceptance* of the identified hazard as an actual problem. An early acceptance that a hazard (e.g., looming crisis) exists is an indispensable prerequisite for initiating coping measures and consequently for managing the crisis quicker and better (Weick, 1993; Coutu, 2002). In this context, the cognitive challenge of (non) acceptance and the associated phenomenon of denial of (potential) dangers are widely discussed in the literature (Hamel & Valikangas, 2003). According to Hamel and Valikangas (2003, p. 55), from an organizational perspective, future events and developments are "less unknowable than […] unthinkable, less inscrutable than unplatable."

Further, in coping with negative crisis events, it is crucial for an organization to see the positive in a negative situation, i.e., *finding a sense* even in times of crisis (Coutu, 2002; Vargo & Seville, 2011). Thereby the organization can take advantage of a crisis by identifying opportunities. This is also discussed under the term sensemaking, because sensemaking does not only mean the ability to make sense of (negative) events but also to act accordingly and initiating the correct response (Weick et al., 2005), i.e., being able to *develop and implement short-term solutions* (Heinze, 2013). The latter is also discussed under the term *bricolage*, which is defined as the ability to improvise and creatively solve problems (Kendra & Wachtendorf, 2003; Mallak, 1998).

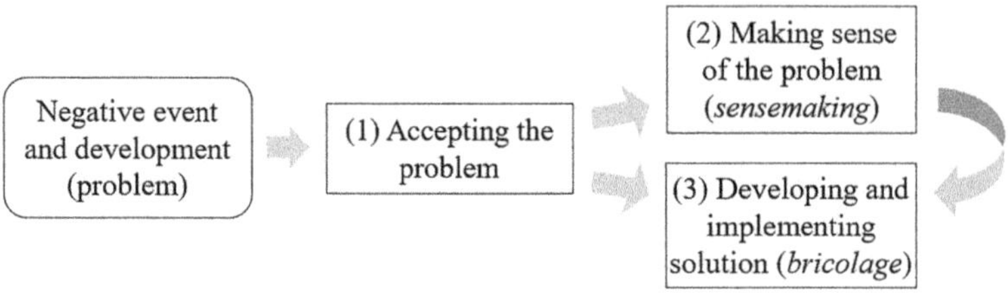

Fig. 7.5 Resilience capabilities to cope. (Source: The authors)

Figure 7.5 summarizes the key abilities during the coping phase, where the ability to accept a problem is a requirement for being able to make sense of the problem and to (simultaneously) come up with a solution to cope with the problem.

Resilience Capabilities to Adapt

To ensure long-term survival, the capability to adapt to an ever-changing environment is of central importance, which is widely understood as the key characteristic of the resilience concept. This also includes a long-term organizational development through learning and knowledge building (Limnios et al., 2014). The adaptive capacity extends to different levels (e.g., organization, individual) and fields of action (e.g., strategic, operational).

At the **organizational level**, the *ability to reflect* past or current events and developments appropriately is key to react appropriately to them (*ability to act*) and to learn from them (*ability to learn*) (Daudelin, 1997; Edmondson, 2002). According to Daudelin (1997), reflection can be prescribed as a process of thinking about the meaning of a problem with the aim to draw appropriate conclusions (e.g., identifying opportunities, producing new knowledge). Therefore, organizational learning, based on past or currents events, leads to adaption and gives guidance for future behavior. In this context, numerous studies found out that organizations are better in coping with challenges when they experienced negative events and build knowledge based on those experiences (lessons learned) (Durst et al., 2020; Rochlin et al., 1987; Roberts et al., 2005). Either this is based on learning from own (near) mistakes or from observing the competitors and their (near) mistakes (Madsen, 2009). However, research found that organizations often fail to implement the lessons learned in their future action (Vaughan, 2005). Therefore, research emphasized the importance of an in-depth and root cause analysis to figure out what went wrong as well as the ability and willpower to actually change something (Haunschild & Sullivan, 2002).

At the **strategic level**, the focus is on a regular review of the strategic business direction (i.e., strategy, goals, and business model) and their adaption when needed. This includes being open for new opportunities and alternatives, which is of special importance in a dynamic market environment with increasing market dependencies, technological progress and change, regulatory requirements, geopolitical shocks, and further disruptions. Thereby sustainable business models are of particular importance, since empirical studies found evidence that these organizations have a higher level of resilience as they are able to cope with potential hazards more quickly and effectively (Ortiz-de-Mandojana & Bansal, 2016). This is because sustainable organizations can identify threatening situations and mitigate their negative effects better than less sustainable organizations, since social and environmental practices (e.g., investing in reliable and high-quality goods and services) can lead to trust in customer relationships. As a result, based on the insights of stakeholder theory, sensitive information are more openly shared with the organization, leading them to being better in perceiving market changes (e.g., new technologies, price changes, changing customer tastes) and anticipating shocks (e.g., impending strikes) (Harrison et al., 2010).

At the **operational level**, adapting operational processes and structures is important for managing disruptions. By designing a resilient supply chain, an organization can significantly reduce vulnerability and disruptions in the value and supply chain (Sheffi, 2005). Accordingly, a resilient organization should be able to adapt (at short notice) their goods and services and their business processes to reflect the changing environment (also Ling-yee & Ogunmokun, 2008). Summarized under the term flexibility, it is understood as the degree of flexibility with regard to procurement, production, and sales. Besides flexibility, the ability to adapt daily business is largely determined by the organization's redundancy since the existence of resources enables operational adaptability.

7.3 Maturity Models

7.3.1 Origin and Application Areas

Originally growing out of **quality management** (Wendler, 2012; Kübel, 2013), maturity models have become widely known since the introduction of the **capability maturity model** (CMM) in 1991 in the field of software development (Schleinzer, 2014). Ever since, maturity models have been developed for countless disciplines. Their **increasing dissemination and application** are due not only to software vendors but also to project management organizations, management consultancies, industry associations, and research institutions, which develop and offer specific maturity models (Ahlemann et al., 2005). Overall, maturity models are applicable to more than 20 domains, which are strongly dominated by software development and software technology (Wendler, 2012; Kübel, 2013). The second largest domain – albeit by a large margin – is represented by the public sector and project management (Wendler, 2012). In the context of strategic management, maturity models were hardly used for a long time. Nevertheless, there is an increasing trend in the recent past (Wendler, 2012).

In the **resilience domain** are **only some proposals for maturity models** existing (Caralli et al., 2011). These cover a wide range of topics, such as resilience safety culture (Trinh & Feng, 2022), cybersecurity resilience maturity measurement (Mbanaso et al., 2019), business model resilience (Radic et al., 2022), and operational resilience (Allen, 2011; McFarlane et al., 2017) but also organizational resilience (McManus et al., 2007; Stephenson, 2010; Gracey, 2020).

The mentioned models and initiatives have not been directed toward organizational resilience in SMEs in particular. Only one model, the SME resilience model by Vargas-Florez et al. (2020), focuses on resilience in SMEs. The authors developed a maturity model based on the structure of the maturity cycle of a company and tested their model by semi-structured interviews with three Mexican SMEs (Vargas-Florez et al., 2020). Nevertheless, the study concludes stating that the model is still under construction and that it is mainly focused on Latin American countries.

The lack of an appropriate organizational resilience maturity model – which measures the resilience determinants as proposed by our definition – results in the need for the development of an organizational resilience maturity model for SMEs. That development will be presented in Sect. 7.4, after a few basics about maturity models have been discussed.

7.3.2 Purpose

Maturity models are used to measure the maturity of an object of investigation, e.g., in an organization (Ahlemann et al., 2005, 12f). For this purpose, the models define capability levels based on a ranking list, which ranges from an initial level through further graduated maturity levels to an optimized level (Pullen, 2007). In these maturity levels, maturity models express the fulfillment of universal, sequential requirements. In this way, maturity models offer organizations a simple but effective way to measure the quality of their processes (Wendler, 2012). Therefore, in practice, maturity models are **popular instruments for determining one's own performance** (Becker et al., 2009; Kübel, 2013). They enable an evaluation and comparison of a specific area, based on objective criteria, such as external requirements, internal targets, or benchmarking references (De Bruin et al., 2005; Kübel, 2013).

Beyond determining the status quo, maturity assessments particularly promote a **continuous improvement** process and support the internal learning process in organizations (Grönert et al., 2014). Thus, based on the maturity model, concrete goals and progress can be formulated – which the organization should implement within a defined period of time – in order to reach the next higher maturity level (Hillson, 1997; Hirsch et al., 2014). In this improvement process, each process area is evaluated individually according to the underlying maturity scale. This results in the greatest possible flexibility in the selection of improvement measures. After all, the available resources and the targeted development goals are decisive for the selection of the improvement practices to be implemented (Tubis & Werbińska-Wojciechowska, 2021).

In addition to the derivation of improvement measures, maturity models support the **monitoring** of their implementation and success (Hillson, 1997; Hirsch et al., 2014). Repeated surveys are used to determine the current status, which provides information about the effectiveness of the measures and forms the basis for determining subsequent improvement activities. In this way, maturity models promote a well-founded and goal-oriented approach to the development of organizations, so that they represent a helpful decision-making tool for optimization (Kübel, 2013).

7.3.3 Structure

Given the fact that maturity models consist of a structured set of elements that describe an evolutionary path of improvement – from immature to mature processes – maturity models typically include three key features: maturity levels, dimensions, and objects (or criteria) (Limat, 2022).

1. *Maturity Levels*

All maturity models have a fix number of maturity levels **for a specific domain** or the various dimensions of the object of investigation (Kübel, 2013; Schleinzer, 2014). Generally, maturity models include **between three and six maturity levels**. These express stages on a (typical, desired, anticipated, or logical) path of development, which range from an initial stage to complete maturity (Schleinzer, 2014). To express the semantics of each developmental stage, maturity levels are given an alphanumeric or a descriptive name according to their ranking (Kübel, 2013). In addition, each maturity level should have a clear description of its objective and characteristics (Fraser et al., 2002).

2. *Dimensions*

The dimensions are specific areas of capability, based on which the maturity model is structured (Limat, 2022). Maturity models that refer to only one dimension are called one-dimensional (Wendler, 2012). However, mostly maturity models describe various characteristics of the objects under consideration and thus are multidimensional (Wendler, 2012; Kübel, 2013). Dimensions may include specific capabilities, process areas, and other design objects to subdivide the area of interest. To determine the concrete dimensions, in intensively discussed application areas, existing taxonomies can be used. In unexplored areas and at a high level of detail, explorative procedures are recommended (e.g., expert interviews, case study analyses, brainstorming, Delphi method) (De Bruin et al., 2005; Kübel, 2013). Often, processes are chosen (also called management categories, activities, attributes, characteristics, or factors) (Becker et al., 2009). Thereby, the dimensions are to be described in such a way that one can obtain consistent and verifiable statements about their state (Kübel, 2013). They are specified either by means of qualitative descriptions or by means of evaluation elements or measurement criteria (practices and activities) (De Bruin et al., 2005; Schleinzer, 2014). It is of relevance that they are well distinguishable from each other. The dimensions of the model must not overlap and should at the same time provide a complete picture of the objects under investigation (Kübel, 2013).

3. *Objects (Criteria)*

The maturity levels for the individual dimensions are assessed using objects or individual criteria, also known as indicators or items (Kübel, 2013; Limat, 2022). They describe the possible manifestations of the dimensions, by subsuming the various abilities and characteristics of the individual dimensions (Kübel, 2013; Limat, 2022). Depending on the area of interest, the respective descriptions can be phenomenal (i.e., describing, measuring), causal (i.e., analyzing cause-effect relationships), or actional (i.e., formulating prescriptions for action) (Ahlemann et al., 2005; Kübel, 2013).

Normally, the maturity level is determined based on predefined evaluation methods. Thus, observations are collected at a certain point in time and subsequently evaluated (Becker et al., 2009; Schleinzer, 2014). Generally, the criteria are evaluated through self-assessment by the companies. However, an independent assessment by an external auditor is also possible. For the assessment, the various maturity models consist of collections of questions and criteria (Vanini & Rieg, 2021). The assessment can be carried out with qualitative or quantitative instruments. In practice, questionnaires with Likert scales or scoring models are mainly used (Fraser et al., 2002; Schleinzer, 2014). While the simplest criteria use a two-part "yes/no" scale, with the disadvantage that a single indicator does not allow gradation into multiple maturity levels, the most meaningful and accurate scales have a narrative anchor for each individual maturity level (Kübel, 2013).

7.4 Development of a Resilience Maturity Model for SME

For the development of a maturity model, it is necessary to define the development framework. In order to design the desired resilience maturity model for SMEs in a comprehensible and theoretically sound way (Becker et al., 2009; De Bruin et al., 2005), this work uses the process model for the development of maturity models by Becker et al. (2009). The authors offer guidance for a methodologically sound development and evaluation of maturity models. Complementary to their process model, the recommendations for the development of maturity models by the authors De Bruin et al. (2005) are taken into account. Thus, this work overcomes a weakness of many existing (resilience) maturity models, whose development process is – if at all – often only incompletely documented (Becker et al., 2009; De Bruin et al., 2005; Knackstedt et al., 2009; Wendler, 2012). Figure 7.6 summarizes the phases included in the generic **development framework**.

Fig. 7.6 Model development phases. (Source: The authors)

7.4.1 Definition of the Scope

The **first step,** in the development process of a maturity model, is to define the scope, which includes both, on the one hand, the **focus of the maturity model** and the other hand the **relevance of the problem** (De Bruin et al., 2005; Limat, 2022).

Regarding the first aspect, the **focus** of the maturity model, it is important to define the following:

- The domain (e.g., a managerial area of responsibility or a sub-discipline)
- The target group (e.g., internal or external audience, academia, or practitioners) (Becker et al., 2009; De Bruin et al., 2005; Knackstedt et al., 2009)

The focus of the maturity model, which is going to be developed in this paper, is given by supporting SMEs with a tool for tackling the complex task of improving their organizational resilience. Consequently, the target group addresses in particular an internal audience in SMEs, especially managers and decision-makers. The aim is to provide them with an easy-to-use self-assessment tool:

1. Firstly, to **determine their organizations' resilience** using objective criteria for assessing the here and now, respectively, the as-is situation
2. Secondly, to **derive improvement measures** by enabling the derivation of a roadmap for improving the domain position
3. And thirdly, to **monitor the effectiveness of the improvement measures** undertaken

The assessment, as well as the improvement, should be easily realized by SMEs, requiring minimal extra resources (Yigit Ozkan & Spruit, 2022). Since SMEs lack resources such as time, money, and expertise (Vargas-Florez et al., 2020; Koppel & Tšernikova, 2022; Yigit Ozkan & Spruit, 2022), the self-assessment helps to keep costs down. Furthermore, it raises the understanding and awareness of organizational resilience (Yigit Ozkan & Spruit, 2022).

Regarding the second aspect, concerning the **relevance** of the problem, it is important to highlight the specific need for the maturity model. This can result, for example, either from the relevance of the addressed area itself or from specific assignments (Becker et al., 2009; Knackstedt et al., 2009). Often, the relevance of the problem is founded particularly on assessing and comparing companies in terms of their capabilities in specific domains (Becker et al., 2009; De Bruin et al., 2005).

In the context of this work, the relevance of the problem results from the practical relevance of organizational resilience itself. The fact that organizations and their functioning and long-term existence are increasingly threatened by adversities and unexpected events urgently calls for SMEs to emphasize on their resilience, in order to survive and to foster future performance and success. As stated before, the literature does not provide a tool – such as a resilience maturity model – which supports SMEs in the complex task of improving their organizational resilience. Thus, the relevance of the problem is underlined by the lack of a complete and theoretically derived resilience maturity model, as a tool for a quick and easy resilience self-assessment and improvement. Therefore, the goal is to develop a resilience maturity model specifically for organizational resilience in SMEs. The model aims to assist organizations in understanding their organizational resilience better and further to enable the improvement of their domain capabilities.

7.4.2 Comparison of Existing Maturity Models

In the second step of the applied process model, a comprehensive literature review of existing resilience maturity models is used, to establish a basis for the following development strategy of the model.

The development of a new maturity model is only recommended if existing models do not fully support the scope of application (Mettler, 2010). Considering the variety of existing maturity models as well as the high number of new developments, it should first be carefully checked whether adequate solutions are already available (Becker et al., 2009; Wendler, 2012). Generally, the use of a standardized or normed maturity model is recommended, because that usually ensures the further development of the competence model (Ahlemann et al., 2005). Therefore, an **extensive review of** existing literature referring to **maturity models for (organizational) resilience** was conducted. The results are summarized in Table 7.1. As mentioned in Sect. 7.3.1, in the resilience domain are only some proposals for maturity models existing. Therefore, beyond organizational resilience maturity models, similar frameworks have also been included.

Despite the number of alternative resilience maturity models and similar frameworks, it was not possible to identify a maturity model that captures the requirements, such as the following:

- Being developed in a comprehensible and theoretically sound way
- Addressing explicitly SMEs
- Measuring the resilience determinants as proposed by our definition
- Being freely available for an easy and quick self-assessment

Table 7.1 Review of existing maturity models concerning (organizational) resilience

Year	Author	Title of the model
2022	Radic et al.	Business Model Resilience Framework
2022	GRC 2020	Risk and Resilience Management Maturity Model
2020	**Gracey**	**Organizational Resilience Maturity Framework (ORM3)**
2020	Vargas-Florez et al.	**SME** Resilience Model
2017	McFarlane et al.	Maturity Framework for Operational Resilience
2013	**Lee et al.**	**Tool to Measure and Compare Organizations' Resilience**
2012	ASIS International	Organizational Resilience Maturity Model
2010	**Stephenson**	**Model of Organizational Resilience**
2007	McManus et al.	Framework for Assessing and Improving the Resilience of Organizations

Nevertheless, the review provides a deep understanding of relevant domain issues, which supports the development of a more comprehensive model, specific to the domain of organizational resilience in SMEs.

7.4.3 Development Strategy

The basic development strategies distinguish between the following:

- Completely new development
- Advancement of existing maturity models (e.g., CMM)
- The combination of several models to form a new maturity model (e.g., CMMI)
- The transfer of structures (e.g., Project RMM) or contents (e.g. ACMM) of existing maturity models to new application areas (Becker et al., 2009; Knackstedt et al., 2009)

Following the findings of the literature review on existing resilience maturity models, in accordance with the problem definition, the new development was decided as a development strategy.

The identified maturity models served as a starting point for the design process, since they already cover aspects of organizational resilience measurement (Becker et al., 2009). Furthermore, by using this approach, the maturity model will be built on accepted and proven standards (Limat, 2022), such as the typical structure of maturity models. Moreover, it was expected that parts of the domain contents could be applied, or at least expediently transferred, to our problem area. This concerns, e.g., the classification of maturity levels as well as the descriptions of individual maturity degrees (Becker et al., 2009).

Meanwhile, the basic model architecture is driven by the resilience determinants for SMEs that were elaborated in Sect. 7.2 of this paper. While the resilience determinants provide the key areas, also named dimensions, their detailed characteristics will shape the measurement criteria in the maturity model.

7.4.4 Design of the Maturity Model

Once the scope and the starting point for the design of the model have been defined, the content of the model must be decided. This **fourth step** forms the central phase of the model development process and consists of an iterative maturity model development, in which the **individual design dimensions** and the **associated design criteria** are continuously shaped.

It "is necessary to identify what needs to be measured in the maturity assessment and how this can be measured. Identification of domain components is critical for complex domains as this enables a deeper understanding of maturity, without which the identification of specific improvement strategies is difficult. The goal is to attain domain components and sub-components that are mutually exclusive and collectively exhaustive" (De Bruin et al., 2005, p. 7). Appropriate procedures for this step include the following:

- Literature review
- Expert interview
- Delphi method
- Analysis of existing theories and models
- Iterative modeling
- Semi-structured interviews

Often, the basis for the core elements of the maturity model is formed by extensive literature research supplemented by consultation with domain experts (Becker et al., 2009; De Bruin et al., 2005; Kübel, 2013). In order to derive the evaluation criteria, literature analyses and explorative research methods – such as the Delphi method and creativity techniques – are widely used (Becker et al., 2009; Knackstedt et al., 2009).

For the development of the resilience maturity model in this paper, a systematic **literature review** – of scientific papers, studies by management consultancies, as well as professional journals – was carried out to identify capabilities and characteristics that have an impact on organizational resilience. Eleven **semi-structured interviews** with experts from small and medium-sized enterprises (duration of 44 to 70 minutes each) extended and validated the criteria for the model development. Using those resilience determinants for SMEs – derived from the literature review and interviews – as a starting point for the model development ensures that the principles recognized in literature and practice serve to analyze organizational resilience.

The development of the maturity model took place in three iterations:

1. In the **first iteration**, an initial architecture of the maturity model was designed. To enable a differentiated analysis of resilience in SMEs, the maturity model comprises the three resilience determinants (which were elaborated in Sect. 7.2 of this paper): resilience resources, resilience organization, and resilience capabilities. They provide the **model dimensions**. Each dimension will be characterized in more detail by various criteria.

   Consequently, the resilience maturity model is like most maturity models, constructed as a multidimensional model that describes various characteristics of the object under consideration (Wendler, 2012; Kübel, 2013). Thus, the model overcomes a weakness of the widely accepted one-dimensional models. The latter represent maturity as a series of one-dimensional linear stages. Using that form of assessment, the result is "an 'average' maturity stage being provided for the entity" (De Bruin et al., 2005, p. 6). This form of assessment "does not adequately represent maturity within complex domains, providing little guidance to an organization wishing to improve the 'as-is' position" (De Bruin et al., 2005, p. 6).
2. Following the basic structural decision of the first iteration, the individual characteristics for the dimensions are to be developed for the content of the architec-

ture. Therefore, in the **second iteration**, the **criteria** assigned to the dimensions were worked out in detail. A total of 26 criteria were identified in which the various capabilities and characteristics can be subsumed. Table 7.2 presents the dimensions and their criteria.

> To meet audience needs, the model design therefore needs to strike an appropriate balance between an often complex reality and model simplicity. A model that is oversimplified may not adequately reflect the complexities of the domain and may not provide sufficient meaningful information for the audience. Whilst a model that appears too complicated may limit interest or create confusion. In addition, a model that is too complicated raises the potential for incorrect application resulting in misleading outcomes (De Bruin et al., 2005, p. 6).

3. Once the content of the model is decided, it is necessary to identify how it can be measured. In the **third iteration**, the architecture of the maturity model is finalized by defining the **maturity levels** – for the domain organizational resilience itself, as well as for the dimensions (domain components) and their criteria (domain subcomponents).

   Typically, maturity models contain three to six maturity levels, which describe stages on a development path from initial stage to full maturity (Mettler, 2010). While the number of maturity levels may vary from model to model, it is important that the selected "stages are distinct and well-defined, and that there is a logical progression through stages. Stages should also be **named with short labels** that give a clear indication of the intent of the stage. **Stage definitions** should be developed to expand stage names and provide a summary of" the stage (De Bruin et al., 2005, p. 6).

   For the resilience maturity model, five maturity levels were defined, ranging from Level 0: Nonexistent to Level 4: Continuously improved. Thus, the model outlines a development path which starts at a complete lack of awareness for resilience management and ends at the highest level with holistically implemented resilience measures that are widely accepted, monitored, and updated. Figure 7.7 illustrates the maturity levels with their labels and definitions.

The **definitions of maturity levels** are formulated universally, without addressing specific attributes or dimensions, and the maturity level achievement is quantified as the average of the degree of fulfillment of the assessed criteria. Following the maturity model of Trinh and Feng (2022) as well as Hirsch et al. (2014), the model is based on the idea that the achieved maturity level for organizational resilience is determined by the number and extent of criteria that are already implemented (Hirsch et al., 2014).

In addition to an overall assessment for the entity, the chosen approach, with domain components and domain subcomponents, enables the provision of more differentiated maturity assessments within the complex domain of organizational resilience. By providing additional layers of detail, the model enables separate maturity assessments for a number of discrete areas. The layers can be represented by the

Table 7.2 Dimensions and their criteria

Dimensions Domain components = Resilience determinants	Criteria Domain subcomponents

Resilience resources	Quantitative (financial resources)
	  Financial potential
	  Financial performance
	Qualitative (personnel resources)
	  Cognitive level
	  Behavioral level
	  Relational level

Resilience organization	Proactive resilience management system
	  Systems and processes for environmental observation and scanning
	  Systems and processes for identifying unexpected events and critical developments
	  Systems and processes for preparing for unexpected events and critical developments
	  Corporate culture (e.g., risk culture)
	Reactive resilience management system
	  Principles, procedures, and measures (rules) to cope with unexpected events and critical developments
	  Crisis communication

Resilience capabilities	Resilience capabilities to anticipate
	  Ability to anticipate
	  Ability to identify weak signals
	  Ability of situation awareness
	  Ability to interpret the data correctly
	  Ability to assign meaning to (negative) events
	Resilience capabilities to cope
	  Ability to accept a problem
	  Ability to make sense of a problem and act/initiate the correct response
	  Ability to develop and implement short-term solutions through innovation and improvision
	Resilience capabilities to adapt
	  Organizational adaptive capacity
	    Ability to reflect appropriately
	    Ability to act appropriately
	    Ability to learn
	  Strategic adaptive capacity
	    Ability to adapt business model
	    Ability to exercise environmental and social changes
	  Operational adaptive capacity
	    Flexibility
	    Redundancy

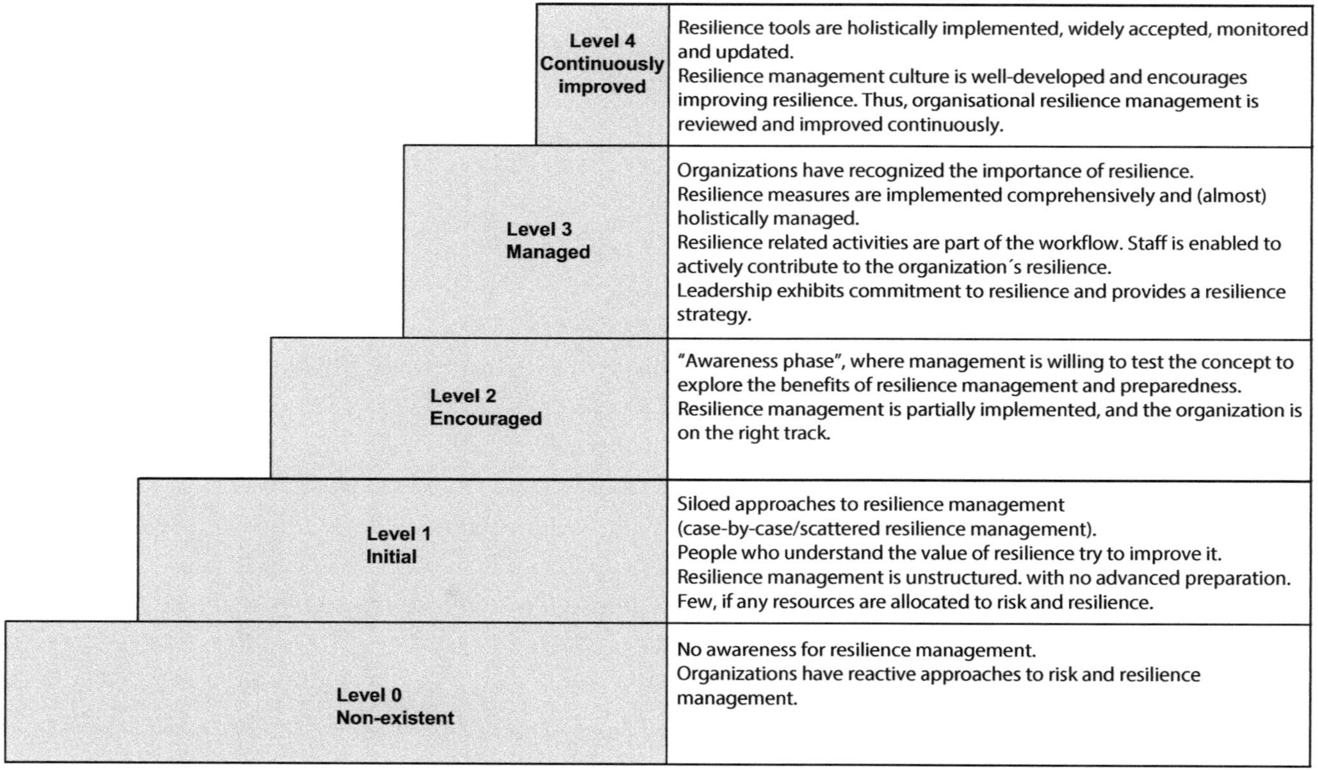

Fig. 7.7 Maturity levels (stages and definitions in accordance with De Bruin et al., 2005; Stephenson, 2010; ASIS International, 2012; Hirsch et al., 2014; GRC, 2020)

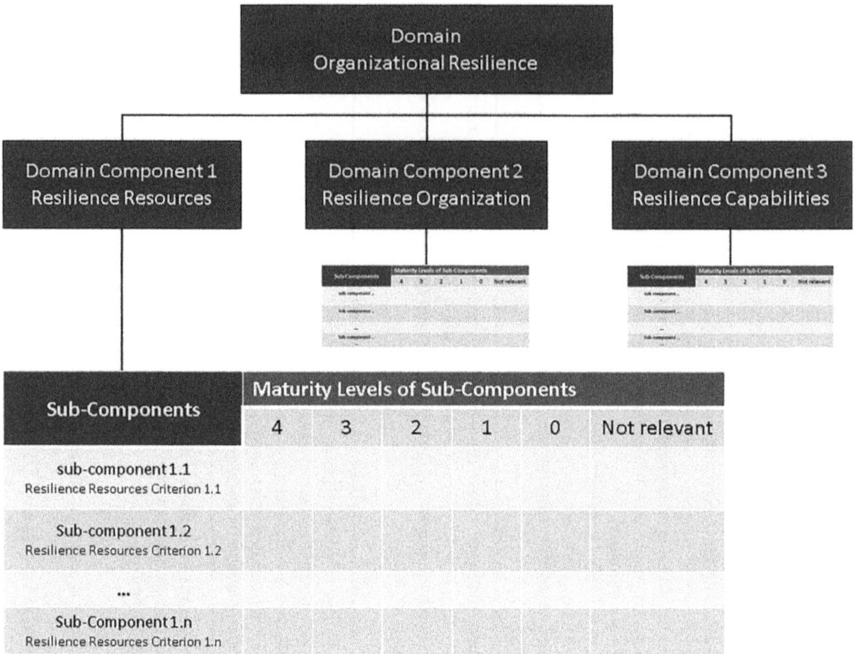

Fig. 7.8 Model layers. (Source: Developed by the authors)

domain, domain components, and subcomponents. Figure 7.8 illustrates how these layers can be designed.

> The results obtained from a layered model enable an organization to gain a deeper understanding of their relative strengths and weaknesses in the domain and to target specific improvement strategies thereby enabling more efficient resource allocation (De Bruin et al., 2005).

A **domain component** – in our model the dimensions that are represented by the resilience determinants – is a major, independent aspect of the given domain organizational resilience. Domain components enable an initial clustering of results for the model audience (De Bruin et al., 2005).

Domain subcomponents – in our model the criteria – are specific capability areas within the domain components. Their identification is recommended for complex domains (De Bruin et al., 2005). The additional layers of detail are as follows:

1. Firstly, assists in the development of the **assessment instrument**
2. Secondly enables richer analysis of maturity results by providing further detail and thus enabling targeted maturity level improvements (De Bruin et al., 2005)
3. Thirdly improves the ability to present maturity results in a manner that meets the needs of the target audience (De Bruin et al., 2005), especially the "ability to

drill-down through the maturity assessment enables model assessment reports to be tailored to varying needs of multiple audiences" (De Bruin et al., 2005, p. 6, 8)

When designing a model, the number of domain components and subcomponents should be kept low to minimize perceived complexity in the model and ensure the independence of the components (De Bruin et al., 2005, p. 7).

Next it is necessary to determine how the **measurement of the achieved maturity level** can occur. This applies to the instrument used in conducting an assessment and the inclusion of appropriate measures within this instrument (De Bruin et al., 2005). With respect to determining the assessment instrument, the domain components and subcomponents provide good guidance. We generated a catalog of 26 criteria (domain subcomponents), covering all three resilience determinants derived from the systematic literature research, to create the organizational resilience measurement instrument (as illustrated in the Appendix).

Regarding the application method, self-assessment, third party assessment, and certified practitioners are generally applicable (De Bruin et al., 2005). Considering the context of SMEs and their limited resources, the maturity model of this paper uses the method of self-assessment, so that it can be carried out by managers, decision-makers and employees. Respondents are asked to rate the criteria according to a five-point Likert scale, which was designed in conformity with the maturity levels (0 – Nonexistent; 4 – Continuously improved). "The use of **Likert scales** [...] can improve reliability and consistency of response and enables results to be easily mapped to maturity stages" (De Bruin et al., 2005, p. 9).

In the chosen assessment model, as the weights or relative importance of determinants and their criteria have not been examined, the **equal weights method** was employed. The final score for organizational resilience is then determined as an **average score** of all its criteria. That requires minimal knowledge of the decision-maker's priorities and minimal input from the decision-maker (Trinh & Feng, 2022), which is useful in the context of SMEs, as they are very versatile. Therefore, this paper can only develop a prototype for a maturity model, which must be adapted by SMEs to their individual needs, e.g., by using weights.

Using the **dimension of resilience resources** and the associated criteria as an example, if a specific criterion falls in the Nonexistent level 0, it scores 0; if it falls in the Initial level 1, it scores 1; and so on. The maturity level in the dimension resilience resources can be scored using Eq. 7.1.

$$\text{Score of resilience resources} = \frac{1}{n}\sum_{i=1}^{n}\left(\text{resilience resources criterion } i\right) \tag{7.1}$$

If the final score is 3, the score of resilience resources leads to the maturity level 3 – Managed; if the final score is 3.5, the score of resilience resources leads to the maturity level 4 – Continuously improved.

Once the same procedure is repeated in all domain components, it is possible to perceive the maturity level of organizational resilience at the domain level. The overall score of the **maturity of organizational resilience** can be determined as an average score of all dimensions, thus the three resilience determinants (Eq. 7.2).

$$\text{Organizational resilience maturity level} = \frac{1}{n}\sum_{i=1}^{n}(\text{Criterion } i) \tag{7.2}$$

$$= 1/3\begin{pmatrix} score\ of\ resilience\ resources + score\ of\ resilience\ organization \\ +score\ of\ resilience\ capabilities \end{pmatrix}$$

Accordingly, if the overall score of organizational resilience is 0, the maturity level is 0 – Nonexistent; if it falls between 1 and 2, the maturity level of organizational resilience is at the Encouraged level 2; and so forth (Trinh & Feng, 2022).

It is worthwhile to note that the various domains – resilience resources, resilience organization, and resilience capabilities – could have different levels of organizational resilience maturity. Evaluating them individually enables resources to be allocated more efficiently to achieve an advanced status regarding resilience (Trinh & Feng, 2022). In this context, it is important to mention that the targeted maturity level does not have to reach the maximum everywhere. The level to be achieved is a management decision that depends, among other things, on the availability of resources and other goals of the organization. This goes hand in hand with the view of the International Organization for Standardization (ISO). According to ISO, "there is no absolute measure or definite goal for resilience – organizations can only be more or less resilient" (ISO 22316: 2017, Introduction).

Finally, the developed model should be tested, validated, and further sharpened by experts. For this purpose, the model development concept specifies the evaluation and transfer in the next step.

7.4.5 Evaluation/Transfer

Normally, the actual development of the maturity model is followed in the fifth step by an evaluation and transfer of the development results. This way the model is tested for validity and generalizability. Validity is assessed for both, good translation of constructs and completeness (De Bruin et al., 2005). By conducting interviews in the previous step, a first validation step was already taken, although broad acceptance could not yet be ensured with this.

Basically, progression through some phases may be iterative. Dependent upon the "test" results, it may be necessary to revisit and adjust decisions made in earlier phases. This basic idea about development paths of maturity models is also captured by De Bruin et al. (2005) in their evolutionary phases of a model's life cycle. Therein, the authors consider **three purposes** for which a model may be applied and assign them to a development path:

1. **Descriptive**

   "If a model is purely descriptive, the application of the model would be seen as single point encounters with no provision for improving maturity […]. This type of model is good **for assessing the here and now** i.e. the as-is situation" (De Bruin et al., 2005).

2. **Prescriptive**

   "A prescriptive model [...] **indicates how to approach maturity improvement** in order to positively affect business value i.e. enables the development of a road-map for improvement" (De Bruin et al., 2005).

3. **Comparative**

   "A comparative model **enables benchmarking** across industries or regions" (De Bruin et al., 2005).

> First, a model is descriptive so that a deeper understanding of the as-is domain situation is achieved. A model can then be evolved into being prescriptive as it is only through a sound understanding of the current situation that substantial, repeatable improvements can be made. Finally, for a model to be used comparatively it must be applied in a wide range of organizations in order to attain sufficient data to enable valid comparison (De Bruin et al., 2005).

The proposed organizational resilience maturity model, which is illustrated in the Appendix, forms a sound basis for the first development phases of a descriptive and partially prescriptive model. Following the required evaluation and transfer, applying the model in various case studies could not only result in validation but also enable the evolution of the model up to the comparative phase.

7.5 Summary

The increasing frequency of adversities and unexpected events threatens the functioning and long-term existence of organizations. That applies in particular to SMEs, which are still dominating the corporate landscape. This urgently calls for SMEs to address and strengthen their resilience.

Since the term resilience is widely used, it was necessary to derive a solid understanding of the definition and concept. Taking the process-oriented view, the authors define organizational resilience as the ability of an organization to anticipate, cope, and adapt to challenging conditions (e.g., crisis, disturbance, shock, or other adverse events and environmental developments) with the aim of withstanding or bouncing back and emerging from them strengthened and more resourceful.

One way to gain a better understanding in the field of interest – including determining one's situation, improving it, and controlling it – is offered by maturity models. Therefore, this paper reported the development of a maturity model for organizational resilience in SMEs. Thus, this paper expands the existing literature about organizational resilience by proposing a (quantitative) maturity model that supports facilitating the understanding of organizational resilience in SMEs.

Based on an extensive review of literature about organizational resilience, supplemented by expert interviews, the components for the maturity model were identified. The authors specify organizational resilience, using three determinants: resilience resources, resilience organization, and resilience capabilities. Their detailed design was explained and transferred into a catalog of criteria for the maturity model. As a result, the developed model consists of 5 maturity levels, 3 assessment domains, and 26 detailed assessment criteria. The level of organizational resilience is assessed through the proposed five-point Likert scale, resembling the defined maturity levels, ranging from 0 (Nonexistent) to 4 (Continuously improved).

By using the developed model to assess organizational resilience, it is evident that an organization can obtain different scores in terms of the resilience dimensions – resilience resources, resilience organization, and resilience capabilities – and their criteria. Thus, the assessment results can support organizations to better recognize the specific resilience areas and resilience practices required and thereby allocate resources efficiently in order to achieve an advanced status with regard to organizational resilience.

With regard to the survey method, the self-assessment is recommended. On the one hand, the model is particularly intuitive and simple to implement, which is especially advantageous for SMEs, considering their limited resources. On the other hand, the model provides theoretical insights into the maturity characteristics of organizational resilience. Thus, the proposed model is useful in practical terms because it enables managers and decision-makers to determine the current level of organizational resilience. Moreover, it provides guidance to identify actions required before a higher maturity can be achieved. Beyond their own information and planning support, managers and decision-makers can also use the model to communicate resilience issues more easily to their employees. For example, in workshops, the model can offer participants a clear view of the status quo, strengths and weaknesses of their organizations' resilience capabilities.

This contribution has several limitations. It becomes evident that managing and improving organizational resilience is a broad and complex topic. Although the proposed factors have been systematically derived from the literature, each organization should consider the maturity model specific to its field of action.

Since SMEs are very diverse, it is not possible to create a maturity model with factors that are equally valid for all SMEs. This results in the first limitation that the domains and criteria for assessing and enhancing organizational resilience have not been prioritized, which implies that all criteria have the same weight. However, individual organizations are expected to decide which aspects are most relevant to them. Therefore, the organization using this maturity model could either apply the equations provided in this chapter or develop a scale of their importance. For this purpose, the proposed maturity model contains various resilience factors, which can be prioritized by SMEs in their specific context via a weighting factor. Likewise, it is possible to remove factors from the evaluation with a weighting of 0.

Conversely, there is the possibility that relevant criteria are missing in the context of certain SMEs. Due to the comprehensible derivation of the model, adjustments – such as criteria addition – should be easy to perform. The adaptability of the model does also play a role with regard to the ever-changing and dynamic nature of threats and risks, due to which it is crucial to incorporate emerging resilience capabilities and standards. This will ensure the maintainability of the assessment of the model and support it to be future proof.

Beyond the weighting and addition of criteria, it is important to consider that maturity models do still have blind spots. Therefore, it is not advisable to make decisions solely based on the organizational resilience maturity model. Maturity models represent a complementary source of information and for objective location determination and derivation of further development and measurement.

A further limitation is that the proposed model was solely derived theoretically from literature research, supplemented by expert interviews. It has not been tested from a practical point of view. Therefore, it would be worthwhile to conduct a case study or rather several case studies, in order to demonstrate the application of the proposed model and validate the factors in practice.

For example, several SMEs – of similar size and industry – can be selected for assessment and comparison. Application will provide additional insight into the relevance and usefulness of the proposed model. The practical relevance of the organizational resilience maturity model could be further increased by large-scale studies to assess benchmark scores from different industries and regions.

Finally, this chapter provides a theoretical contribution that deserves future empirical investigation. The conceptual development of the organizational resilience maturity model offers a ready platform and methodology for further research and comparisons within the assessment of the maturity of organizational resilience management in SMEs.

Appendix

Appendix

Maturity Model for an Resilience Maturity Assessment

Self-Assessment Example

(1) Resilience Resources	4	3	2	1	0	not relevant
quantitative (financial ressources)						
Financial potential *(high liquidity, e.g. cash and cash equivalent)*	x					
Financial performance *(e.g. adequate/low debt coverage, high equity ratio)*		x				
qualitative (personnel resources)						
cognitive level *(abilities, skills, experience, qualifications, know-how & strong values, optimism, hope, sense of purpose)*				x		
behavioral level *(rules, rehearsed routines and patterns)*					x	
relational level *(social and network relationships)*						x
sum total	4	3	0	1	0	
Maturity Level Resilience Resources				2		

(2) Resilience Organization	4	3	2	1	0	not relevant
proactive resilience management system						
systems and processes for environmental observation and scanning *(to detect "weak signals", supplemented by information gathering through interviews, market research, surveys)*		x				
systems and processes for identifying unexpected events and critical developments *(e.g. scenario analysis of key performance indicators, simulation methods, stress tests)*			x			
systems and processes for preparing for unexpected events and critical developments *(emergency plans, risk handbooks and guidelines including roles and responsibilities, predefined communication procedures)*			x			
corporate culture *(organizations norms, values, behaviours and underlying assuptions such as optimism, mindfulness, trust, respect; risk and error culture)*				x		
reactive resilience management system						
Principles, procedures and measures (rules) to cope with (predefined specific or) unexpected events and critical developments					x	
crisis communication *(to internal and external stakeholders e.g. by protocols, mail, social media)*			x			
sum total	0	3	6	1	0	
Maturity Level Resilience Organization				2		

(3) Resilience Capabilities	4	3	2	1	0	not relevant
Resilience capabilities to anticipate						
ability to anticipate				x		
ability to identify weak signals				x		
ability of situation awareness *(perceive potential threat)*				x		
ability to interpret the data correctly *(mindfulness: attention, sensitization, awareness of internal and external adversities)*				x		
ability to assign meaning to (negative) events *(sensemaking)*				x		
Resilience capabilities to cope						
ability to accept a problem *(no denial od dangers)*				x		
ability to make sense of a problem and act/initiate the correct response (sensemaking)				x		
ability to develop and implement short term solutions through innovation and improvisation (Bricolage)				x		
Resilience capabilities to adapt						
organizational adaptive capacity						
ability to reflect appropriately *(past or current events e.g. itendifying opportunities, prooducing new knowledge)*				x		
ability to act appropriately *(ability and willpower)*				x		
ability to learn *(lessons learned, e.g. through in depth and root cause analysis)*				x		
strategic adaptive capacity: Ability to adapt to environmental changes						
ability to adapt business model				x		
ability to exercise environmental and social practices (ESG)				x		
operational adaptive capacity: Ability to adapt daily business (flexibility, redundancy)						
Flexibility *(regarding procurement, productin and sales)*				x		
Redundancy *(existence of resources enables operational adaptability)*				x		
sum total	0	0	0	15	0	
Maturity Level Resilience Capabilities				1		
Organizational Resilience Maturity Level				2		

Scale legend:

4 - Continuously improved
3 - Managed
2 - Encouraged
1 - Initial
0 - Non-existend

References

Aguilar, F. J. (1967). *Scanning the business environment*. Macmillan.

Ahlemann, F., Schroeder, C., & Teuteberg, F. (2005). Kompetenz- und Reifegradmodelle für das Projektmanagement: Grundlagen, Vergleich und Einsatz (ISPRI-Arbeitsbericht No. 01/2005). Osnabrück: Univ. FB Wirtschaftswiss. Organisation u. Wirtschaftsinformatik.

Allen, J. (2011). Measures for managing operational resilience. *EDPACS, 44*(6), 1–6. https://doi.org/10.1080/07366981.2011.643192

Alliger, G. M., Cerasoli, C. P., & Tannenbaum, S. I. (2015). Team resilience: How teams flourish under pressure. *Organizational Dynamics, 44*(3), 176–184.

Amann, B., & Jaussaud, J. (2012). Family and non-family business resilience in an economic downturn. *Asia Pacific Business Review, 18*(2), 203–223.

Ansoff, H. I. (1975). Managing strategic surprise by response to weak signals. *California Management Review, 18*(2), 21–33.

Appelt, D. (2016). *Sensemaking und Sensegiving in der Sanierung* (1st ed.). Springer Fachmedien Wiesbaden.

Ashmos, D. P., & Huber, G. P. (1987). The systems paradigm in organization theory: Correcting the record and suggesting the future. *The Academy of Management Review, 12*(4), 607–621.

ASIS International. (2012). *Maturity model for the phased implementation of the organizational resilience management system*. Retrieved from https://webstore.ansi.org/preview-pages/ASIS/preview_ANSI+ASIS+SPC.4-2012.pdf.

Bamberger, I., & Wrona, T. (2013). Strategische Unternehmensführung: Strategien, Systeme, Methoden, Prozesse (2. Aufl.). Vahlens Handbücher der Wirtschafts- und Sozialwissenschaften. München: Vahlen.

Barney, J. B. (1991). Firm resources and sustained competitive advantage. *Journal of Management, 17*(1), 99–120.

Becker, J., Knackstedt, R., & Pöppelbuß, J. (2009). Entwicklung von Reifegradmodellen für das IT-Management. *Wirtschaftsinformatik, 51*(3), 249–260. https://doi.org/10.1007/s11576-009-0167-9

Boers, B., & Henschel, T. (2022). Crisis management: A necessary evil or useful tool? The role of socioemotional wealth in the crisis management of family firms. *Mrev Management Revue, 33*(4), 397–428. https://doi.org/10.5771/0935-9915-2022-4-397

Burke, R. J. (2005). Effects of 9/11 on individuals and organizations: Down but not out! *Disaster Prevention and Management: An International Journal, 14*(5), 629–638. https://doi.org/10.1108/09653560510634052

Burnard, K., & Bhamra, R. (2011). Organisational resilience: Development of a conceptual framework for organisational responses. *International Journal of Production Research, 49*(18), 5581–5599. https://doi.org/10.1080/00207543.2011.563827

Caralli, R. A., Allen, J. H., & White, D. W. (2011). The CERT resilience management model: A maturity model for managing operational resilience. In *SEI series in software engineering*. Addison-Wesley. Retrieved from https://learning.oreilly.com/library/view/-/9780132565905/?ar

Chapman, M. T., Lines, R. L. J., Crane, M., Ducker, K. J., Ntoumanis, N., Peeling, P., et al. (2020). Team resilience: A scoping review of conceptual and empirical work. *Work & Stress, 34*(1), 57–81. https://doi.org/10.1080/02678373.2018.1529064

Coutu, D. L. (2002). How resilience works. *Harvard Business Review, 80*(5), 46–56.

Crovini, C. (2022). Crisis management and risk management in SMEs: Towards an integrated early warnings system. In S. Durst & T. Henschel (Eds.), *Management for Professionals Ser. Crisis management for Small and Medium-Sized Enterprises (SMEs): Strategies for external crises* (pp. 215–233). Springer International Publishing AG.

Daft, R. L., & Weick, K. E. (1984). Toward a model of organizations as interpretation systems. *The Academy of Management Review, 9*(2), 284–195.

Daudelin, M. W. (1997). Learning from experience through reflection. *Organizational Dynamics, 24*(3), 36–48. https://doi.org/10.1016/s0090-2616(96)90004-2

De Bruin, T., Rosemann, M., Freeze, R. D., & Kulkarni, U. (2005). *Understanding the main phases of developing a maturity assessment model*. Australian conference on information systems.

de Carvalho, A. O., Ribeiro, I., Cirani, C. B. S., & Cintra, R. F. (2016). Organizational resilience: A comparative study between innovative and non-innovative companies based on the financial performance analysis. *International Journal of Innovation, 4*(1), 58–69. https://doi.org/10.5585/iji.v4i1.73

Doubek, C., Exler, M. W., & Situm, M. (2016). Aktueller Stand von Früherkennungssystemen: Eine systematische Übersicht zu Ansätzen zwecks Früherkennung von strategischen Unternehmenskrisen. *Krisen-, Sanierungs- Und Insolvenzberatung.*, (5), 204–210.
Duchek, S. (2020). Organizational resilience: A capability-based conceptualization. *Business Research, 13*(1), 215–246. https://doi.org/10.1007/s40685-019-0085-7
Durst, S., & Henschel, T. (2021). COVID-19 as an accelerator for developing strong(er) businesses? Insights from Estonian small firms. *Journal of the International Council for Small Business, 2*(1), 1–29. https://doi.org/10.1080/26437015.2020.1859935
Durst, S., Heinze, I., Henschel, T., & Nawaz, N. (2020). Unlearning: A systematic literature review. *International Journal of Business and Globalisation, 24*(4), 472–495.
Edmondson, A. C. (2002). The local and variegated nature of learning in organizations: A group-level perspective. *Organization Science, 13*(2), 128–146. https://doi.org/10.1287/orsc.13.2.128.530
Ergün, I. (2014). Risikoberichterstattung in den Lage- und Konzernlageberichten deutscher Groß- und Außenhandelsunternehmen. Schriftenreihe Schriften zum betrieblichen Rechnungswesen und Controlling: Bd. 126. Hamburg: Kovač.
Fahlenbrach, R., Rageth, K., & Stulz, R. (2021). How valuable is financial flexibility when revenue stops? Evidence from the COVID-19 crisis. *The Review of Financial Studies, 34*(11), 5474–5521. https://doi.org/10.3386/w27106
Fink, A., Marr, B., Siebe, A., & Kuhle, J.-P. (2005). The future scorecard: Combining external and internal scenarios to create strategic foresight. *Management Decision, 43*(3), 360–381. https://doi.org/10.1108/00251740510589751
Fraser, P., Moultrie, J., & Gregory, M. (2002). The use of maturity models/grids as a tool in assessing product development capability. In *Managing technology for the new economy: St John's College, Cambridge, UK, 18–20 August 2002 ; proceedings* (pp. 244–249). IEEE Service Center. https://doi.org/10.1109/IEMC.2002.1038431
Freeman, S. F., Hirschhorn, L., & Triad, M. M. (2003). Moral purpose and organisational resilience: Sandler O'Neill & Partners, L.P. in the Aftermath of September 11, 2001. *Academy of Management Proceedings*, (1), B1–B6. https://doi.org/10.5465/ambpp.2003.13792457
Gittell, J. H., Cameron, K., Lim, S., & Rivas, V. (2006). Relationships, layoffs, and organizational resilience. *The Journal of Applied Behavioral Science, 42*(3), 300–329. https://doi.org/10.1177/0021886306286466
Gracey, A. (2020). Building an organisational resilience maturity framework. *Journal of Business Continuity & Emergency Planning*. (Band 13 Heft 4), *13*, 313–327.
GRC 2020. 2023 Fusion - Internetdokument - Risk-and-Resiliency-Management-Maturity-Model.
Grönert, T., Pöppelbuß, J., & Breiter, A. (2014). Reifegradbestimmung der IT-Governance: Eine Fallstudie zur Anwendbarkeit des COBIT 5 PAM in der öffentlichen Verwaltung. In E. Plödereder, L. Grunske, E. Schneider, & D. Ull (Eds.), *Informatik 2014. Big data - Komplexität meistern (1513–1525)*. Springer.
Hamel, G., & Valikangas, L. (2003). The quest for resilience. *Harvard Business Review, 81*(9), 52–63.
Harrison, J. S., Bosse, D. A., & Phillips, R. A. (2010). Managing for stakeholders, stakeholder utility functions and competitive advantage. *Strategic Management Journal, 31*(1), 58–74.
Haunschild, P. R., & Sullivan, B. N. (2002). Learning from complexity: Effects of prior accidents and incidents on Airlines' learning. *Administrative Science Quarterly, 47*(4), 609–643. https://doi.org/10.2307/3094911
Heinze, I. (2013). Entrepreneur sense-making of business failure. *Small Enterprise Research, 20*(1), 21–39. https://doi.org/10.5172/ser.2013.20.1.21
Heinze, I., Henschel, T., & Hirt, J. (2023). *Risky Stories – Storytelling strategisch im Risiko-, Krisen- und Fehlermanagement anwenden*. Springer Gabler. https://doi.org/10.1007/978-3-658-40310-2
Henschel, T., & Salzmann, J. (2021). Best Practice im Krisenmanagement von KMU. *Controller Magazin*, (4), 35–41.

Herdmann, F. (2022). Preparing for crises: Enhancing resilience. In S. Durst & T. Henschel (Eds.), *Management for Professionals Ser. Crisis Management for Small and Medium-Sized Enterprises (SMEs): Strategies for external crises* (pp. 193–214). Springer International Publishing AG.

Hillmann, J., & Guenther, E. (2021). Organizational resilience: A valuable construct for management research? *International Journal of Management Reviews, 23*(1), 7–44. https://doi.org/10.1111/ijmr.12239

Hillson, D. (1997). Towards a risk maturity model. *The Internatoinal Journal of Project & Business Risk Management*, (1), 35–45. Retrieved from http://risk-doctor.com/pdf-files/rmm-mar97.pdf

Hirsch, B., Weber, J., Schulte, N., Huber, R., & Schuster, K. (2014). Zielorientierte Steuerung in Behörden: Masterplan für den öffentlichen Sektor. In *Steuerung & Controlling in öffentlichen Institutionen*. E. Schmidt. Retrieved from http://site.ebrary.com/lib/alltitles/docDetail.action?docID=11012908

Hoitsch, H.-J., Winter, P., & Bächle, R. (2005). Risikokultur und risikopolitische Grundsätze: Strukturierungsvorschläge und empirische Ergebnisse. *Controlling Und Management, 49*(2), 125–133.

Hong, P., Huang, C., & Li, B. (2012). Crisis management for SMEs: Insights from a multiple-case study. *International Journal of Business Excellence, 5*(5), 535–553.

Horne, J. F., & Orr, J. E. (1998). Assessing behaviors that create resilient organizations. *Employment Relations Today, 24*(4), 29–39. https://doi.org/10.1002/ert.3910240405

International Standardization Organisation. ISO 22316:2017 - Security and resilience.

Jacka, M. J. (2017). Resilience through crisis. *Internal Auditor, 2*(74), 26–31. Retrieved from https://www.iia.nl/sitefiles/ia/resilience%20through%20crisis.pdf

Kampmann, A., & Pedell, B. (2022). Using storytelling to promote organizational resilience: An experimental study of different forms of risk communication. *Schmalenbach Journal of Business Research, 74*(4), 695–725. https://doi.org/10.1007/s41471-022-00143-x

Kendra, J. M., & Wachtendorf, T. (2003). Elements of resilience after the World Trade Center disaster: Reconstituting New York City's Emergency Operations Centre. *Disasters, 27*(1), 37–53. https://doi.org/10.1111/1467-7717.00218

Kersten, H., & Klett, G. (2017). *Business Continuity und IT-Notfallmanagement*. Springer Fachmedien Wiesbaden. Retrieved from https://link.springer.com/content/pdf/10.1007/978-3-658-19118-4.pdf

Knackstedt, R., Pöppelbuß, J., & Becker, J. (2009). Vorgehensmodell zur Entwicklung von Reifegradmodellen. *Wirtschaftsinformatik Proceedings*, (44).

Koppel, T., & Tšernikova, O. (2022). Managing Crisis in SMEs. In S. Durst & T. Henschel (Eds.), *Management for Professionals Ser. Crisis Management for Small and Medium-Sized Enterprises (SMEs): Strategies for external crises* (pp. 47–58). Springer International Publishing AG.

Kübel, M. (2013). *Corporate M&A*. Springer Fachmedien Wiesbaden. https://doi.org/10.1007/978-3-8349-3970-8

Lee, A. V., Vargo, J., & Seville, E. (2013). Developing a tool to measure and compare organizations' resilience. *Natural Hazards Review, 14*(1), 29–41. https://doi.org/10.1061/(ASCE)NH.1527-6996.0000075

Lengnick-Hall, C. A., & Beck, T. E. (2005). Adaptive fit versus robust transformation: How organizations respond to environmental change. *Journal of Management, 31*(5), 738–757. https://doi.org/10.1177/0149206305279367

Lengnick-Hall, C. A., & Beck, T. E. (2009). Resilience capacity and strategic agility: Prerequisites for thriving in a dynamic environment. In C. P. Nemeth, E. Hollnagel, & S. Dekker (Eds.), *Ashgate studies in resilience engineering* (Preparation and restoration) (Vol. 2, pp. 61–92). CRC Press. (Original work published 2009).

Lengnick-Hall, C. A., Beck, T. E., & Lengnick-Hall, M. L. (2011). Developing a capacity for organizational resilience through strategic human resource management. *Human Resource Management Review, 21*(3), 243–255. https://doi.org/10.1016/j.hrmr.2010.07.001

Levinthal, D., & Rerup, C. (2006). Crossing an apparent chasm: Bridging mindful and less-mindful perspectives on organizational learning. *Organization Science, 17*(4), 502–513. https://doi.org/10.1287/orsc.1060.0197

Lewin, A. Y., Massini, S., & Peters, C. (2011). Microfoundations of internal and external absorptive capacity routines. *Organization Science, 22*(1), 81–98.

Limat, C. (2022). Disruptionspotenzial künstlicher Intelligenz: Ein Reifegradmodell zur Einführung ganzheitlicher KI-Initiativen in Unternehmen. *Wirtschaftsinformatik & Management, 14*(1), 60–67. https://doi.org/10.1365/s35764-021-00379-y

Limnios, E. A. M., Mazzarol, T., Ghadouani, A., & Schilizzi, S. G. M. (2014). The resilience architecture framework: Four organizational archetypes. *European Management Journal, 32*(1), 104–116. https://doi.org/10.1016/j.emj.2012.11.007

Ling-yee, L., & Ogunmokun, G. O. (2008). An empirical study of manufacturing flexibility of exporting firms in China: How do strategic and organizational contexts matter? *Industrial Marketing Management, 37*(6), 738–751. https://doi.org/10.1016/j.indmarman.2007.05.007

Linnenluecke, M. K. (2017). Resilience in business and management research: A review of influential publications and a research agenda. *International Journal of Management Reviews, 19*(1), 4–30. https://doi.org/10.1111/ijmr.12076

Luthans, F., Youssef, C. M., & Avolio, B. J. (2007). *Psychological capital: Developing the human competitive edge*. Oxford University Press.

Luthans, F., Avey, J. B., Avolio, B. J., & Peterson, S. J. (2010). The development and resulting performance impact of positive psychological capital. *Human Resource Development Quarterly, 21*(1), 41–67.

Madni, A. M., & Jackson, S. (2009). Towards a conceptual framework for resilience engineering. *IEEE Systems Journal, 3*(2), 181–191. https://doi.org/10.1109/JSYST.2009.2017397

Madsen, P. M. (2009). These lives will not be lost in vain: Organizational learning from disaster in U.S. Coal Mining. *Organization Science, 20*(5), 861–875. https://doi.org/10.1287/orsc.1080.0396

Mallak, L. A. (1998). Measuring resilience in health care provider organizations. *Health Manpower Management, 24*(4–5), 148–152. https://doi.org/10.1108/09552069810215755

Mbanaso, U. M., Abrahams, L., & Apene, O. Z. (2019). Conceptual Design of a Cybersecurity Resilience Maturity Measurement (CRMM) Framework. *The African Journal of Information and Communication (AJIC)*. Advance online publication. https://doi.org/10.23962/10539/27535

McFarlane, D., Srinivasan, R., Puchkova, A., Thorne, A., & Brintrup, A. (2017). A maturity framework for operational resilience and its application to production control. In T. Borangiu, D. Trentesaux, A. Thomas, & O. Cardin (Eds.), *Service orientation in Holonic and multi-agent manufacturing: Proceedings of SOHOMA 2017* (pp. 51–62).

McManus, S., Seville, E., Brunsden, D., & Vargo, J. (2007). *Resilience management: A framework for assessing and improving the resilience of organisations*. Retrieved from Resilient Organisations Research Group; University of Canterbury. Department of Accounting and Information Systems website: http://ir.canterbury.ac.nz/handle/10092/9488.

Mettler, T. (2010). Supply-Management im Krankenhaus: Konstruktion und Evaluation eines konfigurierbaren Reifegradmodells zur zielgerichteten Gestaltung. Zugl.: Sankt Gallen, Univ., Diss., 2010 (1. Aufl.). Göttingen: Sierke.

Meyer, A. D. (1982). Adapting to environmental jolts. *Administrative Science Quarterly, 27*(4), 515–537.

Müller, S., & Uschkurat, M. (2021). Krisenresilienz von Unternehmen. Krisen-, Sanierungs- Und Insolvenzberatung. Advance online publication. https://doi.org/10.37307/j.1868-7784.2021.06.03.

Müller, S., & Uschkurat, M. (2022). Informationen zur Krisenresilienz von Unternehmen. Krisen-, Sanierungs- Und Insolvenzberatung. Advance online publication. https://doi.org/10.37307/j.1868-7784.2022.01.04.

Ortiz-de-Mandojana, N., & Bansal, P. (2016). The long-term benefits of organizational resilience through sustainable business practices. *Strategic Management Journal, 37*(8), 1615–1631. https://doi.org/10.1002/smj.2410

Penadés, M. C., Núñez, A. G., & Canós, J. H. (2017). From planning to resilience: The role (and value) of the emergency plan. *Technological Forecasting and Social Change, 121*, 17–30. https://doi.org/10.1016/j.techfore.2016.12.004

Pullen, W. (2007). A public sector HPT maturity model. *Performance Improvement, 46*(4), 9–15. https://doi.org/10.1002/pfi.119

Radic, M., Herrmann, P., Haberland, P., & Riese, C. R. (2022). Development of a business model resilience framework for managers and strategic decision-makers. *Schmalenbach Journal of Business Research, 74*(4), 575–601. https://doi.org/10.1007/s41471-022-00135-x

Ramelli, S., & Wagner, A. F. (2020). Feverish stock price reactions to COVID-19. *The Review of Corporate Finance Studies, 9*(3), 622–655.

Rerup, C. (2009). Attentional triangulation: Learning from unexpected rare crises. *Organization Science, 20*(5), 876–893.

Roberts, K. H., Madsen, P. M., & Desai, V. M. (2005). The space between in space transportation: A relational analysis of the failure of STS-107. In W. Starbuck & M. Farjoun (Eds.), *Organization at the Limit: Lessons from the Columbia disaster* (pp. 81–97). Blackwell. (Original work published 2005).

Rochlin, G. I., La Porte, T. R., & Roberts, K. H. (1987). The self-designing high-reliability organization: Aircraft carrier flight operations at sea. *Naval War College Review, 40*(4), 76–92. Retrieved from https://www.jstor.org/stable/44637690

Scharfenkamp, N. (1987). *Organisatorische Gestaltung und wirtschaftlicher Erfolg: Organizational Slack als Ergebnis und Einflussfaktor der formalen Organisationsstruktur. Mensch und Organisation* (Vol. 13). Walter de Gruyter. Retrieved from https://doi.org/10.1515/9783110867053

Schleinzer, A. (2014). *Entwicklung eines Reifegradmodells für das unternehmensweite Risikomanagement (Diplomarbeit)*. Technische Universität Wien. Retrieved from https://publik.tuwien.ac.at/files/PubDat_229801.pdf

Schulman, P. R. (1993). The negotiated order of organizational reliability. *Administration & Society, 25*(3), 353–372.

Seville, E., Brunsdon, D., Dantas, A., Le Masurier, J., Wilkinson, S., & Vargo, J. (2008). Organisational resilience: Researching the reality of New Zealand organisations. *Journal of Business Continuity & Emergency Planning, 2*(3), 258–266. Retrieved from https://www.ingentaconnect.com/content/hsp/jbcep/2008/00000002/00000003/art00006

Sheffi, Y. (2005). Preparing for the big one [supply chain management]. *Manufacturing Engineer, 84*(5), 12–15.

Shepherd, D. A., & Williams, T. A. (2014). Local venturing as compassion organizing in the aftermath of a natural disaster: The role of localness and community in reducing suffering. *Journal of Management Studies, 51*(6), 952–994. https://doi.org/10.1111/joms.12084

Shepherd, D. A., Williams, T., Wolfe, M., & Patzelt, H. (2016). *Learning from entrepreneurial failure: Emotions, cognitions, and actions*. Cambridge University Press.

Shin, J., Taylor, M. S., & Seo, M.-G. (2012). Resources for change: The relationships of organizational inducements and psychological resilience to employees' attitudes and behaviors toward organizational change. *Academy of Management Journal, 55*(3), 727–748.

Sitkin, S. B. (1992). Learning through failure: The strategy of small losses. *Research in Organizational Behavior, 2*(14), 231–266.

Somers, S. (2009). Measuring resilience potential: An adaptive strategy for organizational crisis planning. *Journal of Contingencies and Crisis Management, 17*(1), 12–23. https://doi.org/10.1111/j.1468-5973.2009.00558.x

Staw, B. M., Sandelands, L. E., & Dutton, J. E. (1981). Threat rigidity effects in organizational behavior: A multilevel analysis. *Administrative Science Quarterly, 26*(4), 501–524.

Stephenson, A. V. (2010). *Benchmarking the resilience of organisations*.

Sutcliffe, K. M., & Vogus, T. J. (2003). Organizing for resilience. In K. S. Cameron, J. E. Dutton, & R. E. Quinn (Eds.), *Positive organizational scholarship: Foundations of a new discipline* (1st ed., pp. 94–110). Berrett-Koehler. Publ (Original work published 2003).

Teixeira, E. D. O., & Werther, W. B. (2013). Resilience: Continuous renewal of competitive advantages. *Business Horizons, 56*(3), 333–342. https://doi.org/10.1016/j.bushor.2013.01.009

Tognazzo, A., Gubitta, P., & Favaron, S. D. (2016). Does slack always affect resilience? A study of quasi-medium-sized Italian firm. *Entrepreneurship & Regional Development, 28*(9–10), 768–790.

Trinh, M. T., & Feng, Y. (2022). A maturity model for resilient safety culture development in construction companies. *Buildings, 12*(6), 733. https://doi.org/10.3390/buildings12060733

Tubis, A. A., & Werbińska-Wojciechowska, S. (2021). Risk management maturity model for logistic processes. *Sustainability, 13*(2), 1–19. https://doi.org/10.3390/su13020659

Vanini, U., & Rieg, R. (2021). Risikomanagement: Grundlagen - Instrumente - Unternehmenspraxis. https://doi.org/10.34156/9783791045269-1.

Vargas-Florez, J., Ruiz-Cantisani, M. I., Castro-Zuluaga, C. A., & Marquez-Gutierrez, M. (2020, July 27). SMEs´ resilience model based on maturity cycle. In *Proceedings of the 18th LACCEI international multi-conference for engineering, education, and technology: Engineering, integration, and alliances for a sustainable development. "Hemispheric cooperation for competitiveness and prosperity on a knowledge-based economy"*. Latin American and Caribbean Consortium of Engineering Institutions. https://doi.org/10.18687/LACCEI2020.1.1.304

Vargo, J., & Seville, E. (2011). Crisis strategic planning for SMEs: Finding the silver lining. *International Journal of Production Research, 49*(18), 5619–5635. https://doi.org/10.1080/00207543.2011.563902

Vaughan, D. (2005). System effects: On slippery slopes, repeating negative patterns, and learning from mistake? In W. Starbuck & M. Farjoun (Eds.), *Organization at the Limit: Lessons from the Columbia disaster* (pp. 41–59). Blackwell. (Original work published 2005).

Vogus, T. J., & Sutcliffe, K. M. (2007). Organizational resilience: Towards a theory and research agenda. In *2007 IEEE international conference on systems, man and cybernetics* (pp. 3418–3422). IEEE. https://doi.org/10.1109/ICSMC.2007.4414160

Weick, K. E. (1993). The collapse of sensemaking in organizations: The Mann Gulch disaster. *Administrative Science Quarterly, 38*(4), 628–652.

Weick, K. E., & Sutcliffe, K. M. (2001). *Managing the unexpected* (1st ed.). Jossey-Bass.

Weick, K. E., & Sutcliffe, K. M. (2006). Mindfulness and the quality of organizational attention. *Organization Science, 17*(4), 514–524. https://doi.org/10.1287/orsc.1060.0196

Weick, K. E., Sutcliffe, K. M., & Obstfeld, D. (1999). Organizing for high reliability: Processes of collective mindfulness. *Research in Organizational Behavior*, (21), 81–124.

Weick, K. E., Sutcliffe, K. M., & Obstfeld, D. (2005). Organizing and the process of sensemaking. *Organization Science, 16*(4), 409–421.

Weiss, M., Högl, M., & Hartmann, S. (2015). Team-Resilienz verstehen: Konzeption eines empirischen Forschungsprojektes. *Wirtschaftspsychologie*, (4), 44–52.

Wendler, R. (2012). The maturity of maturity model research: A systematic mappin. *Information and Software Technology, 54*, 1317–1339.

Wildavsky, A. B. (1988). *Searching for safety*. Transaction Publishers.

Williams, T. A., Gruber, D. A., Sutcliffe, K. M., Shepherd, D. A., Zhao, E. Y. (2017). Organizational response to adversity: Fusing crisis management and resilience research streams. https://doi.org/10.5465/annals.2015.0134

Yigit Ozkan, B., & Spruit, M. (2022). Adaptable security maturity assessment and standardization for digital SMEs. *Journal of Computer Information Systems*, 1–23. https://doi.org/10.1080/08874417.2022.2119442

A Perspective on Resilient and Sustainable Financial Strategies for SMEs

8

Anke Haag

8.1 Introduction

The aim of this chapter is to focus on resilience in the context of sustainability and the access to finance for SMEs. Sustainability is becoming more and more important for society, policy makers and companies. To reach the aim of reducing greenhouse gas emissions and stopping global warming, a range of regulations and directives have been enacted by the European Commission within the last years. These regulations and directives set challenges for companies and have an impact on the reporting of their economic activities. The regulations are also addressed to financial institutions which lead to a stronger focus on sustainability issues of (potential) borrowers. Consequently, sustainability issues will become more and more important for the availability of capital. Listed SMEs are directly addressed by the EU regulations. However, even SMEs that might not be addressed by the EU regulations are well advised to know the requirements and standards on reporting sustainable activities to maintain their chances to have access to bank finance. This is what is meant by sustainable financial resilience in the context of this section. It means the proactive and reactive adaptability and flexibility of companies to the challenges of sustainability and the associated impact on access to finance.

The chapter starts with a short presentation of selected milestones that raised the awareness of the need for sustainability in the world and formed the basis for the regulations that are discussed in Sect. 8.3. Since the chapter is primarily addressed to practitioners and has a focus on sustainability financial resilience, it does not discuss all existing regulations in the context of sustainability. It also does not dive deeply into the issues of banking regulation. This would exceed the framework of

A. Haag (✉)
Technische Hochschule Mittelhessen, Giessen, Germany
e-mail: anke.haag@w.thm.de

S. Durst, T. Henschel (eds.), *Small and Medium-Sized Enterprise (SME) Resilience*, Management for Professionals, https://doi.org/10.1007/978-3-031-50836-3_8

this chapter and miss the main aim of it. It presents fundamental regulations and directives that have an impact on the nonfinancial disclosure of companies. This is important for understanding the requirements on providing information about the sustainability of a company. Section 8.4 highlights the sustainability risks that are assessed by financial institutions and therefore have an impact on the access to finance for SMEs. Section 8.5 picks up the main regulations, merges them to concrete challenges for companies, and derives recommendations to deal with these challenges. The chapter ends with a conclusion and presents a checklist for practitioners to handle the discussed challenges and become resilient in the context of sustainability and the access to finance.

8.2 The Long Way to Sustainability

In the early 1970s, the Club of Rome stated that the Earth system cannot support the rates of economic and population growth much beyond the year 2100 (Meadows et al., 1972). In 1983, the UN formed the World Commission on Environment and Development (WCED), also known as Brundtland Commission. The aim was to analyze the interrelationship between human activity and the environment as well as their implications for economic and environmental policy. The work of the WCED resulted in the so-called Brundtland Report "Our Common Future" (1987). The Brundtland Report not only highlighted the importance of sustainability and a sustainable transition but also established it as a key factor of economic development policy (World Commission on Environment and Development, 1987).

In the Earth Summit in Rio de Janeiro in 1992, member states agreed to set up certain goals to achieve sustainable development. The aim was to "(…) stabilise greenhouse gas concentrations in the atmosphere at a level that would prevent dangerous anthropogenic interference with the climate system" (United Nations, 1992).

In the 2015 Paris Agreement on Climate Change (COP21), countries reconfirmed the target to keep the average global temperature increase well below 2 °C and as close as possible to 1.5 °C above pre-industrial levels (United Nations, 2015).

To support the sustainable transition, the UN developed the "Agenda 2030" (2030 Agenda for Sustainable Development) which includes 17 Sustainable Development Goals (SDGs). These goals address areas of particular importance for the planet and humanity and are to be achieved around the world by 2030. The 17 SDGs seek to strengthen the social, economic, and environmental dimensions of sustainable transition (United Nations, 2015).

It is often stated that the success of sustainable development depends on the successful shift from fossil energy to renewable or carbon-free energies. In this regard, all states need to establish mechanisms and regulations for a successful sustainable transition (United Nations, 2015). To measure or identify sustainable issues, these are classified as environmental, social, and governmental issues (ESG) (United Nations, 2004).

The increasing importance of ESG aspects is also reflected in regulatory frameworks of the EU and its institutions. It has an extensive impact on companies of all size and age. In the "2030 Climate target plan," the EU member states agreed on (1) a greenhouse gas emissions reduction of at least 55%, (2) an increase of at least 32% of renewable energy sources, and (3) a rise of at least 32.5% energy efficiency, all compared to 1990 (EU-Commission, 2020a).

All of this has consequences on the regulations of companies which in turn also affect SMEs. SMEs are well advised to know these regulations in order to be able to build sustainable financial resilience.

8.3 Selected Regulations in the Context of Sustainability

Section 8.2 has highlighted some of the main regulations to achieve climate neutrality in the EU by 2050. These regulations are also intended to promote sustainable business practices. The financial service industry is considered as one important key player in helping to fund the sustainable transition. Governments and companies intend to reach the SDGs by allocating capital for activities that foster sustainability. However, additional private investments will be needed to reach the ambitious aims.

Sustainable investments became very popular for private investors within the last decade (Forum nachhaltige Geldanlagen, 2022). The rising popularity also promoted the phenomenon of greenwashing in the marketplace for sustainable investments. Greenwashing is a misleading or false communication about the impact of sustainability on a firm or financial instrument. It commonly occurs when firms declare to be greener than they are (EU-Commission, 2020c).

Uncertainty about the actual sustainable impact of a firm or financial instrument may lead to reservations from private investors concerning sustainable investments and could become a threat for the whole sustainable transformation. Therefore, the European Green Deal and the Action Plan on Financing Sustainable Growth contain a range of regulations that seek for an increasing transparency of sustainability criteria for the decision-making processes concerning investments.

Action Plan: Financing Sustainable Growth

To achieve the aims of the Agenda 2030, around 520 billion Euros in additional private and public investment per year will be needed by 2030 (EU-Commission, 2021a).

For this purpose, the EU Commission launched the Action Plan: Financing Sustainable Growth in 2018. The plan includes three main fields of action:

1. reorient capital flows towards sustainable investment in order to achieve sustainable and inclusive growth;
2. manage financial risks stemming from climate change, resource depletion, environmental degradation and social issues; and
3. foster transparency and long-termism in financial and economic activity. (EU-Commission, 2018)

Several legislative acts were adopted to put the plan into action. Two important legislative acts in the context of this paper are the EU Taxonomy (Regulation (EU)

2020/852) which will be explained in more detail later and the Sustainable Finance Disclosure Regulation (Regulation (EU) 2019/2088). The Sustainable Finance Disclosure Regulation (SFDR) seeks to enhance transparency *in the financial market and prevent greenwashing. It addresses financial market participants like investment firms, provider of* insurance-based investment products, or financial advisors. *Those market participants must provide information* about sustainability matters like sustainability risk policies, adverse sustainability impacts, or the integration of sustainability risks (EU-Commission, 2020b).

European Green Deal

The European Green Deal entails the commitment of all EU member states to become the first climate-neutral continent by 2050. This includes the aim to reduce greenhouse gas emissions by 55% compared to 1990 levels (EU-Commission, 2019). As one part of the European Green Deal, the European Commission pledges to review the nonfinancial reporting standards of Directive 2013/34/EU of the European Parliament and of the Council (DIRECTIVE (EU) 2022/2464). Directive 2013/34/EU addresses annual and consolidated financial statements and related reports such as management reports. It was amended in 2022 by the Corporate Sustainability Reporting Directive (DIRECTIVE (EU) 2022/2464) which will be discussed in the following.

Corporate Sustainability Reporting Directive (CSRD)

For corporations outside the financial services sector, the most important applicable regulations are the Corporate Sustainability Reporting Directive (CSRD) and the EU Taxonomy.

The CSRD is derived from the Nonfinancial Reporting Directive (NFRD). It entered into force on January 5, 2023, and expands the nonfinancial reporting standards as well as the scope of entities obliged to report.

Since 2018, NFRD required public interest companies (e.g., banks and insurers) with more than 500 employees to report on issues about environmental pollution, social responsibility, human rights, and diversity (NFRD report). These firms will have to apply the new rules for the first time in the financial year 2024, for reports to be published in 2025. In addition, other large companies as well as listed SMEs will have to publish CSRD reports from 2026 to 2027, respectively, for the financial year 2025 and 2026, respectively (EU-Commission, 2022). A detailed overview about the set of required companies, criteria, and first reporting year is available in Table 8.1.

The CSRD addresses a by far broader set of companies than the NFRD. While around 500 entities were obligated to publish an NFRD report in Germany (Europe: ~12,000 entities), the CSRD will apply to around 15,000 entities (Europe: ~50,000 entities) (Kaiser-Neubauer, 2022; EU-Commission, 2021b).

The CSRD not only applies to more corporates than the NFRD; it also includes more comprehensive and more harmonized reporting standards than the NFRD. In particular, the CSRD reporting requires information on:

Table 8.1 Timeline Transposition CSRD

Category	Criteria	Start date
Public interest companies (e.g., banks and insurers)	More than 500 employees	Reporting in 2025 for the financial year 2024
Listed entities, as well as large entities	Meets two of three criteria: 1. More than 250 employees 2. More than €40 million net turnover 3. More than €20 million balance sheet total	Reporting in 2026 for the financial year 2025
SMEs listed on a regulated EU market (excluding micro-undertakings)	Meets two of three criteria: 1. An average of 50 employees during the financial year 2. Net turnover: €8 million 3. Balance sheet total: €4 million	Reporting in 2027 for the financial year 2026

Source: DIRECTIVE (EU) 2022/2464 (Article 5); Directive 2013/34/EU (Article 3 paragraph 4, 3,2)

- The resilience of the company's business model and strategy for sustainability risks
- Plans ensuring compatibility regarding climate neutrality targets by 2050
- Time-bound sustainability goals including targets for reducing greenhouse gas emission and progress in achieving those targets
- Sustainability incentive systems for administrative, management, and supervisory bodies
- Principal sustainability including actions taken to manage these risks (DIRECTIVE (EU) 2022/2464; Art. 19a Directive 2013/34/EU)

The CSRD seeks to enhance transparency about the actual contribution to solve ecological and social challenges. This is linked to the so-called double materiality which is already a part of the NFRD but becomes clearer and more mandatory in the CSRD. The double materiality contains an outside-in perspective (financial materiality) and an inside-out perspective (impact materiality). The inside-out perspective comprises the impact of sustainability issues on the business itself and the value of the company. The outside-in perspective expounds the company's environmental and social impact (EU-Commission, 2022).

EU Taxonomy

Clear definitions for environmentally sustainable economic activities are pivotal to direct capital flows toward sustainable investments. Such definitions are given by the EU Taxonomy which entered into force in 2020. The EU Taxonomy is a *classification system for economic activities. It is intended to protect inventors from greenwashing, to help companies to determine and even enhance their own sustainability status, and to reallocate investments to sustainable projects.*

The EU Taxonomy Regulation sets mandatory requirements for disclosure: In 2022, companies that fall under the scope of the NFRD as well as financial market participants that fall under the scope of SFRD must disclose for the first time for the financial year 2021. From the financial year 2024 onwards, the number of companies required to disclose will expand according to the CFRD (as illustrated in Table 8.1).

Following the EU Taxonomy, an economic activity is environmentally sustainable (or "aligned" with the EU Taxonomy) when it substantially contributes to one or more of the following environmental objectives: climate change mitigation; climate change adaptation; the sustainable use and protection of water and marine resources; the transition to a circular economy; pollution prevention and control; and the protection and restoration of biodiversity and ecosystems. Additionally, it must not significantly harm any of the environmental objectives, is carried out in compliance with the minimum safeguards, and complies with certain technical screening criteria (EU-Commission, 2020c). The EU Commission will publish delegated regulations for the technical screening standards for all six environmental objectives step by step. From the financial year 2024 onwards, the disclosure must include all six environmental objectives.

To make sure, that the taxonomy addresses all relevant sectors, the identification of economic activities is oriented to the EU classification "Nomenclature européenne des activités économiques" (NACE). This means that NACE code forms the basis of eligible activities under the EU Taxonomy. It is important to know that business activities are only eligible for alignment assessment if they are listed in the NACE (and therefore in the EU Taxonomy).

Reportable entities must provide three "sustainable" key performance indicators (KPI): the turnover generated from taxonomy-aligned activities, the capital expenditures (CapEx), and the operating expenditures (OpEx) related to environmentally sustainable processes or assets. The KPI are specified in the COMMISSION DELEGATED REGULATION (EU) 2021/2178 from July 2021.

Where It All Comes Together—The Sustainability Finance Strategy

The EU Taxonomy and the disclosures of SFRD and CSRD are two important pillars for a sustainable financial framework according to the Action Plan: Financing Sustainable Growth from 2018. The third pillar is built by investment tools such as standards and green labels to increase transparency and mitigate greenwashing for sustainability-oriented investors.

Based on these three pillars, the European Commission published the new Strategy for Financing the Transition to a Sustainable Economy (Sustainability Finance Strategy) in 2021 as illustrated in Fig. 8.1 (EU Commission, 2021c).

The strategy contains four key areas which mainly address the financial sector for achieving the aspired transition:

1. The strategy provides instruments and policies that enable companies of all economic sectors to finance their transition plans whatever their starting point.

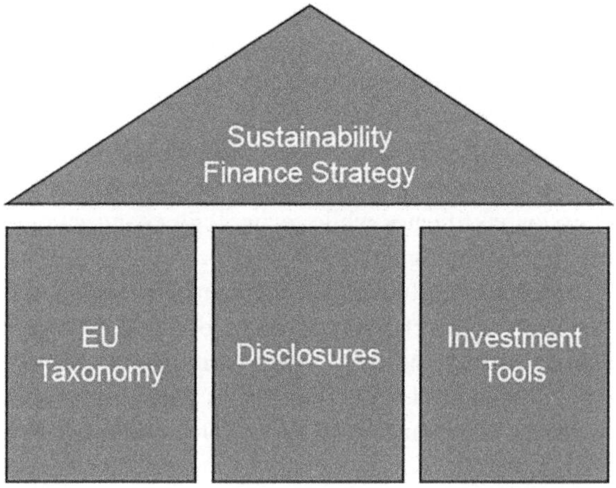

Fig. 8.1 Sustainability Finance Strategy. (Source: Own illustration)

2. The strategy considers the needs of individuals as well as SMEs and enables them better access to sustainable finances.
3. The strategy defines how the financial sector can contribute to reach the aims of the EU Green Deal while becoming more resilient and proactive against greenwashing.
4. The strategy points out how to support an international consensus about the ambitious agenda of sustainable finance (EU Commission, 2021c).

Key area 3 addresses the increase of the economic and financial resilience against sustainability risks. This includes the integration of sustainability risks in financial reporting standards; the systematic and transparent capture of relevant sustainability risks in credit ratings and credit outlooks; and the integration of sustainability risks in risk management systems of banks, including climate change stress tests by banks (EU Commission, 2021c). While these measures have a direct impact on financial institutions, they also have an influence on SMEs.

8.4 Sustainability Risks

The Sustainability Finance Strategy focuses on sustainability risks. Consequently, it is advisable to discuss what is meant by this term. According to the European Commission, a sustainability risk means "(…) an environmental, social or governance event or condition that, if it occurs, could cause a negative material impact on the value of the investment" (EU-Commission, 2020b). Sustainability risks are often also referred to as ESG risks. From the perspective of a financial institution, sustainability risks "(…) have or may potentially have significant negative impacts on the assets, financial and earnings situation, or reputation (…)" (BaFin, 2019). Basically, two main categories of sustainability risks can be distinguished: physical risks and transition risks.

Physical risks arise from natural hazards (e.g., heatwaves, floods, storms, droughts, etc.) but also from long-term climate changes and have a direct impact on assets and/or productive capacity. They may also have indirect negative impacts on supply chains or business models.

Transition risks arise from policy or technology changes on the way to a low-carbon economy. Policy changes might result in increased prices or shortage of emission certificates while technology changes could result in the replacement of existing technologies (BaFin, 2019).

Financial institutions such as banks are affected by both risks in several ways. They can be affected directly, e.g., by flood damage to a bank building. Banks can also be affected indirectly when their customers are reacting to sustainability risks, e.g., through production disruptions, changes in sales opportunities, or damages to buildings or production facilities. This can result in higher loan defaults for banks (BaFin, 2019).

While nonfinancial institutions are required to publish the KPIs CapEx and OpEx to prove their sustainability, financial institutions are required to publish another KPI: the Green Asset Ratio. This is based on the delegated regulation (EU) 2021/2178 that supplements the EU Taxonomy. From the financial year 2023 onwards, financial institutions must disclose the proportion of exposures related to taxonomy-aligned activities compared to their total assets. The Green Asset Ratio shall demonstrate to what extent a financial institution provides loans for taxonomy-aligned activities (EU-Commission, 2021d).

Consequently, banks must assess the taxonomy conformity of their borrowers. They are required to systematically identify, disclose, and manage sustainability risks as part of their risk management. This includes regular climate stress testing by supervisors as well as banks (European Central Bank, 2020).

8.5 The "Sustainable Financial Challenge" for SMEs

The previous sections have highlighted the importance of a sustainable transition for the planet, the society, and the economy. Moreover, they have illustrated some of the main financial regulations to achieve the sustainable targets of the EU Commission. The achievement of these ambitious aims is a challenge for financial as well as nonfinancial institutions.

Sustainable financial resilience in the context of this article means the proactive and reactive adaptability and flexibility of companies to these challenges.

This section picks up the main challenges and provides suggestions for a resilient handling of these challenges for SMEs.

It was demonstrated that the CSRD will become mandatory for many companies and increases the requirements on reporting standards. In a first step, companies should assess whether they must provide a CSRD report or not. If so, these companies must know the reporting requirements of the CSRD. Among others, the CSRD requires information on the resilience of the company's business model and strategy for dealing with sustainability risks. This means that companies must know their sustainability risks and need to demonstrate how to manage these risks. This has an impact on the risk management system of these companies. Risks must be identified, measured, and classified.

The provision of information about sustainability risks and nonfinancial information presupposes the availability of the relevant information and data. Many companies still do not have standardized processes to deliver these data (Henschel et al., 2022; PricewaterhouseCoopers, 2022). Consequently, companies need to adjust existing or establish new processes and systems to be able to collect and provide necessary data for their reporting.

Another requirement of the CSRD is the disclosure of time-bound sustainability targets including targets for reducing greenhouse gas emission, and progress in achieving those targets. This requires the definition of precise sustainability targets as well as the measurement of their achievement. The CSRD also requires reporting on sustainability incentive systems for administrative, management, and supervisory bodies. To fulfill these requirements, many companies need to initially establish sustainability incentive systems as a study of PricewaterhouseCoopers from 2022 has demonstrated (PricewaterhouseCoopers, 2022).

However, even if a company is not required to provide a CSRD reporting, it is advisable to become familiar with the requirements of the nonfinancial disclosure. This is justified by the increasing consumer awareness for ecological and sustainable entrepreneurship. Sustainability reporting can be considered as an effective tool to enhance a company's reputation (Gomez-Trujillo et al., 2020; Kim, 2019).

The EU Taxonomy sets mandatory requirements on disclosure. The classification system for economic activities intends to increase transparency and comparability of sustainability issues and to prevent greenwashing. Consequently, even companies that voluntarily decide to provide nonfinancial disclosure are well advised to apply the requirements of the EU Taxonomy. This allows detailed insights in their actual environmental impact and the sustainable contribution of its economic activities.

Important to notice is the fact that the EU Taxonomy does not define sustainability on a company level. It defines sustainability and technical screening criteria for separate economic activities. Consequently, an entire company cannot be defined as sustainable but some or even all its underlying activities can be.

To find out whether an economic activity can be considered as sustainable or not, it must be checked for its eligibility. Only those activities that have defined technical screening criteria are taxonomy eligible. This check can be very challenging. A good approach is to categorize all activities (and not only the main business activities) according to the NACE codes which form the basis of eligible activities and technical screening criteria under the EU Taxonomy. However, the descriptions of the taxonomy do not always correspond precisely to the scope of each NACE code. The EU Commission itself published the information that "the NACE codes should only be understood as indicative and should not prevail over the specific definition of the activity provided in its description" (EU Commission, 2021e).

Activities that can be defined as eligible must be checked for taxonomy alignment in a next step. Taxonomy aligned are eligible economic activities that make a

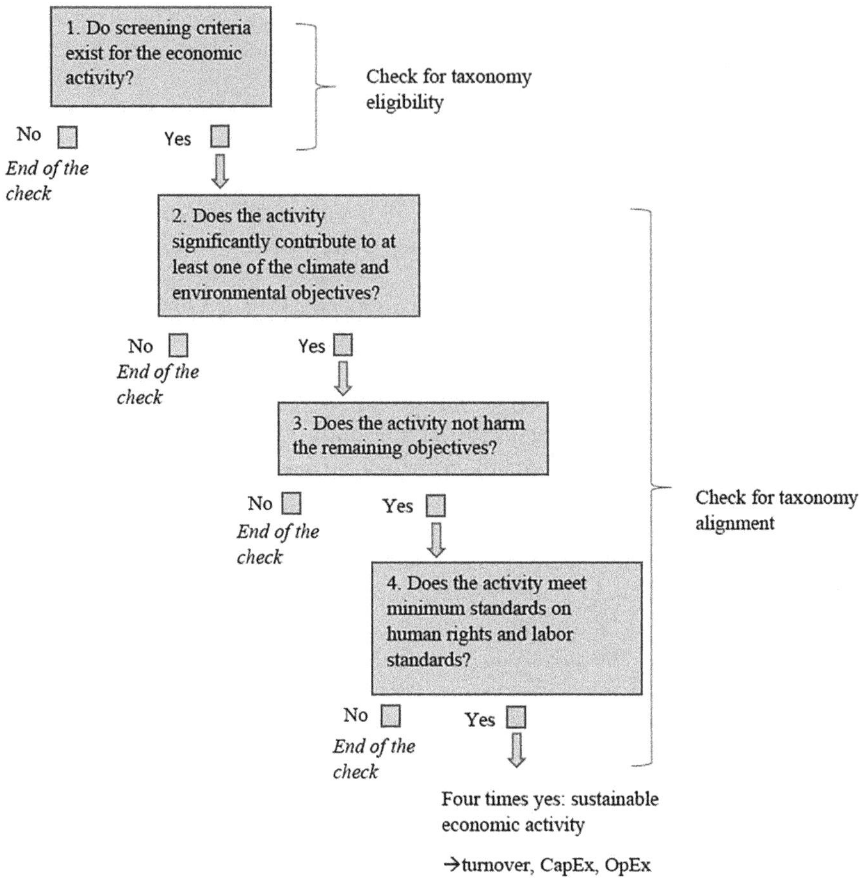

Fig. 8.2 Check for taxonomy eligibility and alignment. (Source: Own illustration)

substantial contribution to at least one of the climate and environmental objectives, do not harm the remaining objectives, and meet minimum standards on human rights and labor standards (EU-Commission, 2020c). How to check for taxonomy eligibility and alignment is illustrated in Fig. 8.2.

For eligible and aligned economic activities, turnover, CapEx, and OpEx must be reported (EU-Commission, 2020c). To be able to derive the respective shares for eligible and aligned economic activities, a company is well advised to install a good data management, clearly defined processes, and technical solutions.

As mentioned above, even companies that are not required to provide a CSRD reporting might benefit from providing a nonfinancial reporting corresponding to the EU regulations. This can be justified by growing customer awareness for sustainability and growing regulation pressure. A nonfinancial reporting which is adapted to the EU regulations and requirements increases transparency and facilitates comparability for customers, suppliers, and investors. It might protect against greenwashing accusation and attract investors looking for sustainable investments.

The access to finance will become more and more reliant on sustainability issues. That applies for private investors as well as financial institutions. Financial institutions must disclose a Green Asset Ratio—the proportion of exposures related to taxonomy-aligned activities compared to their total assets. The Green Asset Ratio shall demonstrate to what extent a financial institution provides loans for taxonomy-aligned activities. This means that financial institutions must check the taxonomy conformity of their borrowers (EU-Commission, 2021d). Consequently, even companies that are not obliged to report on sustainability issues will need such a reporting when applying for a loan. Companies that have included sustainability in their strategy and are able to provide relevant data will improve their negotiation position with lenders (Englert et al., 2023).

Moreover, financial institutions must analyze to what extent sustainability risks affect the default risk of potential borrowers. This means that financial institutions will define general risk indicators or sustainability ratings to evaluate these risks (European Central Bank, 2020).

As a consequence, sustainability risks may make loans more expensive for borrowers (Englert et al., 2023). However, it is also possible that financial institutions apply exclusion criteria to deny a loan application to reduce their own sustainability and reputation risks (Global Sustainable Investment Alliance, 2020). Companies that (voluntarily) provide nonfinancial disclosure to demonstrate their sustainable activities will have better access to finance in the future (Englert et al., 2023). This presupposes that companies know, measure, and report their sustainability risks and sustainable economic activities.

This highlights the connection between sustainability and finance. Sustainability will become more and more important for the access to finance. SMEs that are aware of this and create the necessary transparency about sustainable issues will build up a sustainable financial resilience that might become essential in the future (Awaysheh et al., 2020; Bigot & Germon, 2021; Henschel et al., 2022).

8.6 Conclusion and Checklist for Sustainable Financial Resilience

All this demonstrates that even companies that are not required to provide a CSRD reporting are well advised to report on their sustainable activities. To enable transparency and comparability, these companies should also know and apply the regulations and recommendations of the European Commission. This is important for the company's reputation as well as their access to finance. Therefore, it is important to be familiar with the relevant regulations as early as possible. Resilience is the key to a successful future of a company. This also applies for resilience in the context of sustainability challenges. The active confrontation with these challenges and regulations can mitigate uncertainty and make companies more resilient. A clear demonstration of one's own sustainable economic activities and standpoint can ensure a sustainable access to finance. For all this, companies need resources—human resources as well as financial resources. They may need to build up special know-how, new structures, new data management, and/or new IT solutions. However, all of this can be considered as an investment in a sustainable and resilient future.

In this paper, selected sustainable regulations and challenges are illustrated. Moreover, recommendations for meeting these challenges to build up sustainable financial resilience are provided. The paper ends with Table 8.2 that merges the challenges with appropriate actions and provides a path to increase sustainable financial resilience.

Table 8.2 Checklist on how to deal with selected sustainable challenges

Challenge	Suggestions for resilient actions
CSRD will become mandatory for many companies	☐ Clarify if company is required to provide a CSRD reporting
CSRD brings higher reporting requirements/nonfinancial reporting	☐ Become familiar with the requirements of the nonfinancial disclosure ☐ Adopt a sustainability strategy ☐ Know your sustainability risks ☐ Adopt your risk management and processes to collect information about sustainability risks and nonfinancial data ☐ Set time-bound sustainability target and measure the achievement ☐ Establish sustainability incentive systems
Increasing consumer awareness for ecological and sustainable issues	☐ Be aware of the positive impact of sustainability on the company's reputation ☐ Provide a sustainability reporting (even if it is not required)
EU Taxonomy defines technical screening criteria and preconditions for sustainable activities	☐ Screen all economic activities (not only the main business economic activities) for eligibility ☐ Know NACE codes and descriptions of EU Taxonomy ☐ Check technical screening criteria for all eligible activities to verify the alignment
Reporting of turnover, CapEx, and OpEx for eligible and aligned economic activities	☐ Define processes to measure the share of turnover, CapEx, and OpEx for eligible and aligned activities ☐ Provide necessary technical standards
Financial institutions must check the taxonomy conformity of their borrowers	☐ Access to finance will more and more depend on sustainability issues in the future ☐ Know, measure, and report sustainability risks and sustainable economic activities—this data will become necessary for a loan application ☐ Financial institutions might apply exclusion criteria to deny a loan application to reduce their own sustainability and reputation risks ☐ Know, measure, and report sustainability risks and sustainable economic activities ☐ Provide a sustainability strategy
Additional resources are needed	☐ Build up special know-how, new structures, new data management, and/or new IT solutions ☐ Make a finance plan

Source: Own illustration

References

Awaysheh, A., Heron, R., Perry, T., & Wilson, J. (2020). On the relation be-tween CSR and financial performance. *Strategic Management Journal, 41*(6), 965–987.

BaFin. (2019). *Guidance notice on dealing with sustainability risks.* https://www.bafin.de/SharedDocs/Downloads/EN/Merkblatt/dl_mb_Nachhaltigkeitsrisiken_en.pdf?__blob=publicationFile&v=5. Accessed 26 Mar 2023.

Bigot, G., & Germon, R. (2021). Resilience, digitalization, and CSR's three pillars to develop robust post-COVID MSMEs. *Journal of the International Council for Small Business, 2*(3), 167–171.

Englert, M., Glang, P., Mahlendorf, M. (2023). Was bringt's? Der Effekt einer positiven ESG-Darstellung bei der klassischen Bankfinanzierung. Der Be-trieb No. 7: 337–342.

European Central Bank. (2020). *Guide on climate-related and environ-mental risks: Supervisory expectations relating to risk management and disclosure.* https://www.bankingsupervision.europa.eu/ecb/pub/pdf/ssm.202011finalguideonclimate-relatedandenvironmentalrisks~58213f6564.en.pdf. Accessed 25 Apr 2023.

EU-Commission. (2018). *Action plan: Financing sustainable growth, (COM (2018) 97 final).* https://eur-lex.europa.eu/legal-content/EN/TXT/PDF/?uri=CELEX:52018DC0097&from=EN. Accessed 26 Feb 2023.

EU-Commission. (2019). *The European Green Deal, (COM (2019) 640 final).* https://eur-lex.europa.eu/resource.html?uri=cellar:b828d165-1c22-11ea-8c1f-01aa75ed71a1.0002.02/DOC_1&format=PDF. Accessed 26 Feb 2023.

EU-Commission. (2020a). *Stepping up Europe's 2030 climate ambition - Investing in a climate-neutral future for the benefit of our people, (COM (2020) 562 final).* https://eur-lex.europa.eu/legal-content/EN/TXT/PDF/?uri=CELEX:52020DC0562&from=DE. Accessed 26 Feb 2023.

EU-Commission. (2020b). *REGULATION (EU) 2019/2088, sustainability-related disclosures in the financial services sector.* https://eur-lex.europa.eu/legal-content/EN/TXT/PDF/?uri=CELEX:02019R2088-20200712. Accessed 06 May 2023.

EU-Commission. (2020c). *REGULATION (EU) 2020/852, EU-Taxonomy.* https://eur-lex.europa.eu/legal-content/EN/TXT/PDF/?uri=CELEX:32020R0852. Accessed 06 May 2023.

EU-Commission. (2021a). *The EU sustainable finance framework.* https://thedocs.worlbank.org/en/doc/8dea75f98f65a824e389bdbd422f06d8-0430012022/related/Andreas-Rajchl-EU-Commission.pdf. Accessed 7 Apr 2023.

EU-Commission. (2021b). *Sustainable finance and EU taxonomy: Com-mission takes further steps to channel money towards sustainable activities.* https://ec.europa.eu/commission/presscorner/detail/en/IP_21_1804. Accessed 1 Mar 2023.

EU-Commission. (2021c). *Strategy for financing the transition to a sustainable economy.* https://eur-lex.europa.eu/resource.html?uri=cellar:9f5e7e95-df06-11eb-895a-01aa75ed71a1.0001.02/DOC_1&format=PDF. Accessed 27 Mar 2023.

EU-Commission. (2021d). *COMMISSION DELEGATED REGULATION (EU) 2021/2178 of 6 July 2021 supplementing Regulation (EU) 2020/852 of the European Parliament and of the Council.* https://eur-lex.europa.eu/legal-conent/EN/TXT/PDF/?uri=CELEX:32021R2178&from=DE. Accessed 08 Apr 2023.

EU-Commission. (2021e). *COMMISSION DELEGATED REGULATION (EU) 2021/2139 of 4 June 2021 supplementing Regulation (EU) 2020/852 of the European Parliament and of the Council.* https://eur-lex.europa.eu/legal-content/EN/TXT/PDF/?uri=CELEX:32021R2139. Accessed 20 May 2023.

EU-Commission. (2022). *DIRECTIVE (EU), 2022/2464 Corporate Sustainability Reporting Directive.* https://eur-lex.europa.eu/legal-content/EN/TXT/PDF/?uri=CELEX:32022L2464&from=DE. Accessed 25 Mar 2023.

Forum nachhaltige Geldanlagen. (2022). Marktberichte nachhaltige Geld-anlagen. Deutschland, Österreich und die Schweiz. https://www.umweltbundesamt.de/daten/private-haushalte-konsum/konsum-produkte/gruene-produkte-marktzahlen/marktdaten-bereich-finanzen#freiwillige-kompensation-von-treibhausgasemissionen. Accessed 1 Mar 2023.

Global Sustainable Investment Alliance. (2020). *Global sustainable in-vestment review 2020.* https://www.gsi-alliance.org/wp-content/uploads/2021/08/GSIR-20201.pdf. Accessed 25 Apr 2023.

Gomez-Trujillo, A. M., Velez-Ocampo, J., & Gonzalez-Perez, M. A. (2020). A literature review on the causality between sustainability and corporate reputation: What goes first? *Management of Environmental Quality: An International Journal, 31*(2), 406–430.

Henschel, T., Florio, C., Jharni, S., & Stellmacher, M. (2022). The impact of corporate social responsibility on advancing the enterprise risk management performance relationship in small and medium-sized enterprises. *Journal of the International Council for Small Business, 3*(4), 321–328.

Kaiser-Neubauer, Ch. (2022). *Klimacheck für Betriebe*. SZ-online, 15.03.2022. https://www.sueddeutsche.de/kolumne/nachhaltigkeitsbericht-umweltbilanz-eu-1.5547738. Accessed 14 Mar 2023.

Kim, S. (2019). The process model of corporate social responsibility (CSR) communication: CSR communication and its relationship with consumers' CSR knowledge, trust, and corporate reputation perception. *Journal of Business Ethics, 154*(4), 1143–1159.

Meadows, D., Randers, J., & Behrens, W., III. (1972). *Limits to economic growth: A report for the Club of Rome's project on the predicament of mankind.* Universe Books.

PricewaterhouseCoopers. (2022). *EU-Taxonomie – Nichtfinanzielle Be-richterstattung im Wandel.* https://www.pwc.de/de/im-fokus/accounting-reporting/eu-taxonomie-nachhaltigkeitsberichterstattung-im-wandel.html. Accessed 22 Apr 2023.

United Nations. (2015). *Paris Agreement.* https://unfccc.int/sites/default/files/english_paris_agreement.pdf. Accessed 27 Feb 2023.

United Nations. (1992). *United Nations framework convention on climate change.* https://unfccc.int/resource/docs/convkp/convger.pdf. Accessed 27 Feb 2023.

United Nations, The Global Compact. (2004). *Who cares wins: Connecting the financial markets to a changing World United Nations.* https://www.unglobalcompact.org/docs/issues_doc/Financial_markets/who_cares_who_wins.pdf. Accessed 16 Jul 2023.

World Commission on Environment and Development. (1987). *Report of the World Commission on environment and development: Our common future.* https://sustainabledevelopment.un.org/content/documents/5987our-common-future.pdf. Accessed 27 Feb 2023.

Playing to Win: Enhancing Resilience in SMEs with Gamification 9

Ilka Heinze

9.1 Introduction

In today's dynamic and unpredictable business environment, small and medium-sized enterprises (SMEs) face numerous challenges that can significantly impact their sustainability and success as they are particularly subjected to resource constraints and hence more vulnerable to external shocks (Ratten, 2020). In recent years, studies on the resilience of SMEs[1] are increasing, however, there are still some gaps in the literature. Conz et al. (2017) state that it is widely unknown which strategies positively or negatively influence the resilience of such enterprises and that results are largely indecisive.

However, there is already some evidence that achieving resilience in SMEs is not without its obstacles. Limited resources, constrained budgets, and a lack of specialized training programs pose significant challenges for SME leaders and their teams (Chhatwani et al., 2022; Conz et al., 2017; Pathak et al., 2023). Traditional approaches to training and development often fall short in addressing the unique needs of SMEs, leaving them vulnerable to disruptions and unable to harness their full potential (Heinze & Henschel, 2021). Lately, gamification and serious games as new approaches to create engaging and immersive learning experiences have gained recognition as powerful tools for training and development (de Rosa & De Gloria, 2021; Friedrich et al., 2020; Hawthorn et al., 2021; Hellström et al., 2023; Löffler

[1] Enterprises with <250 employees and ≤ € 50 m turnover or ≤ € 43 m balance sheet total fall under the EU definition (https://single-market-economy.ec.europa.eu/smes/sme-definition_en)

I. Heinze (✉)
Hochschulen Fresenius, Berlin, Germany
e-mail: ilka.heinze@hs-fresenius.de

S. Durst, T. Henschel (eds.), *Small and Medium-Sized Enterprise (SME) Resilience*, Management for Professionals, https://doi.org/10.1007/978-3-031-50836-3_9

et al., 2021; Silic et al., 2020), offering a unique blend of entertainment and education by its combination of playfulness and technology.

This chapter contributes to knowledge by (1) provision of a framework of multiple layers of resilience and their interactions in SME; (2) introduction of the offerings held by serious games and gamification as a transformative learning approach; and (3) discussion of key benefits, strategies, and considerations for implementing gamified processes and serious games in SMEs to develop and strengthen their resilience capabilities.

Through a combined analysis of relevant literature and practical insights, this chapter will provide valuable guidance for SME leaders, trainers, and professionals seeking effective methods to enhance resilience within their organizations. By embracing the power of gamification, SMEs can unlock new avenues for growth, innovation, and sustainable success in an ever-evolving business landscape. In the following, I will provide an overview of organizational resilience and explain its significance for SMEs. Thereafter, both concepts serious games and gamification will be defined and their application in order to support learning, skill development, and behavior change as well as their potential organizational development will be discussed. In the core part, I will present a conceptual framework that illustrates the application of serious games and gamified processes for resilience building. Specific resilience factors that can be targeted through gamification and serious games, such as adaptability, resourcefulness, and agility will be identified, and ways to foster learning, problem-solving, and decision-making skills necessary for developing resilience are discussed. The chapter concludes with a summary of key points discussed in the chapter, emphasizing on the potential of serious games in fostering organizational resilience in SMEs as well as challenges and limitations SMEs might face with the implementation. Furthermore, areas for future research in the context of gamified processes to increase SMEs' organizational resilience are highlighted.

9.2 The Concept of Resilience and its SME Particularities

In the following, light will be shed to the general understanding of resilience and its characteristics that apply to SMEs. First, several theories of the concept will be introduced, followed by a discussion of research focused on single as well as multiple levels of resilience. Finally, I conclude with the presentation of a conceptual framework that is suitable for capturing the multiple levels of resilience, both in their entirety and the interactions between these levels.

9.2.1 Understanding Resilience and its Characteristics for SMEs

Following Bruhn (2021) who based her definition on the works of Bengel and Lyssenko (2016), resilience should be understood as a dynamic process consisting of human-environment interaction and developing over time. A resilient system can maintain or limit its functionality in a tolerable and gradual manner in the wake of external or internal adversities (Zander, 2019). Typical practices are persistence, adaption, or transformation, encompassing preparedness, risk avoidance, as well as flexible response capabilities (Buyl et al., 2022). Additionally, Bonß (2015) raises an intriguing question about the interpretation and significance of resilience for vulnerable or already disrupted systems, stating that on the one hand, resilience stands for a fundamental defense against changes and the restoration of "old" states of normality, while on the other hand, resilience can also refer to a successful adaptation to irreversibly changed conditions. This implies that systems must undergo self-transformation to survive and discover new states of normality. Also, Buyl et al. (2022) draw attention to the fact that resilient behavior goes beyond a mere "bouncing back."

9.2.2 Layer of Individual Resilience: Personal Resources and Entrepreneurial Resilience

Early research focused on individual employee resilience, drawing from positive psychology (DesJardine et al., 2019). According to Duchek et al. (2021), individuals possess personal resilience resources that support their ability to navigate through crises. These resources include certain traits, skills, and supportive factors that help individuals cope with challenging situations. While some of these resources may be innate, others can be acquired and developed over time. Key resources for individual resilience include optimism, mindfulness, and social support. Another research strand relevant to this chapter encompasses studies on the resilience of entrepreneurs. Since many small and medium-sized enterprises (SMEs) are owner-managed, their individual resilience is also of great importance. Ahmed et al. (2022) studied stress, resilience, and coping together in order to understand how entrepreneurs develop psychological resilience and demand future research in regard to the nature of stress, examination of other life domains, resilience as an outcome of entrepreneurship, individual differences in resilience trajectories, as well as the dark side of resilience. The potential risk of negative effects of entrepreneurial resilience have also been highlighted by Hartmann et al. (2022), who—similarly to Ahmed et al.—carried out a systematic review of the literature and put forward their agenda for future research. The researchers raise the question on how psychological resilience can help to facilitate the sustainable functioning of the new venture during initiation, engagement in, and performance of entrepreneurial endeavors and suggest further research focused on the link between entrepreneurs' psychological resilience and organizational resilience. Research by Pathak et al. (2023) indicates an effect of entrepreneurial resiliency is manifested in various forms affecting the way SMEs deal with adversities. The authors propose a framework based on seven characteristics of entrepreneurial resilience, such as a resilient mindset, a sense of duty, resiliency as a business routine, resource-based behavior, time-based behavior, and pursuing a focus.

9.2.3 Layer of Team Resilience: The Role of Effective Teamwork

Turning to the team level, Duchek et al. (2021) state that it is crucial to establish a shared foundation for effective teamwork. Collaboration within a team depends not only on the individual abilities and characteristics of team members but also on collective resources that foster a positive team environment. These resources include shared values, trust and respect among team members, and a positive team climate. Furthermore, Hillmann (2021) draws attention to a certain stream of research that focuses on the role of managers and employees for organizational resilience, highlighting the highly diverse nature of papers, covering aspects such as positive relationships at work, the role of CEOs, the importance of well-treated employees, of social ties of organizational members to the role of strategic human resources. Furthermore, she pays attention to positive organizational behavior that creates optimal work conditions for people, groups, as well as the whole organization and the distinction of definitions of resilience being either state-like or trait-like. State-like resilience is defined as a positive dynamic capability to cope with adversities and risks (Luthans, 2002) that can be developed through training, whereas a trait-like resilience is defined as a relatively stable characteristic of the individual, group, or the organization (Coutu, 2002).

9.2.4 Layer of Organizational Resilience: Capacities Required on Firm Level

The review provided by Hillmann (2021) also addresses organizational resilience. The author identifies another stream of research focused on additional factors that can have influence on organizational resilience, such as different facilitation of social, financial, and human capital in female- and male-owned businesses (Danes et al., 2009), as well as in family and nonfamily businesses (Amann & Jaussaud, 2012). Additionally, learning is an especially important prerequisite for smaller businesses (Glover, 2012). Further factors are creativity (Richtnér & Löfsten, 2014) as well as social resources, mindset, and engagement in resourcefulness (Williams & Shepherd, 2016). Similarly, Duchek et al. (2021) highlight the fragmented nature of emerging literature, aiming to provide insights from a variety of research areas, such as crisis and risk management, organizational ambidexterity, organizational reliability, business model adaptability, and corporate social responsibility (CSR). The authors sum up that organizational resilience requires several capabilities, including time, capital, and human resources, and that the examination of these capabilities asks for a process perspective, based on more qualitative and ethnographic approaches. Similarly, Hillmann (2021) raises the question of how organizational resilience can be facilitated by human development, such as education of managers to perceive threats as opportunities and take on a more positive behavior in times of crisis and adversity.

9.2.5 SME Resilience from a Multilevel Perspective

Sullivan-Taylor and Branicki (2011) take a closer look at the size of organizations and found that size interrogates the relationship between resilience capabilities, such as flexibility and adaptation. The authors state that SMEs might take a different approach to resilience, due to lack of resourcefulness. Less capacity to identify and deal with problems in order to avoid adversity hinders SMEs in their ability to build up organizational resilience. Duchek et al. (2021) focus on strengthening resilience to prepare organizations for turbulent times by provision of a multilevel design to manage resilience. Raetze et al. (2021) highlight that resilience in organizations must be examined as a multilevel construct consisting of individual, team-based, and organizational levels with respective interactions. Although there are similarities in the abilities and behaviors required at each level, specific resources and developmental approaches are needed. Hillmann (2021) states that currently, resilience serves as an overarching "umbrella" concept, defined by Hirsch and Levin (1999) as a collection of paradigms derived from different research areas that lack a unified theoretical framework and are seemingly disconnected. The wide range of research findings focusing on resilience in an SME context provided above are in support of Hillmann's proposal. Major influences on multiple layers of resilience in SMEs are summarized in Fig. 9.1.

The framework represents resilience as a multilevel dynamic process consisting of human-environment interaction (Bengel & Lyssenko, 2016; Bruhn, 2021) maintaining or limiting its functionality in a tolerable and gradual manner as a response to external or internal adversities. The external environment is qualified by the

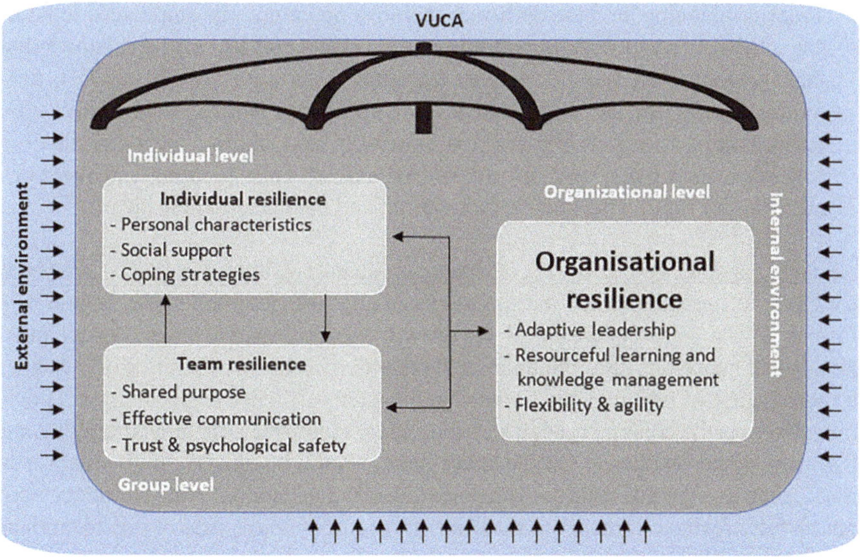

Fig. 9.1 Framework of multiple layers of resilience and their interactions in SME

acronym VUCA that stands for Volatility, Uncertainty, Complexity, and Ambiguity, representing a concept used to describe the unpredictable and rapidly changing nature of the business and organizational environments (Stiehm & Townsend, 2002). The three levels of resilience are built on their major capacities and explained as follows:

1. Drawing on Ahmed et al. (2022), DesJardine et al. (2019), Duchek et al. (2021), Hartmann et al. (2022), and Pathak et al. (2023), individual (or psychological) resilience is based on (1) personal characteristics such as optimism, mindfulness, adaptability, self-confidence, and a sense of purpose; (2) social support as availability of relationships, networks, and resources that provide emotional, informational, and practical assistance; and (3) coping strategies as problem-solving skills, positive reframing, seeking social support, practicing self-care, and maintaining a balanced lifestyle.
2. Following Coutu (2002), Duchek et al. (2021), Hillmann (2021), and Luthans (2002), team resilience is mainly based on (1) shared purpose that is collectively understood and embraced by team members and hence enabling the team to navigate challenges and setbacks effectively; (2) effective communication and collaboration effecting in strong communication skills, open dialogue, and collaborative problem-solving; and (3) trust and psychological safety that create an environment where individuals feel comfortable taking risks, expressing their opinions, and learning from failures.
3. As stated by Amann and Jaussaud (2012), Danes et al. (2009), Duchek et al. (2021), Glover (2012), Hillmann (2021), Richtnér and Löfsten (2014), and Williams and Shepherd (2016), crucial building blocks for organizational resilience in SMEs are (1) adaptive leadership, involving proactive decision-making, strategic planning, and the ability to mobilize and empower employees to navigate challenges and seize opportunities; (2) resourceful learning and knowledge management, including continuous learning, fostering a growth mindset, promoting knowledge exchange, and leveraging lessons learned from past experiences (success or failure); and (3) flexibility and agility, involving flexible processes, structures, and operations, as well as agile systems and practices allowing for rapid adjustments, innovation, and openness to new ideas.

All these capacities collectively contribute to enhance resilience in SMEs and hence are likely to strengthen their abilities to effectively navigate challenges, sustain performance, and seize opportunities for growth and success. However, important to note is that capacities also influence each other across the three levels. For instance, a shared sense of meaning and purpose at the team resilience level can have a positive effect on the coping strategies of individual employees, thereby strengthening their individual resilience. On the other hand, even with existing individual resilience, such as high self-efficacy, the potential of organizational-wide resilience may not be fully realized if there are insufficient resources on the side of organizational resilience, such as a lack of openness to new ideas, which in turn may negatively affect individual resilience. Therefore, it is crucial to acknowledge the interplay between the multiple layers of resilience when discussing possible interventions to enhance resilience in SMEs. Therefore, in the following, I propose an approach that is capable to represent all three layers of resilience through gamification and at the same time to promote the interest and motivation of SME members to engage with the topic of resilience through suitable actions in a playful manner.

To conclude, resilience is defined as a dynamic process involving human-environment interaction and the ability to maintain or limit functionality in the face of adversities. SME resilience practices include persistence, adaptation, and transformation, encompassing preparedness, risk avoidance, and flexible response capabilities. The interpretation of resilience in vulnerable or disrupted systems highlights the need for self-transformation and adaptation to irreversibly changed conditions. At the individual level, personal resilience resources such as optimism, mindfulness, and social support play a crucial role. Research on entrepreneurial resilience emphasizes the importance of psychological resilience for sustainable functioning and the need for further exploration. At the team level, collaboration relies on shared values, trust, and a positive team climate. Organizational resilience in SMEs is influenced by factors such as social, financial, and human capital, learning, creativity, and engagement in resourcefulness. Training of employees and education of managers to perceive challenges as opportunities and exhibit positive behavior during crises are likely to address resilience at the three levels of individual, team, and organizational resilience. The main challenge for SMEs is how to create an environment that motivates and encourages employees as well as their managers to spend their scarce resources to build and develop resilience-enhancing competencies. Therefore, in the following section, I will introduce the concepts of serious games and gamification as a potential solution for SMEs.

9.3 The Potential of Gamification and Serious Games for Organizational Development

In this section, the concepts of gamification as well as serious games will be defined. Additionally, it will be highlighted how such concepts can be applied to promote learning, skill development, and behavior change at the individual and team level. Furthermore, the potential of gamification for the purpose of organizational development will be discussed.

9.3.1 Learning and Skill Development with Playful Activities

Following Metz and Becker (2022), serious games are playful activities specifically designed for educational or training purposes. They utilize game mechanics, simulations, and interactive elements to create immersive learning environments. Serious games aim to facilitate the acquisition of knowledge, skills, and competencies by providing engaging and authentic scenarios. By adopting a playful approach, serious games aim to make the learning experience more enjoyable and effective, promoting active participation, problem-solving, decision-making, and the transfer of learned concepts into real-world applications. These games can cover a wide range of topics and serve as a medium for analyzing decision processes, fostering appropriate behaviors, and facilitating reflection in vocational or professional education. Gamification refers to the application of game elements and techniques, involving elements such as competition, challenges, rewards, and interactive experiences to enhance motivation, engagement, and learning in nongame contexts. By incorporating gamelike features, gamification aims to make tasks or learning experiences more enjoyable, stimulating, and effective, ultimately influencing behavior, promoting skill development, and fostering innovation.

To decide for the best approach to apply gamified solutions in an organizational context, we must be more precise in regard to definitions. Thus, serious games are defined as stand-alone educational games designed for specific learning objectives, whereas gamification can be applied to any nongame contexts by incorporating game elements in order to enhance motivation and engagement. Serious games provide a complete gaming experience, while gamification enhances existing activities with gamelike features.

9.3.2 Applications in Business and Management Contexts

In recent years, both serious games and gamification have been introduced to various business and management contexts, starting out in marketing, followed by personnel management, lean management, project management, innovation management, change management, business process modelling (Strahringer & Leyh, 2017), and risk management (Henschel & Heinze, 2023; Schönbohm & Jülich, 2016). Stieglitz (2017) clusters the application of gamification into the fields of supporting business processes, knowledge acquisition, and behavior influence. According to the author, the first domain, business processes, covers various processes that can benefit from gamification approaches, including regular operations as well as special actions and events. Stieglitz (2017) further states that in recent years, companies have started to modernize their communication and collaboration infrastructure and create unified central solutions for the entire organization. In this context, enterprise social networks are playing an increasingly important role (Stieglitz & Meske, 2012). These platforms pose significant challenges for management as employees need to be motivated to use them meaningfully, and the resulting knowledge must be stored in a way that allows retrieval and utilization. Gamification can be applied here to support the achievement of desired goals. Employees can be encouraged to complete their profiles through progress indicators, and badges or points can increase activity or channel it in specific directions (Koch et al., 2013). The fundamental conditions of voluntary and autonomous use of social networks provide a good basis for integrating gamification elements sensibly. Gamification could be used intentionally and temporarily, for example, to support the implementation of enterprise social media. Likewise, evaluation and ranking systems can help identify good ideas. For the second domain, knowledge acquisition, Stieglitz (2017) draws attention to the importance to distinguish between individual and collective learning situations. In individual knowledge acquisition, individuals can engage with subject matter and perform exercises independently. Immediate feedback, benchmarking results against other users, and achieving new levels of knowledge are likely gamification elements. In collective scenarios, the immediate exchange and collaboration among learners takes precedence, as it is intended to promote the generation of knowledge. Similarly, gamification elements can help increase motivation to generate contributions or evaluate the quality of content (Stieglitz & Meske, 2012). In collective scenarios, competitive motives can also play a stronger role, such as comparing the learning achievements of different participants (Teh et al., 2013). For the last domain, influence of behavior, Stieglitz (2017) provides an example focused on energy-saving habits, including competitive approaches like informing individuals that they consume more electricity than a specific comparison group. The healthcare sector is another example. In recent years, devices and applications designed to optimize one's health-related behavior, such as step counters and calorie trackers and blood pressure monitors, have been on the rise. Stieglitz (2017) states that these approaches incorporate playful elements extensively, employing benchmarking, providing immediate feedback on movement and nutrition, and awarding points for individual achievements. A recent study by Jackson et al. (2020) introduces the principles of resilient healthcare through a serious video game, aiming to engage clinicians, promote idea sharing, and encourage reflection on practice. The game, called Resilience Challenge, presents clinical dilemmas that players must navigate. The authors state that Resilience Challenge is a promising tool to stimulate reflections on clinical work, although its effectiveness in communicating resilient healthcare principles to clinicians yielded mixed results.

All these findings demonstrate that both serious games as stand-alone applications and gamification as an enhancement to work processes have significant potential for organizational development. While many experimental studies currently focus on large companies or research institutions, both serious games and gamified business processes present a great opportunity to address resource scarcity, particularly in SMEs. Due to their motivational aspects, employees are more likely to learn autonomously, and desired behaviors can be trained without constant managerial involvement. Therefore, in the following section, I will provide an overview of major elements necessary to design and implement gamified processes and interactions to foster resilience in SMEs on multiple levels.

9.4 Considerations for Design and Implementation of Gamified Resilience Management in SMEs

In this section, I will first introduce major game components that are likely to increase motivation and encouragement of SME employees and managers to enhance their resilience competencies. Furthermore, I will present a step-by-step approach to implement gamified processes or interactions that ensures the successful realization of such a project in SMEs.

9.4.1 Major Aspects of Game Design

Before deciding for a certain playful process of interaction, it is necessary to understand the different levels and components of games and their likely impact on our users. Friedrich et al. (2020) provide an overview of the aspects of gamification and state that gamification can be broken down into three aspects: game dynamics, mechanics, and components (see Table 9.1). The most tangible forms of gamification are the game components, such as points, rankings, levels, or quests, that are integrated into a system. These components give rise to game mechanics, which serve as incentives, such as challenges, competition, feedback, rewards, or cooperation, and in turn create various motivational dynamics. These dynamics, which are the most abstract form of gamification, cannot be directly implemented or controlled but have a significant influence on motivation (Shpakova et al., 2016).

In their literature review, Shpakova et al. (2016) state that the commonly mentioned components of gamification include badges, levels, leaderboards, and points. These elements are widely recognized and visually represented, requiring no further discussion regarding their categorization. Avatars and virtual goods also align well with these requirements. Collections and teams are additional elements that can be visually represented and have the potential to promote different mechanics in the system. Ranks, representing status, could be visualized through badges but could also be considered as a distinct element. Other elements such as achievements, content unlocking, countdown clocks, gifting, progress bars, and quests show a very strong relationship to game mechanics and therefore might have been reclassified within other existing categories.

Table 9.1 Aspects of gamification

Components	Mechanics	Dynamics
Achievements	*Internal*:	Constraints
Avatars	Challenges	Emotions
Badges	Chance	Narrative
Collections	Competition	Progression
Content unlocking	Cooperation	Relationships
Countdown clock	Meaningful stories	
Gifting	Time pressure	
Leaderboards	*External*:	
Levels	Feedback	
Points	Levels	
Progress bar	Performance graphs	
Quests	Virtual goods	
Ranking	Rewards	
Teams	Status	
Virtual goods		

Adopted from Friedrich et al. (2020)

The mechanics, which comprise the second category of the gamification aspects, are defined by their interactions and effects on users, involving some form of action. Friedrich et al. (2020) distinguish between elements that draw on intrinsic motivation and elements linked to extrinsic motivation. In the first category fall elements such as challenges, chances, competition, cooperation, meaningful stories, and time pressure, whereas the elements fall in the latter one. The distinction is of high practical relevance, as intrinsic incentives should be preferred over extrinsic ones because they tap into individuals' internal motivation and enjoyment of the task itself, fostering long-term engagement and satisfaction. Unlike extrinsic incentives, which rely on external rewards or punishments, intrinsic incentives promote a sense of autonomy, mastery, and purpose, leading to higher creativity, productivity, and overall well-being.

Turning to the highest level of gamification elements, known as dynamics, Shpakova et al. (2016) report about challenges in its review due to differing interpretations. While some view dynamics as aspects of the game that cannot be directly managed, others see them as emotional responses of users or conceptual models of game components and experiences. In nongaming contexts, it is crucial to consider the models of behavior and engagement that creators aim to foster, making it more appropriate to characterize this level as conceptual models of game components and user engagement that cannot be directly managed. The types of engagement listed on the third level include expression, relationship/fellowship, and discovery/curiosity, which align with social engagement types such as expression, collaboration, and exploration. Additional elements like progression, narrative, and fantasy can be seen as conceptual models of components, while sensations, submission games, emotions, and game design atoms are either irrelevant or redundant for nongame contexts and hence are excluded by the authors. However, Friedrich et al. (2020) only partly agree with Shpakova et al. (2016), developing their own interpretation as presented in Table 9.1.

Considering all three aspects of gamification—components, mechanics, and dynamics—is crucial for implementing gamification to support resilience in SMEs. The identified components, such as badges, points, ranks, and virtual goods, provide visual representation and engagement. Mechanics, including intrinsic incentives like challenges and cooperation, tap into internal motivation, fostering long-term engagement and satisfaction. Extrinsic incentives, such as feedback, reward, and status, might be relevant especially for quick wins and for certain types of culture and organizational environments. Dynamics, such as progression and relationships, promote social engagement and the development of conceptual models of user behavior. The question that must be answered now is how to leverage these elements in order to strengthen resilience in SMEs by encouraging participation, ensuring motivation, and enhancing a sense of purpose. There is no general right or wrong, as each SME is of a unique nature; therefore, I propose a step-by-step approach to develop and implement gamified interactions and processes that will be presented in the following.

9.4.2 Step-by-Step Approach for SMEs to Design and Implement Gamification to Enhance Resilience

As discussed above, not only the concept of resilience with its interdependencies between the several resilience levels as well as further internal and external influences is of a rather complex nature. Also, the various dynamics, mechanics, and components of gamification show that some thoughts must be spend on the setup in advance. Therefore, I cannot resist to put forward that "failing to plan is planning to fail," a phrase that is commonly attributed to either Benjamin Franklin or Winston Churchill, although there is no definitive evidence that they actually said it. However, the quote nicely emphasizes a well-known problem in organizational development: lack of diagnosis and lack of a process model. Therefore, in the following, I will present some basic key considerations for designing and implementing gamification in general and as an enhancement for enterprise resilience explicitly in SMEs.

Schmidt et al. (2017) introduce a process model that integrates diagnosis and is based on the integration of scientific knowledge with numerous practical experiences from the gamification context. It explains the inputs, methodology, and outcomes of each project step in a total of six phases. The model is especially recommended as it is not exclusively designed for digital games. The authors state that while digital solutions are often the obvious choice, project teams should foster an open and creative culture that considers non-digital solution components as well. Therefore, their approach also includes developing solutions beyond the commonly seen forms of gamification, such as points and badges. Instead, it allows for a departure from specific manifestations in order to achieve true innovation. The model presented by Schmidt et al. (2017) follows a sequential "input-throughput-output" framework with six phases in total (see Fig. 9.2). Each phase has specific goals, participants, and iterative processes. The output of one phase becomes the input for the next, with documentation and planning being essential components. The model emphasizes a gradual reduction of uncertainty throughout the phases by separation of creation and production.

The aim of Phase 1, exploration, is to build an understanding of the gamification project, its goals, functions, criteria, expectations, as well as a discussion about the motivation and potential benefits and drawbacks. The proposed step-by-step process, financial arrangements, and scope of design are discussed. This phase also focuses on building trust, reducing uncertainties, and forming the basis for mutual decision-making regarding the proposed gamification. In Phase 2, the analysis starts after the decision to proceed and relies on a multi-perspective examination of the use case, surrounding processes, and users that take center stage. Based on planning in Phase 1 as well as on the information gathered in Phase 2, in Phase 3, ideation, data is compared, validated, and, if necessary, revised in a design process that includes initial concept sketches, and project strategic objectives. It is not uncommon for the ideas generated earlier to be completely replaced based on the insights gained. For example, in a gamification project, a planned usability measure may lead to a revision of user training. The ideation phase significantly reduces uncertainties for the further progress of the gamification project. Turning to Phase 4,

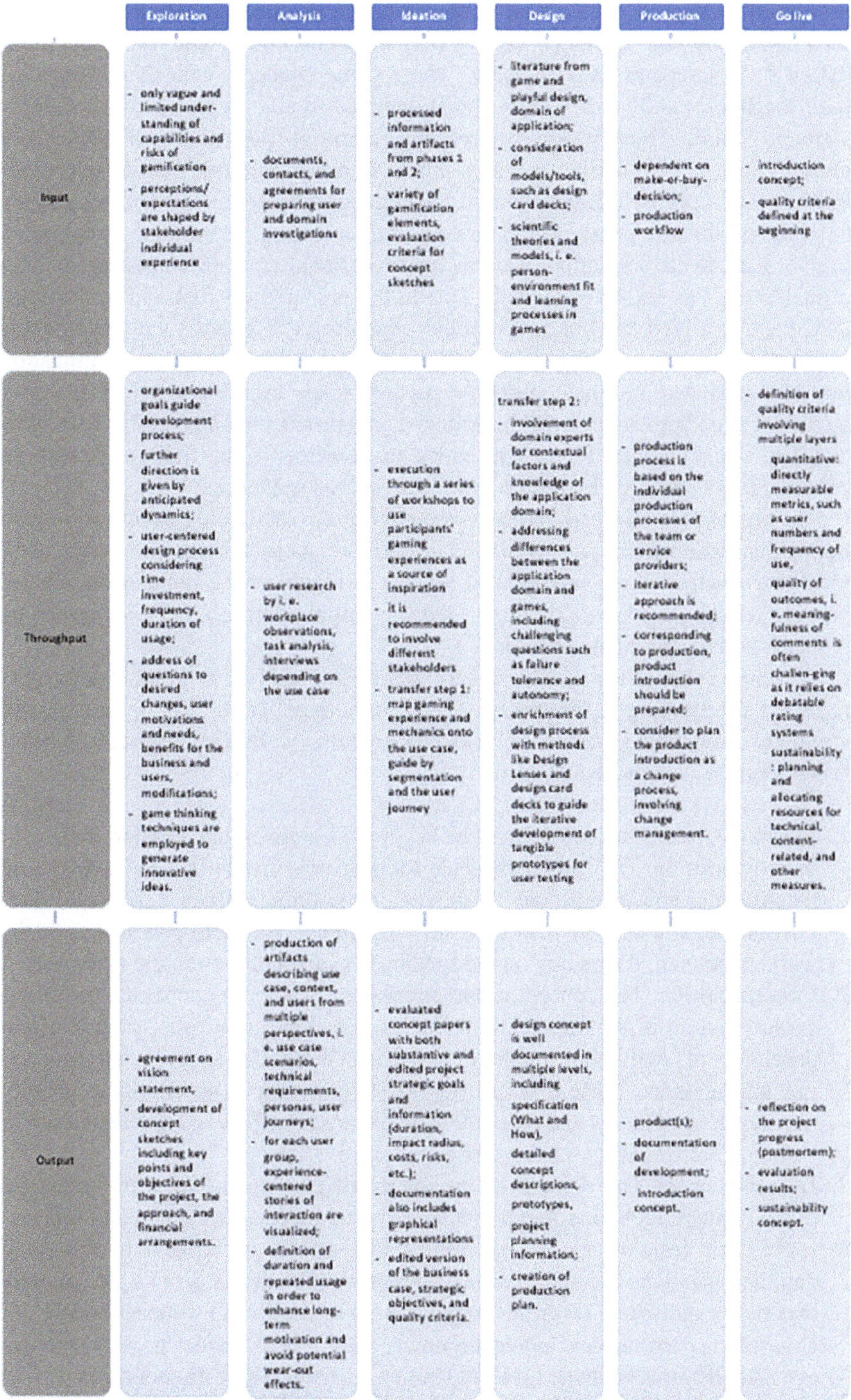

Fig. 9.2 Process model for implementation of gamification based on Schmidt et al. (2017)

design, following the decision on a concept paper, the design phase transforms the idea into a complete design concept. A playful mindset once again forms the foundation of this second transfer phase, where game concepts with their dynamics, their mechanics and elements are operationalized to align with the organization's strategic goals and the use case of enhancing enterprise resilience. Like the previous phase, Phase 4 is primarily a creation phase. Iterative prototypes are developed to evaluate and approach the content and experience-oriented goals. In Phase 5, we enter the production phase, which involves implementing the design concept into a usable and effective solution, such as an educational concept consisting of both digital as well as real-live elements. Due to the preparatory work and documentation, there is a high level of predictability regarding the duration and costs of this phase. Go live is the starting point of Phase 6. In this final phase, the gamification will be introduced into the context, the planned goals from Phase 1 will be evaluated, necessary adjustments will be arranged, and product maintenance tasks will be handled. The following Fig. 9.2 provides an overview of the framework with its essential tasks clustered by project phases as well as sequences.

The process model clearly presents the importance of aligning gamification with both organizational goals and context. Furthermore, it ensures that all relevant technical, logistical, and resource-related aspects in regard of the implementation are brought to light. Furthermore, due to the sequential approach, complexity can be reduced, and resources are spared.

To achieve this, it is crucial to clearly define and analyze relevant stakeholders right at the beginning of the project. Based on Schmidt et al. (2017), for a project aiming to implement gamification to enhance enterprise, resilience groups of stakeholders can be categorized as follows:

1. *Business Group*: This group includes key representatives and decision-makers of the organization. They are responsible for developing, defining, and considering the strategic and operational objectives of the project. They collaborate with internal departments such as HR, IT, compliance and data protection, or the workers council, depending on the specific organization's structure and needs.
2. *Concept Group*: The concept group consists of experts in gamification, serious games, and all disciplines relevant for organizational resilience, such as talent development, well-being, employee assistance, but also change management and risk management. These experts bring their knowledge in areas such as interaction design, pedagogy, and psychology to ensure the effective implementation of gamification strategies for enterprise resilience.
3. *Domain Group*: The domain group comprises participants from the organizational context, including users, domain experts, process designers, and supervisors. Their insights and knowledge of the subject are crucial in designing gamified solutions tailored to enhance enterprise resilience. In an SME, domain experts for individual resilience might consist of health and wellness coaches or counselors, personal development trainers, employee assistance program providers, and HR professionals; for team resilience, again HR professionals as well as team leaders or supervisors, project managers, and peer mentors or coaches; and

for organizational resilience, it's the business owners or top-level executives who drive the overall resilience strategy and decision-making within the SME, furthermore risk management experts who identify and mitigate potential risks that may impact the organization, HR professionals or organizational development specialists who assess and enhance the organization's resilience culture, and—last but not least—external consultants or advisors who specialize in organizational resilience for SMEs.

4. *Trades Group*: The trades group encompasses professionals from various disciplines involved in media production and media technology. These professionals play a vital role in executing the practical aspects of implementing gamification, such as developing the necessary media assets and utilizing appropriate technologies.

In each phase of the project, certain groups may take a leading role, depending on their expertise and responsibilities. Additionally, a project leader should be appointed to guide the overall process, providing guidance and coordination without holding an individual content-related position.

Taken together, the implementation of the proposed framework as well as the definition of stakeholders relevant for the gamification project is supposed to counteract the phenomenon of "failing to plan is planning to fail," that is often characteristic for SMEs, due to their scarce resources. Gamification aims to increase motivation and participation; however, it also poses challenges and limitations during the adoption and implementation. Fischer et al. (2017) discuss common problems from an institutional perspective. Translating their findings into the SME context means that SME owners, managers, HR professionals, as well as external consultants and advisors should be aware of factors such as:

1. Employee heterogeneity: In gamified workplace settings, employees are given more control over their learning and development process. However, not all employees may be ready for this or have the necessary individual prerequisites. Varying knowledge levels, learning preferences, and even organizational culture can impact the effectiveness of gamification. Similarly, individuals have different preferences for game styles, as demonstrated by research on player types (Bartle, 1996). Therefore, it is crucial to thoroughly assess the individual prerequisites and expectations of employees before implementing gamification in the workplace.
2. Distraction from work: Game elements can also have a negative impact on workplace settings, particularly when the game concept overshadows the primary work objectives. Gamification is a form of motivational design intended to enhance employee engagement. It is not necessary for employees to be consciously aware of the game mechanics; instead, these elements can operate on a subconscious level. Therefore, it is essential to ensure that the work goals of employees and the tasks to be accomplished remain at the forefront of work planning and implementation.

3. Data security and privacy rights: In virtual gamified work scenarios, employees leave behind digital footprints, such as progress or status indicators, social connections, and more. The information generated can be utilized for personalizing and adapting work processes (work analytics). However, employees are becoming more aware of data protection concerns. Hence, it is crucial to handle the generated personally identifiable data responsibly, as it is a fundamental success factor in digital work environments and the gamification of work processes.

To summarize, the design and implementation of gamification in SMEs require careful consideration to build or enhance resilience throughout the organization at various levels. Schmidt et al. propose a process model that integrates scientific knowledge and practical experiences to guide the implementation of gamification. The model emphasizes the importance of considering both digital and non-digital components and encourages innovative approaches. The process consists of six phases, allowing for a gradual reduction of uncertainty. Key stakeholders, including the business group, concept group, domain group, and trades group, play vital roles in designing gamified solutions tailored to enhance enterprise resilience. Challenges in SMEs include employee heterogeneity, potential distractions from work objectives, as well as data security and privacy concerns. Thorough assessment of employee prerequisites and expectations, prioritizing work goals, and responsible handling of personally identifiable data are essential for successful gamification implementation in the workplace. By following this framework and involving relevant stakeholders, SMEs can effectively harness gamification to strengthen resilience across the organization.

9.5 Conclusion

This chapter contributes to knowledge by (1) provision of a framework of multiple layers of resilience and their interactions in SME; (2) introduction of the offerings held by serious games and gamification as a transformative learning approach; and (3) discussion of key benefits, strategies, and considerations for implementing gamified processes and serious games in SMEs to develop and strengthen their resilience capabilities. Therefore, it provides valuable guidance for SME leaders, HR professionals, organizational development experts as well as risk managers and external consultants and advisors seeking effective methods to enhance resilience within their organizations. By embracing the power of gamification and serious games, SMEs can unlock new avenues for growth, innovation, and sustainable success in an ever-evolving business landscape. The chapter began with an overview of organizational resilience and its significance for SMEs, followed by a discussion of serious games and gamification as tools for learning, skill development, and behavior change. In accordance with the requirements of enterprise resilience defined as a multilevel dynamic umbrella concept, a theoretical framework has been presented, illustrating the application of gamified processes for resilience building, targeting specific factors such as adaptability, resourcefulness, and agility. Challenges and limitations in implementing gamification in SMEs were acknowledged, including employee heterogeneity, potential negative effects on workplace setting, and data security concerns.

In conclusion, the potential of playful elements and interactions in fostering resilience in SMEs should not be overlooked. Gamified approaches offer opportunities to address resource scarcity and promote autonomous learning and behavior change. However, further exploration, research, and practical applications are required to fully understand and leverage the benefits of gamification and serious games in the context of SME resilience. By carefully considering the proposed framework, following a step-by-step approach to design and implement playful interactions, involving relevant stakeholders, and addressing the identified challenges, SMEs can effectively harness gamification to strengthen resilience throughout their organizations, ultimately enhancing their ability to navigate and thrive in a dynamic business environment.

References

Ahmed, A. E., Ucbasaran, D., Cacciotti, G., & Williams, T. A. (2022). Integrating psychological resilience, stress, and coping in entrepreneurship: A critical review and research agenda. *Entrepreneurship: Theory and Practice, 46*(3), 497–538. https://doi.org/10.1177/10422587211046542

Amann, B., & Jaussaud, J. (2012). Family and non-family business resilience in an economic downturn. *Asia Pacific Business Review, 18*(2), 203–223. https://doi.org/10.1080/13602381.2010.537057

Bartle, R. (1996). Hearts, clubs, diamonds, spades: Players who suit MUDs. *Journal of MUD Research*, 1–19. http://www.researchgate.net/publication/247190693_Hearts_Clubs_Diamonds_and_Spades_Players_who_suit_MUDs

Becker, W., & Metz, M. (2022). *Digitale Lernwelten – Serious games und gamification*. Springer.

Bengel, J., & Lyssenko, L. (2016). Resilienz und Schutzfaktoren.. In Bundeszentrale für gesundheitliche Aufklärung.

Bonß, W. (2015). Karriere und sozialwissenschaftliche Potenziale des Resilienzbegriffs. In *Resilienz im Sozialen* (pp. 15–31). Springer Fachmedien Wiesbaden. https://doi.org/10.1007/978-3-658-05999-6_2

Bruhn, H. (2021). Resilienz-Konzept und Kritik. In *Forschungsprojekt RESIST – Resilienz im Strafvollzug*. Universität Siegen.

Buyl, T., Gehrig, T., Schreyögg, J., & Wieland, A. (2022). Resilience: A critical appraisal of the state of research for business and society. *Schmalenbach Journal of Business Research, 74*(4), 453–463. https://doi.org/10.1007/s41471-022-00151-x

Chhatwani, M., Mishra, S. K., Varma, A., & Rai, H. (2022). Psychological resilience and business survival chances: A study of small firms in the USA during COVID-19. *Journal of Business Research, 142*, 277–286. https://doi.org/10.1016/j.jbusres.2021.12.048

Conz, E., Denicolai, S., & Zucchella, A. (2017). The resilience strategies of SMEs in mature clusters. *Journal of Enterprising Communities, 11*(1), 186–210. https://doi.org/10.1108/JEC-02-2015-0015

Coutu, D. L. (2002). How resilience works. *Harvard Business Review*, 46–51.

Danes, S. M., Lee, J., Amarapurkar, S., Stafford, K., Haynes, G., & Brewton, K. E. (2009). Determinants of family business resilience after a natural disaster by gender of business owner. *Journal of Developmental Entrepreneurship, 16*(4), 333–354.

de Rosa, F., & De Gloria, A. (2021). Design methodology of analytical games for knowledge acquisition. *International Journal of Serious Games, 8*(4), 3–23. https://doi.org/10.17083/IJSG.V8I4.456

DesJardine, M., Bansal, P., & Yang, Y. (2019). Bouncing Back: Building resilience through social and environmental practices in the context of the 2008 global financial crisis. *Journal of Management, 45*(4), 1434–1460. https://doi.org/10.1177/0149206317708854

Duchek, S., Geithner, S., & Scheuch, I. (2021). Resilienzförderung in Organisationen Individuen, Teams und Unternehmen für turbulente Zeiten stärken. *Zeitschrift Für Führung Und Organisation (Zfo), 3*, 128–133. www.wiso-net.de

Fischer, H., Heinz, M., Schlenker, L., Münster, S., Follert, F., & Köhler, T. (2017). Die Gamifizierung der Hochschullehre – Potenziale und Herausforderungen. In S. Strahringer & C. Leyh (Eds.), *Gamification und serious games* (HMD ed., pp. 113–125). Springer Fachmedien GmbH. https://doi.org/10.1007/978-3-658-16742-4_9

Friedrich, J., Becker, M., Kramer, F., Wirth, M., & Schneider, M. (2020). Incentive design and gamification for knowledge management. *Journal of Business Research, 106*(November 2017), 341–352. https://doi.org/10.1016/j.jbusres.2019.02.009

Glover, J. (2012). Rural resilience through continued learning and innovation. *Local Economy, 27*(4), 355–372. https://doi.org/10.1177/0269094212437833

Hartmann, S., Backmann, J., Newman, A., Brykman, K. M., & Pidduck, R. J. (2022). Psychological resilience of entrepreneurs: A review and agenda for future research. *Journal of Small Business Management, 60*(5), 1041–1079. https://doi.org/10.1080/00472778.2021.2024216

Hawthorn, S., Jesus, R., & Baptista, M. A. (2021). A review of digital serious games for tsunami risk communication. *International Journal of Serious Games, 8*(2), 21–47. https://doi.org/10.17083/ijsg.v8i2.411

Heinze, I., & Henschel, T. (2021). Risk(ing) sophistication: Towards a structural equation model for risk management in small and medium-sized enterprises. *International Journal of Entrepreneurship and Small Business, 44*(4), 386–412.

Hellström, M. M., Jaccard, D., & Bonnier, K. E. (2023). A systematic review on the use of serious games in project management education. *International Journal of Serious Games, 10*(2), 3–24. https://doi.org/10.17083/ijsg.v10i2.630

Henschel, T., & Heinze, I. (2023). Gamifizierte Anreize für das Risikomanagement in KMU. *Controlling Zeitschrift Für Erfolgsorientierte Unternehmenssteuerung, 34*(Special Issue Summer 2023), 74–78.

Hillmann, J. (2021). Disciplines of organizational resilience: Contributions, critiques, and future research avenues. *Review of Managerial Science, 15*(4), 879–936. https://doi.org/10.1007/s11846-020-00384-2

Hirsch, P. M., & Levin, D. Z. (1999). Umbrella advocates versus validity police: A life-cycle model. *Organization Science, 10*(2), 199–212. https://doi.org/10.1287/orsc.10.2.199

Jackson, J., Iacovides, J., Duncan, M., Alders, M., Maben, J., & Anderson, J. (2020). Operationalizing resilient healthcare concepts through a serious video game for clinicians. *Applied Ergonomics, 87*. https://doi.org/10.1016/j.apergo.2020.103112

Koch, M., Ott, F., & Oertelt, S. (2013). Gamification von business software – Steigerung von motivation und partizipation. In M. Koch & F. Ott (Eds.), *Schriften zur soziotechnischen integration* (Vol. 3, pp. 1–32). Universität der Bundeswehr.

Löffler, E., Schneider, B., Asprion, P. M., & Zanwar, T. (2021). CySecEscape 2.0 – A virtual escape room to raise cybersecurity awareness. *International Journal of Serious Games, 8*(1), 59–70. https://doi.org/10.17083/ijsg.v8i1.413

Luthans, F. (2002). The need for and meaning of positive organizational behavior. *Journal of Organizational Behavior, 23*(6), 695–706. https://doi.org/10.1002/job.165

Pathak, M. D., Kar, B., Panigrahi, R. R., & Shrivastava, A. K. (2023). Role of entrepreneurial resilience in SMEs to promote marketing and entrepreneurship amid Covid19 challenges. *Journal of Research in Marketing and Entrepreneurship*. https://doi.org/10.1108/JRME-04-2022-0050

Raetze, S., Duchek, S., Maynard, M. T., & Kirkman, B. L. (2021). Resilience in organizations: An integrative multilevel review and editorial introduction. *Group and Organization Management, 46*(4), 607–656. https://doi.org/10.1177/10596011211032129

Ratten, V. (2020). Coronavirus (Covid-19) and entrepreneurship: Cultural, lifestyle and societal changes. *Journal of Entrepreneurship in Emerging Economies, 13*(4), 747–761. https://doi.org/10.1108/JEEE-06-2020-0163

Richtnér, A., & Löfsten, H. (2014). Managing in turbulence: How the capacity for resilience influences creativity. *R and D Management, 44*(2), 137–151. https://doi.org/10.1111/radm.12050

Schmidt, R., Brosius, C., & Herrmanny, K. (2017). Ein Vorgehensmodell für angewandte Spielformen. In S. Strahringer & C. Leyh (Eds.), *Gamification und serious games* (HMD ed., pp. 15–29). Springer Fachmedien GmbH. https://doi.org/10.1007/978-3-658-16742-4_2

Schönbohm, A., & Jülich, A. (2016). On the effectiveness of gamified risk management workshops: Evidence from German SMEs. *International Journal of Serious Games, 3*(2), 67–82. https://doi.org/10.17083/ijsg.v3i2.117

Shpakova, A., Dörfler, V., & Macbryde, J. (2016). The role(s) of gamification in knowledge management (EURAM 2016). In *16th annual conference of the European academy of management.*

Silic, M., Marzi, G., Caputo, A., & Bal, P. M. (2020). The effects of a gamified human resource management system on job satisfaction and engagement. *Human Resource Management Journal, 30*(2), 260–277. https://doi.org/10.1111/1748-8583.12272

Stieglitz, S. (2017). Enterprise gamification – Vorgehen und Anwendung. In S. Strahringer & C. Leyh (Eds.), *Gamification und serious games* (HMD ed., pp. 3–13). Springer Fachmedien GmbH. https://doi.org/10.1007/978-3-658-16742-4_1

Stieglitz, S., & Meske, C. (2012). Maßnahmen für die Einführung unternehmensinterner Social Media. *HMD – Praxis Der Wirtschaftsinformatik, 287*, 36–42.

Stiehm, J. H., & Townsend, N. W. (2002). *The U.S. Army War College. Military education in a democracy*. Temple University Press.

Strahringer, S., & Leyh, C. (2017). *Gamification und serious games. Grundlagen, Vorgehen und Anwendungen*. Springer Vieweg. https://doi.org/10.1007/978-3-658-16742-4_7

Sullivan-Taylor, B., & Branicki, L. (2011). Creating resilient SMEs: Why one size might not fit all. *International Journal of Production Research, 49*(18), 5565–5579.

Teh, N., Schuff, D., Johnson, S. L., & Geddes, D. (2013). Can work be fun? Improving task motivation and help-seeking through game mechanics. In *International conference on information systems (ICIS).*

Williams, T. A., & Shepherd, D. A. (2016). Building resilience or providing sustenance: Different paths of emergent ventures in the aftermath of the Haiti earthquake. *Academy of Management Journal, 59*(6), 2069–2102. https://doi.org/10.5465/amj.2015.0682

Zander, M. (2019). Resilienz. Socialnet. Das Netz Für Die Sozialwirtschaft. https://www.socialnet.de/lexikon/Resilienzfoerderung

Organisational Resilience in German Leasing Companies

10

Christian Glaser

10.1 Introduction

"It is not the strongest of the species that survives, nor the most intelligent that survives. It is the one that is the most adaptable to change." This quote by scientist Charles Darwin goes back more than 200 years, yet it is more relevant now than ever. One might simply change the word "change" with "crises" and the result is a justification for the need for a systematic organisational resilience.

Resilience describes the process and capacity of a company to address major acute and strategic challenges through responsiveness and reinvention to achieve organisational renewal (Herbane, 2019, p. 478).

Today's globalised world is often described with the acronym VUCA consisting of volatility, uncertainty, complexity and ambiguity (Bennett & Lemoine, 2014). The term refers to the US army and was introduced by Bennis and Nanus in the mid-1980s (Bennis & Nanus, 1985). During the last 10–15 years, there were numerous acute and strategic challenges: the subprime crisis with the subsequent financial and Euro crisis; the economic crisis and now lately the Covid-19 outbreak with worldwide lockdowns and severe effects on the global economy; and the war in Ukraine with an increase in inflation, sudden supply chain disruptions and potential energy shortages. Furthermore, there is still a potential risk with the looming Taiwan conflict and its (potential) impact on global supply chains, military operations and the global economic situation. All of these events underline the importance of resilient entrepreneurship.

Small and medium-sized enterprises (SMEs), in most countries defined as organizations with less than 250 employees (OECD, 2005), are the backbone also of the German leasing market (IfM, 2018; Bisnode, 2020; BaFin, 2020a). The German

C. Glaser (✉)
University of Heilbronn, Germany

S. Durst, T. Henschel (eds.), *Small and Medium-Sized Enterprise (SME) Resilience*, Management for Professionals, https://doi.org/10.1007/978-3-031-50836-3_10

leasing industry is regulated by the German banking supervision since 2009. Therefore, the risk management practice of those companies is greatly shaped by regulative aspects. In the following, major findings of a study conducted by the author on risk management practices in the German leasing industry ($n = 40$) are presented, focusing on the aspect of organisational resilience.

Resilience focusing on SMEs in general and in the context of regulated industries such as the German leasing industry in particular is widely overlooked and at best in its infancy. Therefore, this article aims to shed more light on this highly relevant field of research and is coming up with practical proposals how organisation resilience might be increased in small and medium-sized companies.

The need for resilience is comparably high in the German financial industry. The president of the German banking regulation agency BaFin, Mark Branson, stated in late 2022 that the financial industry is currently not in the most difficult but probably in the most complex phase of recent years. He therefore stressed the importance of organisational resilience (Branson, 2022).

10.2 Theoretical Background

Over the last years, resilience has been recognized as a key factor in entrepreneurial success, and subsequently, also academic interest in this research area increased (van der Vegt et al., 2015; Bullough et al., 2014; Corner et al., 2017).

However, there is still much room for research when focusing on resilience in many different ways: First, it is the respective context, often driven by the impacts of disasters such as Covid-19. Secondly, the specific focus on SME's resilience is often missing in the rare academic research (Bhamra, 2016; Doern, 2016; Parnell, 2015; Verreynne et al., 2018). Furthermore, this also includes an understanding of the response on internal crises and external adversity which also seem to be little researched (Doern, 2016; Herbane, 2010).

There are different focus areas on resilience in the few academic researches such as differences between banks, systemic resilience of banks and focus on SMEs and performance during crises. The following Table 10.1 summarizes exemplary research from selected, predominantly peer-reviewed journals that have some relation to German leasing SMEs or whose findings are transferable to German leasing SMEs.

10.2.1 Resilience, Crisis and Business Continuity Management

Resilience is a subject of study in different academic fields and disciplines. In general, it describes a situation in which a system enhances its capabilities against internal or external shocks or crises (Khajehpour et al., 2022; Sahebjamnia et al., 2018). Resilience is defined as the situation when a system is able to recover and return to its original state (Rose, 2017; Dormady et al., 2019). Organisational resilience is defined as the ability to anticipate key opportunities and events from emerging

Table 10.1 Summary of literature on resilience

Researcher (year)	Subject	Country	Key findings
Markman and Venzin (2014)	Resilience and stamina of the banks during the subprime crisis	–	Large banks are less resilient than small banks.
Ghouse et al. (2022)	Comparison of resilience of 12 Islamic banks and 21 conventional banks	Pakistan, Bangladesh, Indonesia, Malaysia, UAE and Turkey	Conventional banking sector was more resilient to the economic downturn in the context of Covid-19 than the Islamic banking industry.
Dovern et al. (2010)	Resilience of the German banking system to macroeconomic shocks	Germany	German banking system is comparably resilient in macroeconomic shocks.
Anani and Owusu (2023)	Analysis of 22 quarters from Q1–2017 to Q2–2022 of 450 US commercial banks	USA	Banks with robust regulatory capital ratios are less risky.
Vallascas and Keasey (2012)	Analysis of bank resilience to systemic shocks	153 listed European banks from 17 countries (15 EU countries as well as Norway and Switzerland)	For the systemic risk "small is beautiful" in terms of the maximum exposure of a single bank
Acciarini et al. (2021)	Organisational resilience in the Covid-19 pandemic	Italy (four case studies in different industries)	Development of strategic skills such as digital skills is associated to companies with a high level of resilience
Herbane (2019)	Variance of formalisation of activities to enhance resilience	256 UK SMEs	Variations reflect differences in firm location, personal networks, the influence of external crisis events and entrepreneurs' attitudes

trends, constantly adapting and changing, rapidly bouncing back from disaster and remaining stable in a turbulent environment (Coutu, 2002; Fiksel, 2003, 2006; Hamel & Valikangas, 2003; Sutcliffe & Vogus, 2003; Stewart & O'Donnell, 2007; Marcos, 2008).

Crises are typically rooted in an event that is relatively unpredictable and has the potential to threaten and/or negatively impact the company's performance (Coombs & Holladay, 2006; Parnell, 2015; Boers & Henschel, 2021; Glaser, 2022). According to Mitroff and Alpaslan (2003) and Gorge (2006), the following different forms of crises can be differentiated:

- Physical crises (accidents, product recalls or loss of utilities due to fire, broken water pipe, etc.)
- Natural disasters (earthquake, flood or storm)
- Economic crises (economic recession or loss of a major customer)

- Legal and reputational crises (Internet defacement or malicious rumours)
- Personnel crises (staff illness or death, industrial action or staff criminality)
- External criminal crises (terrorism or malicious product tampering)
- Information crises (cybercrime or information theft)

They can be triggered internally or externally, for example, reaching from human-made disasters such as the subprime crisis in 2007/2008 or Russia's attack of Ukraine since 2022 up to nature-made crises such as hurricane Katrina, Fukushima or Covid-19.

Crises as described above have the potential to destroy a society or economic prosperity although there are some organizations that not only withstand but even prosper in such economic situations (Markman & Venzin, 2014). These organisations are resilient.

10.2.2 Definition of Resilience, Crises and Business Continuity Management

The International Monetary Fund (IMF) has identified 145 banking crashes, 204 monetary collapses and 72 sovereign debt crises since 1970, and Kindleberger (1989) has spotted 48 financial meltdowns between the Dutch Tulip Mania in 1637 and the Great Recession in 1929 (Markman & Venzin, 2014).

The German Leasing Industry in a Nutshell

The German finance leasing market has been regulated by the banking supervision since the end of 2009. Similar to credit institutions, finance leasing companies also have to comply with the "Minimum Requirements of Risk Management" (MaRisk) and the "German Banking Act" (KWG). More than 50% of the externally financed investments in 2021 were financed via leasing. The newly concluded leasing contracts in 2021 amounted to more than 70 billion EUR (BDL, 2022). As the leasing industry is greatly shaped by SMEs, a special focus on these firms is of great importance.

Dovern et al. (2010) analysed the profit and loss data of banks of a period of 39 years and found that the German banking system is comparably resilient in macroeconomic shocks. This probably also includes the German leasing industry which is typically included in the banking industry and which is also regulated by the German banking supervision.

Dependency on Decision-Makers

There seems to be reasonable consensus within the literature that the main reasons for business failure are management incompetence, poor decision-making and inexperience (e.g., Haswell & Holmes, 1989, p. 73; Allen, 1995; Hodgetts & Kuratko, 1998; Kharbanda & Stallworthy, 1985; Laitenen, 1992; Peterson et al., 1983; Zimmerer & Scarborough, 1994). However, these reasons seem to be too simplistic and too broad. Argenti therefore stated, "While everyone agrees that bad management is the prime cause of failure, no one agrees what 'bad management' means nor how it can be recognized except that after the company has collapsed, then everyone agrees how badly managed it was" (Argenti, 1976, p. 3).

Small Is Beautiful in Terms of Resilience

Markman and Venzin (2014, p. 1105) found in their analysis of the subprime crisis that large banks are despite their size, resources and economies of scale surprisingly less resilient than small banks. They furthermore did not find a significant link between product or market diversification and resilience and stressed mainly the impact of a bank's management on its resilience. Based on their analysis of financial and nonfinancial crises, they concluded that resilience is conceptualised as a firm's ability to "adapt, endure, bounce back and then thrive despite a catastrophic event".

Vallascas and Keasey (2012) showed furthermore for the systemic risk that "small is beautiful" in terms of the maximum exposure of a single bank. The smaller the individual default, the smaller is the systemic risk. The same is true for a lessee of a leasing firm.

Not only the field of organisational resilience in the German leasing industry is heavily under-researched but also the broader field of organisational resilience in the banking industry which can lead to economic stagnation and bankruptcies of banks (Prorokowski, 2011). Khajehpour et al. (2022) furthermore highlighted the importance of banks to the state economy.

Close Connection to Change Management

Herbane (2019) identified four clusters among SMEs: Attentive Interventionists, Light Planners, Rooted Strategists and Reliant Neighbours. Thereof, Attentive Interventionists are most resilient and showing the highest degree of resilience formalisation and capability to cope with crises. Rooted Strategists, at the other extreme, show the lowest level of resilience formalisation and the highest level in relying on personal networks.

It was found that market and learning-oriented SMEs tend to be more innovative and resilient (Salavou et al., 2004).

Ates and Bititci (2011) demonstrated that change management process capability is fundamental to creating resilience in SMEs. They based their findings on interviews with 232 senior managers among 37 manufacturing SMEs across Europe.

Focus on Performance

The term resilience describes a company's ability to recover from shocks and adapt to disruptions (Roundy et al., 2017). It addresses different managerial constructs including performance (Carmeli & Markman, 2011). At that same time, it cannot be observed or measured directly (Gittell et al., 2006; Levine et al., 2018; DesJardine et al., 2019). Therefore, there need to be some "work-around" measurements such as performance, growth, financial resources or company rating. For larger companies, also the development of the stock price might be an indication of the robustness of resilience (Xia et al., 2022).

The presence of formal processes and planning are seen as an element of resilience (Corey & Deitch, 2011; Spillan & Hough, 2003).

Resilience in Times of Covid-19

Anani and Owusu (2023) showed in their research of the Covid-19 crisis that banks with robust regulatory capital ratios are less risky, which means that they have a lower insolvency risk than less capitalised banks. This finding is probably not surprising and underlines the importance of banking supervisions efforts with the equity ratios as well as the strict analysis of risk-bearing capability calculations.

Xia et al. found in their analysis of the Covid-19 pandemic that especially digital finance has positive effects on corporate resilience. This seems to be particularly valid for small firms, non-state-owned enterprises and low cash holding firms (Xia et al., 2022, p. 1).

Resilience in SMEs

SMEs, in general, have limited resources such as time, money and human capital (Van Gils, 2005). Furthermore, they lack the skills and capability in long-term strategic change to drive resilience because they are more caught in operative troubleshooting (Ates & Bititci, 2011). Change in SMEs is typically driven by the external environment such as the customers (Soderquist et al., 1997; Hudson-Smith & Smith, 2007).

The much-cited VUCA world with its inevitable adversarial developments requires the entrepreneurial ability to recover from shocks and adapt to new disruptions. This is typically subsumed under the term resilience (Roundy et al., 2017). In particular, access to fresh liquidity in the form of banks and financial services firms is very critical for firm survival (Musso & Schiavo, 2008). This is especially true for small and medium-sized enterprises.

Sullivan-Taylor and Branicki (2011) showed in their research a size effect when considering resilience relationships among different companies. A one-size-fits-all approach seems not to be appropriate.

Ates and Bititci (2011, p. 5614) researched 37 SMEs across Europe focusing on change management. They came up with a research proposition of elements that negatively impact resilience in SMEs. Those negative factors reach from slow reactions, high levels of resistance to change, old-fashioned leadership style (command and control) instead of participative leadership, lack of long-term planning, etc. The following Fig. 10.1 summarizes the major factors negatively impacting resilience in SMEs. It could be a useful guide for German leasing SMEs, which could have a negative impact on their resilience and should therefore be avoided when managing change.

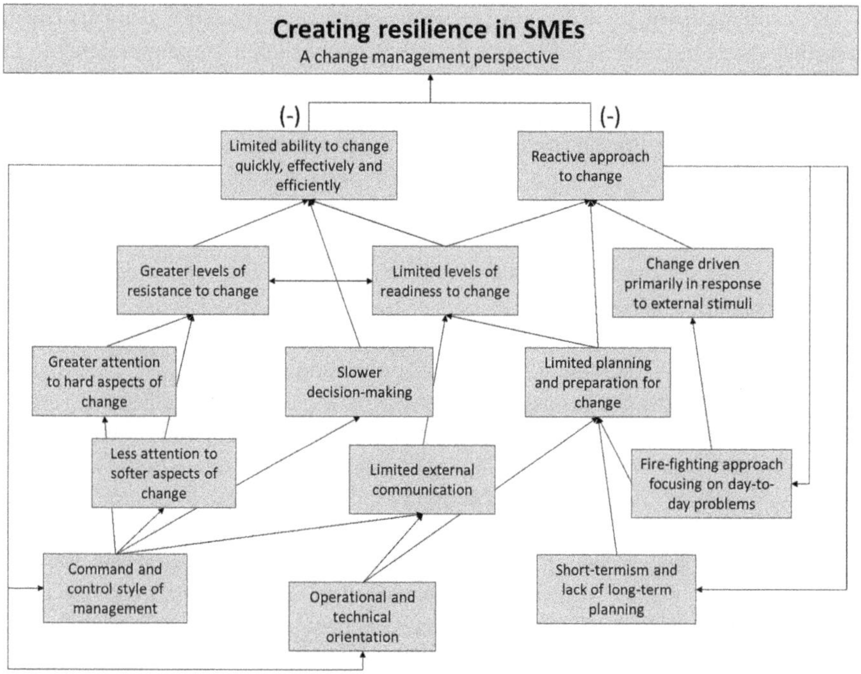

Fig. 10.1 Factors negatively impacting resilience in SMEs. (Source: Adapted from Ates and Bititci (2011, p. 5614))

10.3 Methodology

In the following, the methodological choices of the referred empirical research are presented and justified. Furthermore, the major considerations of the sample selection are briefly described.

10.3.1 Data Collection and Research Approach

As the state of research in organisational resilience of German leasing companies is nascent and the main domains of this research are hard to measure in a quantitative way, a qualitative research approach was chosen (Edmondson & McManus, 2007; Khan et al., 2016). In-depth expert interviews with chief risk officers or (owner) managers including brief background information were preferred rather than other qualitative approaches such as case studies, ethnography or focus groups. Through these in-depth interviews, nascent research areas could be explored (Edmondson & McManus, 2007; Tsang, 2014; Zachariadis et al., 2013). Interviews were conducted between April and September 2017 and covered mainly the practical resilience including risk management organisation, the operations and resources perspective as well as reporting.

Research could be seen as cross-sectional, which actually means that the chosen non-random samples were taken in a snapshot rather than a longitudinal mode. In building theory, the researcher relied on induction. Characteristically for research in a nascent knowledge area, the aim of this inquiry was to identify patterns that might be transferred to a resulting framework. To ensure plausibility and feasibility of the proposed framework, four additional interviews were conducted with managers of German leasing firms (Glaser, 2018).

10.3.2 Sample Selection

For the present research topic, non-probability sampling was applied as the samples were self-selected by the researcher. Potential interviewees were chosen based on the list of approved leasing firms by the German banking supervision. This seems to be appropriate as also no statistical inferences about the characteristics of the population were drawn. On the basis of this sample, one is still able to generalize about the population, however not on a statistical basis (Saunders et al., 2009).

To be included in the sample, different criteria needed to be achieved. Besides others, only companies with the permission by the German banking supervision (BaFin/Bundesbank) to offer finance leasing and persons either responsible for risk management or general managers were interviewed. The whole sample added up to 35 small and medium-sized and 5 large German leasing firms. The following Table 10.2 shows demographic variables for each interviewee.

10.3.3 Analysis of Qualitative Data

There are numerous approaches to analyse qualitative data. Considering the underlying research philosophy as well as the status quo of research and the form of data, grounded analysis was chosen. While in the other major data analysis approach, content analysis, a positivist framework forms the basis (Easterby-Smith et al., 2015, p. 188), critical realism and grounded theory seem to be highly compatible (Kempster & Parry, 2014; Levers, 2013; Oliver, 2011). Instead of (merely) testing and elaborating existing theory, grounded analysis is open to build theory from themes and categories based or "grounded" in the data. This means that a systematic analysis is needed to identify theories (Charmaz, 2006). Therefore, grounded analysis takes a more holistic approach than content analysis as it derives structure within a more inductive environment by comparing different data fragments rather than analysing data purely deductively in a pre-existing structure (Easterby-Smith et al., 2015, p. 191). Through this, grounded analysis is open to new discoveries. It is mainly about the understanding of context. Additionally, there are different cycles in data analysis to address questions arising from previous analysis until "data saturation" is achieved.

Table 10.2 Demographics of each interviewee

	Size cluster	Employees	New contact volume p.a. (mio. EUR)	Owner-managed	Part of a group (>2 firms, total >250 employees)	Bank-depending	Captive/ primarily sales financing	Business focus
1	Micro	3	3	Yes	No	No	No	IT for medical industry
2	Micro	4	17	No	Yes	Yes	No	Universal
3	Micro	7	30	Yes	No	No	No	Used machines
4	Micro	7	35	No	Yes	No	Yes	Machines
5	Micro	9	34	Yes	No	No	No	Universal
6	Micro	9	40	Yes	No	No	No	Universal
7	Small	10	130	Yes	No	Yes	No	Universal
8	Small	10	3	Yes	No	No	No	Universal
9	Small	10	36	No	No	No	No	Universal
10	Small	12	25	Yes	No	No	No	Universal
11	Small	14	33	Yes	No	No	No	Used premium cars
12	Small	20	200	No	Yes	Yes	Yes	Machines
13	Small	20	4	No	No	No	No	Fleet cars
14	Small	22	36	Yes	No	No	No	Medical technology
15	Small	25	20	No	No	No	No	IT
16	Small	25	175	Yes	No	No	No	Cars, boats and vintage cars
17	Small	27	140	No	Yes	Yes	Yes	Machines
18	Small	28	100	Yes	No	No	No	Universal
19	Small	30	66	Yes	No	No	No	Universal
20	Small	31	66	No	No	Yes	No	Cars, agri, machines, medical
21	Small	32	85	No	Yes	No	No	IT
22	Small	40	70	No	Yes	Yes	No	Cars
23	Small	42	130	Yes	No	No	No	Universal
24	Small	42	80	Yes	No	No	No	Universal
25	Small	43	120	No	Yes	Yes	No	Universal
26	Medium	50	65	Yes	No	No	No	IT
27	Medium	69	150	No	Yes	No	No	Universal

(continued)

Table 10.2 (continued)

	Size cluster	Employees	New contact volume p.a. (mio. EUR)	Owner-managed	Part of a group (>2 firms, total >250 employees)	Bank-depending	Captive/ primarily sales financing	Business focus
28	Medium	70	230	No	No	Yes	No	Universal
29	Medium	79	90	Yes	No	No	No	Universal
30	Medium	80	161	Yes	No	No	No	Universal
31	Medium	120	300	No	Yes	Yes	No	Agri, cars, machines, yachts
32	Medium	140	500	No	Yes	No	Yes	Cars
33	Medium	160	613	No	Yes	Yes	Yes	Trucks
34	Medium	165	500	No	Yes	No	Yes	Industries of holding
35	Medium	220	1000	No	Yes	Yes	No	Food and agri
36	Large	390	714	No	Yes	Yes	No	Universal
37	Large	690	1045	No	Yes	Yes	No	Universal
38	Large	800	600	No	Yes	Yes	Yes	Universal
39	Large	900	1000	No	Yes	Yes	No	Universal
40	Large	2500	8900	No	Yes	Yes	No	Universal

Source: Own illustration

10.4 Research on Risk Management in the Leasing Industry

Based on 40 interviews among German leasing companies of different sizes, thereof 35 SMEs, the author of this paper focused on enterprise-wide risk management. The research outcome is widely in agreement and corresponds with the few, existing literature on risk management in leasing firms, although those studies differed in design and sample. The central research outcome on the risk management practice of German leasing companies in general is summarised in the following seven theses before the upcoming chapters focus on organisational resilience in particular:

1. Regulation can be seen as the central driver of risk management practice.
2. Risk management decisions of leasing firms are mainly based on single exposure level.
3. The vast majority of leasing firms does not have an integrated approach to risk management.
4. Lack of know-how and a high degree of informality strongly influence the risk management practice of leasing SMEs.
5. Scarcity of resources can be seen as a driving force in every management decision of leasing SMEs.

6. Organisational learning shows clear room for improvement and is often conducted in a rather unstructured way.
7. The business organisation is shaped by strong dependencies on key players and by flat hierarchies.

An in-depth research of the risk management practice revealed that German leasing firms have different levels of risk management sophistication. With increasing firm size, the level of sophistication is increasing. Small firms are typically lacking know-how as well as key resources like time, money and IT equipment. Especially compared to larger firms, it is important to state that SMEs need their own solutions and processes as they are not just "the smaller version of large firms" and their methods can therefore not be handed down to them (Shrader et al., 1989; Virdi, 2005, p. 5).

The presented seven theses will serve as a guideline for further investigations in the context of organisational resilience and the special focus on public investigations in the following chapter.

10.5 Resilience in the Leasing Industry

10.5.1 Regulation as Driver of Resilience

All of the interviewed SMEs and all large firms have a risk management system in place as this is a core requirement of the banking supervision and its "Minimum Requirements of Risk Management" (MaRisk). Furthermore, 34 out of the 35 interviewed SMEs and all large firms have a contingency planning in place. Surely, the banking regulation led to a professionalisation of risk management and in its bug wave also resilience in leasing companies. Also, more formal processes and procedures were promoted. Many companies implemented written contingency plans as well as schedules of responsibilities and a risk management team. However, it can be seen that the degree of formality of risk management depends strongly on the company size. This was also confirmed in earlier studies in other industries (Durst & Ferenhof, 2016; Falkner & Hiebl, 2015; Henschel, 2008).

However, those SMEs having established a contingency planning mainly focus on IT. Only a handful of SMEs extended their contingency planning to other "emergencies" arising, for example, due to liquidity shortages, absences of key players etc. On the one hand, it does not seem to be surprising that the main focus is on IT, as for a financial service company, such as a leasing firm, this often is the central "Achilles' heel". On the other hand, a pure focus on IT might often also neglect other important areas. For example, clear substitution plans and competences might be necessary in case of unplanned absences of key players as well as pre-defined measures in case of liquidity gaps.

As all of those SMEs with a more extensive contingency planning are part of a group, it might be concluded that the group influence results more likely in a more extensive contingency plan. In one case, a medium-sized SME even went one step further and developed a crisis management system:

> Crisis management goes one step further as we decide there how to react in case a certain event might trigger a crisis in our group. This can be production downtimes or, in a global context, political crises where we need (in an extreme case) to get our employees out of a certain country.

Such a crisis management might be seen as a very advanced form of organisational resilience and is probably, for most German leasing SMEs, too sophisticated. If only for political crises and questions on how to bring back employees do not seem to be relevant for most SMEs that are acting only on the German market.

10.5.2 Isolated, Small-Scale Decisions Based on Single Exposures

The smaller a leasing company, the more focus is typically on single exposures and single events. The decisions are mainly made by the owner-manager and not discussed in a management team. SMEs tend to focus on simple tools and to a certain degree on their gut feeling instead of applying highly sophisticated stochastic models. Surely, the regulative requirements strengthened the meaning of portfolio-based considerations. Nevertheless, portfolio management is rather seldom used by SMEs. The reasons vary from missing high-volume business and no universal approach with the possibility to diversify or simply to a lack of experience in building up portfolio management and reporting. Larger firms, on the other hand, focus more on portfolio-driven views and have an expert team more often in charge when evaluating the risk management performance.

Not only the little IT resources can be seen as a key factor for highly manual control activities, often based on individual data processing like Excel, Access or even handwritten lists. Additionally, missing knowledge and experience in the use of such tools and methods is one key explanation to consider. Several studies showed that although structures for managing risks are widely implemented, reactive risk behaviour is still dominant (e.g., Bömelburg et al., 2012; Klein & Höfner, 2011; Neyer & Hofeditz, 2014). The usage of early warning signals which are essential for a proactive approach to crisis management show a clear size effect: The larger a company, the more probable it is that early warning indicators are used.

10.5.3 No Integrated Approach to Resilience

An integrated approach to organizational resilience means more than simply keeping a few contingency plans for the major IT tasks. It involves a close connection of all major tasks such as strategic planning and especially management behaviour and status quo reporting.

In all of the interviewed SMEs, crisis management and risk management—which form the basis for organisational resilience—are undertaken by the same person. In larger firms, there were some firms having separate risk and crisis managers and different committees. Also, the few SMEs which stated that their risk management is connected with strategic planning only have at best a partial connection in place. Although some of the interviewed small firms described their approach as integrated as risk/crisis management and other core functions such as strategic planning (if performed at all) are mainly undertaken or at least accounted by the same person—for example, the owner-manager, with the ultimate decision power and responsible for risk and crisis management—it showed that it is not integrated.

Although organisational resilience is perceived as important by most of the interviewed SMEs, an integrated approach with a harmonisation with the planning process and other strategic elements is missing. To a high degree, a lack of knowledge leads to ineffective solutions in risk and crisis management and the missing use of new tools and methods. The lack of knowledge might also be seen as the major reason why most SMEs were erroneously convinced of having an integrated instead of a rather isolated approach to risk and crisis management.

10.5.4 Lack of Know-How and High Degree of Informality

SMEs employ less academics with mostly less external experience than larger firms. Decisions are mainly made by the (owner) manager and also, alternatives seem to be underestimated. Furthermore, most SMEs are anxious of losing flexibility (which is one of their core competitive advantages) when applying formal methods in risk management more intensively. As also external consultants are only seldom hired, the risk managers depend heavily on their informal network in between the leasing industry as well as their contact to the federal association of German leasing firms (BDL) and the external auditors. Risk management practices in SMEs are more informal than in larger firms. This can be especially seen in the different steps of the risk management process but also in informal meetings as well as informal exchange of ideas with colleagues in the leasing industry, for example, on competition analysis but also on risk identification and fraud prevention.

When it comes to new situations for SMEs' managers, they frequently use their personal network to manage risky situations. In "normal" risk situations, this might be helpful; in crisis situations, relying mainly on informal networks might be very dangerous.

The typically flat hierarchies promote informal processes and measures, whereas strict rules and process descriptions put pressure on more formal processes. Also, the strict rules of the banking supervision increase the importance of formal crisis management. One of the interviewed SMEs therefore also stated in this context:

> While we were able to handle things on an informal basis in the past, we are now forced more often to get processes described and created in a more formal way.

Some SMEs are therefore afraid of losing their high degree of flexibility and refuse strict limits as they see their unique selling proposition and their fast and uncomplicated decision-making process in jeopardy, otherwise.

Those SMEs which are more established and on the brink of becoming a large firm tend to have more often a formal risk and crisis management in place. They are also more advanced in the life cycle typology and focus on integrated and formal processes and tools. The different checks and policies are shaped greatly by the own experiences with crises. It is therefore closely connected with the topic of organisational learning, respectively learning from failure.

10.5.5 Scarcity of Resources

The scarcity of resources influences different levels of the organization and the risk management system, for example, recruiting, IT, liquidity and funding, etc. Especially since the financial crisis in 2008, the importance of risk acceptance increased as fewer banks were willing to take the full risks from the leasing firms. Due to scarce resources, leasing firms now had to decide either to take the risks on their own or decline the requests.

With increasing risk acceptance, also the vulnerability for crises increases and consequently also the need for a well-working crisis management system. Whereas larger leasing firms are mainly afraid of economic crises and fraud cases, small leasing firms see also other sources of crises such as problems in recruitment and dependency on single key players or family disputes.

SMEs seem to be stuck in operative challenges. None of the interviewed small or micro firms mentioned a strategic challenge as their currently striking key task. On the other hand, the interviewed medium-sized along with the large firms focus more on the future development of the company in general and the risk and crisis management in particular in their key challenges of digitalisation as well as achieving a proof of concept of risk management activities. Additionally, their goal is to eliminate the strong emotional influence in the daily risk management and strengthen its objectivity. Only with a transparent risk management, it is possible to achieve best results also for crisis management.

10.5.6 Unstructured Organisational Learning

Organisational learning and back testing are undertaken at best in an unstructured way. It is highly subjective and not sufficiently documented. Although the processes and models are typically simple and no highly complex validation and learning cycle would be necessary, also simple post calculations of contracts or alpha and beta errors do not exist. Merely for fraud cases, several SMEs built up a database to learn from failures and modify processes and tools.

Smallman (1996) stressed the importance of organisational learning for an enterprise-wide approach to risk management by stating that it is "the lynch pin of holistic risk management" (Smallman, 1996, p. 16). This statement seems to be valid for organisational resilience too, learning from failures and losses not only from own ones but also from others. Only with an appropriate corporate culture, organisational resilience might be effective enough to allow a fast and structured response to crises. Most of the crises are foreshadowing. Therefore, the connection between event identification and reporting tasks as well as process descriptions and changes in processes might be in the focus. The feedback loop with the organisational learning is also closely connected to back testing, as well as basic risk management tasks or policies.

Organisational learning is therefore as important as the severity of a crisis might be quickly existence threatening on the one hand, but on the other hand, similar risky situations might occur und resemble each other. The following quote of Mark Twain is in line with this view: "History doesn't repeat itself, but it does rhyme".

10.5.7 Strong Dependency on Key Players

Probably the most underestimated risk also goes along with scarce resources: dependency on key players/human resources risk (HR risk). In comparison to large firms, SMEs more often encounter a strong dependency on key players as specialists are rare and not all jobs have adequate substitutes. The flat hierarchies on the other hand make it easier for managers to establish a company-wide risk culture by simply acting as role models and having a basic documentation on it.

The banking regulation with its focus on enterprise-wide documentations of core processes and tasks also helped many SMEs to decrease the dependency on key players as those core requirements are now transparent.

In smaller owner-managed firms, the owner is typically involved in all decisions whereas larger firms tend to manage risks collectively through expert boards of directors. In some cases, the owner-manager is supported by a small management team—in crisis situations this might be also a crisis team—although this is rather an exception for most of the researched SMEs. Besides the personal experience and educational background, the personality of the manager takes an important role. The positive side of this situation is a fast and flexible decision-making, and the negative side is the strong dependency as well as the risk of lonesome decisions without any other expert who might intervene if necessary.

The following chapter focuses on public investigations through the German banking supervision. During those investigations, a leasing company's risk management including crisis management is checked considering its compliance with regulative requirements.

10.6 Public Investigations Through Banking Supervision

The German leasing industry is regulated by the German banking supervision since 2009. Therefore, the risk management practice of German leasing firms is greatly shaped by regulative aspects such as the "Minimum Requirements of Risk Management" as well as the "Supervisory Requirements for IT in Financial Institutions". Compliance with regulative requirements is checked via regulative reporting, regular annual audits and public audits by the banking regulation.

Public Audits by the Banking Supervision

Public audits of German leasing companies are typically conducted by Deutsche Bundesbank on behalf of Bundesanstalt für Finanzdienstleistungsaufsicht (BaFin). Those audits are based on § 44 Kreditwesengesetz (German Banking Act) and can be due to a particular reason as well as routine audits without any particular reason. The latter was a reaction to the bankruptcy of Herstatt Bank in 1974 which was hit by devise speculations and rumours in the context of an upcoming public audit by the banking supervision. At this time, public audits equalled a general stigmatisation of the audited institute—no matter of the audit's results.

Public audits might be on general risk management topics or on particular focus topics where the banking supervision is aiming to gain a better understanding how certain topics are handled in practice. Besides random selections, the banking supervision might also react to newspaper notifications or other reports on drawbacks such as in the Libor affair with institutes like Deutsche Bank or the Wirecard affair with non-existing EUR 1.9 billion of cash (Hesse, 2013; Storbeck et al., 2020).

Focus Areas of Banking Regulation

The vast majority of areas are directly connected to risk management and related topics such as credit processes, IT-related topics such as contingency plans, business continuity management, etc. The regulatory focus topics are chosen annually by the European Central Bank (ECB) and the German banking supervision derives its own topics, mostly in congruence to those of the ECB.

All of the actions are aiming to achieve the banking supervision's goals (Glaser, 2020a):

- Ensuring operational capability, stability and integrity of the German financial market
- Compliance with respective laws and regulation
- Ensuring operational capability of solvency at all times; protection of customers' account deposits

Room for Improvement

Reports of public audits show that organisational resilience and especially crisis management are well documented in the meantime for IT topics. However, "dry runs" and tests are often incomplete. Therefore, the banking supervision comes up regularly with amendments (i.e., new regulations) and clarifications (of existing regulations) to constantly improve the crisis management and especially to adapt it to changed environments. Especially in the context of IT, one might see the increasing importance to be prepared against information crises such as cybercrime and information theft through hackers.

As leasing companies operate nearly fully digital, information crises have become the most important field for crisis management over the last years. Other important threats are personnel crises especially for smaller companies that sometimes depend existentially on one or only a few key players and also legal and reputational crises. Especially changes in the legal environment might easily endanger the business model of a leasing company. Economic crises are another important category. On a customer level, the credit risk is normally carefully checked; however, on a global level, it is hard to predict an economic recession or global crisis. The other crises named in Sect. 10.2.1 such as physical crises, natural disasters and external criminal crises are less important for most leasing SMEs compared to the aforementioned ones.

Focus on Covid-19 and War in Ukraine

The banking supervision aims to have an up-to-date picture of the situation of the financial market in general and the leasing market in particular. Therefore, besides public investigations, they also send out investigative letters with questions on current market situations and the company's prognosis. In the Covid-19 crisis and the war in Ukraine, especially for large firms with a certain relevance to the financial system, the Federal Financial Supervisory Authority (BaFin) held regular videoconferences. For system relevant banks, the cycle was even shorter for sure. However, among the participants, there was no leasing SMEs, and most of the participants were banks or large leasing companies belonging to a bank holding with a certain relevance to the financial system.

In the midst of the Covid-19 crisis, the European Banking Association (EBA) as the European standard setter with relevance for the German banking supervision, too, emphasized the importance of crisis management. Also, declarations on the liquidation planning of institutes as well as Covid-19 policies were published by the EBA. The BaFin published FAQs and other information on regulatory measures and sanctions, but also journal papers on the significance of the Covid-19 crisis (BaFin, 2020b, c, d, e).

The following chapter summarises selected findings on risk management in general and crisis management in particular in the German leasing industry with a focus on SMEs' organizational resilience.

10.7 Framework on Organizational Resilience for Leasing Firms

The presented framework on organisational resilience aims to improve the risk and crisis management processes in a transparent and structured way regardless of the company's size. It was developed on the basis of the conducted 40 interviews by the author of this research. The core element is surely the underlying risk strategy which is typically derived from the business strategy and the global risk strategy and must include detailed information to what extent which risks are accepted and how they should be handled. And of course, it needs to be defined at what moment the crisis management is taking over. The risk strategy is typically closely connected to a risk analysis with the essential risks and its probability of occurrence. The exact characteristics of resilience are also strongly depending on the underlying motivation: Is it intrinsic or is it purely compliance driven? This means: Is the main driver self-interest by the management or is it the regulatory pressure?

The typical starting point is a transparent definition of severity and crises events. This also includes the differentiation between disruption/interruption of operations, contingency/emergency, crisis and catastrophe (with ascending severity). In a first step, the focus is on the criticality of processes and applications or functions before potential events that might harm those areas are connected in a second step.

In the operations and resources perspective, selected measures—depending strongly on the underlying critical processes and tasks and interrelationships with other areas, applications and processes—are included. It needs to be addressed which maximum downtimes are acceptable for the respective tasks, what thresholds are acceptable when it comes to malperformance, but also which alternatives exist in case a process cannot be performed as desired/expected.

Besides formal written documentations and plans, this also includes checks, policies and internal environment. Surely, the banking regulation led to a professionalisation of risk management in leasing companies. Also, more formal processes and procedures were promoted. Nevertheless, it can be seen that the degree of formality of risk management depends strongly on the company size. Especially in small and medium-sized firms, knowledge is mostly informal (Henschel et al., 2015) and therefore also risk management is supposed to be more difficult to establish. On the other hand, it is more difficult in larger firms to implement the right "instinct" which is in line with the risk strategy, which is essential as there is often no time during crises to carefully re-evaluate measures or read in which job instruction everything is written. In every crisis situation, employees and managers need to decide certain things independently as not every eventuality can be foreseen.

The corporate risk appetite needs to be reflected in the different steps of risk and crisis management at every time. This also includes outsourced tasks that need to be considered carefully and particularly in the risk management system.

In the reporting perspective, it is essential to constantly compare the status quo to the corporate objectives. This is also more than simply checking whether a crisis or a catastrophe occurred. It is also about early warning systems and interruptions with the potential for a crisis, so-called near misses. It is also about learning from failures (own ones and ones from others), gaining a feeling for crises as well as finding the right balance between formality and flexibility. It is about making failures "learnable" and moving the decision-makers as well as all other employees from the unknown to the known. Only what is known can also be actively managed!

The planning dimension focuses on the potential impact of crises on the company's plan fulfilment. Besides forecasts or scenario analyses for the status quo, this also involves strategic planning aspects such as decisions on activities in new markets or with new products or potential mergers and acquisitions. Furthermore, this might also involve larger changes of organisational structures and processes. In this dimension, it is important to also involve stakeholders to a certain extent.

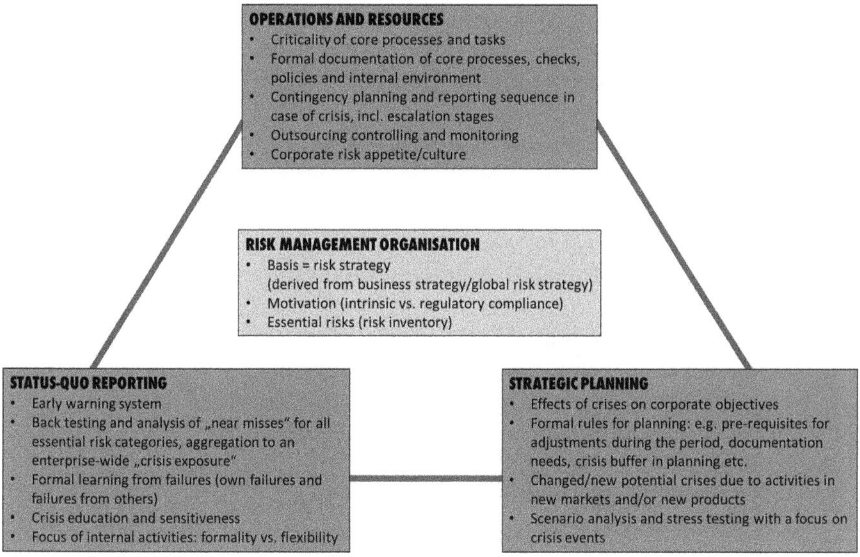

Fig. 10.2 Framework on organisational resilience for leasing firms. (Source: Own illustration)

The following Fig. 10.2 presents a proposed framework for organisational resilience that is following a framework by the author of this article on enterprise-wide risk management for German leasing firms (Glaser, 2020b).

The presented framework cannot eliminate all crises and does not make risk management useless. Instead, it should be seen as an early draft for first more conscious steps to an active risk and crisis management. Due to the characteristics of crises, interruptions and catastrophes and the huge variety and origins, it is more important to get started than aiming at the 100% solution. A large benefit is already achieved when a certain awareness for crises is created. This is why organisational resilience is a core part of a good governance!

10.8 Self-Assessment on Resilience

Based on the framework presented in Fig. 10.2 and practical experiences of the author, the following "Practitioner Checklist" is supposed to support leasing companies (and companies from other industries as well) in their efforts to identify sources of crises and finally implement an organisational resilience with a certain risk and crisis management in practice:

Practitioner Checklist on Organisational Resilience

Step 1: Identification of critical tasks, processes and functions

- Definition of criticality in terms of profitability, legal aspects and time criticality
  - What is the maximum loss the company might bear without getting existential problems?
  - Which deadlines or other legal requirements are endangered when certain processes or tasks cannot be performed as planned?
  - What is the maximum downtime for different tasks?
- What alternatives exist for critical processes?
- In which cases is a strong dependency without any substitute partner/solution prevailing?
- What thresholds are in place? Where is the brink of "normal" interruptions and a crisis?
- Are all tasks and functions included, also outsourced jobs?

Step 2: (Early warning) indicators for crisis management

- Dependency on key players
  - Employee fluctuation (esp. in critical departments such as sales)
  - Number of identified key players (employees in critical jobs without substitute)
  - Days of absence
- Avoiding dependencies
  - Are there any limits for certain business partners?
  - Is there a careful outsourcing controlling in place?
  - Do internal auditors of the leasing company also include outsourced activities in their audit landscape?
  - Is management carefully considering dependencies in its strategic roadmap?
  - Are there any sole dependencies due to no acceptable alternatives? What are the company's immediate measures and drawer plans to deal with this in line with the risk strategy?
- IT environment and processes
  - Outsourcing ratio (no. of outsourced, critical tasks/activities)
  - Number of non-integrated, different IT systems
  - Degree of formality of internal activities: formal vs. informal
  - Core processes documented
  - Age/availability of IT infrastructure
  - Self-invented IT system vs. standard-ERP by well-known software provider
  - Backup infrastructure
- Liquidity situation
  - Available revolving credit line (contractually agreed)
  - Development of the own credit rating by external banks
  - Number of different bank partners
  - Credit spread for own credit lines

  - Volume of overdue payments by customers
- Risk culture
  - How can the lived risk culture be classified?
  - Is the way of working characterised by rules and prohibitions or is there a lot of freedom for the individual employees?
  - How is regular reconciliation carried out to ensure that decisions made independently are in line with the company and the risk strategy?
  - Is risk orientation carried out holistically “from the gatekeeper to the boss”?
- Focus on planning
  - How is the strategic planning organised?
  - Despite all the planning efforts, is there still enough room for unplanned issues?
  - How much focus is there on responding appropriately to certain circumstances rather than the illusion of being able to predict everything?
  - To what extent does the factor of antifragility find applications in the strategic orientation of the company? This could possibly make numerous planning steps obsolete.

The points considered in step 1 of the presented practitioner checklist on organisational resilience are essentially open questions and can be answered completely differently depending on the individual, critical aspects and processes. The indicators mentioned in step 2, however, are transformed in the following “Self-Assessment on Organisational Resilience” template. Based on the results of this assessment, the leasing firms see transparently where any areas for improvement are and where resilience is already comparably strong.

For each question, a scoring between 1 (lowest) and 4 (highest) is supposed to be assigned. To avoid that the middle score is chosen too often, four grades are chosen.

Self-Assessment on Organisational Resilience

Instruction: Please answer the following questions for the considered company by assigning scores between 1 and 4.

(a) *IT Infrastructure and Processes*

How frequent and how severe were computer crashes, system breakdowns and IT downtimes in the last 12 months?

(1 = not at all; 2 = very seldom and only minor effect; 3 = happened several times with an effect only on few departments; 4 = happens frequently with considerable effects to the whole company)

How would you describe the age and availability of the IT infrastructure?

(1 = state of the art; 2 = quite new with strict maintenance intervals; 3 = infrastructure works mostly, but maintenance intervals have expired; 4 = outdated infrastructure, hard to find experts to fix the system in case of problems)

To what degree are non-integrated, different IT-systems used?

(1 = one major ERP system for all critical processes; 2 = only very few other applications that are, however, connected via standard interfaces; 3 = several different IT systems that are mainly connected via standard interfaces to one leading ERP system; 4 = numerous non-integrated systems with different leading systems and double entry of data depending on different departments)

How formal are core processes and the backup infrastructure documented and checked? Are continuity tests undertaken regularly?

(1 = highly formal, at least once a year for all critical processes; 2 = formal for most processes, tests are undertaken from time to time; 3 = mainly informal, tests are undertaken sporadically and unstructured; 4 = no formal documentation and no tests at all)

To what degree are outsourced services and facilities used?

(1 = nothing outsourced at all; 2 = only very few outsourcing with carefully selected and well-certified partners; 3 = outsourcing plays an important role and dependencies on outsourcing partners exist; 4 = numerous outsourced tasks, the leasing firm has no knowledge to perform the tasks on its own again)

(b) *Crisis Culture*

Are "near misses" in all areas reported and their sources carefully tracked?

(1 = mandatory for every department; 2 = on a voluntary basis, depends on the criticality; 3 = sporadical talks, employees are asked to report on them; 4 = no reporting at all)

Is a company-wide, formal knowledge sharing and mistake culture lived?

(1 = very well established with additional events such as regular round table sessions or jour fixes for department-wide exchange; 2 = partly, depends strongly on each department leader and superior; 3 = first measures to step away from egoistic views; 4 = culture of fear with blaming and knowledge hiding widely spread)

How frequent are internal changes in processes, checks and procedures due to learnings from failures?

(1 = frequently, all over the company; 2 = quite frequently, depending strongly on the department; 3 = partly, but clear measures and responsibilities of superiors to ensure transparency; 4 = very seldom, no structured reaction and no formal learning from failures)

(c) *Restart Phase*

What is the degree of formality for internal activities?

(1 = highly formal, all important decisions need to be audit proof and follow the rules; 2 = mainly formal, only in few situations, informal and spontaneous activities/overrides are common; 3 = mainly informal with only few rules, but more and more formalized due to regulative pressure; 4 = highly informal, management decides on their own with a high degree of flexibility, no global policy or rules in place)

To what degree are core processes documented?

(1 = all core processes are documented and constantly checked and updated; 2 = most processes are documented and updated once a year; 3 = only few documented processes, no mandatory update; 4 = (specialist) knowledge is mainly undocumented and typically in the head of the employees)

Is a contingency planning in place and considers all critical areas (on the basis of a protection requirements analysis)?

(1 = well-established and considering all critical areas; 2 = in place but not covering all essential areas; 3 = only considering IT risks, no other areas at all; 4 = no contingency planning at all)

(d) *Coordination Effort with Partners*

To what extent are critical tasks outsourced?

(1 = not at all; 2 = only very few outsourcing and carefully selected partners with certifications; 3 = several critical tasks are outsourced, there are contractual regulations but no additional checks or minimum requirements of outsourcing partners; 4 = numerous activities to stay flexible and make use of partner's expertise instead of building up own expertise)

Does the contingency planning also consider outsourced activities?

(1 = all outsourced activities are considered and annual floor checks undertaken; 2 = partly, focus on most critical outsourced tasks; 3 = only on special purpose when risks are striking; 4 = no, focus only on internally performed tasks)

(e) *Liquidity Situation and Credit Terms*

To what extent is a contractually agreed, revolving credit line available?

(1 = the company might be able to cover its costs without receiving any cash-in for more than 6 months; 2 = the company is able to cover its costs for more than 3 months; 3 = the company is only able to cover its costs for 1 month; 4 = no available, contractually agreed credit line)

How is the own credit rating (that is compiled by banks) developing? How is the credit spread for own credit lines developing?

(1 = improvement with positive outlook; 2 = slightly improving or unchanged, outlook stable; 3 = slightly downgrading or unchanged, outlook negative; 4 = clear downgrade, outlook negative)

How is the volume of overdue payments by customers developing?

(1 = decreasing volume in all branches; 2 = slightly decreasing or stable on a low level; 3 = slightly increasing or stable on a high level; 4 = clear increase in all major branches and rating classes)

(f) *Dependency on Key Players*

How is the level of employee fluctuation in knowledge-critical departments, such as sales?

(1 = constant on a low level; 2 = slightly increasing but still on a low level; 3 = constant on a medium level; 4 = strongly increasing and/or on a high level)

How is the level of absence days in knowledge-critical departments, such as sales?

(1 = constant on a low level; 2 = slightly increasing but still on a low level; 3 = constant on a medium level; 4 = strongly increasing and/or on a high level)

How is the level of (external) training days, especially in departments with critical specialist knowledge, such as legal department?

(1 = constant on a high level; 2 = slightly decreasing but still on a high level; 3 = constant on a medium level; 4 = strongly decreasing and/or on a low level)

How is the level of lost customers to former sales reps (customer "stealing" through fluctuated employees)?

(1 = constant on a low level; 2 = slightly increasing but still on a low level; 3 = constant on a medium level; 4 = strongly increasing and/or on a high level)

How is the level of employees "lost" to direct competitors (employee "stealing" through direct competitors)?

(1 = constant on a low level; 2 = slightly increasing but still on a low level; 3 = constant on a medium level; 4 = strongly increasing and/or on a high level)

How high is the proportion of key players without direct substitutes?

(1 = very low, all key players have assigned direct substitutes who also serve as holiday replacement to stay updated; 2 = quite low, assigned substitutes to the vast majority of key players; 3 = moderate, substitution planning for most key players, degree of practical tests, for example, due to holiday replacements, depends on each department; 4 = high, substi-

tutes are assigned by management on special purpose only when key player is absent, based on availability of substitutes)

What is the focus of employee education: specialist or rather generalist?

(1 = generalist; 2 = centralistic education with specific expert's focus; 3 = focus on expert's knowledge that is covered by several employees—"expert's group"; 4 = specialist with large expert knowledge and little up to no direct substitutes)

What is the effect of the sudden absence of a key player such as department leader, sales rep, general manager?

(1 = more work for substitute, but clearly defined tasks and responsibilities; 2 = most tasks are documented, substitute needs some time to keep the critical processes running; 3 = negative effect is seen clearly in the financial figures, large degree of improvisation necessary with time-intense search for substitute and substitute's start-up phase; 4 = existence-threatening situation, search for external substitutes takes very long)

When calculating the average score for each of the questions and/or the categories, it becomes quite obvious where improvement potentials and where critical areas are. Based on the criticality, the companies should prioritise their actions. Scores between 1 and 2 might be assigned due to a low severity and no immediate action necessary, whereas scores between 3 and 4 might be an indicator for very critical developments and the need for immediate action and countermeasures.

Like in the classical risk management as well, the risk handling is typically oriented on the criticality, that is, the risk/loss potential, and the respective probability

Table 10.3 Different levels of organisational resilience

Low level of resilience	High degree of resilience
Key players are not fully transparent, and no substitution plans are in place.	Key players are made transparent with clearly assigned substitutes.
Neither formal learning from failures nor regular continuity tests	Formal learning from failures and frequent continuity tests for all critical processes
IT systems are outdated and mainly non-integrated and no backup location is available.	Modern IT system with very few different sub-systems/databases is in place including a well-working backup location.
High degree of informality—knowledge tacit, not explicit	Focus on formal and documented processes.
No available, contractually agreed revolving credit line	Contractually agreed, revolving credit line with sufficient volume to cover costs for a longer period
No crisis management team ("crisis committee") and no definition of crisis "thresholds" and no pre-defined reporting lines	Crisis committee and clear definition of crisis, frequent scenario analyses and stress tests including crisis events as well as pre-defined reporting lines
Neither contingency planning for all core processes nor outsourcing controlling	Contingency planning for all core processes and outsourcing controlling
No limits for certain levels of dependencies of certain stakeholders/third parties, etc.	Strict limits for levels of dependencies of certain stakeholders/third parties, etc.

Source: Own illustration

of occurrence. Therefore, different countermeasures might be selected when handling the different processes, departments and/or tasks. Also, the success of the chosen measures should be closely monitored in a designated crisis risk reporting.

Based on the presented checklist with the self-assessment and the earlier presented framework on risk and crisis management, one can see clear differences among the different leasing companies and the respective anchorage of organisational resilience in the operative tasks and processes. Companies with a high level of resilience seem to consider most of the mentioned points and try to achieve the maximum effect, whereas small companies often show a less formal approach to resilience. If they consider crises situations at all, they are often only reacting when a severe situation occurs. They are typically focused strongly on very few key areas and no formal resilience or documented processes, and contingency plans are existent. Due to the high degree of informality, operations stay tacit and are not getting explicit which makes organisational resilience very difficult.

The following Table 10.3 presents a summary of selected resilience characteristics of the two extremes, a high and low level of organisational resilience.

10.9 Conclusion

In general, SMEs are more vulnerable for crises and disasters. This is also true for leasing companies. Customers reduce their investments—at least capital-widening investments and not replacement investments—and banks tend to apply stricter rules and higher prices for their fundings. At the same time, a crisis can create market opportunities that can best be addressed with innovative and proactive employees. In this case, the flexible and quick decision-making of SMEs is beneficial.

On the way of becoming resilient "masters of disasters", the presented framework on organisational resilience is supposed to help leasing SMEs to apply a structured management and decision-making approach. This approach is supposed to be more than simply regulatory compliance. Instead, it focuses on an economic-driven, enterprise-wide approach that is congruent with the risk management strategy and processes. By becoming more and more resilient to crises, SMEs have more time to take the upcoming chances and turn the crisis into the ramp-up stage for sustainable growth.

It is not without cause that the Greek word "krisis" does not only describe a hopeless situation but rather the turning point of a dangerous situation. Also the Chinese word for crisis, namely, "weiji 危机" consists of "wei 危" that means danger and "ji 机" that means opportunity (Glaser, 2019). The close connection of crisis and strategic planning illustrates the importance of an integrated approach to CM for companies of all sizes and all industries. For leasing companies, the regulatory aspects require even more a structured and enterprise-wide approach to crisis management (Glaser, 2022).

References

Acciarini, C., Boccardelli, P., & Vitale, M. (2021). Resilient companies in the time of Covid-19 pandemic: A case study approach. *Journal of Entrepreneurship and Public Policy, 10*(3), 336–351.

Allen, K. (1995). *Launching new ventures – An entrepreneurial approach*. Upstart.

Anani, M., & Owusu, F. (2023). Regulatory capital and bank risk-resilience amid the Covid-19 pandemic: How are the Basel reforms faring? *Finance Research Letters, 52*, 103591.

Argenti, J. (1976). *Corporate collapse – The causes and symptoms*. Halstead Press.

Ates, A., & Bititci, U. (2011). Change process: A key enabler for building resilient SMEs. *International Journal of Production Research, 49*(18), 5601–5618.

BaFin. (2020a). *Liste der zugelassenen Finanzierungsleasing- und Factoringinstitute*. As of June 15, 2020. https://www.bafin.de/SharedDocs/Downloads/DE/Liste/Unternehmensdatenbank/dl_li_fidi_leas_fac.html

BaFin. (2020b). Coronakrise, EBA erläutert Leitlinien zu allgemeinen. July 10, 2020. Zahlungsmoratorien. https://www.bafin.de/SharedDocs/Veroeffentlichungen/DE/Meldung/2020_Corona_andereBehoerden/meldung_2020_07_10_corona_virus_74_EBA_Leitlinien_allgemeine_Zahlungsmoratorien.html;jsessionid=735A0B1295ED43B79F28E1A4ED33EFBD.1_cid370

BaFin. (2020c). Covid-19-Lage: Neue Entwicklungen und wichtige Informationen der BaFin. July 6, 2020. https://www.bafin.de/DE/Aufsicht/CoronaVirus/CoronaVirus_node.html

BaFin. (2020d). Corona-Krise: BaFin erläutert veränderte aufsichtliche Anforderungen. March 24, 2020. https://www.bafin.de/SharedDocs/Veroeffentlichungen/DE/Pressemitteilung/2020/pm_200324_corona-krise_aufsichtliche_anforderungen.html

BaFin. (2020e). Corona-Virus ist ein erhebliches Risiko für den Finanzsektor. March 17, 2020. https://www.bafin.de/SharedDocs/Veroeffentlichungen/DE/Fachartikel/2020/fa_bj_2003_Corona.html

Bennett, N., & Lemoine, G. (2014, January–February). What VUCA really means for you. *Harvard Business Review*. https://hbr.org/2014/01/what-vuca-really-means-for-you

Bennis, W. G., & Nanus, B. (1985). *Leaders: Strategies for taking charge*. Harper & Row.

Bhamra, R. (2016). *Organisational resilience: Concepts, integration and practice*. Taylor & Francis Group.

Bisnode. (2020). *Firmendatenbank*. https://www.hoppenstedt-firmendatenbank.de/

Boers, B., & Henschel, T. (2021). Entrepreneurial orientation and crisis: How family firms manage the COVID-19 pandemic. *Rethinking Finance, 1*(3), 65–72.

Bömelburg, P., Zähres, R., Beyer, G., & Schöffel, C. P. (2012). Risikomanagement im Mittelstand - Eine aktuelle Bestandsaufnahme. *Der Betrieb, 65(21), 1161–1166.*

Branson, M. (2022, November 14). *Die Banken sollten ihre Resilienz aufrechterhalten*. BaFin.com. https://www.bafin.de/SharedDocs/Veroeffentlichungen/DE/Meldung/2022/meldung_2022_11_14_EuroFinanceWeek_P.html

Bullough, A., Renko, M., & Myatt, T. (2014). Danger zone entrepreneurs: The importance of resilience and self-efficacy for entrepreneurial intentions. *Entrepreneurship: Theory and Practice, 38*(3), 473–499.

Bundesverband Deutscher Leasing-Unternehmen (BDL). (2022). *Marktbericht 2022*. https://jahresbericht.leasingverband.de/leasing-markt-und-umfeld/marktbericht-2022/

Carmeli, A., & Markman, G. D. (2011). Capture, governance, and resilience: Strategy implications from the history of Rome. *Strategic Management Journal, 32*(3), 322–341.

Charmaz, K. (2006). Constructing grounded theory: A practical guide through qualitative research. Sage, London.

Coombs, W. T., & Holladay, S. J. (2006). Unpacking the halo effect: Reputation and crisis management. *Journal of Communication Management, 2*(10), 123–137.

Corey, C. M., & Deitch, E. A. (2011). Factors affecting business recovery immediately after Hurricane Katrina. *Journal of Contingencies & Crisis Management, 19*(3), 170–181.

Corner, P. D., Singh, S., & Pavlovich, K. (2017). Entrepreneurial resilience and venture failure. *International Small Business Journal, 35*(6), 687–708.

Coutu, D. (2002). How resilience works. *Harvard Business Review, 80*(5), 46–51.

DesJardine, M., Bansal, P., Yang, Y. (2019). Bouncing back: building resilience through social and environmental practices in the context of the 2008 global financial crisis. *Journal of Management, 45(4), 1434–1460.*

Doern, R. (2016). Entrepreneurship and crisis management: The experiences of small businesses during the London 2011 riots. *International Small Business Journal: Researching Entrepreneurship, 34*(3), 276–302.

Dormady, N., Roa-Henriquez, A., & Rose, A. (2019). Economic resilience of the firm: A production theory approach. *International Journal of Production Economics, 208*, 446–460.

Dovern, J., Meier, C. P., & Vilsmeier, J. (2010). How resilient is the German banking system to macroeconomic shocks? *Journal of Banking and Finance, 34*(8), 1839–1848.

Durst, S., Ferenhof, H. A. (2016). Knowledge risk management in turbulent times. In: North K, Varvakis G (eds.) Competitive strategies for small and medium enterprises. Springer, Cham, p 195–209

Easterby-Smith, M., Thorpe, R., & Jackson, P. R. (2015). *Management and business research (5th ed.). London: Sage.*

Edmondson, A. C., McManus, S. E. (2007). Methodological fit in management field research. *Academy of management review, 32(4), 1246–1264.*

Falkner, E. M., Hiebl, M. R. W. (2015). Risk management in SMEs: a systematic review of available evidence. *Journal of Risk Finance, 16(2):122–144.*

Fiksel, J. (2003). Designing resilient, sustainable systems. *Environmental Science and Technology, 37*(23), 5330–5339.

Fiksel, J. (2006). Sustainability and resilience: Toward a systems approach. *Sustainability: Science, Practice and Policy, 2*(2), 1–8.

Ghouse, G., Ejaz, N., Bhatti, M. I., & Aslam, A. (2022). Performance of islamic vs conventional banks in OIC countries: Resilience and recovery during Covid-19. *Borsa Istanbul Review, 22*, S60–S78.

Gittell, J. H., Cameron, K., Lim, S., Rivas, V. (2006). Relationships, layoffs, and organizational resilience. *The Journal of Applied Behavioral Science, 42(3), 300–329.*

Glaser, C. (2018). Risikofaktoren im Leasing und deren ganzheitliches Management: Ergebnisse einer empirischen Studie kleiner und mittelständischer Unternehmen. *Finanzierung Leasing Factoring, 65*(5), 210–217.

Glaser, C. (2019). *Risiko im management.* Springer.

Glaser, C. (2020a). Knoweldge Risk Management in German Leasing Companies. In: Durst, S., Henschel, T. (2020) Knowledge Risk Management: From Theory to Praxis. Springer, Cham, p.159–183.

Glaser, C. (2020b). BaFin-Sonderprüfungen nach §44 KWG. Wiesbaden, Springer.

Glaser, C. (2022). Crisis management in German leasing companies. In S. Durst & T. Henschel (Eds.), *Crisis management for small and medium-sized enterprises (SMEs)* (pp. 165–190). Springer.

Gorge, M. (2006). Crisis management best practice – Where do we start from? *Computer Fraud & Security, 2006*(6), 10–13.

Hamel, G. A., & Valikangas, L. (2003). The quest for resilience. *Harvard Business Review, 81*(9), 52–63.

Haswell, S., & Holmes, S. (1989). Estimating the small business failure rate: A reappraisal. *Journal of Small Business Management, 27*(3), 68–74.

Henschel, T. (2008). Sophistication of risk management practices in German SMEs. *Controller Magazin, 33(1):83–90.*

Henschel, T., Durst, S., Busch, S. (2015). Praxis des Risikomanagements: deutsche, chinesische und schottische kleine und mittlere Unternehmen. *Zeitschrift für Risk, Fraud & Compliance (ZRFC), 10(6), 246–255.*

Herbane, B. (2010). Small business research: Time for a crisis-based view. *International Small Business Journal, 28*, 43–64.
Herbane, B. (2019). Rethinking organizational resilience and strategic renewal in SMEs. *Entrepreneurship & Regional Development, 31*(5–6), 476–495.
Hesse, M. (2013). LIBOR Probe Could Cost Deutsche Bank Billions. Accusations Against Jain. Spiegel International. *February, 4, 2013.* https://www.spiegel.de/international/business/libor-probe-could-cause-deutsche-bank-billions-of-euros-a-881388.html
Hodgetts, R. M., & Kuratko, D. F. (1998). *Effective small business management*. Dryden Press.
Hudson-Smith, M., & Smith, D. (2007). Implementing strategically aligned performance measurement in small firms. *International Journal of Production Economics, 106*(2), 393.
Institut für Mittelstandsforschung (IfM). (2018). *KMU insgesamt gemäß KMU-Definition der EU-Kommission.* https://www.ifm-bonn.org/statistiken/unternehmensbestand/#accordion=0&tab=0
Kempster, S., Parry, K. (2014). Critical Realism and Grounded Theory. In Edwards PK, O'Mahoney J, Vincent S (Eds.) Studying organizations using critical realism: A practical guide (pp. 86–108). Oxford: Oxford University Press.
Khajehpour, M., Sedaghatparast, E., & Rabieh, M. (2022). Designing a comprehensive model of organizational resilience in the banking industry of Iran. *Asian Journal of Economics and Banking, 6*(1), 69–87.
Kharbanda, O. P., & Stallworthy, E. A. (1985). *Corporate failure: Prediction, panacea and prevention*. McGraw-Hill.
Khan, M. J., Hussain, D., Mehmood, W. (2016). Why do firms adopt enterprise risk management (ERM)? Empirical evidence from France. *Management Decision, 54(8):1886–1907.*
Kindleberger, C. (1989). Manias, Panics and Crashes: A history of Financial Crises. 2nd ed. New York: Basic Books.
Klein, M., & Höfner, A. (2011). Proaktives Risikomanagement im Mittelstand. Eine Option zur frühzeitigen Ableitung von Krisen - und Insolvenzprognosen. *Zeitschrift für Krisen-, Sanierungs- und Insolvenzberatung, 7(1), 5–12.*
Laitenen, E. K. (1992). Prediction of failure of a newly founded firm. *Journal of Business Venturing, 7*(4), 323–340.
Levers, M.-J. D. (2013). Philosophical paradigms, grounded theory, and perspectives on emergence. *SAGE Open, 3(4), 1–6.* https://doi.org/10.1177/2158244013517243
Levine, R., Lin, C., Xie, W. (2018). Corporate resilience to banking crises: The roles of trust and trade credit. *Journal of Financial and Quantitative Analysis, 53(4), 1441–1477.*
Marcos, J. (2008). *Organisational resilience: The key to anticipation, adaptation and recovery* [online]. Available from http://www.som.cranfield.ac.uk/som/dinamic-content/cced/documents/org.pdf. Accessed: January 3, 2023.
Markman, G. M., & Venzin, M. (2014). Resilience: Lessons from banks that have braved the economic crisis—And from those that have not. *International Business Review, 23*(6), 1096–1107.
Mitroff, I. I., & Alpaslan, M. C. (2003). Preparing for evil. *Harvard Business Review, 81*(April), 109–115.
Musso, P., & Schiavo, S. (2008). The impact of financial constraints on firm survival and growth. *Journal of Evolutionary Economics, 18*(2), 135–149.
Neyer, B., & Hofeditz, M. (2014). Risikomanagement im herstellenden Mittelstand. *Zeitschrift Führung und Organisation, 83(4), 227–232.*
OECD. (2005). *OECD SME and entrepreneurship outlook: 2005.* https://stats.oecd.org/glossary/detail.asp?ID=3123
Oliver, C. (2011). Critical realist grounded theory: A new approach for social work research. *British Journal of Social Work, 42(2):371–387.*
Parnell, J. A. (2015). Crisis management and strategic orientation in small and medium-sized enterprises (SMEs) in Peru, Mexico and the United States. *Journal of Contingencies & Crisis Management, 23*(4), 221–233.
Peterson, R. A., Kozmetsky, G., & Ridgeway, N. M. (1983). Perceived causes of small business failures: A research note. *American Journal of Small Business, 8*(1), 15–19.

Prorokowski, L. (2011). Recovery from the current banking crisis: Insights into costs and effectiveness of response regulations. *Qualitative Research in Financial Markets, 3*(3), 193–223.

Rose, A. (2017). *Defining and measuring economic resilience from a societal, environmental and security perspective*. Springer.

Roundy, P. T., Brockman, B. K., & Bradshaw, M. (2017). The resilience of entrepreneurial ecosystems. *Journal of Business Venturing Insights, 8*, 99–104.

Sahebjamnia, N., Torabi, S. A., & Mansouri, S. A. (2018). Building organizational resilience in the face of multiple disruptions. *International Journal of Production Economics, 197*, 63–83.

Salavou, H., Baltas, G., & Lioukas, S. (2004). Organizational innovation in SMEs: The importance of strategic orientation and competitive structure. *European Journal of Marketing, 38*(9–10), 1091–1112.

Saunders, M., Lewis, P., Thornhill, A. (2009). Research Methods for Business Students, 5th edn. Financial Times Prentice Hall, Harlow.

Shrader, C. B., Mulford, C. L., Blackburn, V. L. (1989). Strategic and operational planning, uncertainty, and Performance in small firms. *Journal of Small Business Management 27(4):45–60.*

Smallman, C. (1996). Risk and organizational behaviour: a research model. *Disaster Prevention and Management 5(2):12–26.*

Soderquist, K., Chanaron, J. J., & Motwani, J. (1997). Managing innovation in French small and medium-sized enterprises: An empirical study. *Benchmarking for Quality Management and Technology, 4*, 259.

Spillan, J., & Hough, M. (2003). Crisis planning in small businesses: Importance, impetus and indifference. *European Management Journal, 21*(3), 398–407.

Stewart, J., & O'Donnell, M. (2007). Implementing change in a public agency: Leadership, learning and organisational resilience. *International Journal of Public Sector Management, 20*, 239.

Storbeck, O., McCrum, D., Palma, S. (2020). Wirecard fights for survival as it admits scale of fraud. Financial Times June 22, 2020. https://www.ft.com/content/2581fda5-8c89-46b5-9acf-ba8a88d74d88

Sullivan-Taylor, B., & Branicki, L. (2011). Creating resilient SMEs: Why one size might not fit all. *International Journal of Production Research, 49*(18), 5565–5579.

Sutcliffe, K. M., & Vogus, T. (2003). Organizing for resilience. In K. S. Cameron, J. E. Dutton, & R. E. Quinn (Eds.), *Positive organizational scholarship: Foundations of a new discipline* (pp. 94–110). Berrett-Koehler.

Tsang, E. W. (2014). Case studies and generalization in information systems research: A critical realist perspective. *The Journal of Strategic Information Systems, 23(2):174–186.*

Vallascas, F., & Keasey, K. (2012). Bank resilience to systemic shocks and the stability of banking systems: Small is beautiful. *Journal of International Money and Finance, 31*, 1745–1776.

van der Vegt, G. S., Essens, P., Wahlström, M., & George, G. (2015). Managing risk and resilience. *Academy of Management Journal, 58*(4), 971–980.

Van Gils, A. (2005). Management and governance in Dutch SMEs. *European Management Journal, 23*(5), 583.

Verreynne, M.-L., Ho, M., & Linnenluecke, M. (2018). Guest editorial. *International Journal of Entrepreneurial Behavior & Research, 24*(7), 1122–1128.

Virdi, A. A. (2005). Risk management among SMEs. http://www.cpaireland.ie/docs/default-source/business-resource/icaew-risk-management-among-smes.pdf?sfvrsn=2. Accessed 12 Aug 2018.

Xia, Y., Qiao, Z., & Xie, G. (2022). Corporate resilience to the COVID-19 pandemic: The role of digital finance. *Pacific-Basin Finance Journal, 74*, 101791, 1–21.

Zachariadis, M., Scott, S. V, Barrett, M. I. (2013). Methodological Implications of Critical Realism for Mixed-Methods Research. *MIS quarterly, 37(3):855–879.*

Zimmerer, T. W., & Scarborough, N. M. (1994). *Essentials of small business management*. Macmillan.

11 Building Resilience: Pillars of Workforce Agility at Organizational and Individual Levels in SMEs

Karin Reinhold

11.1 Introduction

In today's dynamic and unpredictable business landscape, small and medium-sized enterprises (SMEs) face numerous challenges that can impact their growth and survival. Various approaches and models have been proposed and implemented to address the challenges posed by global competition and market dynamics (Sherehiy et al., 2007). One of the key factors that contribute to the success of SMEs in such environments is their ability to adapt and prosper in the face of adversity, which requires a high level of agility and resilience. Researchers see agility as a strategy that enables organizations to survive and thrive in highly competitive business landscape (Holbeche, 2018, 2019; Storme et al., 2020). Resilience, on the other hand, refers to the ability of an organization, team, or individual to bounce back from setbacks (such as crises or disruptions), learn from failures, and effectively navigate through change and uncertainty (Gunasekaran et al., 2011; Soomro et al., 2022). The resilience of an organization depends on three essential pillars: its leadership and culture, the strength of its established networks and relationships that can provide support, and the strategic positioning of the organization to be prepared for change (Seville, 2016). Interestingly, research results have shown that during crises, businesses find the people aspects of the crisis one of the most challenging (Brown et al., 2015; Soomro et al., 2022). Workforce resilience encompasses various dimensions and can be described as a capability, capacity, characteristic, outcome, or process, sometimes a combination of these (Seville, 2018). It refers to the employees' ability to recover quickly from adverse events or crises (Brusset & Teller, 2017), enabling the workforce to be agile in using the opportunities from adverse

K. Reinhold (✉)
Department of Business Administration, Tallinn University of Technology, Tallinn, Estonia
e-mail: karin.reinhold@taltech.ee

S. Durst, T. Henschel (eds.), *Small and Medium-Sized Enterprise (SME) Resilience*, Management for Professionals, https://doi.org/10.1007/978-3-031-50836-3_11

circumstances: resilient individuals are able to adapt, remain focused, and navigate difficult situations with a positive mindset. Workforce agility and resilience are therefore interconnected concepts that contribute to an organization's ability to continue to be successful in a dynamic and uncertain environment.

This chapter explores the concept of workforce agility within SMEs, focusing on both the organizational and individual levels, in order to ensure resilience. The chapter emphasizes the importance of developing and fostering agility as fundamental pillars for SMEs to thrive in today's unpredictable market. It highlights the significance of viewing resilience and agility as interconnected concepts that require a holistic approach for effective implementation.

The chapter begins by discussing the concept of workforce agility and highlights the differences between individual and organizational pillars of agility. After that, the chapter gives an in-depth overview of the main pillars at the individual level describing the key elements necessary for employees to adapt and thrive in a rapidly changing work environment. These pillars include proactivity, flexibility and adaptability, resilience, learning agility, collaborative mindset, competence, self-motivation, and self-management. Subsequently, the chapter examines the organizational pillars of agility by exploring the role of leadership; encouragement of flexibility, autonomy, and empowerment; and discussing the significance of providing employees with learning and development opportunities and describing the importance of communication and information sharing. It highlights the need for strategic agility and technology enablement and addresses the role of employee well-being and work-life balance in promoting resilience and agility, emphasizing the need for supportive policies and practices. Finally, the chapter presents the challenges faced by SMEs in relation to resilience and agility, considering their limited resources and organizational structures, but also gives examples of certain advantages for SMEs, such as greater flexibility and closer employee relationships.

11.2 Concept of Workforce Agility

Creating a universally accepted definition of workforce agility remains a challenge for researchers due to varying perspectives. Different authors approach workforce agility either as a set of abilities and work skills or as the attitudes and behaviors exhibited or expected from employees in a dynamic and uncertain business environment (Muduli, 2017). However, regardless of the viewpoint, all definitions emphasize how employees respond to and adjust to change (Alavi et al., 2014) and also involve attributes such as proactivity, initiative, and the ability to anticipate and address problems (Alavi & Abd-Wahab, 2013; Sherehiy & Karwowski, 2014). According to Tessarini and Saltorato (2021), workforce agility is defined as:

> workers' ability to adjust to a fast-changing, flexible and uncertain work environment through proactive and adaptive knowledge, skills, behaviours, and attitudes.

Taking into account the definition, it can be stated that workforce agility from SMEs' resilience perspective refers to the ability of employees within SMEs to quickly adapt and respond to changes, challenges, and opportunities in their work environment. It involves being flexible, proactive, and responsive in the face of uncertainties and market fluctuations. Workforce agility is an important component of resilience for SMEs as it enables them to effectively navigate through disruptions and maintain their competitive edge (Zhou et al., 2022). Resilient individuals and teams are better equipped to manage stress, maintain focus and optimism, problem-solve, and maintain a sense of purpose and motivation.

The pillars of agility can be described at individual and organizational level (Holbeche, 2019; Robertson et al., 2015; Tessarini & Saltorato, 2021; Walter, 2020). Individual-level workforce agility refers, according to the definition presented above, to the ability of individual employees to adjust, learn, and respond effectively to changes in the work environment. Organizational-level agility focuses on the capacity of the organization as a whole to quickly and efficiently respond to market dynamics and technological developments. It involves creating an environment that promotes collaboration among employees with diverse skills and attitudes, encourages autonomy, gives empowerment, and ensures the organization has the necessary competencies to navigate and adapt to a rapidly evolving business landscape. In summary, individual-level agility primarily focuses on the agility of individual employees and their ability to perform successfully in a changing work environment. It pertains to their skills, mindset, and behaviors. In contrast, organizational-level agility encompasses a broader scope, involving the entire organization, its structures, processes, culture, and systems.

Table 11.1 describes the main differences of these two perspectives by scope of impact, scale and complexity, decision-making authority, structural considerations, and time horizon.

While individual-level and organizational-level agility are distinct, they are interconnected and mutually reinforcing. In the next subchapters, the main pillars on both individual and organizational levels are described.

11.2.1 Pillars of Agility: Individual Level

The individual pillars of workforce agility encompass seven key elements that contribute to the development of an agile workforce. These pillars are shortly defined in Table 11.2.

Proactivity relates to the level of engagement in activities that benefit the organization and workers themselves. This attribute depends greatly on other pillars: self-motivation and self-management, and also autonomy to make important decisions and solve problems (Muduli & Pandya, 2018; Sherehiy & Karwowski, 2014; Tamtam & Tourabi, 2020). Motivated and curious workers are better at detecting and responding to change (Storme et al., 2020). In addition, collaboration is a strong indicator of proactivity, given that it is essential to share goals and improve the work system, usually composed by people with different skills and attitudes (Qin &

Table 11.1 The differences between individual and organizational pillars of agility

	Individual level	Organizational level
Scope of impact	Focuses on the agility of individual employees and their ability to adapt and perform in a changing work environment. It pertains to their skills, mindset, and behaviors	Encompasses a broader scope, involving the entire organization, its structures, processes, culture, and systems
Scale and complexity	Operates at a relatively smaller scale, primarily addressing the agility of one employee	Involves managing and coordinating multiple individuals, teams, departments, and functions across the entire organization
Decision-making authority	Allows employees to make agile decisions within their assigned roles and responsibilities. They can autonomously adapt their work methods, priorities, and approaches to meet changing circumstances	Involves strategic decisions made by leaders and managers to steer the organization in response to external or internal changes. It requires decision-making processes that consider the organization's overall goals and objectives
Structural considerations	Can be influenced by personal traits, competencies, and development efforts. Employees can enhance their agility through continuous learning, skill building, and self-awareness	Is influenced by various structural factors such as the organization's size, structure, resources, technology, and overall adaptability. It requires creating an agile infrastructure that supports rapid decision-making, information flow, collaboration, and innovation
Time horizon	Focuses mainly on short-term adaptability, enabling employees to quickly respond to immediate challenges	Encompasses both short-term and long-term perspectives. It involves building strategic capabilities, anticipating future trends, and proactively positioning the organization to thrive in a dynamic environment

Based on Ajgaonkar et al. (2022), Eilers et al. (2022), Tessarini and Saltorato (2021) and Holbeche (2018)

Nembhard, 2015). Flexibility and adaptability, on the other hand, include behaviors, attitudes, or skills that involve embracing and actively participating in changes related to work conditions, tasks, and expectations. At an individual level, flexibility and adaptability encompass several aspects:

- The ability to determine when or where work is conducted.
- Proactivity and resilience when interacting with individuals from diverse cultural backgrounds or with different experiences.
- The capacity to handle a variety of tasks, even concurrently (Qin & Nembhard, 2015; Sherehiy & Karwowski, 2014; Tamtam & Tourabi, 2020).

Resilience, in relation to agility, is closely intertwined with proactivity, flexibility, and adaptability and encompasses positive attitudes toward change, new technologies, innovative ideas, and alternative approaches to work (Muduli & Pandya, 2018). Within the context of agility, resilience stands in contrast to resistance (Qin & Nembhard, 2015). It also pertains to the ability to effectively navigate and handle

Table 11.2 Pillars of agility at individual level

Pillar	Short description
Proactivity	A proactive approach toward work, involving taking initiative, anticipating problems, finding solutions of change-related problems, and actively seeking opportunities for improvement
Adaptability and flexibility	The ability to quickly adjust and respond to changing circumstances (e.g., during market fluctuations), rapid response to different tasks and work context, and multi-functionality
Learning agility	A willingness and ability to continuously acquire new knowledge, skills, and competencies to adapt to evolving job requirements and technologies
Resilience	The capacity to bounce back from setbacks, cope with stress, and maintain a positive attitude in challenging situations and tolerance to unexpected work environments
Collaborative mindset	The readiness to collaborate and work effectively with colleagues, teams, and diverse groups of people, fostering cooperation, communication, and knowledge sharing
Cognitive skills	Possessing strong problem-solving, critical thinking, and decision-making abilities, enabling individuals to analyze complex situations and make informed choices
Self-motivation and self-management	Having the drive and discipline to manage one's time, tasks, and priorities effectively while maintaining a high level of motivation and commitment

Based on Alavi et al. (2014), Biron et al. (2011), Muduli (2016), Qin and Nembhard (2015), Sherehiy (2008), Sherehiy and Karwowski (2014), Tessarini and Saltorato (2021) and Walter (2020)

unexpected and potentially stressful situations (Sherehiy & Karwowski, 2014). However, there are some studies available that have examined the impact of workforce agility on employee health. In this regard, Braun et al. (2017) highlight that the demands and pressures associated with increased organizational agility can contribute to high-stress conditions, which could potentially be mitigated through individual resilience.

Learning agility of the workforce refers to the ability and willingness of individuals and teams to quickly learn, adapt, and apply new knowledge and skills in different situations. It encompasses the capacity to acquire and integrate new information, embrace feedback, and continuously develop one's capabilities. A workforce that demonstrates learning agility is open to change and proactively seeks opportunities for growth and development. Learning agile individuals are not only receptive to new ideas and perspectives but also have the ability to transfer and apply their learning to different contexts, enabling them to navigate challenges, take advantage from opportunities, and stay ahead.

Collaborative mindset is characterized by a strong belief in the value of collaboration and a willingness to actively engage with others (Eilers et al., 2022; Stabe & Wolf, 2003). Individuals with a collaborative mindset understand that their own success is interconnected with the success of the team and the organization as a whole. They actively seek opportunities to collaborate, share ideas, and contribute their skills and expertise to collective efforts. They demonstrate openness to different perspectives, listen actively, and engage in constructive dialogue to find innovative solutions. Individuals with a collaborative mindset value cooperation, trust, and respect in their interactions with colleagues. They proactively seek feedback and offer support. This mindset enables individuals to contribute effectively to cross-functional teams (Gore & Kess, 2011; Markovic et al., 2021; Münnich et al., 2022).

Competence, which is based on cognitive skills, can be evaluated based on the speed at which new ideas, knowledge, technologies, and work procedures are understood and developed. Additionally, the ability to effectively handle emerging and complex information technologies, as well as various resources and tools, serves as an indicator of competence (Muduli, 2016; Patil & Suresh, 2019; Qin & Nembhard, 2015). Consequently, it is assumed that individuals who continually enhance their skills, knowledge, and procedural expertise are more aligned with the principles of workforce agility (Muduli, 2016; Sherehiy & Karwowski, 2014).

Self-motivation and self-management are key attributes of an agile workforce at the individual level. Self-motivation refers to the ability of individuals to drive themselves forward, set goals, and maintain a proactive and enthusiastic attitude toward their work (Sherehiy & Karwowski, 2014; Tamtam & Tourabi, 2020). Agile individuals possess a strong sense of purpose, intrinsic motivation, and a growth mindset, allowing them to take initiative, seek challenges, and persist in the face of obstacles. They are self-driven and continuously seek opportunities for learning and development. Self-management, on the other hand, refers to an individual's ability to effectively organize, prioritize, and manage their own work (Sherehiy & Karwowski, 2014; Tamtam & Tourabi, 2020). Agile individuals possess excellent time management skills, can adapt to changing priorities, and make autonomous decisions. They demonstrate discipline and accountability, meet deadlines, and maintain a high level of productivity. They are proactive in identifying and addressing potential obstacles and seek feedback to improve their performance. Agile individuals excel in self-motivation and self-management by leveraging their intrinsic motivation, goal-setting abilities, and effective time and task management skills. They take ownership of their work, demonstrate a high degree of responsibility, and have a strong work ethic. They embrace autonomy and show resilience in the face of challenges, continually seeking opportunities for growth and improvement.

These pillars collectively contribute to individuals' agility, enabling them to navigate dynamic work environments, embrace change, and continuously adapt and grow in their roles. Furthermore, individual agility is closely interconnected with organizational agility, as both levels of agility complement and reinforce each other. In the next subchapter, the organizational pillars are discussed.

11.2.2 Pillars at Organizational Level

At the organizational level, several important pillars contribute to employees' agility which are shortly defined in Table 11.3.

Table 11.3 Pillars of agility at organizational level

Pillar	Short description
Leadership and culture	Effective leadership that promotes a culture of agility, encourages innovation, provides clear direction, and supports employees in adapting to change
Continuous learning and development	Emphasizing a culture of lifelong learning and providing opportunities for employees to acquire new knowledge, skills, and competencies. This pillar promotes adaptability and equips employees with the ability to quickly acquire and apply new information
Autonomy and empowerment	Granting employees a sense of ownership and autonomy over their work, allowing them to make decisions and take initiative. Promoting proactivity refers to the active engagement in activities that bring benefits to both the organization and the employees themselves
Flexibility encouragement	Encouraging flexibility in work arrangements, such as remote work options, flexible schedules, and cross-functional assignments. This pillar enables employees to respond effectively to changing demands and work in diverse settings
Communication and information sharing	Fostering a collaborative work environment that encourages effective communication, teamwork, and knowledge sharing. This pillar promotes agile decision-making, problem-solving, and innovation through enhanced collaboration among employees
Strategic agility	Developing a growth mindset, promoting a positive attitude toward change, and encouraging employees to be open to new ideas and perspectives
Technology enablement and competence	Leveraging technology and digital tools to enhance efficiency, collaboration, and innovation within the workforce. This pillar involves providing employees with the necessary digital skills and resources to adapt to technological advancements.
Engagement and well-being	Prioritizing employee well-being, both physical and mental, and supporting resilience-building practices. This pillar involves promoting work-life balance, stress management, and fostering a supportive and inclusive work environment

Based on Biron et al. (2011), Muduli (2017), Tessarini and Saltorato (2021) and Walter (2020)

Developing a more *agile culture* necessitates the adoption of novel routines and the introduction of management processes, which can arise from a combination of transformative elements like *leadership and strategy*, as well as transactional activities such as *training and development*. Senior managers, in particular, play a vital role in spearheading the cultivation of agile thinking and practices, setting an example for others within the organization (Pulakos et al. 2019; Thomas & Suresh, 2023). In an agile context, leadership goes beyond traditional hierarchical structures and encompasses qualities such as vision, adaptability, collaboration, and empowerment. Promoting organizational agility involves shifting away from rigid top-down control imposed by line managers and empowering business entities to operate as flexible and interconnected units (Pulakos et al., 2019). One way to achieve this is by delegating additional tasks and strategic authority to micro-level organizational units. Agile leaders inspire and motivate their teams, fostering a culture of innovation, continuous learning, and adaptability. They provide clear direction and purpose, aligning their teams' efforts with organizational goals. Agile leaders create an environment of psychological safety, where individuals feel comfortable taking risks and sharing innovative ideas. Effective agile leaders also promote collaboration, facilitate open communication, and support the development of high-performing teams (Susanty et al., 2022).

In situations where external and internal factors impact the business environment (such as recently experienced COVID-19 pandemics or ongoing Russian-Ukrainian War), it becomes necessary for employees to acquire new skills and effectively apply them in practical settings—providing *learning opportunities* in organizations becomes crucial. Organizational learning encompasses both the direct and indirect knowledge acquired through work experience and the creation of an environment that encourages continuous learning among employees, fostering self-development and proactive behaviors. Such environment promotes the acquisition of new skills and knowledge transfer. Moreover, the development of cognitive skills, such as problem-solving and logical reasoning, plays an important role in agility through the learning process (Qin & Nembhard, 2015).

One of the training practices closely linked to workforce agility is the qualification of employees to perform a variety of tasks, commonly referred to as cross-training. Cross-training has been studied and implemented mainly in the field of operations management, particularly in settings such as factories and serial production lines (Qin & Nembhard, 2015; Hopp et al., 2004). This practice facilitates greater flexibility by enabling workers to adapt and fulfill different roles based on the specific needs and demands of the organization. Furthermore, employees with a broader skill set are generally less prone to experiencing fatigue, musculoskeletal disorders, and stress associated with repetitive tasks as they are rotating their tasks regularly (Padula et al., 2017; Rao Pabolu & Shrivastava, 2021; Van Wyk et al., 2018).

Autonomy and empowerment are fundamental principles in agile organizations, fostering an environment where individuals have the freedom to make decisions and take ownership of their work (Kahl et al., 2023; Muduli, 2016; Muduli, 2017; Stray et al., 2018). In an agile context, autonomy means providing individuals with the authority and responsibility to make independent choices and take action. It enables employees to utilize their skills, knowledge, and expertise to contribute to the organization's goals. To elaborate further, Scott and Davis (2007) differentiate between two forms of power: legitimate power and endorsed power. Legitimate power is rooted in hierarchical structures and derives from formal authority granted by managers. On the other hand, endorsed power refers to an informal sphere of autonomy and freedom that is supported by managers. In this regard, the cultivation of collaborative practices becomes crucial. Empowerment involves giving individuals the confidence and support to take on challenges, innovate, and make meaningful contributions. Agile organizations empower their employees by providing them with the resources, information, and trust needed to stand out in their roles (Muduli, 2016). This empowerment not only enhances employee engagement and job satisfaction but also promotes creativity and problem-solving skills. By fostering autonomy and empowerment, agile organizations utilize the potential of their workforce, resulting in increased innovation, agility, and overall organizational success (Box 11.1).

Box 11.1: Empowerment and Agility in Agile Organizations: A Study from Estonia (Idasaar, 2020)

A study from Estonia (Idasaar, 2020) *among employees, specialists and managers in agile organizations about employee's psychological and structural empowerment and employee's forms of agility (proactivity, adaptivity and resilience).* The results showed that all components of psychological empowerment moderately influence workforce agility. Structural empowerment, on the other hand, showed weak to moderate influence on workforce agility. However, it was confirmed that psychological empowerment acts as a significant mediator for structural empowerment. The results also revealed that psychological empowerment significantly affects workforce agility, with perceived competence and perceived control being the most influential elements, followed by goal adoption. Based on the findings, it can be concluded that individuals with higher levels of empowerment are more proactive, adaptable, and resilient in their work environment.

Technology enablement and competence play a vital role in fostering agility within organizations. Agile organizations leverage technology to automate routine tasks, improve communication and information sharing, and enable real-time decision-making (Walter, 2020). By adopting agile-friendly technologies such as cloud computing, collaborative platforms, and project management tools, organizations can create a digital ecosystem that supports agility (Saputra, 2022). The organization should ensure that employees have access to the necessary technology tools, software, by providing licenses or subscriptions and guarantee the infrastructure that supports the efficient use of technology. Additionally, developing technological competence among employees is essential. It involves providing training and resources to enhance digital literacy, technical skills, and the ability to leverage technology effectively. This competence empowers employees to embrace technological advancements, adapt to changing digital landscapes, and leverage technology as a catalyst for agility. In addition, in order to establish sustainable workforce resilience and agility, it is essential to prepare employees for the digital future by providing continuous reskilling opportunities. Throughout this process, the focus should be on leveraging human strengths within collaborative relationships, both among individuals and between individuals and machines (Holbeche, 2019).

Encouraging flexibility within the workforce is another important aspect of fostering workforce agility. At the organizational level, flexibility refers to the organization's ability to reorganize its workforce to respond to changes (Alavi, 2016; Qin & Nembhard, 2015). Organizations can promote flexibility by offering flexible work arrangements, such as remote work options or flexible hours, which allow employees to balance their personal and professional life (Tessarini & Saltorato, 2021).

Both agility and resilience rely on strong *collaboration and communication*. Agile organizations foster a culture of open communication, transparency, and cross-functional collaboration, enabling teams to work together seamlessly and share knowledge and insights. This collaborative mindset enhances organizational resilience by facilitating the exchange of information, rapid decision-making, and coordinated responses during times of disruption (Holbeche, 2019; Tessarini & Saltorato, 2021).

The *strategic agility* mindset is a cognitive framework that involves having a forward-thinking perspective, a proactive attitude, and a willingness to embrace change (Ludviga & Kalvina, 2023; Munteanu et al., 2020). This mindset encourages organizations to be agile in their decision-making processes, anticipate future trends, and explore new opportunities. A core aspect of the strategic agility mindset is the willingness to embrace innovation. Organizations with a strategic agility mindset actively seek out new ideas, technologies, and processes to drive innovation. They encourage a culture of experimentation, where failure is seen as a learning opportunity (Ajgaonkar et al., 2022).

Workforce agility and organizational resilience are interconnected also through employee *engagement and well-being*. Agile organizations prioritize employee empowerment, well-being, and work-life balance, which contribute to higher levels of engagement and resilience. Engaged and resilient employees are more likely to adapt, persevere, and contribute to the overall resilience of the organization. Resilience-based practices for employees are designed to enhance their well-being and help them cope with challenges and work-related stress as well as avoid burnout. These practices focus on building personal resilience, fostering a positive work environment, and promoting overall employee well-being (Jennings et al., 2013; Ludviga & Kalvina, 2023). They can include workshops, seminars, or online courses that teach techniques such as stress management, emotional regulation, problem-solving, and mindfulness. Another way to support employees' well-being is creating a supportive work environment that prioritizes mental health, e.g., offering employee assistance programs, counselling services. For example, Jennings et al. (2013) implemented an intervention that introduced various practices to cultivate mindful awareness, starting with foundational exercises like body and breath awareness and expanding to activities promoting a mindful approach in daily routines (e.g., standing, walking, and being present). In Pipe et al.'s (2012) study, they implemented an intervention known as the "Transforming Stress" workshop. This workshop specifically addressed the influence of stress on the interconnected aspects of the body, mind, and spirit. It offered participants a range of techniques to enhance their ability to self-regulate stress responses by transitioning into a more harmonious physiological state.

Work-life balance should be encouraged by promoting flexible work arrangements, such as telecommuting, flexible hours, or compressed workweeks. Supporting employees in maintaining a healthy balance between work and personal life can contribute to their overall well-being and resilience. It is important to implement wellness initiatives that focus on physical health, such as fitness programs, health screenings, healthy eating options, and ergonomic workstations. Physical well-being is closely linked to resilience and can positively impact employees' ability to handle challenges (Gómez-Borges et al., 2022; Robertson et al., 2015) (Box 11.2).

Box 11.2: Organizational resilience and Employees' Personal Resilience: A Case-Study from Estonia (Liiv, 2023)

A case-study from Estonia (Liiv, 2023) *among 3 organizations: one from public sector and two from private sector (a large company and a small company) about the influence of organizational resilience on the relationship between employees' personal resilience and burnout*: The study revealed that organizational resilience influences the relationship between employee resilience and burnout. Employees with lower levels of resilience and low organizational support experience moderate symptoms of burnout. However, when employees have high personal resilience, burnout is absent. Interestingly, for those employees who have high personal resilience and high organizational resilience, their level of burnout somewhat increases. They have the energy to cope with difficulties, and when supported by the organization, their level of effort increases. When organizational resilience is weaker, the relationship between burnout and personal resilience is somewhat weaker as well, indicating that personal resilience has a lesser impact on reducing burnout.

These pillars collectively create an organizational ecosystem that fosters a workforce with agility and resilience. As described above, this requires a comprehensive approach that addresses various aspects of organizational culture, leadership, training, technology enablement, flexibility, and employee well-being.

11.3 Challenges and Advantages for SMEs

Developing workforce agility can present several challenges in SMEs compared to large companies. Here are some of the reasons which can be highlighted as follows (Alavi, 2016; Bessant et al., 2001; Chan et al., 2019; Do et al., 2022; Gunasekaran et al., 2011; Soomro et al., 2022):

- Limited resources: SMEs often have limited financial and human resources, which can make it challenging to invest in training and development programs necessary for building workforce agility.
- Lack of specialized human resource functions: SMEs may not have dedicated specialized personnel to focus on workforce development and agility initiatives, resulting in limited expertise and resources to drive these efforts effectively.
- Resistance to formalization: SMEs often value informality and flexibility, which can lead to resistance in adopting formalized processes and structures that are essential for systematically developing workforce agility.
- Limited scale for internal mobility: SMEs may have fewer job positions and limited opportunities for internal mobility and career advancement. This can make it difficult for employees to gain diverse experiences and develop the agility required for adapting to different roles or functions.

- Lack of formalized processes: Due to limited resources, SMEs may have less well-defined and formalized processes and systems for talent management, performance evaluation, and succession planning. This can impede the systematic development of workforce agility.
- Resistance to change: SMEs, particularly family-owned or long-established businesses, may have a more traditional and risk-averse culture, making it challenging to foster a culture of agility and adaptability that embraces change and innovation.
- Limited exposure to external networks: SMEs often have limited external networks and partnerships compared to larger companies, which can restrict employees' exposure to diverse perspectives, best practices, and new ideas that can enhance their agility.
- Operational focus: SMEs often prioritize operational efficiency and short-term goals due to resource constraints and market demands. This focus may limit the time and attention available for long-term workforce development initiatives, including agility building efforts.

It is important to note that while these challenges exist, SMEs also possess certain advantages, which can be leveraged to foster agility in different ways. Some of them are described as follows (Alavi, 2016; Bessant et al., 2001; Chan et al., 2019; Do et al., 2022; Gunasekaran et al., 2011; Soomro et al., 2022):

- Flexibility and adaptability: SMEs are often more flexible in their operations and decision-making processes. This allows them to respond quickly to market changes and emerging opportunities, leveraging their smaller size and fewer bureaucratic layers.
- Enhanced innovation: Workforce agility promotes a culture of innovation and creativity. In SMEs, employees can have more direct involvement in decision-making and innovation processes, leading to faster idea generation, experimentation, and implementation. Additionally, in contrast to larger organizations, SMEs generally have shorter decision-making processes due to less bureaucracy and fewer layers of approval. Quick decision-making enables prompt responses to challenges and opportunities, facilitating adaptive behaviors.
- Cross-functional collaboration: SMEs typically have smaller teams and fewer hierarchical barriers, fostering more frequent collaboration across different functions and departments. This cross-functional collaboration enables employees to gain exposure to diverse perspectives and skills, enhancing their agility by developing a broader understanding of the organization.
- Learning opportunities: SMEs often provide employees with diverse responsibilities and exposure to various aspects of the business. This multifaceted experience allows individuals to learn and develop a wide range of skills, fostering agility and adaptability to different roles and tasks.
- Greater autonomy and ownership: Employees in SMEs often have more autonomy and ownership over their work, which empowers them to take initiatives, make decisions, and adapt quickly to changes. This sense of ownership fosters a culture of agility and accountability.

- Enclosed work environment: SMEs typically have a smaller employee base, leading to closer relationships and more personal connections among colleagues. This supportive work environment promotes effective communication, collaboration, and knowledge sharing, enhancing agility through the rapid flow of information.
- Opportunity for skill diversification: SMEs often provide employees with opportunities to take on different roles. This diversification of skills and responsibilities helps individuals develop agility by broadening their capabilities and adaptability to evolving needs.
- Entrepreneurial mindset: SMEs are often driven by an entrepreneurial spirit and a willingness to take risks. This mindset encourages employees to embrace change, explore new ideas, and continuously seek improvement, contributing to a culture of agility and innovation.
- Direct impact and recognition: In SMEs, employees can witness the direct impact of their contributions on the organization's success. This sense of purpose and recognition can fuel intrinsic motivation, leading to higher levels of engagement, commitment, and agility.

Overall, the advantages of developing workforce agility in SMEs derive from their inherent characteristics, including flexibility, innovation focus, collaborative culture, and opportunities for skill diversification. Leveraging these advantages can enable SMEs to cope with challenges in dynamic and unpredictable business landscapes.

Table 11.4 presents the key messages for SME managers or owners who wish to develop or maintain an agile workforce.

11.4 Conclusions

Workforce resilience and agility play crucial roles in the success and sustainability of SMEs. As SMEs navigate through changing business landscapes, workforce resilience enables employees to effectively cope with challenges, bounce back from setbacks, and adapt to new circumstances. Workforce agility, on the other hand, empowers employees and organizations to respond quickly, innovate, and take advantage of opportunities, enhancing their competitive edge. In SMEs, developing workforce resilience and agility can be particularly beneficial due to the inherent advantages that SMEs possess, such as flexibility, innovation focus, and closer employee relationships. These advantages allow SMEs to foster a culture that promotes continuous learning, cross-functional collaboration, and employee empowerment, which are vital for building resilience and agility.

To cultivate workforce resilience and agility in SMEs, it is essential to invest in employee development programs and promote a supportive and inclusive work environment. Additionally, managers in SMEs need to play a critical role in setting a good pattern in resilient and agile behaviors while also providing the necessary resources and opportunities for growth.

Table 11.4 Key messages for managers and owners of SMEs

Key messages: How to get started? Eight points for managers and owners of SMEs
1. *Understanding the agile mindset:* Emphasize the importance of embracing an agile mindset in the organization through encouraging open communication, flexibility, and adaptability among employees
2. *Aligning agile practices with business goals:* Communicate the importance of agility and resilience in achieving long-term success and ensure that agile practices align with the company's strategic objectives
3. *Developing agile leadership*: Train managers to lead in an agile environment and empower their teams and encourage leadership that allows to coach employees rather than follow traditional top-down management
4. *Building structural and psychological empowerment:* Ensure that the organizational structure supports agile practices and decision-making; foster a work environment that empowers employees to take ownership of their work and decisions through autonomy and competence
5. *Investing in employee learning and development*: Encourage a culture of continuous learning and growth through providing training and resources to enhance employees' skills and competencies and sharing success stories across the organization
6. *Establishing strong team dynamics*: Foster collaboration and teamwork among employees through creating a supportive and inclusive work environment where diverse perspectives are valued
7. *Encouraging innovation and embracing technology*: Invest in technology and tools that facilitate collaboration and efficiency, support a culture of experimentation, appreciate learning from failures, and encourage innovation
8. *Prioritizing employee well-being*: Recognize the importance of work-life balance and employee well-being through offering wellness programs and supporting mechanisms to manage stress and burnout

While the challenges in developing workforce resilience and agility in SMEs may include limited resources, structural constraints, and resistance to change, the potential benefits outweigh these obstacles. By prioritizing the development of workforce resilience and agility, SMEs can position themselves to navigate uncertainties, take advantage of emerging opportunities, and be successful in dynamic and competitive markets.

References

Ajgaonkar, S., Neelam, N. G., & Wiemann, J. (2022). Drivers of workforce agility: A dynamic capability perspective. *International Journal of Organizational Analysis., 30*(4), 951–982. https://doi.org/10.1108/IJOA-11-2020-2507

Alavi, S. (2016). The influence of workforce agility on external manufacturing flexibility of Iranian SMEs. *International Journal of Technological Learning, Innovation and Development, 8*, 111. https://doi.org/10.1504/IJTLID.2016.075185

Alavi, S., & Abd-Wahab, D. (2013). A review on workforce agility. *Research Journal of Applied Sciences, Engineering and Technology., 16*, 4195–4199. https://doi.org/10.19026/rjaset.5.4647

Alavi, S., Wahab, D. A., Muhamad, N., & Shirani, B. A. (2014). Organic structure and organisational learning as the main antecedents of workforce agility. *International Journal of Production Research, 52*(21), 6273–6295. https://doi.org/10.1080/00207543.2014.919420

Bessant, J., Francis, D., Meredith, S., Kaplinsky, R., & Brown, S. (2001). Developing manufacturing agility in SMEs. *International Journal of Technology Management., 22*(1–3), 28–54. https://doi.org/10.1504/ijmtm.2000.001374

Biron, M., Farndale, E., & Paauwe, J. (2011). Performance management effectiveness: Lessons from world-leading firms. *International Journal of Information Technology and Management – IJITM, 22*, 1294–1311. https://doi.org/10.1080/09585192.2011.559100

Braun, T. J., Hayes, B. C., DeMuth, R. L. F., & Taran, O. A. (2017). The development, validation, and practical application of an employee agility and resilience measure to facilitate organizational change. *Industrial and Organizational Psychology, 10*(4), 703–723. https://doi.org/10.1017/iop.2017.79

Brown, C., Stevenson, J., Giovinazzi, S., Seville, E., & Vargo, J. (2015). Factors influencing impacts on and recovery trends of organisations: Evidence from the 2010/2011 Canterbury earthquakes. *International Journal of Disaster Risk Reduction, 14*, 56–72.

Brusset, X., & Teller, C. (2017). Supply chain capabilities, risks, and resilience. *International Journal of Production Economics, 184*(10), 59–68. https://doi.org/10.1016/j.ijpe.2016.09.008

Chan, C. M., Teoh, S. Y., Yeow, A., & Pan, G. (2019). Agility in responding to disruptive digital innovation: Case study of an SME. *Information Systems Journal, 29*, 436–455.

Do, H., Budhwar, P., Shipton, H., Nguyen, H.-D., & Nguyen, B. (2022). Building organizational resilience, innovation through resource-based management initiatives, organizational learning and environmental dynamism. *Journal of Business Research, 141*, 808–821. https://doi.org/10.1016/j.jbusres.2021.11.090

Eilers, K., Peters, C., & Leimeister, J. M. (2022). Why the agile mindset matters. *Technological Forecasting and Social Change, 179*, 121650. https://doi.org/10.1016/j.techfore.2022.121650

Gómez-Borges, A., Zuberbühler, M. J. P., Martínez, I. M., & Salanova, M. (2022). Self-care at work matters: How job and personal resources mediate between self-care and psychological well-being. *Journal of Work and Organizational Psychology, 38*(3), 231–239. https://doi.org/10.5093/jwop2022a15

Gore, A., & Kess, P. (2011). Collaboration in agile networks: Developing a Nordic model. *International Journal of Agile Systems and Management, 4*, 379–393. https://doi.org/10.1504/IJASM.2011.043128

Gunasekaran, A., Rai, B. K., & Griffin, M. (2011). Resilience and competitiveness of small and medium size enterprises: An empirical research. *International Journal of Production Research, 49*(18), 5489–5509. https://doi.org/10.1080/00207543.2011.563831

Holbeche, L. S. (2018). Organisational effectiveness and agility. *Journal of Organizational Effectiveness: People and Performance, 5*(4), 302–313. https://doi.org/10.1108/JOEPP-07-2018-0044

Holbeche, L. S. (2019). Shifts in organizational culture when implementing agility. *Journal of Creating Value, 5*(2), 124–138.

Hopp, W. J., Tekin, E., & Other, M. P. (2004). Benefits of skill chaining in serial production lines with cross-trained workers. *Management Science, 50*(1), 83–98.

Idasaar, M. (2020). *Tööjõu agiilsus ja selle seos psühholoogilise ja struktuurse võimestamisega.* Master thesis, TalTech.

Jennings, P. A., Frank, J. L., Snowberg, K. E., Coccia, M. A., & Greenberg, M. T. (2013). Improving classroom learning environments by cultivating awareness and resilience in education (CARE): Results of a randomized controlled trial. *School Psychology Quarterly, 28*, 374–390. https://doi.org/10.1037/spq0000035

Kahl, J., de Klerk, S., & Whiteoak, J. (2023). Managing empowerment: Adjusting organisational units' autonomy to achieve corporate agility. *Journal of Organizational Effectiveness: People and Performance*. https://doi.org/10.1108/JOEPP-05-2022-0126

Liiv, K. (2023). *Organisatsiooni säilenõtkuse mõju töötajate säilenõtkuse ja läbipõlemise vahelisele seosele*. Master thesis, TalTech.

Ludviga, I., & Kalvina, A. (2023). Organizational agility during crisis: Do employees' perceptions of public sector organizations' strategic agility Foster employees' work engagement and Well-being? *Employee Responsibilities and Rights Journal*. https://doi.org/10.1007/s10672-023-09442-9

Markovic, S., Koporcic, N., Arslanagic-Kalajdzic, M., Kadic-Maglajlic, S., Bagherzadeh, M., & Islam, M. (2021). Business-to-business open innovation: COVID-19 lessons for small and medium-sized enterprises from emerging markets. *Technological Forecasting and Social Change, 170*, 120883, ISSN:0040-1625. https://doi.org/10.1016/j.techfore.2021.120883

Muduli, A. (2016). Exploring the facilitators and mediators of workforce agility: An empirical study. *Management Research Review, 39*(12), 1567–1586. https://doi.org/10.1108/MRR-10-2015-0236

Muduli, A. (2017). Workforce agility: Examining the role of organizational practices and psychological empowerment. *Global Business and Organizational Excellence, 36*(5), 46–56. https://doi.org/10.1002/joe.21800

Muduli, A., & Pandya, G. (2018). Psychological empowerment and workforce agility. *Psychological Studies, 63*(3), 276–285. https://doi.org/10.1007/s12646-018-0456-8

Münnich, M., Schlüter, J., & Marinkovic, M. (2022). Cultural transformation of industries through creation of new collaboration concepts driven by employee engagement. In *2022 IEEE international conference on Industrial Engineering and Engineering Management (IEEM), Kuala Lumpur, Malaysia* (pp. 0011–0016). https://doi.org/10.1109/IEEM55944.2022.9989872

Munteanu, A.-I., Bibu, N., Nastase, M., Cristache, N., & Matis, C. (2020). Analysis of practices to increase the workforce agility and to develop a sustainable and competitive business. *Sustainability, 12*, 3545. https://doi.org/10.3390/su12093545

Padula, R. S., Comper, M. L. C., Sparer, E. H., & Dennerlein, J. T. (2017). Job rotation designed to prevent musculoskeletal disorders and control risk in manufacturing industries: A systematic review. *Applied Ergonomics, 58*, 386–397. https://doi.org/10.1016/j.apergo.2016.07.018

Patil, M., & Suresh, M. (2019). Modelling the enablers of workforce agility in IoT projects: A TISM approach. *Global Journal of Flexible Systems Management, 20*(2), 157–175. https://doi.org/10.1007/s40171-019-00208-7

Pipe, T. B., Buchda, V. L., Launder, S., Hudak, B., Hulvey, L., Karns, K. E., & Pendergast, D. (2012). Building personal and professional resources of resilience and agility in the healthcare workplace. *Stress and Health, 28*, 11–22. https://doi.org/10.1002/smi.1396

Pulakos, E. D., Kantrowitz, T., & Schneider, B. (2019). What leads to organizational agility: It's not what you think. *Consulting Psychology Journal: Practice and Research, 71*(4), 305–320.

Qin, R., & Nembhard, D. A. (2015). Workforce agility in operations management. *Surveys in Operations Research and Management Science, 20*(2), 55–69. https://doi.org/10.1016/j.sorms.2015.11.001

Rao Pabolu, V. K., & Shrivastava, D. (2021). A dynamic job rotation scheduling conceptual framework by a human representing digital twin. *Procedia CIRP, 104*, 1367–1372, ISSN:2212-8271. https://doi.org/10.1016/j.procir.2021.11.230

Robertson, I. T., Cooper, C. L., Sarkar, M., & Curran, T. (2015). Resilience training in the workplace from 2003 to 2014: A systematic review. *Journal of Occupational and Organizational Psychology, 88*(3), 533–562. https://doi.org/10.1111/joop.12120

Saputra, N. (2022). Synergizing digital competence and team work for accelerating workforce agility. In *5th international seminar on Research of Information Technology and Intelligent Systems (ISRITI)* (pp. 601–606).

Scott, W. R., & Davis, G. F. (2007). *Organizations and organizing: Rational, natural, and open systems perspectives*. Pearson Prentice Hall.

Seville, E. (2016). *Resilient organizations: How to survive, thrive, and create opportunities through crisis and change*. Kogan Page.

Seville, E. (2018). Building resilience: How to have a positive impact at the organizational and individual employee level. *Development and Learning in Organizations: An International Journal, 32*(3), 15–18. https://doi.org/10.1108/DLO-09-2017-0076

Sherehiy, B. (2008). *Relationships between agility strategy, work organization and workforce agility*. University of Louisville.

Sherehiy, B., & Karwowski, W. (2014). The relationship between work organization and workforce agility in small manufacturing enterprises. *International Journal of Industrial Ergonomics, 44*(3), 466–473. https://doi.org/10.1016/j.ergon.2014.01.002

Sherehiy, B., Karwowski, W., & Layer, J. K. (2007). A review of enterprise agility: Concepts, frameworks, and attributes. *International Journal of Industrial Ergonomics, 37*(5), 445–460. https://doi.org/10.1016/j.ergon.2007.01.007

Soomro, M. A., Ali, M. H., Tan, K. H., Kumar, A., & Sinniah, S. (2022). Workforce resilience in the post-COVID-19 era: Differences based on manufacturing–service orientation and firm size. *Production Planning & Control*. https://doi.org/10.1080/09537287.2022.2106446

Stabe, M., & Wolf, P. (2003). Towards a collaborative mindset – How to leave the thinking box? In *Proceedings of the 10th ISPE international conference on concurrent engineering research and application, enhanced interoperable systems* (pp. 1165–1170).

Storme, M., Suleyman, O., Gotlib, M., & Lubart, T. (2020). Who is agile? An investigation of the psychological antecedents of workforce agility. *Global Business and Organizational Excellence, 39*(6), 28–38. https://doi.org/10.1002/joe.22055

Stray, V., Moe, N. B., & Hoda, R. (2018). Autonomous agile teams: Challenges and future directions for research. In *Proceedings of the 19th international conference on agile software development: Companion* (pp. 1–5). Association for Computing Machinery.

Susanty, A. I., Budiharjo, E., & Winarto, W. (2022). Achieving an agile organisation in an Indonesian telecommunications company: Investigation on leadership impact and mediation variables. *Journal of Science and Technology Policy Management*. https://doi.org/10.1108/JSTPM-07-2021-0095

Tamtam, F., & Tourabi, A. (2020). A framework for measuring workforce agility: Fuzzy logic approach applied in a Moroccan manufacturing company. *Advances in Science, Technology and Engineering Systems Journal, 5*(3), 411–418. https://doi.org/10.25046/aj050352

Tessarini, G., & Saltorato, P. (2021). Workforce agility: A systematic literature review and a research agenda proposal. *Innovar, 31*(81), 155–168. https://doi.org/10.15446/innovar.v31n81.95582

Thomas, A., & Suresh, M. (2023). Readiness for agile-sustainability in health-care organizations. *International Journal of Quality and Service Sciences*. https://doi.org/10.1108/IJQSS-06-2022-0056

Van Wyk, A. E., Swarts, I., & Mukonza, C. (2018). The influence of the implementation of job rotation on employees' perceived job satisfaction. *International Journal of Business and Management, 13*, 89.

Walter, A.-T. (2020). Organizational agility: Ill-defined and somewhat confusing? A systematic literature review and conceptualization. *Management Review Quarterly, 71*. https://doi.org/10.1007/s11301-020-00186-6

Zhou, Q., Edafioghor, T., Wu, C.-H., & Doherty, B. (2022). Building organizational resilience capability in small and medium-sized enterprises: The role of high-performance work systems. *Human Resource Management Journal*. https://doi.org/10.1111/1748-8583.12479

12 Enterprise Risk Management and Resilience in SMEs During COVID-19 Pandemic: The Case of Italian Dealerships

Cristina Florio and Laura Brotto

12.1 Introduction

COVID-19 pandemic urged companies to operate in a *new normal* business environment, where market dynamics were characterized by distinctive economic, social and business transformations (Corpuz, 2021). The way in which companies have responded to the challenges posed by said transformations has heavily affected their business and determined whether they have thrived, survived or exited the market. In management literature, Enterprise Risk Management (ERM) is recognized as the key to anticipate and bear risks at the organizations' best (COSO, 2004, 2017), and to contribute building organizational resilience, which in turn is considered as inevitable in the current business environment (Ferrell, 2021; Natale et al., 2022; Xie & Wu, 2022).

Extant literature underlines that small and medium enterprises (SMEs) are the most affected by disruptions, as they are "*are structurally weaker and exposed to the danger of failure when facing unexpected risks*" (Verbano & Venturini, 2013, p. 194). They are particularly vulnerable to external and internal threats, being ineffective in risk identification, assessment and monitoring (Manas et al., 2021). Extant literature has widely underlined that SMEs often suffer from internal constraints related to the paucity of the financial, managerial and information resources necessary to face risks and uncertainty and thus mitigate shocks (Curran & Blackburn, 2011; Dvorski Lacković et al., 2022; Raghavan, 2005). COVID-19 pandemic challenged SMEs more than any other crisis did before and forced them to take

C. Florio (✉)
University of Verona, Verona, Italy
e-mail: cristina.florio@univr.it

L. Brotto
Quintegia, Treviso, Italy

S. Durst, T. Henschel (eds.), *Small and Medium-Sized Enterprise (SME) Resilience*, Management for Professionals, https://doi.org/10.1007/978-3-031-50836-3_12

decisions *in the dark*, without formal risk management[1] processes and resiliency plans (Westby & Lamb, 2020).

Despite growing research on SMEs in the last decade, risk management practices in this context remain "*a 'spot' subject*" (Verbano & Venturini, 2013, p. 194), and only few studies deal with the questions of how ERM is actually implemented in SMEs, what are its basic components and characteristics in business practice and whether companies use ERM frameworks' guidance while implementing it (de Araújo Lima et al., 2020; Crovini et al., 2021). Similarly, research on organizational resilience has grown significantly in recent years (Duchek, 2020; Hillmann, 2021; Hillmann & Guenther, 2021; Linnenluecke, 2017; Williams, 2017); however, the remaining focused on large companies instead of SMEs (Utami et al., 2021).

Still, SMEs deserve specific attention because of their role in the economy. In Europe, they represent 99.8% of the total number of companies, employ almost 84 million workers and produce 57% of total gross value added (European Commission, 2017; Statista, 2021). Consistently with this impressive data, they are meant to be "*the engine of economic growth in the industrialized world*" (Massaro et al., 2016, p. 258).

With such premise, this chapter aims to understand how ERM has evolved during the pandemic and helped SMEs to increase strategic and operational resilience. In detail, the study delves into the ERM system designed by SMEs and the role it played during the COVID-19 period in increasing strategic and operational resilience against future shocks. As an outcome of the analysis conducted, a checklist is provided for SMEs' self-assessment of their capability to develop operational and strategic resilience before, during and after a disruptive event, by leveraging risk management tools and practices.

To achieve its purpose, this study adopts a qualitative methodology and relies on data collected from in-depth interviews to professionals who work in 10 selected Italian SMEs. Italy was among the first countries to be hit by COVID-19 pandemic and applied massive and long-lasting restrictions to business activities. It is thus not surprising that 91% of Italian SMEs[2] were moderately to highly impacted by the COVID-19 crisis (Eurostat, 2023). Data was analysed by referring to the risk management typology developed by Henschel (2010) and the different forms and timings of organizations' dynamic resilience (Annarelli & Nonino, 2016; Colberg, 2022; Vogus & Sutcliffe, 2007). More in detail, this study focuses on the Italian automotive industry, a sector of fundamental importance for the national economic wellbeing and which is recently undergoing massive changes. A key actor of the automotive supply chain is represented by dealerships, i.e., the organization which brings into connection the Original Equipment Manufacturers (OEMs) and the buyers (customers). Dealerships are mostly SMEs, and during COVID-19 disruption,

---

[1] For the sake of simplicity, in this chapter, the expressions "ERM" and "risk management" are used interchangeably.

[2] Small and medium enterprises (SMEs) are those companies having less than 250 employees, an annual turnover up to 50 million euros or a balance sheet total of maximum 43 million euros (Eurostat, 2023).

they suffered the impact of several types of risks: supply risk, since there was shortage of vehicles produced by OEMs and of spare parts; demand risk, due to the fluctuation in demand causing uncertainty and making it difficult to plan sales; and financial risks associated with the decrease in sales and disruptions in supply and demand (Eldem et al., 2022). With all the features mentioned, this setting is considered both suitable and interesting for performing an analysis on ERM and resilience building in SMEs.

The study contributes to the management literature as it provides evidence on the usefulness and evolution of risk management processes to help SMEs respond to the COVID-19 disruption and build resilience against future shocks. Indeed, extant literature is meagre on practical examples and experiences of SMEs on how organizational resilience capacity can be achieved. Focusing on the automotive industry, the few extant studies on the impact of COVID-19 pandemic on the automotive sector mainly focus on the effect of the pandemic and the current megatrends on the industry players (Hoeft, 2021; Simonazzi et al., 2020; Wang & Wells, 2020), on the automotive supply chain in different countries and on OEMs reaction to related disruptions (Eldem et al., 2022). To the best of these authors' knowledge, only one study has investigated how dealerships reacted to the COVID-19 pandemic in Switzerland, with a focus on SMEs sustainability (Block et al., 2021). No research paper is found to study the impact of the pandemic on dealerships and the consequent adaptation and evolvement of their ERM strategies to improve organizational resilience. This study aims to fill this knowledge gap, thus responding to the research calls raised to analyse the impact of the application of ERM on organizational resilience (Arfiansyah, 2021).

Moreover, the study brings practical implications to professionals like SMEs' owners, general managers and CFOs who are sceptical in implementing risk management processes in their organization but, at the same time, are looking for ways to increase their business resilience. The checklist designed may help them to understand the status of their company and possible room for improvement.

The rest of the chapter is structured as follows. Section 12.2 develops the theoretical background of reference and review relevant literature on ERM and resilience within SMEs. Section 12.3 provide a short description of the automotive industry, with a focus on dealerships and the COVID-19 pandemic. Section 12.4 explains the research design, while Sect. 12.5 presents the research findings and offers a self-assessment checklist. Finally, Sect. 12.6 offers a few concluding remarks to highlight the contributions of the study.

12.2 Theoretical Background and Literature Review

12.2.1 Organizational Resilience and SMEs

In the current volatile world, organizational resilience must be contemplated as an inevitable (Ferrell, 2021; Natale et al., 2022; Xie & Wu, 2022). According to the management literature, resilience can be defined by assuming three different perspectives. First, resilience is viewed as a business ability to restore its operations and capacity to the pre-crisis perceived normality. However, it is also recognized that a *new normal* is likely to be established after a pandemic shock (Corpuz, 2021). Second, resilience is defined as the business ability to introduce gradual changes through the improvement of existing products, procedures and operations. According to this view, resilience is a dynamic process subject to constant evolution that affects firms' capabilities (Hamel & Valikangas, 2003). Third, resilience is defined basing on the transformative effects of a crisis: businesses are incentivized to engage in changes that are urgent and drastically different from their existing business models, resulting in innovations in products, services and partnerships (Brockner & James, 2008; Buliga et al., 2016; Dahles & Susilowati, 2015). In turn, innovation helps the company to achieve desirable performance in a turbulent environment (Bustinza et al., 2019). The time in which the organization understands how to respond to a shock is called *phoenix phase*. It involves coping and learning, breakdown and reorganization periods to maintain robust and stable functions and innovate through improvements and new creations (Ritter & Pedersen, 2020). Innovation is thus an important mean for businesses to survive and remain resilient in the face of external perturbations (Wang et al., 2020), becoming an important source of sustainable competitive advantage (Hamel & Valikangas, 2003). In this regard, Taleb (2021) introduced the concept of *antifragility*, defined as a system's capability to face stressors, shocks and volatility and thrive. When disruptions occur in an antifragile environment, the effects and impacts are only positive (Bravo & Hernández, 2021).

Furthermore, Spedding and Rose (2007) identified two forms of resilience: *static resilience*, which entails the ability of a system or an entity to continue its functions in the face of shocks, and *dynamic resilience*, which refers to the capacity of an entity or system to quickly recover from a shock (Jayasinghe et al., 2022). As well underlined by Simms et al. (2022, p. 4), adopting the dynamic resilience lenses is key when "*the disruption/threat is recurring and ongoing as in the case of the persistent COVID-19 pandemic*". Furthermore, Annarelli and Nonino (2016) divide dynamic resilience into strategic and operational resilience. *Operational resilience* is related to organizational defences and robustness to remain safe and stable (Iborra et al., 2020). By achieving operational resilience, the firm can offer a wide range of services and products within a short period, focusing on its business stabilization and survival (Baharin et al., 2021; Lampel et al., 2014), resisting, responding and recovering from the disruption (Annarelli & Nonino, 2016; Colberg, 2022; DesJardine et al., 2019; Duchek, 2019). In turn, *strategic resilience* deals with resilience inputs at the firm level, i.e., the firms' engagement in exploring opportunities through adaptability (Biggs et al., 2015), responsiveness (Williams et al., 2013) and flexibility (Iborra et al., 2020). Both forms of resilience are linked to *organizational ambidexterity* (Raisch et al., 2009), i.e., the dynamic capability to create, extend and modify company's basic resources (Helfat & Peteraf, 2003; Teece, 2018), so to achieve a competitive advantage by simultaneously exploiting existing competencies and exploring new opportunities (Iborra et al., 2020; Roffia & Dabić, 2023).

Finally, literature is aligned in maintaining that organizational resilience should be assessed: (a) before the disruptive event occurs (*ex-ante resilience*), in what can be considered a proactive phase of anticipation going on daily to consider resilience concerning businesses' readiness to identify and address potential negative effects arising from shocks; (b) during the disruption (*during the crisis resilience*), when there is the response and adaptation on what to consider during the crisis period; and (c) after the disruption (*ex-post resilience*), i.e., the reactive phase to gather insights on how the company survived (Colberg, 2022; Vogus & Sutcliffe, 2007).

Although it is well known that organizations are striving to implement strategies to create more resilient future operations (Ferrell, 2021; Natale et al., 2022; Xie & Wu, 2022), empirical evidence on resilience is scarce and mixed. Resilience characteristics are usually temporary since they tend to change over time and circumstances (Manurung & Widodo, 2022). This brings to lacking consensus about what elements constitute resilience capability and universal means for measuring resilience (Levine, 2014): indeed, in extant literature, there is no agreement on whether resilience is created or achieved (Hillmann, 2021), whether it is a capability (Battisti et al., 2019) or a characteristic of organizations (Colberg, 2022; Välikangas, 2010), and whether it is a reactive (persist, regenerate and recover) or proactive (anticipating and adaptive) instrument (Colberg, 2022). What is more, extant studies on resilience models focus on large organizations with formal structures and well-established organizational processes, thus being mostly irrelevant to SMEs (Manurung & Widodo, 2022). SMEs need to consider all the possible disturbances in their strategic decisions to successfully manage risks and pursue their medium- to long-term survival and success (Crovini et al., 2021). Indeed, in this highly variable and dynamic environment, an enterprise cannot be a static entity; otherwise, it will lose its competitive advantage. Conversely, the ability to resist and reconfigure by modifying strategies and organizational structure (if necessary), leveraging control tools, financial resources and information systems infrastructure, is essential for SMEs' survival (Roffia & Dabić, 2023).

Extant literature on SMEs' resilience provides conflicting views. According to one standpoint, the ability of SMEs to be resilient in face of crises is reduced because of a lack of planning for crises; unstructured procedures; limited internal resources such as managerial expertise; narrow customer base; low bargaining power; and dependence on key stakeholders (Branicki et al., 2017; Smallbone et al., 2012). SMEs are meant to be more vulnerable to the destructive effects of risks due to their *liability of smallness* (de Araújo Lima et al., 2020). For this reason, an effectual learning approach is necessary for SMEs, because these companies need to adapt fast to the changing market conditions, by learning from shocks in order to maintain their revenues and shield from losses (Simms et al., 2022). According to a different perspective, however, SMEs have the capability to develop significant resilience because they are more flexible, innovative and better able to respond quickly to changing environments (Branicki et al., 2017; Williams & Vorley, 2014).

12.2.2 Enterprise Risk Management and SMEs

Resilience and ERM strategies are emerging as keystones to business success (Assibi, 2022) in the face of a "*new normal*" business environment created by COVID-19 (Corpuz, 2021). ERM is used by organizations to reduce the negative effects of risks and to optimize the benefits resulting from disruptive situations, thus supporting organizations in becoming more resilient in times of uncertainty (Kimbrough & Componation, 2009). More in detail, "*[a]chieving resilience is reliant upon the ability of an organisation to anticipate and manage uncertainty. The conceptual foundation for this rests on an awareness of the organisation's operating environment and its connections within that environment*", where awareness is facilitated by "*the effective integration of risk management*" (Dahms, 2010, p. 23).

With its holistic approach, ERM goes beyond a conventional risk perspective and incorporates response capabilities that allow the company to identify and exploit opportunities as market conditions change and thereby impose a more favourable risk profile (Andersen, 2008). An effective ERM process not only considers *downside risk*, frequently associated with insurance and hedging activities aimed at mitigating financial losses, but also attempts to enhance firm value through evaluation of business opportunities, i.e., of *upside risk* which primarily focuses on business resilience through investments and operational innovations (Callahan & Soileau, 2017). It is of utmost importance that the ERM program is embedded in the vision, mission and strategic planning (COSO, 2017), thus "*developed during the conceptual stage and implemented even before the system is operational*"; conversely, if the ERM implementation "*is delayed until the beginning of operations, it can [still] identify emerging risks new threats, weaknesses, and exposures to prioritize them and propose an improvement process*", but it might fail to shield the organization from the imminent disruptions (Louisot, 2015, p. 86). Both COSO (2017) and academic studies (Arfiansyah, 2021; Bogodistov & Wohlgemuth, 2017) argue that in the long term, ERM will strengthen organizational resilience by improving the agility with which the organization adapts to changing business circumstances.

According to Assibi (2022), implementing ERM means that firms need to use a broader range of processes, tools and people that make up the organization to identify what risks are most important for their future wellbeing and then take proactive steps towards optimizing resiliency. This is exactly what makes ERM adoption so challenging for SMEs: indeed, SMEs often lack the financial, managerial and information resources to implement effective risk identification, assessment and monitoring processes, and thus to be able to face emerging risks and uncertainty (Brustbauer, 2016; de Araújo Lima et al., 2020; Raghavan, 2005). ERM systems can be implemented in many ways that can significantly differ among SMEs (Dvorski Lacković et al., 2022; Miloš Sprčić et al., 2017). The latter can be classified into three categories according to their attitude to adopt holistic approach to risk management, which is a function of their business planning, performance management, risk management process and risk management organization (Henschel, 2010). *Reactors* have immature risk management and performance measurement systems, whereas their business planning is at a medium level. They do not look into future risky events, do not use an initiative-taking approach to risk management (Glaser, 2019) and tend to react to disruptions in an inappropriate and inconsistent manner (Crovini et al., 2021; Henschel, 2010). In their turn, *defenders* are SMEs which have started implementing components of a comprehensive risk management system, operate in a dynamic business environment and compete intensively with new, small entrants. Business planning, performance measurement and the risk management process are more formalized than in reactors, while the risk management organization tend to have considerable deficits. How defenders can further develop in a positive way depends strongly on the rapidity of environmental changes (Henschel, 2010). Finally, *analysers* tend to undertake a broad analysis of the business environment and have better business planning than defenders and medium or advanced risk management processes' maturity. They have a clear business strategy set out in writing and they rely on external consultants. They are capable to balance their limited adaptability to current market trends and evolutions by their business stability and risk awareness (Crovini et al., 2021; Glaser, 2019; Henschel, 2010). Table 12.1 reports a summary of Henschel (2010) typology.

12.3 The Empirical Setting

The automotive industry is a relevant and interesting setting where the issues of ERM and organizational resilience in SMEs can be explored. Indeed, it is one of the oldest industries in the world and a general indicator of the wellbeing of the economy in many countries, being among the fastest growing and concentrated industries in Europe (Fraser et al., 2013). It is also a significant employer and investor in Research and Development (R&D) projects (Drelich-Skulska & Bobowski, 2021).

The automotive industry has experienced a century of stability in its business model (Fraser et al., 2013), but nowadays, experts refer it as at a crossroad (Hauptmeier, 2010; Simoudis & Zoepf, 2019): on the one hand, there are ongoing *megatrends*, which include Connectivity, Automatization, Sharing and Electrification (CASE); on the other hand, the COVID-19 pandemic hit the automotive industry heavily, to the extent the latter was one of the eight mostly affected industries (Hadi & Supardi, 2020).

The automotive industry plays a significant role in the Italian economy, as it includes 5.528 enterprises and 273.600 direct and indirect employees, representing the 7.3% of all Italian workers in the manufacturing sector (ANFIA, 2023). In 2022, the automotive industry had a turnover of € 86.2 billion, accounting for 9.9% of manufacturing turnover and 5.2% of Italy's Gross Domestic Product. The R&D spending component in the industry is also particularly significant, with an investment value of about € 1.7 billion, accounting for 13.2% of national R&D spending and 18.8% of manufacturing industry spending. Not surprisingly, this industry's competitiveness is higher than that of the manufacturing sector as a whole: in 2022, the national institute of statistics (Istituto Nazionale di Statistica, ISTAT) estimated a competitiveness index of 122.7, being 100 the index for the whole manufacturing industry.

Table 12.1 Henschel (2010) typology

	Reactor	Defender/prospector	Analyser
Business planning	No formal planning methods. Only annual sales plan developed. No look into the future. Accounts and financial statement prepared externally	No sophisticated formal planning methods. Long- and short-term profit and liquidity planning. Medium-term planning horizon. Little use of forecasting methods. Accounts and annual financial statements are prepared internally.	Sophisticated formal planning systems, various subplans linked together and long-term planning horizon. Detailed profit and liquidity planning used in the short term
Performance measurement	No sophisticated performance measurement tools	Greater openness towards modern instruments of performance measurement. No significant difference with the reactor in using traditional performance measurement systems	Modern instruments of performance measurement (e.g., Balanced Scorecard, shareholder value) and use of a knowledge management system. Usage of these instruments for risk management purposes
Risk management process	Identifies only specific familiar risks with a short-term risk time horizon. No formal risk reporting procedure	Slight improvements when compared to reactors. Familiar with narrow set of well-identified risks. No consideration of all risks might rush into costly failures. Major weaknesses in risk reporting and linking of risk management to business planning	Long-term perspective considering all types of risk faced. Risk reviewing frequency at shorter time intervals. Highly advanced link of risk management to business planning
Risk management organization	Little formalization of the responsibilities for risk management, concentrated towards managing director. Informality and no risk assessment methods employed. Missing regulations on replacement/ succession	Initial contingency and replacement planning. Clear weaknesses in succession planning. Informality, no sophisticated assessment methods. Quantitative methods dominating	Risk management implementation and development assigned to controlling unit. Highly sophisticated risk assessment, combining qualitative and quantitative methods. Great involvement of employees in risk assessment. Comprehensive contingency and replacement regulations

In this industry and specific contingency, focusing on dealerships provides interesting insights on ERM and business resilience because they are often SMEs and represent the connecting point between the OEMs (the producers) and the consumers (the buyers) (Fraser et al., 2013; Hoeft, 2021; Thun & Hoenig, 2011; Sturgeon et al., 2009). Being the fundamental link between these two players, dealerships act as retailers and represent the point of contact long after customers have purchased their vehicle. No dealership means no sales (except for the online sales) and no aftersales. During COVID-19, dealerships suffered many types of risks, among which *supply risk*, since there has been shortage of vehicles produced by OEMs and of spare parts that affected the sales of new cars and maintenance; *demand risk*, due to the fluctuation in demand causing uncertainty and making it difficult to plan sales, because consumers in periods of crisis postpone nonessential purchases; *(indirect) manufacturing risk*, because with less demand and hampered supply, OEMs suspended production for some time, leading to increased cost per vehicle produced; *data and information risk*; and *financial risks*, associated with the decrease in sales and disruptions in supply and demand (Accenture, 2020; Eldem et al., 2022). Moreover, *miscellaneous emerging risks* has arisen more recently, like the shortage of semiconductor chips and hence of the product, which led to a revision of the selling approach and an increase in the value of used cars; the Ukrainian war and the consequent rising energy crisis; the changing customer behaviour and the consequent management of the customer experience; and the switch to a direct selling model through an agent instead of the usual indirect selling model through a mandate. To survive and further expand their business, car dealerships must rely on their internal capacity to develop effective and flexible responses to industry challenges and risks (Gurau & Ranchhod, 2007).

The COVID-19 lockdown in Italy as of March 2020 led to a collapse in dealerships' sales monthly of more than 85%, which reached nearly 98% in April 2020 if compared to the same period in 2019. The crisis brought the 2020 market down to 2014 levels, closing the year with less than 1.4 million registered cars. The 2022 results are even worse; the market closed at 1.3 million registered cars (UNRAE, 2023). However, in 2022, the sales network relied on 1.182 dealerships (−2.4% compared to 2021), with total sales of more than € 46 billion, and employed 110.000 direct employees (Italia Bilanci, 2023). The Automotive Dealer Report 2023, a publication dedicated to the economic and financial analysis of the Italian car distribution industry, points out that in 2022, the average turnover of dealerships exceeded 38 million euros, the highest revenue level since 2005 with 1.3 million registered cars (−9.7% with respect to 2021). Such value exceeded by about one million euros the turnover of 2019, a year in which car registrations were almost two million. Despite the decline in sales volume, in 2022, dealerships' revenues grew by an average of 3% and profitability came in at 1.8%. Such positive results are a signal that Italian dealerships were able to recover from the shock generated by the disruption of COVID-19 pandemic. They thus represent an interesting setting to be investigated as regards ERM practices for resilience building.

12.4 Research Methodology

12.4.1 Sampled Dealerships and Interviewed Professionals

Consistently with the purpose of this study and because our aim is to go deep rather than wide (Draper, 2004), a qualitative research approach is adopted by conducting semi-structured interviews in ten Italian dealerships.[3] The latter were identified among small- and medium-sized firms, which according to the definition provided by Eurostat (2023) are those with fewer than 250 employees and an annual turnover of up to € 50 million, or a balance sheet total of no more than € 43 million.

As detailed in Table 12.2, most of the dealerships operate in the north of Italy, whereas 20% operate in the centre of Italy (Tuscany and the province of Rome). Two of the dealerships are controlled by a holding, while half of them are family-owned SMEs. Dealerships have between 43 and 132 employees: in detail, two of them are considered small whereas eight are medium enterprises. A common feature among the dealerships is a flat hierarchy, as the owner is also the general manager. Moreover, there are few business units, limited to sales and business development centre; marketing, aftersales and spare parts; finance; and administration. Each dealership represents between 1 and 11 car brands, with half dealerships that sell premium car brands, whereas the remaining ones are generalist. With only one exception, in 2020, the turnover was heavily affected by the COVID-19 pandemic, with a reduction ranging from −13% to −35% compared to the previous year. Conversely, in 2021, positive changes between 4% and 32% were recorded. The latter were not enough to meet or beat year 2019 turnover; however, they are a signal of prompt and significant recovery.

We adopted purposive sampling technique to reach the most knowledgeable participants in providing the desired information about risk management practices and organizational resilience (Eldem et al., 2022). Because it cannot be taken for granted that SMEs have enough economic resources for hiring a chief risk officer or a chief resilience officer (Aureli & Salvatori, 2013; Crovini et al., 2021; Florio et al., 2022; Gao et al., 2013; Petroni, 1999), interviews were conducted with business owners, general managers and/or financial directors of Italian dealerships. Following Eldem et al. (2022, p. 7), "*the professionals were considered suitable if they had at least five years of working experience in the dealership considered, have managed the COVID-19 outbreak*". Additionally, professionals shall have insights into the strategic and operational resilience decisions, as well as into ERM decisions, the firm is implementing in the post COVID-19 period. Interviews were conducted by phone or video call in January and February 2023 and lasted 50 minutes on average.

The interviewed professionals cover the role of owner of the enterprise (40%), general director (40%) or financial director/treasury manager (20%). Their age span goes from 33 to 63. Most of them hold a degree in economics and business

[3] We gratefully acknowledge the kind collaboration by Tommaso Bortolomiol, chief executive officer of Quintegia S.p.A. (Treviso, Italy), who provided the initial contact with several Italian dealerships.

Table 12.2 Characteristics of sampled dealerships

Dealership #	Foundation year	No employees	No locations	Car brands	Geographic location	2021 turnover (million, €)	2021 vs 2020 (%)	2020 turnover (million, €)	2020 vs 2019 (%)	2019 turnover (million, €)
1	1982	107	9	8	North-east	30.63	+32	23.25	−35	35.77
2	1963	91	3	2	Milan	44.32	+23	36.16	−27	49.53
3	1973	57	6	4	Rome	40.39	+4	38.99	−15	45.87
4	1946	49	1	2	Brescia	36.81	+9	33.74	−22	43.25
5	2009	43	3	1	North-east	28.68	+22	23.60	+23	19.18
6	1960	104	10	11	Veneto	46.12	+19	38.69	−17	46.61
7	1974	83	3	3	Veneto	36.96	+15	32.11	−30	45.87
8	1983	103	7	6	North-east	47.04	+6	44.27	−13	50.88
9	1950	121	8	8	Parma	45.39	+18	38.40	−19	47.40
10	1917	132	9	7	Tuscany	50.27	+25	40.19	−28	55.82

Source: Own elaborations from collected data

management. Regarding their working experience, the oldest interviewees started working in the family dealerships after their studies (40%), whereas the youngest ones (60%) explored different sectors before entering the automotive one. The professionals' working experience in the dealership in which they currently work varies between 7 and 40 years.

12.4.2 Interview Guide and Data Analysis

Prior research by Henschel (2010) was adapted to derive the questions for conducting the interviews. The first part of the interview focused on collecting demographic information of the interviewee (gender, age, education, working experience) and of the company (total revenues per year in the 2019–2022 period, number of employees, car brands represented, showrooms owned, geographical coverage). Following, three sections focus on the business planning processes implemented, the risk governance and risk management practices, and the use of key performance and risk indicators. Finally, there are three sections aimed at identifying the common traits and differences in the risk management and resilience strategies before (until February 2020), during (March 2020 to April 2021) and after (from May 2021) the disruptive event. The focus of the questions was on several major themes: (1) the background and role of the risk management strategies in forecasting a black swan shock (i.e., the pandemic); (2) the initial reaction to the disruptive event together with the business survival plans and the challenges; and (3) how the experience was used in the organization to adapt and improve risk management strategies and accordingly resilience. The questionnaire is attached in Appendix A.

To ensure traceability and mitigate contingent concerns about methodological rigor and inherent subjectivity, the analysis of the empirical material was documented step by step. In the first stage of analysis, the interview transcripts were screened for recognizing the elements of the selected four thematic areas of a holist risk management framework as per Henschel (2010), namely, business planning, performance measurement, risk management process and risk management organization. Accordingly, each author separately examined the transcripts to classify the dealerships as reactors, defenders/prospectors and analysers. No substantially different interpretations arose among the authors. In the second stage of analysis, the strategies and actions applied by interviewed professionals to deal with the pandemic were identified by the authors and discussed through the lens of their contribution to business resilience. To such purpose, the authors relied on the concepts of operational and strategic resilience and its evolution over time, as per the theoretical background of reference.

12.5 Research Findings and Discussion

The following paragraphs present and discuss the findings of the interviews made to the practitioners of the ten selected dealerships. In detail, it describes how ERM was designed and implemented and how it helped face the COVID-19 pandemic and increase business resilience against future shocks. Section 12.5.1 presents the evidence collected in terms of business planning, risk governance, risk management processes and performance indicators. Section 12.5.2 provides concrete examples on how sampled dealerships put in place risk management processes to survive the downturn caused by the pandemic and their capability to increase their organizations' resilience. Finally, Sect. 12.5.3 provides a checklist on resilience building actions for SMEs which practitioners can use to subjectively measure the resilience of their organization.

12.5.1 Enterprise Risk Management

CASE megatrends, COVID-19 and emerging risks uncovered the fact that dealerships were not ready to switch from the "*business as usual*" paradigm to a new way of operating characterized by changing customer behaviour, stock shortage and rising prices. Based on Henschel (2010)'s typology of risk management practices, all the dealerships in the sample can be classified as *defender-type firms*. Table 12.3 reports a summary of the business planning, performance measurement and overall risk management practices adopted by the Italian dealerships.

As regards business planning, most dealerships already work with a master budget, which is mainly used to program yearly projects, monitor costs and forecast contribution margins. The budgeting process is often carried out by the finance and administration department (D2, D3, D4, D6, D7, D8, D9, D10) or managed directly by the owner or the general director (D1, D5). All dealerships start working on the budgeting process in October, when the strategies for the new year are provided by the board of directors based on the firm-specific long-term strategies set and those

Table 12.3 Summary of empirical results from the sampled dealerships

	Summary of empirical results
Business planning	Master budget used to program yearly projects, control costs and forecast contribution margins. Budgeting process developed mostly by finance and administration department. Budget reviewed throughout the year with interim financial statements
Performance measurement	Operating and financial KPIs. Operating KPIs specific to the sector in which they operate; great focus on sales
Risk management process	Mostly qualitative methods. Risk identification through risk maps. Narrow set of well-known risks (strategic, market and financial risks). Link between business planning and risk management not developed
Risk management organization	Risk officer not present; business owner, general manager or financial director in charge of it. Board of directors or general manager responsible for supervising it

Source: Own elaborations from collected data

assigned by the OEMs represented, and the objectives are translated into measurable targets. The main point is to understand the financial needs of the different business units and match them with the forecasted sales because these businesses own a considerable percentage of long-term assets that originate periodical fixed costs. Furthermore, dealerships' profits are normally just a small percentage of the yearly turnover, being around 1.80–2.00% of total revenues on average. Throughout the year, the master budget is generally reviewed and compared frequently with the interim financial statements, i.e., every month or every 3–4 months. Monitoring is run by the board of directors or the general manager, except in those dealerships controlled by a holding. In that case, the whole budgeting process is owned by the holding top management team.

Dealerships use operating and financial KPIs for performance measurement, which are often defined according to the targets set by OEMs since dealerships' variable margins depend on meeting certain commercial objectives. Operational indicators are business specific and include the number of leads converted into actual buyers (D1, D2), new car sales over used cars sales per month (D3, D5, D6), sales generated from a specific campaign (D2, D3, D5, D6, D10), sales of used cars over sales of total cars (D2, D3, D6, D10), sales over inventory for each specific car brand, financial and insurance services sold with either new or used cars (D2, D3, D7, D9), productive hours in the workshop (D7, D9, D10) and workshop productivity, i.e., number of cars repaired (D7, D9). Financial KPIs are the traditional return on equity, return on investments, return on sales and debt to equity ratio. Because dealerships make substantial investments in fixed assets, especially property that is rented or purchased as showrooms, the latter are assessed regularly. Moreover, since dealerships might have a large inventory of vehicles, cash can be tied up for long time. For this reason, working capital, liquidity ratios and inventory turnover of both used and new cars are systematically monitored with a frequency varying between once a month and once every 3 or 4 months. As underlined by D2 referring to COVID-19 times, "*there were times in which we had so many cars that we did not have cash on hand, since as soon as OEMs deliver vehicles, they must be paid, whereas in other months, cash was sitting idle because customers were buying but we missed the product to be delivered to them*".

With reference to risk management process and organization, not surprisingly most dealerships do not implement systematic risk assessment strategies; they are characterized by an *immature risk approach* instead. Only a few dealerships (D2, D7, D10) have adequate measures and strategies in place to deal with disruptions (Crovini et al., 2021). In most cases, the subject responsible for conducting the risk management-related activities is the business owner (D1, D2, D5, D6) or the general manager (D3, D4, D8, D9). In some cases of medium-sized firms, it is the financial director (D7, D10) together with the finance and administration department. The supervision and review of the risk management processes is most of the times assigned to the board of directors and general manager (D1, D2, D3, D4, D5, D6, D8, D9) or centralized by the holding (D7, D10). Overall, the defender typology's risk management becomes visible in the strict control by owners and general managers, and in maintaining a traditional approach when facing environmental changes.

Risk identification in dealerships involves using a risk map (D3, D7, D8, D9, D10) or discussing risks orally during the budgeting process (D1, D2, D4, D5, D6). The general manager of D7 states that "*the key feature of our [D7] budgeting system and risk map is that they are set up in a way which they are visible in real time to every business unit manager so they can be modified and refined whenever needed without passing through the finance department or CEO. A warning message will be displayed to the CFO who can then decide to approve the amendment or not. Of course, approval is needed, but in this way the process is smoother*". This dealership is more advanced than the sample average, as often issues are reported in coordinating information and thus achieving an overview of the current risk position (Henschel, 2006).

Consistently with the defender typology description, dealerships only have a narrow set of well-known, familiar risks, namely, strategic, market and financial risks. Strategic risks refer to the risk that OEMs, from which dealerships totally depend, change their commercial policy: the agency risk is intense nowadays, which involves OEMs switching from an indirect selling model to a direct selling model, meaning that dealers become agents and the sale is realized by the car maker. Market risks involve changing customers' attitudes and needs, product shortage and delivery risk due to the high uncertainty when the vehicle will be delivered to the customer. Financial risks are related with dependence on banks, cash availability, interest rates on financing and the risk of not reaching targets imposed by OEMs, causing a reduction in profits. These businesses tend to compete on price, quality, delivery and service, and to realize their existing strategies, they need to avoid incurring in risks perceived as unnecessary (Miles et al., 1978; O'Regan et al., 2006). It is interesting to note that only in few dealerships (D7, D9, D10), team leaders of different business areas take part in the risk identification process. Risk identification and related issues are inevitably linked to risk assessment and risk monitoring, which results as particularly weak: indeed, all dealerships try to assess the impact of the risks previously recognized on the master budget, but then risk indicators and threshold levels are neither identified nor implemented, and action plans are not designed. In turn, this brings dealerships not to use techniques to optimize and, thus manage, single risks (Henschel, 2006). Moreover, measures that should be implemented if risk values violate the corresponding thresholds are neither planned nor included in the reporting, again confirming that the sampled dealerships are defender-type firms (Henschel, 2006).

Overall, although dealerships have quite developed business planning and performance management systems, the link between the latter and risk management practices is not well developed. Indeed, these companies struggle to adopt a holistic approach to risk management and take risks into account in silos in the short-term budgeting process, while one a few dealerships engage in a discussion within business units. This causes risks to be managed only when they materialize, i.e., when the organization is already exposed to the harmful consequences (Aureli & Salvatori, 2013) and needs to treat threats instead of seizing opportunities.

12.5.2 Resilience Building

Before COVID-19, dealerships had inadequate pandemic preparedness measures in place, and the interviewees admitted they had a high degree of scepticism towards the need to prepare for disasters (Jayasinghe et al., 2022). All the interviewed dealers did not expect COVID-19 could have had such an impact on their businesses. In fact, D4 remarks that "*the pandemic immediately posed a huge threat on our type of business, especially for the fact that we have a large amount of fixed costs, for example, mortgage for the new showroom, utilities, etc., that must be paid no matter what*". They only reacted when the crisis was already coming towards them and realized that two-digit losses of total revenues would have been recorded. D6 admits that "*the unique feature of this crisis is that it originated both financial and operating risks, causing long-lasting effects*". To face such a standstill of the market, dealerships largely relied on risk retention, by holding the risk and keeping it at the current level of impact and probability, and on risk transfer, by reducing its impact and/or probability by transferring it or in some cases sharing a part of it, "pushing" the event out of the organization. These responses are consistent with SMEs having defensive reactions (Brustbauer, 2016; Miles et al., 1978) to disruptions as identified by Guedes et al. (2015) in the Brazilian automotive industry.

How organizations respond to disruptions affects their business for a very long time as it determines whether they will thrive, survive or go out of the market. Sampled dealerships utilized a combination of different coping mechanisms immediately after the crisis started (Kraus et al., 2020). Initially, the dealerships adopted a *persevering* strategy, relying on measures aimed at sustaining the business activities of the company in response to the shock (Wenzel et al., 2020). In the short run, interviewed dealerships engaged in temporary business model adjustments because they could only react within their existing operational and strategic processes (Casadesus-Masanell & Ricart, 2010; Clauss et al., 2022; Kraus et al., 2020): some dealerships reported that they started to serve their clients remotely, by making videocalls or phone calls to explain their products and transforming the physical car showroom in a digital one. Subsequently, the dealerships adopted risk management processes with the aim of improving the antifragility of their business, through understanding the consequences of the disruption in the short and long term, focusing on the parts of the organization which were mainly affected. They developed the ability to manage the change, by leveraging resources already available and (whenever possible) acquiring new resources to shape the most effective and efficient possible solution. In the long run, they realized that the crisis was opening opportunities for strategic renewal; thus, they started to explore solutions for long-term strategic changes and developed *innovating* strategies to build resilience (Kraus et al., 2020; Wenzel et al., 2020).

Interestingly, the interviewees reported that after the initial shock, the new challenges brought by the pandemic and the emerging risks were not only negative but also positive because they opened new scenarios for growth: while they were incurring large expenses to overcome the "*business as usual*" paradigm and bring changes to the company's business model, they had the chance to benefit from business opportunities in a saturated industry such as the automotive one. Novelties related to the COVID-19 pandemic were the *reorganization of dealerships' risk management processes* and a *creation of new professional roles* (such as innovation and change managers); *business model changes*; and an *acceleration of the process of dealerships' digitalization* (e.g., the implementation of virtual showrooms and virtual assistants). D8 states that "*at the beginning and during the pandemic, looking at my peers, the most common reaction was to pause strategies and investments while waiting for more certainty. We decided to do the exact opposite, by realizing that it was the time to initiate an extraordinary restructuring process of the dealership, to deal with a new scenario that became definitive in the end*". In line with a prior study by Battisti et al. (2019), the resilience pattern outcome of dealerships in this study appears to be *sustained performance*: the reason is that small firms have a relative advantage in their capacity to learn fast, compared to large firms (Vossen, 1998), and this allows them to be resilient in uncertain and turbulent environments (Weick & Sutcliffe, 2011). Therefore, SMEs' necessary capabilities for developing business resilience for the future can be summarized in three adjectives: flexibility, adaptability and innovation (Vossen, 1998).

Following the impact of COVID-19, according to the professionals interviewed, the automotive industry is currently experiencing a particular triad of challenges: lack of trust in the system, spending possibilities and product shortage. Below, the major risks for dealerships in 2023 are commented. First, an *inventory risk* (D1, D4, D5, D7) is reported because a high amount of stock owned for fluctuations in OEMs production means high amount of cash tied up that could have been used for more productive activities. Second, lacking stability in *business profitability* is a matter of concern for several dealers (D6, D8, D10) because, on the one hand, the recommended prices for new cars are rising due to OEMs' costs of production, and, on the other hand, there is less demand from the market since inflation makes new cars less affordable for potential customers. Third, *dependence on suppliers* (OEMs) *and customers* is perceived as an increasing risk, currently faced by making attempts to diversify the customer base and the products and services offered, relying on social capital to mitigate the weak bargaining position and performing at their best at delivering high-quality pre- and post-sale services.

In consequence of current challenges, the business model of dealerships is expected to change because they will not get the same revenues from the same business activities. D6 admits "*the business activity carried out by dealerships is a complex job because it is characterized by many fragmented marginalities*". In fact, considering the economic environment in which small- and medium-sized dealerships are operating today, the key to switch from the "*surviving mode*" imposed by the pandemic to "*thriving mode*" is to set strategies and implement ERM processes to increase their business resilience (Agarwal et al., 2022; Branicki et al., 2017; Buliga et al., 2016; Ferrell, 2021). In this regard, D7 states: "*I have realized that there are external factors that inevitably impact my company and its business. What we can take positively from these events is that the company has always showed its ability to constantly change and adapt*".

During this post-COVID-19 period, organizations are experiencing coping and learning, breakdown and reorganization periods to maintain robust and stable functions and innovate through improvements and new creations, living a "*phoenix phase*" (Ritter & Pedersen, 2020). It is therefore argued that organizational learning is a major component in any effort to sustain firm performance during crises and retain a source of competitive advantage when market conditions change (Do et al., 2022; García-Morales et al., 2012). D10 affirms that "*in dealerships today, one cannot think in terms of individual compartments (sales, aftersales, services). All components, on the contrary, must come together to create value; accordingly, very often in the past, dealers have focused heavily on new car sales, while now more than ever, there is a need to create a cross-selling philosophy, including services, building* ad hoc *financial and insurance packages to give concrete answers to customers' spending budgets*". This approach represents an innovative way to identify, assess and manage risks even in smaller companies (Blanc Alquier & Lagasse Tignol, 2006), thus representing a good solution for SMEs as the idea is to create at the end of the process a sort of "*risk memory*" for the managers and owners to exploit consolidated knowledge and the experience learned in facing a specific risk and opportunity (Blanc Alquier & Lagasse Tignol, 2006). D5 remarks that "*COVID-19 has created a scenario where uncertainty is no longer just a risk factor, but it has become the variable that conditions the choices of all players. Dealers, as a result, cannot predict how the market will evolve in the coming months. Changes happen fast, and companies need to move faster like a Ferrari*". From the evidence collected, it seems that sampled small and medium dealerships perceive the need to acquire and develop different capabilities to build resilience: *dynamic and organizational capabilities,* because companies that seek to maximize their internal resources experience stronger resistance to internal and external shocks, sustaining their performance (Do et al., 2022); *leadership capabilities*, through a clear vision and strong commitment in adopting risk management processes by top management, as well as through creating alternatives and "*develop 'prepared minds' cascades throughout the organisation in the planning process*" (Dahms, 2010, p. 23); *ERM capabilities*, through more formal risk management strategies, with a better mapping of risks and by diversifying products and services offered, adopting threshold levels for KPIs and designing new KRIs; *financial capabilities*, through better monitoring of inventory and cash flows, reviewing costs, transforming fixed costs into variable costs, to be augmented or contracted according to the forecasted annual margins; *disaster risk planning capabilities*, working on real-time management systems and scenario analysis since by forecasting the economic and financial impact of shocks somehow likely to occur, it can be understood how to react before these sceneries occur, adopting a prospective view.

According to the interviews performed and the data collected, it is shown that during and in the post-COVID-19 crisis, sampled small and medium dealerships have increased their business resilience and managed to sustain their business activities during the economic downturn, through business model and company's strategies reconfiguration, which continue to be adopted in these days. To build such a resilient system, the interviewed Italian dealerships are putting into practical terms the three steps identified by Assibi (2022). First, they are implementing *forward-facing practices* by using a mix of lagging and leading risk indicators, hence Key Risk Indicators (KRIs), which will be adjusted to provide red flags before a risky event occurs directly related to the firm's risk tolerance levels. Moreover, they are using *dynamic prioritization* of risks, by regularly monitoring them through the company's informative systems. Finally, they are implementing *adaptive responses* through active decision-making based on constantly refreshed KRIs and scenario analyses (Assibi, 2022).

12.5.3 Proposal of a Checklist on Resilience-Building Actions for SMEs

Basing on the empirical results obtained by this study, a checklist is designed for every SME's owner/director which includes self-assessment questions aimed at guiding the latter to evaluate business resilience. In detail, questions focus on both strategic and operational resilience to be critically analysed in three different time periods: before the disruptive event (i.e., ordinary times), during the disruption and after the disruption. Questions are open-ended so that they can be adapted to SMEs operating in every industry and to allow the professionals involved to make their own considerations. The idea is to help professionals to increase their awareness on the state of the art, to identify areas that need improvement and to push them into insightful reasoning on which interventions shall be made to build resilience.

1. Ex-ante Resilience Assessment
   (a) *Strategic Resilience*
      - Is there a long-term vision for the company? Which is its timeframe? Is there a procedure and timeline to set strategies and business targets inside the firm?
      - Is the leadership strong?
      - Is it possible to switch to alternative strategies quickly?
      - Is the company measuring its business' antifragility? In which way?
      - Is there an assessment of core activities and critical levels of sales, revenues and profitability?
      - Are budgets reviewed throughout the year by means of interim financial statements? How often are cash flows reviewed?
      - Is there an assessment of the maximum loss the company might bear without getting survival issues?
      - Are dependencies on certain stakeholders carefully embedded in the company's strategic roadmap?
      - Is there a risk management system?
      - Is the mapping of risks covering all the risks the company might experience or is it considering only certain risk categories?
      - Are scenario analysis and stress tests used? Are contingency plans in place?

- Is there a crisis committee or team?
- Is the risk management process shared? With whom? How is commitment on targets achievement created?

(b) *Operational Resilience*
- Which are the critical tasks, processes and company's functions that guarantee the everyday functioning of the business?
- Are there backup systems to support critical tasks, processes and functions?
- Is there an assessment of the maximum downtime for different tasks before being affected?
- Is there unused capacity (in terms of production, personnel, etc.)?
- Which is the level of flexibility in production, distribution, etc., processes?
- Is the business building efficiency of processes through shortened lead times?
- What about the outsourced processes? Is there a careful outsourcing controlling in place (e.g., for business development centres)?
- Is there an assessment of the key players (i.e., main stakeholders)? How are they (e.g., employees, suppliers, customers)? Is the company's dependence on them properly assessed?
- Is any scenario analysis performed to forecast consequences on lacking support by such stakeholders and to plan for possible solutions?
- Are KPIs defined, computed and interpreted systematically to track the business operating performance (e.g., sales, products sold, lead times, profitability)?
- Are threshold levels for KPIs and KRIs in place?
- Is there a monitoring and warning system for KPIs and KRIs in place?

2. During Crisis Resilience Assessment (Crisis Management)

(a) *Strategic Resilience*
- Is there a strong leadership?
- What are the company's immediate strategic plans to deal with the disruption in line with its risk strategy? Is it possible to switch to alternative strategies quickly?
- What is the magnitude of damage made by the disruption in monetary terms? What is the assessed long-term impact?
- Is it still possible to achieve the business objectives previously fixed? Is it necessary to change the business strategy in the short run?
- Is the company able to keep revenues and profits streams?
- How far are KPIs and KRIs moving from their targets? Are they still above minimum thresholds?

(b) *Operational Resilience*
- What is the assessed impact of the disruption on operations? How often is it reviewed?
- Which are the critical tasks, processes and company's functions to be kept working during the disruption?

- Is it possible to implement quickly new solutions to keep in touch with customers? Is it possible to make some processes and tasks improvements?
- Is it still possible to achieve targeted operating KPIs and KRIs? Are they still above minimum thresholds?

3. Ex-post Resilience Assessment
   (a) *Strategic Resilience*
      - Is there a formal learning process from failures (e.g., written reports, adjusted budget)? Is it shared with all the employees of the company?
      - Which aspects of risk management processes adopted have been assessed to be key for resilience of the firm to survive the disruption?
      - Has the company been able to maintain revenues and profits streams?
      - Is management providing a strong leadership for the future of the company?
      - How are long-term and short-term strategies and objectives affected?
      - Have new strategic risks emerged and recognized by the company?

   (b) *Operational Resilience*
      - Has the company's business plan been improved?
      - Have new operational risks emerged and recognized by the company?
      - Is knowledge formalized through specific processes? Are contingency plans being reviewed considering the disruption?
      - How frequent are internal changes in processes, checks and procedures due to learnings from failures?
      - What is the forecasted time necessary for the organization to recover from the adverse impact? Are operating KPIs and KRIs away from or close to their targets?
      - Which risk management processes and checks at the operative level are in place to enhance resilience to future shocks?

12.6 Conclusion

This study investigates the state of implementation of ERM practices in small and medium Italian dealerships and report on how such practices have been adapted during the COVID-19 crisis to support and build organizational resilience. The research was motivated by the fact that, in these last years, SMEs are facing many disturbances that impact on their way of doing business, their performance and sometimes even their survival. The most recent and severe disruption is the COVID-19 pandemic, which has worsened all the other pre-existing challenges which typically SMEs encounter (Agarwal et al., 2022). An example of these companies are small- and medium-sized car dealerships, which, on top of the pandemic, were already experiencing disruptive shocks synthetized in the acronym CASE. In turn, COVID-19 created new and important challenges for such firms' ERM systems that must be addressed.

Relying on in-depth interviews to professionals of ten Italian small- and medium-sized dealerships, this study finds that SMEs use partially formalized risk management practices and can be classified as *defender type of firms* according to Henschel (2010) typology. Regarding risk governance, usually the business owner, the CFO and/or the general director deals with the processes and then it is discussed and reviewed with the board of directors. In identifying risks, they either use a risk map or discuss them orally during the budgeting process. They have only a narrow set of well-known familiar risks (strategic, market and financial risks) and try to assess the impact of such risks in the master budget. Yet, risk indicators and threshold levels are neither identified nor implemented and action plans are not designed. Although all risks are not predictable, failing to attempt to identify and manage response to risk throughout a firm can have a detrimental impact (Callahan & Soileau, 2017).

During the COVID-19 disruption, however, Italian dealerships implemented *forward-facing practices* using a mix of lagging and leading risk indicators and used a *dynamic prioritization* of risks by regularly monitoring them through the company's informative systems and implemented *adaptive responses* through active decision-making based on constantly refreshed KRIs and scenario analyses (Assibi, 2022). Their *phoenix phase* lasted very little, and dealerships worked intensively for their strategic and operational dynamic resilience. In the period following COVID-19 pandemic, the goal for Italian small and medium dealerships is keeping the flexibility they developed during the crisis and examine not only the threats but also the opportunities that arise from the current situation, for example, a reorientation of their business (Block et al., 2021). At the same time, these companies shall be aware they shall link risk management practices with business strategy and objective setting as recommended by COSO (2017), to have a more complete and clear vision of all the risks the organization faces through a portfolio view of risks and their interdependencies (Thun & Hoenig, 2011). With well-developed risk management processes and a sound firm strategy, SMEs will become better equipped for future disruptions (Crovini et al., 2021). In fact, flexible, innovative and adaptive capabilities play a key role in post-crisis recovery (Engle, 2011) and help the SMEs become antifragile.

With its findings, this chapter provides three contributions to existing SMEs' ERM and resilience literature (Callahan & Soileau, 2017). First, this research answers to the calls for more studies on the practical implementation of risk management practices in SMEs (Aureli & Salvatori, 2013; Callahan & Soileau, 2017; Crovini et al., 2021; Glaser, 2019; Tan & Lee, 2021). Indeed, unique evidence on Italian small and medium dealerships' risk management system is provided, by reporting the exclusive perspective of owners and managers directly involved in the day-to-day operations and fully aware of the complexity of their business (Crovini et al., 2021). Moreover, by adopting Henschel (2010) framework to comment on the gathered data, the study constitutes a practical operationalization of the defender-type firms' typology. Second, further contributions to the literature on the role of ERM in business continuity and resiliency during the COVID-19 crisis are given (Anton & Nucu, 2020; Assibi, 2022), through the evidence brought together on SMEs' reactions to the pandemic disruption. Third, this study contributes to the scarce literature on SMEs' resilience and business model transformation in the post-COVID-19 period (Pongtanalert & Assarut, 2022; Utami et al., 2021), by practically showing how SMEs in the automotive industry adapted to the current business environment and implemented new risk management tools. Moreover, based on the empirical results obtained, a resilience checklist is provided to practitioners to allow them to independently assess their organization's business resilience. Indeed, these research findings could be very useful to SMEs owners who are taking steps to proactive risk management in their business (Tan & Lee, 2021).

Appendix A: The Interview Guide

General information about the interviewee and the company

- Can you tell me about your background education?
- Can you describe your working experience?
- Can you describe your company in terms of year of foundation, turnover, number of employees, number of business units, brands sold, number of showrooms?

Business planning

- How do you set strategies and business targets inside your firm?
- What budgeting system do you use for long-term planning? How many years into the future do you plan?
- What budgeting system do you use for short-term planning?
- How is the budgeting process designed? Can you describe the phases?
- Who supervises and approves the budget?
- How is the budget disseminated inside the firm?

Risk governance and risk management processes

- Is there a risk officer in the company? If not, who is the person responsible for risk management inside the company?
- Do you think the risk management process is of fundamental importance to your company?
- Do you follow a formal framework for risk management?
- How would you describe your risk management process?
- Which risk categories are used to evaluate risks?
- How often and by who are risks identified and reviewed?
- Who supervises and reviews the risk management system?
- Is risk management linked to business planning?
- How are risk management practices disseminated inside the firm?
- What is the amount of budget that is dedicated to risk management practices?

Performance indicators

- Do you use a knowledge management system in your company?
- What Key Performance Indicators (KPIs) do you use to monitor the business activity? Can you provide some examples?
- Do you determine quantitative impacts risks may have on KPIs?
- Do you use Key Risk Indicators (KRIs)? Can you provide some examples?

Company's response to COVID-19

- Before COVID-19:
  - What were the major risks for the automotive industry at the end of 2019 in your opinion? And for dealerships, in particular your firm?
  - Which risk management strategies did you put in place before COVID-19?
  - Did you have a risk response plan for all significant events that could happen?
- During COVID-19
  - Did you expect COVID-19 would have such a huge impact on businesses?
  - Which risk management strategies did you put in place during the lockdown?
  - What operative plans did you put in action during the lockdown?
  - Did your business model change during the pandemic?
- After COVID-19
  - What are the major risks for the automotive industry nowadays in your opinion? And for dealerships, particularly your firm?
  - Did your perception of risk change after the pandemic?
  - Which risk management strategies do you actuate now?
  - How are you dealing with the stock shortage?
  - Do you implement and monitor KPIs and KRIs aimed at identifying emerging risks?
  - How would you define business resilience?
  - Which actions are you putting in place and what should be done to enhance preparedness and resilience of your company to future shocks?
  - Which aspects of risk management processes were key for resilience of your firm?

References

Accenture. (2020, April). *Impact on the automotive industry: Navigating the human and business impact of COVID-19*. https://www.accenture.com/_acnmedia/PDF-121/Accenture-Covid-19-Impact-Automotive-Industry.pdf

Agarwal, V., Mathiyazhagan, K., Malhotra, S., & Pimpunchat, B. (2022). Building resilience for sustainability of MSMEs post COVID-19 outbreak: An Indian handicraft industry outlook. *Socio-Economic Planning Sciences, 85*, 101443.

Andersen, T. J. (2008). The performance relationship of effective risk management: Exploring the firm-specific investment rationale. *Long Range Planning, 41*(2), 155–176. https://doi.org/10.1016/j.lrp.2008.01.002

ANFIA. (2023, March). *Fatturato del settore Automotive in Italia a gennaio 2023*. Retrieved May 9, 2023, from https://www.anfia.it/data/portale-anfia/comunicazione_eventi/comunicati_stampa/2023/01.2023-Approfondimento_ANFIA_Fatturato.pdf

Annarelli, A., & Nonino, F. (2016). Strategic and operational management of organizational resilience: Current state of research and future directions. *Omega, 62*, 1–18.

Anton, S. G., & Nucu, A. E. A. (2020). Enterprise risk management: A literature review and agenda for future research. *Journal of Risk and Financial Management, 13*(11), 281.

Arfiansyah, Z. (2021). The effect of enterprise risk management, knowledge management, and organizational culture on organizational resilience. *International Journal of Contemporary Accounting, 3*(2), 93–114.

Assibi, A. T. (2022). The role of enterprise risk management in business continuity and resiliency in the post-COVID-19 period. *Open Access Library Journal, 9*(6), 1–19.

Aureli, S., & Salvatori, F. (2013). The current state of risk management in Italian small and medium-sized enterprises. In *Proceedings of the 8th international conference of accounting and management information systems* (pp. 15–36). Editura ASE.

Baharin, S. N., Yusof, F., Said, J., & Zahari, A. I. (2021). Assessing organisational resilience of private higher learning institutions. *Malaysian Online Journal of Educational Management, 9*(4), 53–72.

Battisti, M., Beynon, M., Pickernell, D., & Deakins, D. (2019). Surviving or thriving: The role of learning for the resilient performance of small firms. *Journal of Business Research, 100*, 38–50.

Biggs, R., Rhode, C., Archibald, S., Kunene, L. M., Mutanga, S. S., Nkuna, N., et al. (2015). Strategies for managing complex social-ecological systems in the face of uncertainty: Examples from South Africa and beyond. *Ecology and Society, 20*(1), 52.

Blanc Alquier, A. M., & Lagasse Tignol, M. H. (2006). Risk management in small-and medium-sized enterprises. *Production Planning & Control, 17*(3), 273–282.

Block, A., Gellrich, M., & Russ, C. (2021). Effects of the COVID-19 pandemic on SME sustainability: Case study of car dealerships in Switzerland. *European Journal of Applied Business and Management, 7*(1), 58–83.

Bogodistov, Y., & Wohlgemuth, V. (2017). Enterprise risk management: A capability-based perspective. *The Journal of Risk Finance, 18*(3), 234–251.

Branicki, L. J., Sullivan-Taylor, B., & Livschitz, S. R. (2017). How entrepreneurial resilience generates resilient SMEs. *International Journal of Entrepreneurial Behavior & Research, 24*(7), 1244–1263.

Bravo, O., & Hernández, D. (2021). Measuring organizational resilience: Tracing disruptive events facing unconventional oil and gas enterprise performance in the Americas. *Energy Research and Social Science, 80*, 102187.

Brockner, J., & James, E. H. (2008). Toward an understanding of when executives see crisis as opportunity. *The Journal of Applied Behavioral Science, 44*(1), 94–115.

Brustbauer, J. (2016). Enterprise risk management in SMEs: Towards a structural model. *International Small Business Journal, 34*(1), 70–85.

Buliga, O., Scheiner, C. W., & Voigt, K. I. (2016). Business model innovation and organizational resilience: Towards an integrated conceptual framework. *Journal of Business Economics, 86*(6), 647–670.

Bustinza, O. F., Gomes, E., Vendrell-Herrero, F., & Baines, T. (2019). Product–service innovation and performance: The role of collaborative partnerships and R&D intensity. *R&D Management, 49*(1), 33–45.

Callahan, C., & Soileau, J. (2017). Does enterprise risk management enhance operating performance? *Advances in Accounting, 37*, 122–139.

Casadesus-Masanell, R., & Ricart, J. E. (2010). Competitiveness: Business model reconfiguration for innovation and internationalization. *Management Research: Journal of the Iberoamerican Academy of Management, 8*(2), 123–149.

Clauss, T., Breier, M., Kraus, S., Durst, S., & Mahto, R. V. (2022). Temporary business model innovation – SMEs' innovation response to the Covid-19 crisis. *R&D Management, 52*, 294–312.

Colberg, T. (2022). Organisational resilience: Creating ambidexterity in strategic and operational resilience. In *12th International Scientific Conference "Business and Management 2022"*.

Committee of Sponsoring Organizations of the Treadway Commission (COSO). (2004). *Enterprise risk management*. https://www.coso.org/Documents/COSO-ERM-Executive-Summary.pdf

Committee of Sponsoring Organizations of the Treadway Commission (COSO). (2017). *Enterprise risk management, integrating with strategy and performance*. https://www.coso.org/Shared%20Documents/2017-COSO-ERM-Integrating-with-Strategy-and-Performance-Executive-Summary.pdf

Corpuz, J. C. G. (2021). Adapting to the culture of "new normal": An emerging response to COVID-19. *Journal of Public Health, 43*(2), e344–e345.

Crovini, C., Ossola, G., & Britzelmaier, B. (2021). How to reconsider risk management in SMEs? An advanced, reasoned and organised literature review. *European Management Journal, 39*(1), 118–134.

Curran, J., & Blackburn, R. A. (2011). *Researching the small enterprise*. SAGE Publications, Ltd. https://doi.org/10.4135/9781849209847

Dahles, H., & Susilowati, T. P. (2015). Business resilience in times of growth and crisis. *Annals of Tourism Research, 51*, 34–50.

Dahms, T. (2010). Resilience and risk management. *The Australian Journal of Emergency Management, 25*(2), 21–26.

de Araújo Lima, P. F., Crema, M., & Verbano, C. (2020). Risk management in SMEs: A systematic literature review and future directions. *European Management Journal, 38*(1), 78–94.

DesJardine, M., Bansal, P., & Yang, Y. (2019). Bouncing back: Building resilience through social and environmental practices in the context of the 2008 global financial crisis. *Journal of Management, 45*(4), 1434–1460.

Do, H., Budhwar, P., Shipton, H., Nguyen, H. D., & Nguyen, B. (2022). Building organizational resilience, innovation through resource-based management initiatives, organizational learning and environmental dynamism. *Journal of Business Research, 141*, 808–821.

Draper, A. K. (2004). The principles and application of qualitative research. *Proceedings of the Nutrition Society, 63*(4), 641–646.

Drelich-Skulska, B., & Bobowski, S. (2021). Intra-industry trade and implications of the European Union-Japan Economic Partnership Agreement from the perspective of the automotive industry. *Entrepreneurial Business and Economics Review, 9*(2), 183–206.

Duchek, S. (2019). Organizational resilience: A capability-based conceptualization. *Business Research, 13*(1), 215–246.

Duchek, S. (2020). Organizational resilience: A capability-based conceptualization. *Business Research, 13*(1), 215–246.

Dvorski Lacković, I., Kurnoga, N., & Miloš Sprčić, D. (2022). Three-factor model of Enterprise Risk Management implementation: Exploratory study of non-financial companies. *Risk Management, 24*(2), 101–122.

Eldem, B., Kluczek, A., & Bagiński, J. (2022). The COVID-19 impact on supply chain operations of automotive industry: A case study of sustainability 4.0 based on sense–adapt–transform framework. *Sustainability, 14*(10), 5855.

Engle, N. L. (2011). Adaptive capacity and its assessment. *Global Environmental Change, 21*, 647–656.

European Commission. (2017). *Annual report on European SMEs 2016/2017 – Focus on self-employment*. https://op.europa.eu/en/publication-detail/-/publication/0b7b64b6-ca80-11e7-5538e69-01aa75ed71a1/language-en/format-PDF

Eurostat. (2023). *Small and medium-sized enterprises (SMEs) – Structural business statistics*. Eurostat. https://ec.europa.eu/eurostat/web/structural-business-statistics/information-on-data/small-and-medium-sized-enterprises#:~:text=SMEs%20are%20defined%20as%20employing,more%20than%20EUR%2043%20million

Ferrell, C. (2021). *Strengthening operational resilience in a post-pandemic environment*. https://erm.ncsu.edu/library/all-articles

Florio, C., Rossignoli, F., & Melloni, G. (2022). Drivers of ERM in SMEs: Which corporate governance features matter? In C. Florio et al. (Eds.), *Multiple perspectives in risk and risk management* (pp. 141–167). Springer.

Fraser, K., Tseng, B., & Hvolby, H. H. (2013). TQM in new car dealerships: A study from the firms' perspective. *The TQM Journal, 25*(1), 5–17.

Gao, S. S., Sung, M. C., & Zhang, J. (2013). Risk management capability building in SMEs: A social capital perspective. *International Small Business Journal, 31*(6), 677–700.

García-Morales, V. J., Jiménez-Barrionuevo, M. M., & Gutiérrez-Gutiérrez, L. (2012). Transformational leadership influence on organizational performance through organizational learning and innovation. *Journal of Business Research, 65*(7), 1040–1050.

Glaser, C. (2019). Risk management in German leasing SMEs—A qualitative study. In C. Florio et al. (Eds.), *Multiple perspectives in risk and risk management* (pp. 193–209). Springer.

Guedes, E. J. G., Bittar, A. D. V., Di Serio, L. C., & De Oliveira, L. H. (2015). Risk management in the supply chain of the Brazilian automotive industry. *Journal of Operations and Supply Chain Management (JOSCM), 8*(1), 72–87.

Gurau, C., & Ranchhod, A. (2007). Flexible risk management in new product development: The case of small-and medium-sized biopharmaceutical enterprises. *International Journal of Risk Assessment and Management, 7*(4), 474–490.

Hadi, S., & Supardi, S. (2020). Revitalization strategy for small and medium enterprises after Corona virus disease pandemic (covid-19) in Yogyakarta. *Journal of Xi'an University of Architecture & Technology, 12*, 4068–4076.

Hamel, G., & Valikangas, L. (2003). En busca de la resiliencia. *Harvard Business Review, 81*(9), 40–52.

Hauptmeier, M. (2010). The second automobile revolution: Trajectories of the world carmakers in the 21st century – edited by Michel Freyssenet. *British Journal of Industrial Relations, 48*(4), 817–819.

Helfat, C. E., & Peteraf, M. A. (2003). The dynamic resource-based view: Capability lifecycles. *Strategic Management Journal, 24*(10), 997–1010.

Henschel, T. (2006). Risk management practices in German SMEs: An empirical investigation. *International Journal of Entrepreneurship and Small Business, 3*(5), 554–571.

Henschel, T. (2010). Typology of risk management practices: An empirical investigation into German SMEs. *International Journal of Entrepreneurship and Small Business, 9*(3), 264–294.

Hillmann, J. (2021). Disciplines of organizational resilience: Contributions, critiques, and future research avenues. *Review of Managerial Science, 15*(4), 879–936.

Hillmann, J., & Guenther, E. (2021). Organizational resilience: A valuable construct for management research? *International Journal of Management Reviews, 23*(1), 7–44.

Hoeft, F. (2021). Assessing dynamic capabilities of incumbents in the face of unprecedented industry transformation: The case of the automotive industry. *Journal of Strategy and Management, 14*, 259.

Iborra, M., Safon, V., & Dolz, C. (2020). What explains the resilience of SMEs? Ambidexterity capability and strategic consistency. *Long Range Planning, 53*(6), 101947.

Italia Bilanci. (2023). *Automotive dealer study*. https://www.italiabilanci.com/prodotto/automotive-dealer-report-2023-versione-digitale/

Jayasinghe, N., Fernando, S., Haigh, R., Amaratunga, D., Fernando, N., Vithanage, C., et al. (2022). Economic resilience in an era of "systemic risk": Insights from four key economic sectors in Sri Lanka. *Progress in Disaster Science, 14*, 100231.

Kimbrough, R. L., & Componation, P. J. (2009). The relationship between organizational culture and enterprise risk management. *Engineering Management Journal, 21*(2), 18–26.

Kraus, S., Clauss, T., Breier, M., Gast, J., Zardini, A., & Tiberius, V. (2020). The economics of COVID-19: Initial empirical evidence on how family firms in five European countries cope with the corona crisis. *International Journal of Entrepreneurial Behavior & Research, 26*(5), 1067–1092.

Lampel, J., Bhalla, A., & Jha, P. P. (2014). Does governance confer organisational resilience? Evidence from UK employee-owned businesses. *European Management Journal, 32*(1), 66–72.

Levine, S. (2014). *Assessing resilience: Why quantification misses the point*. Overseas Development Institute.

Linnenluecke, M. K. (2017). Resilience in business and management research: A review of influential publications and a research agenda. *International Journal of Management Reviews, 19*(1), 4–30.

Louisot, J. P. (2015). Risk and/or resilience management. *Risk Governance and Control: Financial Markets and Institutions, 5*(2), 84–91.

Manas, N., Zakuan, N., & Setapa, M. (2021). The practices of Enterprise Risk Management (ERM) in Small and Medium Enterprises (SMES) – A literature review. In *E-Proceeding 8th International Conference on Public Policy and Social Science (ICOPS).*

Manurung, I. D. P., & Widodo, E. (2022). Building resilient micro-small enterprises: A case study of MSEs in the midst of the Covid-19 pandemic. *Jurnal Administrasi Bisnis, 11*(2), 1–12.

Massaro, M., Handley, K., Bagnoli, C., & Dumay, J. (2016). Knowledge management in small and medium enterprises: A structured literature review. *Journal of Knowledge Management, 20*(2), 258–291.

Miles, R. E., Snow, C. C., Meyer, A. D., & Coleman, H. J., Jr. (1978). Organizational strategy, structure, and process. *Academy of Management Review, 3*(3), 546–562.

Miloš Sprčić, D., Kožul, A., & Pecina, E. (2017). Managers' support – A key driver behind enterprise risk management maturity. *Zagreb International Review of Economics and Business, 20*(SCI), 25–39.

Natale, A., Poppensieker, T., & Thun, M. (2022). *From risk management to strategic resilience*. McKinsey and Company. [Online]. Available at: https://www.mckinsey.com/capabilities/risk-and-resilience/our-insights/from-risk-management-to-strategic-resilience

O'Regan, N., Ghobadian, A., & Sims, M. (2006). Fast tracking innovation in manufacturing SMEs. *Technovation, 26*(2), 251–261.

Petroni, A. (1999). Mapping the diffusion of advanced risk management practices among Italian small-and medium-sized firms. *Risk Management and Insurance Review, 2*(3), 125–140.

Pongtanalert, K., & Assarut, N. (2022). Entrepreneur mindset, social capital and adaptive capacity for tourism SME resilience and transformation during the COVID-19 pandemic. *Sustainability, 14*(19), 12675.

Raghavan, R. S. (2005). Risk management in SMEs. *The Chartered Accountant, 6*, 528–535.

Raisch, S., Birkinshaw, J., Probst, G., & Tushman, M. L. (2009). Organizational ambidexterity: Balancing exploitation and exploration for sustained performance. *Organization Science, 20*(4), 685–695.

Ritter, T., & Pedersen, C. L. (2020). Analyzing the impact of the coronavirus crisis on business models. *Industrial Marketing Management, 88*, 214–224.

Roffia, P., & Dabić, M. (2023). The role of management control and integrated information systems for the resilience of SMEs. *Review of Managerial Science*, 1–23.

Simms, C., McGowan, P., Pickernell, D., Vazquez-Brust, D., & Williams, A. (2022). Uncovering the effectual-causal resilience nexus in the era of Covid-19: A case of a food sector SME's resilience in the face of the global pandemic. *Industrial Marketing Management, 106*, 166–182.

Simonazzi, A., Sanginés, J. C., & Russo, M. (2020). *The future of the automotive industry: Dangerous challenges or new life for a saturated market?* Institute for New Economic Thinking Working Paper Series No. 141.

Simoudis, E., & Zoepf, S. (2019). *The automotive industry at a crossroads*. Center for Automotive Research at Stanford. [Online]. Available at: https://cars.stanford.edu/blog/automotive-industry-crossroads

Smallbone, D., Deakins, D., Battisti, M., & Kitching, J. (2012). Small business responses to a major economic downturn: Empirical perspectives from New Zealand and the United Kingdom. *International Small Business Journal, 30*(7), 754–777.

Spedding, L. S., & Rose, A. (2007). *Business risk management handbook: A sustainable approach*. Elsevier.

Statista. (2021). *Estimated number of small and medium sized enterprises (SMEs) worldwide from 2000 to 2021*. https://www.statista.com/statistics/1261592/global-smes/

Sturgeon, T. J., Memedovic, O., Van Biesebroeck, J., & Gereffi, G. (2009). Globalisation of the automotive industry: Main features and trends. *International Journal of Technological Learning, Innovation and Development, 2*(1–2), 7–24.

Taleb, N. N. (2021). *Incerto 5-book bundle: Fooled by randomness, the black swan, the bed of procrustes, antifragile, skin in the game*. Random House.

Tan, C., & Lee, S. Z. (2021). Adoption of enterprise risk management (ERM) in small and medium-sized enterprises: Evidence from Malaysia. *Journal of Accounting and Organizational Change, 18*, 100–131.

Teece, D. J. (2018). Business models and dynamic capabilities. *Long Range Planning, 51*(1), 40–49.

Thun, J. H., & Hoenig, D. (2011). An empirical analysis of supply chain risk management in the German automotive industry. *International Journal of Production Economics, 131*(1), 242–249.

Unione Nazionale Rappresentanti Autoveicoli Esteri (UNRAE). (2023). *Analisi del mercato autoveicoli in Italia, UNRAE Book 2022*. UNRAE.

Utami, I. D., Santosa, I., & Leila, M. V. (2021). Priority resilience strategy for micro, small, and medium enterprises for dealing with natural disasters. *International Journal of Disaster Risk Reduction, 55*, 102074.

Välikangas, L. (2010). *The resilient organization: How adaptive cultures thrive even when strategy fails*. McGraw-Hill.

Verbano, C., & Venturini, K. (2013). Managing risks in SMEs: A literature review and research agenda. *Journal of Technology Management and Innovation, 8*(3), 186–197.

Vogus, T. J., & Sutcliffe, K. M. (2007, October). Organizational resilience: Towards a theory and research agenda. In *2007 IEEE international conference on systems, man and cybernetics* (pp. 3418–3422). IEEE.

Vossen, R. W. (1998). Relative strengths and weaknesses of small firms in innovation. *International Small Business Journal, 16*(3), 88–94.

Wang, L., & Wells, P. (2020). Automobilities after SARS-CoV-2: A socio-technical perspective. *Sustainability, 12*(15), 5978.

Wang, C., Cheng, Z., Yue, X. G., & McAleer, M. (2020). Risk management of COVID-19 by universities in China. *Journal of Risk and Financial Management, 13*(2), 36.

Weick, K. E., & Sutcliffe, K. M. (2011). *Managing the unexpected: Resilient performance in an age of uncertainty* (Vol. 8). Wiley.

Wenzel, M., Stanske, S., & Lieberman, M. B. (2020). Strategic responses to crisis. *Strategic Management Journal, 41*(7/18), 3161.

Westby, J. R., & Lamb, L. (2020). Rethinking risk in a post-pandemic world. *Risk Management, 67*(11), 8–9.

Williams, T. (2017). The nature of risk in complex projects. *Project Management Journal, 48*(4), 55–66.

Williams, N., & Vorley, T. (2014). Economic resilience and entrepreneurship: Lessons from the Sheffield City region. *Entrepreneurship and Regional Development, 26*(3–4), 257–281.

Williams, B. D., Roh, J., Tokar, T., & Swink, M. (2013). Leveraging supply chain visibility for responsiveness: The moderating role of internal integration. *Journal of Operations Management, 31*(7–8), 543–554.

Xie, X., & Wu, Y. (2022). Business networks and organizational resilience capacity in the digital age during COVID-19. In *Academy of management proceedings* (Vol. 2022, No. 1, p. 14086). Academy of Management.

13 Increasing Value and Resilience Through Project Risk Management: A Case Study in the IT Consulting Sector

Raffaele Testorelli, Anna Tiso, and Chiara Verbano

13.1 Introduction

Risk is an effect, in terms of a positive or negative deviation from expected outcomes, resulting from uncertainty (ISO 31000, 2018), that can affect economic performance, business continuity, reputation, and environmental and social outcomes of an organization. Risk management (RM) supports companies in achieving their goals, exploring new opportunities, and reducing potential losses in an uncertain and dynamic business environment (ISO 31000, 2018; Radner & Shepp, 1996).

In addition, the current complex business environment is pushing many organizations to develop the ability to be resilient, intended as the capacity of an adapting and/or evolving system to bounce back to dynamic stability after a disturbance (Chroust & Aumayr, 2017), where the focus of resilience is the adaptation of organizations amid continuing and unfolding disruptions (Linnenluecke, 2017). Indeed, resilience includes the system's ability to create new conditions of fitness for itself whenever necessary, reorganizing, reconfiguring, restructuring, and even reinventing when appropriate in response to disruptions (Chroust & Aumayr, 2017; Dahlberg, 2015). Hence, resilience is the capability not only to remain unaffected by random and unpredicted changes but also to manage to take advantage of them (Taleb, 2012).

Becoming resilient may even be more critical for small- and medium-sized enterprises (SMEs) because they are more vulnerable due to challenges such as accessing finance and restrictions due to their limited size (Branzei & Abdelnour, 2010; Tognazzo et al., 2016). The idea of resilience in SMEs is often used to label

R. Testorelli (✉) · A. Tiso · C. Verbano
University of Padova, Padua, Italy
e-mail: raffaele.testorelli@unipd.it; anna.tiso.2@phd.unipd.it; chiara.verbano@unipd.it

S. Durst, T. Henschel (eds.), *Small and Medium-Sized Enterprise (SME) Resilience*, Management for Professionals, https://doi.org/10.1007/978-3-031-50836-3_13

firms' economic performance and responsiveness in light of specific shocks, such as financial crisis and recession (Williams et al., 2013; Muhammedamin et al., 2021).

Managing risk and resilience result to be particularly relevant in projects, where the exposure to risk is high. Indeed, projects are considered the main vehicles to implement companies' strategic objectives of innovation and growth, often entailing significant levels of uniqueness and uncertainty (Shimizu et al., 2012). At the same time, project failure can reveal detrimental for the organization and society as a whole.

Project Risk Management (PRM) is the stream of RM that focuses on managing risk and resilience in projects. PRM is a systematic process that manages intrinsic project risks, fostering the effect of positive events (opportunities) while mitigating those related to negative events (threats) (Borge, 2002; PMI, 2013). For this reason, PRM is a widely used approach by companies to achieve success in their projects (Elkington & Smallman, 2002), with the final aim of creating and protecting value (Willumsen et al., 2019). In particular, the value generated through PRM is defined as the ratio between benefits and costs (European Standards 12973, 2000; Laursen & Svejvig, 2016; Morris, 2013), including both economic and intangible (not monetary) components (Shenhar et al., 2001; Voss et al., 2002).

The academic and managerial interest toward the PRM as a value generation process shed light on several aspects of the topic, highlighting the necessity of investigating the role of multiple stakeholders and the contribution of their perspectives on the value created at the individual, organizational, and society levels (Lepak et al., 2007; Winter et al., 2006). However, while international standards paid greater attention to PRM as a value generation process, the empirical literature reports some conflicting results and gaps, offering a unique opportunity to deepen the theme. In particular, understanding what value can be generated and how it can be enhanced (Andersen, 2014; Willumsen et al., 2019), considering contextual factors (Turner et al., 2010; Willumsen et al., 2019) and the impacts on the overall organization (Andersen, 2016; Sanchez et al., 2009; Serra & Kunc, 2015), would provide a significant contribution to broaden knowledge about the topic, addressing literature gaps and contradictions. Moreover, fostering the creation of value through PRM would enhance the development of resilience in projects.

This study presents the results emerging from a case study in the IT consulting sector, offering some insights on how to tailor the PRM system to maximize value generation and resilience in projects for different stakeholders.

13.2 Theoretical Background

SMEs are seen as a vibrant and innovative source of innovation and have been the main source of new employment growth in many advanced economies. However, SMEs face a high risk of insolvency and many firms struggle to grow as they had planned (Henschel & Lantzsch, 2022).

Although these issues are frequently caused by management errors and weaknesses in organization design, many of these failures can be mitigated through

PRM, resulting in the reduced likelihood of project failure of SMEs and the increased likelihood of leveraging opportunities (Testorelli & Verbano, 2022).

Furthermore, environmental uncertainty has an impact on RM efforts in SMEs (Henschel & Durst, 2016). Becoming resilient is critical for SMEs because they are more vulnerable due to challenges such as accessing finance and restrictions due to their limited size (Branzei & Abdelnour, 2010; Tognazzo et al., 2016) and managing knowledge risks (Durst et al., 2018).

Finally, the concept of resilience is often used to label the economic performance and responsiveness of SMEs in light of specific shocks, such as financial crisis and recession (Muhammedamin et al., 2021; Williams et al., 2013).

From the analysis of the current literature, several approach and perspectives on PRM emerge, highlighting the lack of a shared common definition:

- *Management approach.* According to the management approach, PRM is a systematic process that aims to identify and manage risk, in order to act on its appearance, by implementing systems and procedures to identify, analyze, evaluate, and address the risks inherent to any project (Conroy & Soltan, 1998; Raz & Michael, 2001). It focuses on the identification of specific project events and situations that could impact the original plan, to develop adequate risk responses.
- *Evaluation approach.* A different view is proposed by the evaluation approach, according to which PRM aims at determining risk factors, through the collection and analysis ex post of the information about project risks, addressing them since the initial stage of the project (Bakker, 2010; Jiang & Klein, 2001; Wallace et al., 2004).
- *Contingency approach.* Another interesting perspective is offered by the contingency approach, which focuses mainly on unknown project risks in situations with difficulties in detecting the relevant variables and interactions. It deals with the project capability of managing uncertainties, fostering resilience and adaptability, particularly (1) through constant environmental scanning to recognize unforeseen events when they arise, (2) having a resilient, responsive, and functioning structure at the organizational level, (3) engaging and communicating with stakeholders, and (4) having competent resources with adequate self-awareness and the ability to deal with stressful situations (Besner & Hobbs, 2012; Geraldi et al., 2010; Javani & Rwelamila, 2016; Jun et al., 2011; Sommer & Loch, 2003).
- *Agile and combined approaches.* In certain project types (e.g., software development projects), the agile methodologies are often adopted, to improve adaptability and responsiveness to change. Finally, in recent years, combined approaches to PRM have been introduced.

This variety demonstrates how PRM literature is rich; however, the contribution of the different approaches to value creation and resilience in projects, what and how value is generated through PRM, is still lacking. Moreover, despite the different perspectives provided by the current literature on the role of project stakeholders in the creation of value, the attempts to measure the value generated for them result incomplete. Indeed, project stakeholders can be considered both targets of value creation and potential sources of risk in projects, based on their behaviors, expectations, and perceptions (Javani & Rwelamila, 2016; Lepak et al., 2007). In this regard, Mendelow (1991) classifies stakeholders according to their power and interest in the project; Mitchell et al. (1997) according to their power, urgency, and legitimacy; and Murray-Webster and Simon (2006) evaluate them on their (1) power to influence the project, derived from their position in the organization or from their credibility as leaders or experts; (2) interest in the project; and (3) supportive or resistant attitude toward the project.

13.2.1 Main Concepts

To solve the discrepancies on the definition and measurement of the value generated with PRM among researchers, the current paragraph recalls the fundamental concepts, providing some definitions assumed in the research:

- *PRM economic value*: the ratio between the economic benefits generated through PRM for a project stakeholder and the cost of its implementation (European Standard 12973, 2000; Laursen & Svejvig, 2016; Morris, 2013; Quartermain, 2002).
- *PRM intangible benefit*: utility of the additional intangible benefits generated through PRM, as perceived by a project stakeholder (Laursen & Svejvig, 2016; Scholz & Tietje, 2002; Willumsen et al., 2019).
- *PRM value*: total value generated through PRM for a project stakeholder (economic value and intangible benefit).
- *PRM value generation*: process of value generation through PRM. It is context-specific and depends on the level of analysis and can be an individual, organization, or society (Laursen & Svejvig, 2016; Lepak et al., 2007).

13.2.2 Literature Review

According to a recent systematic literature review on PRM, 83% of papers result to be empirical. The majority adopts alternatively a process perspective with a focus on PRM practices and activities, or a content perspective, analyzing the benefits obtained. Instead, only 31% investigate whether and how the context affects value generation through PRM (Testorelli & Verbano, 2020; Willumnsen et al., 2019; de Carvalho & Rabechini Junior, 2015; Morris, 2013; Besner & Hobbs, 2012; Kutsch, 2008).

In the assessment of the value generated through PRM, five levels of analysis need to be considered: (1) project level, including the individual level related to project team members; (2) company level, related to program and portfolio management; (3) customer level, including customers and customers of customers; (4) business ecosystem level, that involves suppliers, R&D partners, and business partners; and (5) society level, intended as groups of citizens and society as a whole. Although the value generated at one level of analysis can move to others (Lepak et al., 2007), approximately 40% of the literature analyzes only the value generated and captured at the project level. In fewer cases, the analysis is extended to two levels, more frequently the project and the customer levels, or alternatively, the project and the company levels. Finally, only a few papers also consider the business ecosystem or society levels. As opposed to these results, the importance of identifying the expected and actual receivers of the value generated and the impact of this value on each of them is generally acknowledged. Indeed, project stakeholders' conflicting interests and subjective value systems affect their perceptions of the value generated (Lepak et al., 2007; Winter et al., 2006). Although it would be necessary to understand which project stakeholders generate value and how this value is then perceived, just a handful of papers considers the stakeholders' multiple perspectives.

Finally, many authors acknowledge the relevance of measuring the value generated through PRM, but there is limited evidence on how this value can be measured, with a lack of adequate tools to assess the economic value and the additional intangible benefit generated through PRM.

Therefore, some gaps emerge from the current knowledge, highlighting how some aspects of PRM value generation are still overlooked. Further investigations on the influence of the context and of the stakeholders' points of view on the value created in projects are needed, as well as also value measurement requires in-depth research. Moreover, the results contribute to identify the key dimensions that influence the value generation process and the generated value: the context in which projects are conducted (e.g., business sector, company size, process/project organization), the PRM system maturity level (extent to which risk management is embedded within the organization) (Yeo & Ren, 2009), the level of analysis considered, and the specific stakeholder's perspective adopted.

Considering the results highlighted by the literature review, a research opportunity emerged to explore PRM value generation with the final aim of supporting companies in improving value generation and resilience in projects.

Therefore, deepening how to adapt the PRM system to the specific project context would allow to evaluate the effects on the value created and on resilience. Indeed, resilience includes the system's ability to create new conditions of fitness for itself whenever necessary, reorganizing, reconfiguring, restructuring, and even reinventing when appropriate in response to disruptions (Chroust & Aumayr, 2017; Dahlberg, 2015). In addition, as resilience, PRM generates value managing the negative risks, but also catching the existing opportunities. Indeed, resilience is the capability to not only remain unaffected by random and unpredicted changes but also manage to take advantage of them (Taleb, 2012).

More connections between PRM and resilience should be explored in future research.

13.3 Objective and Methodology

The gaps emerging from the literature review highlight the questions about the value generated through PRM, regarding specifically the type of benefits created for project stakeholders and their measurement, the influence of the specific project context. and the improvement perspectives. The final purpose of this research consists of improving value generation and resilience through PRM in projects, promoting both economic and intangible benefits. The analysis and improvement of PRM value generation considers the content and the process, the contextual factors, the levels of analysis, the diverse stakeholders' viewpoints, and the measure of the value.

The research objective is therefore answering the following RQs:

- RQ1: What economic value and intangible (not monetary) benefits are generated through PRM for stakeholders?
- RQ2: How can the economic value and the intangible benefits generated through PRM be measured?
- RQ3: How do contextual factors influence PRM value generation?
- RQ4: How can PRM be improved to increase the value generated?

To investigate all these aspects, a framework was developed. Given the explanatory and exploratory nature of the research objective, a case study and specifically an embedded case study were conducted (Yin, 2013). Indeed, inside the selected company, provided with a PRM system, three different projects were considered. The unit of analysis is the PRM system adopted by the company, and the subunits are the PRM systems implemented in the projects. Moreover, the case study analysis will allow to test and assess the validity of the framework developed for value generation through PRM.

13.3.1 Empirical Framework

The theoretical framework derived from the systematic literature review (Testorelli & Verbano, 2022) lays the foundations for the development of the empirical framework of analysis (Fig. 13.1). It is composed by three main elements, which represent the key dimensions of PRM value generation:

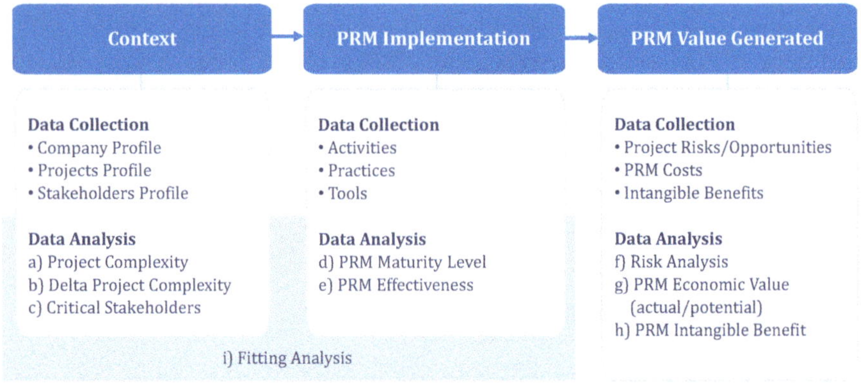

Fig. 13.1 Empirical framework for value generation through PRM

1. *Context*: the project context in which the PRM system was implemented, with a focus on the characteristics of the company, the project, the project stakeholders, and the respondents.
2. *PRM implementation*: the maturity level (defined by the practices, activities, and tools performed) (PMI, 2017; Yeo & Ren, 2009) of the RM and PRM systems adopted, respectively, at the company and at the project level, and the project risks and opportunities.
3. *PRM value generated*: the economic value generated by the PRM system, when compared with the costs of its implementation, and the additional intangible benefit according to project stakeholders.

13.3.1.1 Data Collection

Data have been collected through multiple sources of evidence, including interviews, field notes, project documents, and qualitative and quantitative questionnaires, to guarantee construct validity. Moreover, interviewing at least two respondents for each projects assured internal validity through triangulation (Yin, 2013). Respondents were selected among the project stakeholders, who had a significant understanding about the challenges of PRM and a willingness to be involved. The respondents heterogeneity, in terms of seniority and professional roles, allowed to identify patterns of perceptions from different perspectives and to enhance the reliability of the collected data (Voss et al., 2002). A total of four informants participated in seven interviews, as represented in Fig. 13.2.

Based on the empirical framework, a questionnaire was designed to collect quantitative and qualitative information. It is composed by the three dimensions of the empirical framework (context, PRM implementation, and PRM value generated), divided in further sections.

13.3.1.2 Data Analysis

Data analysis considers nine elements:

- *Project complexity*: Evaluation of the key project characteristics (uncertainty, innovation, novelty, and criticality of stakeholders) on a 7-point Likert-type scale ranging from 1 (very low) to 7 (very high) according to respondents' perceptions (Crispim et al., 2019; Qazi et al., 2016; Yeo & Ren, 2009).
- *Delta project complexity*: Difference in the project complexity perceived by the stakeholders.
- *Critical stakeholders*: Classification of stakeholders, from the project manager's point of view, based on their (1) interest in the project, measured by the degree to which they would be active or passive; (2) their attitude to the project, measured by the degree to which they would "back" (support) or "block" (resist); (3) their power or ability to influence the project, derived from their positional or resource power in the organization, or from their credibility as leaders or experts (Murray-Webster & Simon, 2006). The number of critical stakeholders and the project complexity together define the context criticality.

Unit of Analysis		Sub Unit of Analysis							Respondents			
PRM System	Company Characteristics	Project	Project Description	Project Type	Project Budget *(mil €)*	Team Size *(persons)*	Project Durat. *(months)*	Project Losses *(losses/budget)*	Role	Type	Seniority *(years)*	Interviews *(number, duration)*
Alpha	- **Small service and project oriented company in the IT consulting sector** - Organised according to a combined model (both by projects and by process) - 22 employees, turnover of 2 mil euros (2019) - Agile approach to PRM	α1	**Cost Estimation SW Application**	Small-sized project with a low level of uncertainty and instability and uniqueness and novelty, but with a high level of difficulty in the management of stakeholders	7'	5	8	Low (1.4%)	Project Manager	Project Management Team	2-5	2 (120 min)
									CEO	Top Management	5-10	1 (60 min)
		α2	**Cost Dashboard SW Application**	Small-sized project with a medium-high level of uncertainty and instability, and a high level uniqueness and novelty, but a low level of difficulty in the management of stakeholders	15	4	1.5	Low (0%)	Project Manager	Project Management Team	2-5	1 (60 min)
									Business Analyst	Project Team	1-2	1 (60 min)
		α3	**Order Date Confirmation Automation SW Application**	Small-sized project with a medium level of uncertainty and instability, and a high level uniqueness and novelty, but a low level of difficulty in the management of stakeholders	65	5	3	Low (0%)	Project Manager	Project Management Team	2-5	2 (120 min)
									Business Analyst	Project Team	1-2	1 (60 min)
									Consultant	Project Management Team	1-2	1 (60 min)

Fig. 13.2 Unit/subunits of analysis and respondents

- *PRM maturity level*: Defined, according to the Risk Management-Capability Maturity Model (RM-CMM) (Yeo & Ren, 2009), on the basis of PRM tools, practices and activities implemented (PMI, 2017; Yeo & Ren, 2009).
- *PRM effectiveness*: Evaluated through the risk gap, defined as the ratio between the residual risk and the risk risk-related losses, and the project budget.
- *Risk analysis*: Risks classification into technical/operational, organizational, contractual, financial/economic, and political, based on risk types, sources, responses, and stakeholders involvement (de Camprieu et al., 2007; Dey, 2012; Qazi et al., 2016). Additionally, the initial risk evaluation (probability and expected impact of risk before treatment), the expected risk impact (probability and expected impact of risk after treatment), and the actual risk impact (losses or opportunities actually captured) have been analyzed (Crispim et al., 2019; Qazi et al., 2016; Serpell et al., 2019).
- *PRM economic value generated*: The PRM economic value index (PVI_{econ}) measures the economic value generated through PRM. It is defined as the sum of project risk reductions with the economic opportunities generated by positive risks, over the costs of PRM implementation. Based on Ahmadi-Javid et al. (2020), Laursen and Svejvig (2016), and Serpell et al. (2019), the index was improved by adopting a multistakeholders' perspectives and including the economic impact of positive risks.

$$PVI_{econ} = \frac{\sum_{j=1}^{S}\left(\sum_{i=1}^{N} r_{ij} + o_{ij}\right)}{\sum_{j=1}^{S}\left(\sum_{i=1}^{N} c_{ij}\right)}$$

- where:

(S): number of project stakeholders;
(j): jth project stakeholder, where $j = (1, \ldots, S)$;
(i): ith project risks, where $I = (1, \ldots, N)$;
(r_{ij}): risk reduction of the ith project risk for the jth project stakeholder;
(o_{ij}): economic opportunities for the jth project stakeholder generated through the management of the ith project risk;
(c_{ij}): cost paid by the jth project stakeholder to manage the ith project risk.

If $PVI_{econ} > 1$, the economic benefits are greater than the cost paid for the PRM implementation. On the contrary, $PVI_{econ} <= 1$ means that the economic benefits are equal or lower than the cost. Thus, the higher the PVI_{econ} value, the higher the PRM economic value generated.

- *PRM intangible benefit*: Measured by a multi-attribute utility function (U_{intang}) (Keeney & Raiffa, 1993) that considers a multistakeholders' perspectives. It represents the average perceived utility if additional intangible benefits are generated through PRM. The value of U_{intang} can range from 1 (very low value) to 7 (very high value). The higher the value of U_{intang}, the more intangible benefits perceived by stakeholders.

$$Uj\,\text{intang} = \sum_{i=1}^{n} wij\, uij$$

- where:

(S): number of project stakeholders;
(j): jth project stakeholder, where $j = (1, \ldots, S)$;
(i): ith intangible benefit obtained through PRM;
(w_{ij}) is the relative importance (weight) of the ith intangible benefit to the jth project stakeholder. (w_{ij}) have been determined on the basis of the project stakeholder value system, where $\sum_{i=1}^{J} wij = 1$
(u_{ij}) is the perceived utility of the ith intangible benefit obtained through PRM to the jth project stakeholder (7-point Likert-type scale).

The higher the value of $U_{j\,intang}$, the more the intangible benefits perceived by the jth project stakeholder.

- *Fitting analysis*: The level of fit between the context characteristics and the maturity level of the PRM system implemented in the project were assessed through the risk gap (the difference between the expected risk impact and the actual risk impact over the project budget).

All the analyses are performed with PROValue©, a software specifically developed by the authors of this research to support the data analysis (see Sect. 13.7).

13.3.2 Case Selection and Description

For this case study, an SME based and operating in Italy in the information technology (IT) consulting sector was selected, considering (1) the particular dynamism and uncertainty that characterize this specific sector and (2) that the empirical evidence regarding the contribution of PRM to IT project success thus far is not convincing (de Bakker et al., 2010). To protect the confidentiality, the SME analyzed will be called *Alpha*.

The company is organized according to a combined model (projects and processes), employs 22 people, with a turnover of 2 million euros in 2019. Its main activity is to support the client companies operating in the manufacturing sector with digital transformation, adopting methodologies such as Design Thinking and Agile to conceive innovative solutions. To obtain a broad sample and gain a deeper understanding of the topic applied in this sector, it was necessary to seek heterogeneity among company projects. In this way, it was possible to investigate how PRM systems were adapted and applied to different projects with the aim of generating value. Therefore, three different projects developed by *Alpha* (*Alpha*-1, *Alpha*-2, and *Alpha*-3) have been selected for the analysis, according to the following criteria:

- Different project characteristics.
- PRM implemented.
- Involvement of both internal and external stakeholders in the project.
- Projects finished for at least 6 months, to capture the whole PRM value generated.
- Availability and PM knowledge of at least two project stakeholders.

The three projects have been performed for a customer company operating in the fashion branded eyewear sector and differ in complexity, criticality of stakeholders, and maturity level of the implemented PRM system:

1. *Project Alpha-1* (Cost Estimating SW Application): The objective consists of improving the efficiency and reliability of the cost estimation process for new products, leveraging process digitalization and the management of knowledge about production costs. The project is characterized by a low level of uncertainty, instability, novelty, and uniqueness, but a high level of difficulty in stakeholders' management.
2. *Project Alpha-2* (Cost Monitoring SW Dashboard): The objective consists of controlling production costs through the design, development, and application of a cost dashboard software. The project is characterized by a medium-high level of uncertainty and instability, a high level of novelty and uniqueness, but a low level of difficulty in stakeholders' management.
3. *Project Alpha-3* (ODCA Order Date Confirmation Automation SW Application): The objective consists of improving the production planning through the design and development of an algorithm for the prioritization and control of production orders. The project is characterized by a medium level of uncertainty and instability, a high level of novelty and uniqueness, but a low level of difficulty in stakeholders' management.

13.4 Results

Alpha adopts methodologies such as Design Thinking and Agile to conceive innovative solutions. Accordingly, the agile approach to PRM has been adopted in the analyzed projects, as part of project management activities; the agile approach to PRM aims to perform an initial risk assessment during the pregame and risk reviews during review meetings while reducing the threat of incorrect project output through regular communication with customers, short iterations, and testing (Buganová & Šimíčková, 2019; Fitsilis, 2008; Marle, 2020; Tavares et al., 2019).

The maturity degree of the *Alpha* PRM system is level 3.0 labelled "Defined" (Yeo & Ren, 2009). Given the differences among the selected projects, the PRM system has been implemented with different maturity levels, particularly level 3.0 in *Alpha*-1, and level 2.5 labelled "Initial/Defined" in *Alpha*-2 and *Alpha*-3.

The project manager was responsible for the PRM, with the involvement of *Alpha* internal stakeholders. On the contrary, external stakeholders were not engaged in the PRM activities.

13.4.1 Project Alpha-1: Cost Estimating SW Application

Two project stakeholders were interviewed, one internal to the project team (project manager), and the other external (*Alpha*'s CEO). To begin, the respondents' value system was analyzed to understand the relative relevance of the generated benefits according to each stakeholder interviewed (Fig. 13.3).

The results indicated that both respondents assigned the highest importance to the benefits generated for the customer company, for project management, for the

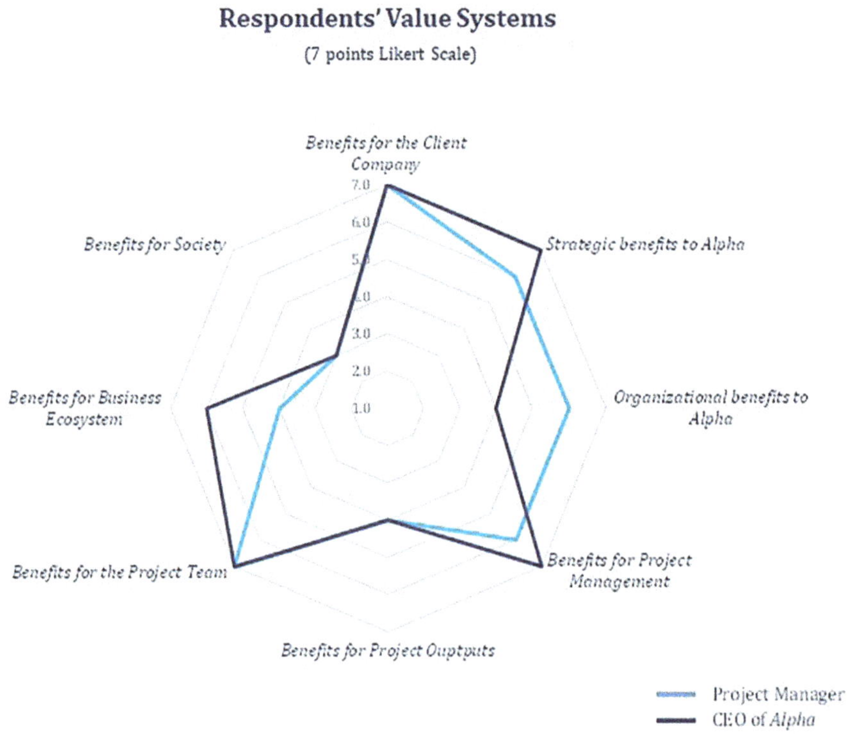

Fig. 13.3 Project *Alpha*-1 – Respondents' value systems

project team, and for *Alpha* (particularly the strategic benefits). Furthermore, the project manager and CEO's different organizational role and professional background were crucial for considering, respectively, the organizational benefit for *Alpha* and the benefits for the business ecosystem as relevant.

The *project complexity* was investigated through the evaluation of the levels of (1) uncertainty and instability, (2) uniqueness and novelty, (3) criticality of stakeholders, and (4) dynamic complexity on a 7-point Likert scale, based on respondents' perspectives (Fig. 13.4). The results indicate that the respondents had similar perceptions, assigning a medium-low overall level of project complexity (3.15 for the project manager, 3.33 for the CEO), coming from the balance of a high level of difficulty in the stakeholder management (average: 5.3), a medium-high level of uniqueness and novelty (average: 5.3), and a low level of uncertainty and instability (average: 2.6).

The *stakeholder analysis* began with the identification of two relevant external project stakeholders in the customer company, assessed according to their (1) interest in the project, (2) their attitude to the project, and (3) their power to influence the project. The score assigned allowed to map the stakeholders into two groups, namely, (1) the saviors, with a high level of interest toward the project and a positive attitude, and (2) a sleeping giant, with a positive attitude, occasionally influential or

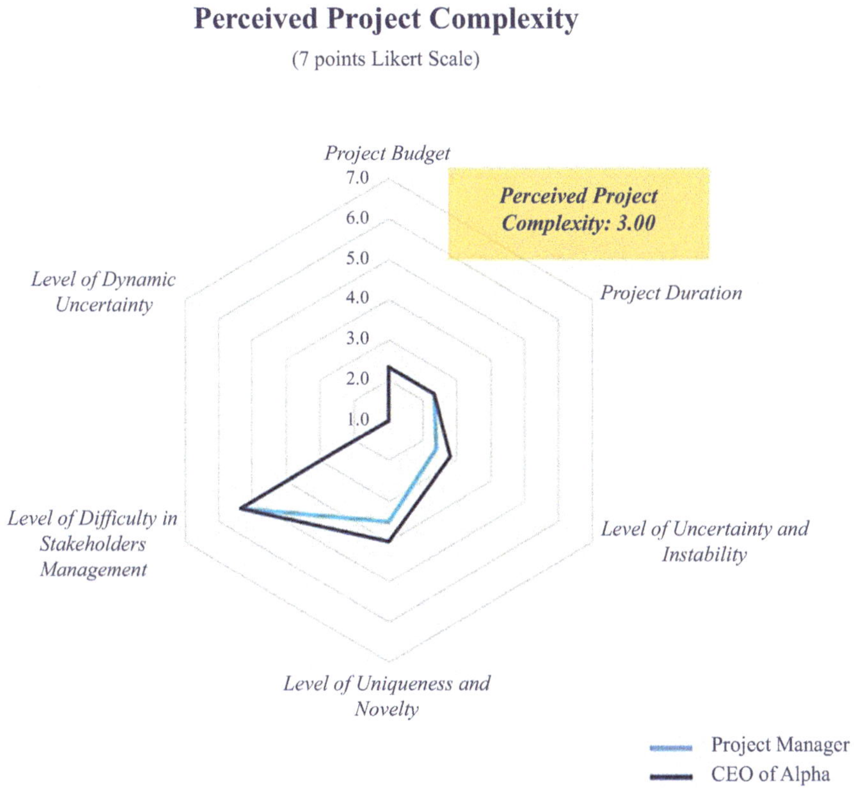

Fig. 13.4 Project *Alpha*-1 – Perceived project complexity

passive, and a low level of interest in the project. The latter revealed to be critical for the project. The three project stakeholders were perceived to have a similar power to influence the project (Fig. 13.5).

An agile approach to PRM has been adopted with a *maturity level* 3 labelled "Defined" (Yeo & Ren, 2009). PRM was implemented in the project through an informal process, as part of the project management activities, with the support of basic PRM techniques. As reported in Fig. 13.6, the following activities were implemented as part of the PRM process: context analysis and planning, risk identification, qualitative risk analysis, response planning, and risk monitoring. *Alpha*'s CEO demonstrated strong commitment and clear sponsorship of PRM, and the project manager facilitated a collaborative teamwork environment and open and transparent communication on the status of project risks within *Alpha*.

The *risks analysis* was conducted collecting quantitative and qualitative information on identified and/or encountered risks, through interviews. Three main risks were defined through PRM:

- *Strategic risk*: Caused by an insufficient level of customer company awareness and alignment about its own needs, generating uncertainty and instability toward

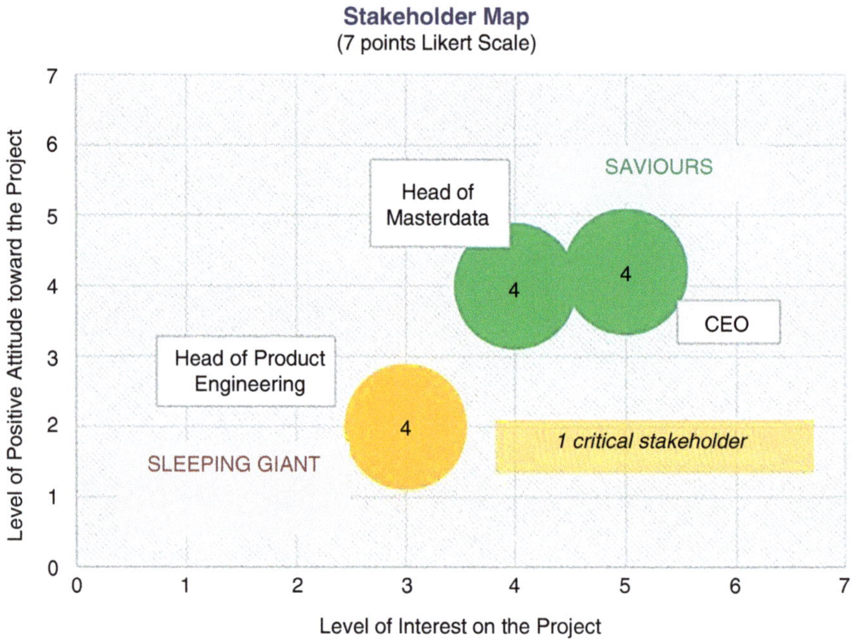

Fig. 13.5 Project *Alpha*-1 – Stakeholder Map

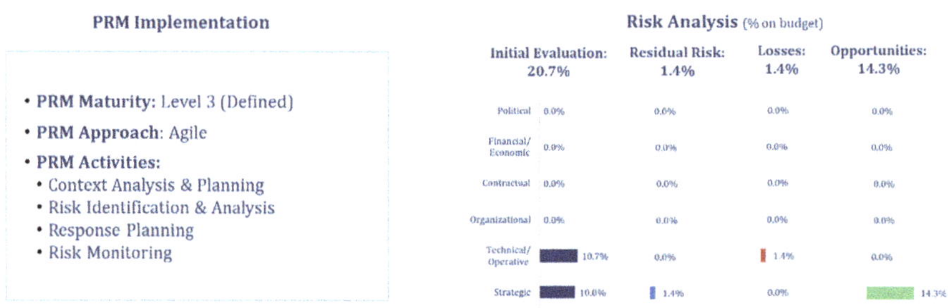

Fig. 13.6 Project *Alpha*-1 – PRM implementation and risk analysis

the scope of the project. The potential consequences were a misalignment of project outputs with the project objectives and expectations of the customer company. The strategic risk was identified, mitigated, and encountered during the project, using a flexible product architecture. Indeed, the project manager solicited formal customer decisions at the critical decision points during the project life cycle. Although the customer company was negatively impacted by the strategic risk (additional costs for scope change), a positive risk was captured by adapting the project to the changes in the context. Therefore, PRM captured the additional business opportunity for *Alpha*, adding a new sprint to the project as a consequence of the scope change (14.3% of the budget).

- *Operative risk*: Generated by the potential misalignment between the project requirements and the software functionalities. Indeed, a misunderstanding about the project requirements by the project team could have led to inadequate functionalities implemented in the software application. The operative risk was identified, mitigated, and encountered during the project, leading to risk-related losses for *Alpha* (1.4% of the budget).
- *Technical risk*: Produced by potential technical difficulties with the integration of the new software application with the existing ICT applications of the customer company. Specifically, the source of risk was an inadequate level of technical analysis performed before the project launch. The technical risk has been identified and fully mitigated through further in-depth technical analysis.

The cost of PRM implementation was paid mainly by *Alpha* as part of the project management activities (4.3% of the project budget). The *PRM economic value*, generated to all the stakeholders, is equal to $PVI_{econ} = 5.50$ (Fig. 13.7). This value is unevenly distributed between stakeholders, with *Alpha* capturing the 55%, both mitigating negative risk and capturing a business opportunity generated by the strategic risk (which led to new activities and a project extension), while the customer company captured the remaining 45% of the economic value mainly through the mitigation of the technical risk. Moreover, the management of the operative risk did not generate value but rather additional costs. However, through a better stakeholder management, the PRM economic value could be lightly higher and estimated in $PVI_{econ} = 5.83$. It is relevant to highlight that despite the small investment in PRM, almost the full value generation potential of the PRM system has been captured.

The PRM *intangible benefit* is equal to $U_{intang} = 3.99$, revealing a perception of medium-high benefit generated, despite the small investment in PRM. This benefit had an impact on the customer company, increasing customer satisfaction and trust; on the project team, with improved team satisfaction, performance, skills, and capabilities in PRM; on project management, leading to a better project alignment with the overall business strategy and improved decision-making, planning, and forecasting (with more adherence to project schedule, budget, and scope); on the company strategic level, fostering the achievement of strategic goals, the mitigation of the risk level, enhancing the brand recognition, and internal stakeholders' satisfaction.

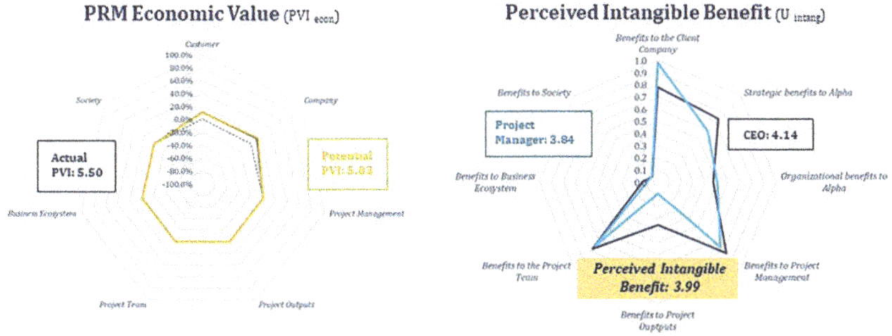

Fig. 13.7 Project *Alpha*-1 – PRM economic value and intangible benefit

13.4.2 Project Alpha-2: Cost Monitoring SW Dashboard

Two project stakeholders were interviewed, both internal to the project team (the project manager and the business analyst). The respondents' value system analysis showed the importance of the benefits generated for the customer company, for the project team, and for *Alpha*, according to both stakeholders. The business analyst perceived as relevant also the benefits for the project outputs, for project management, and for the society, in terms of social and environmental impacts (Fig. 13.8).

Given the innovative nature of the project, respondents agreed on the medium level of *project complexity* (3.42, on a scale from 1, very low, to 7, very high), composed by a very high level of uniqueness and novelty (average 5.6), uncertainty, and instability (average 4.4). However, they disagreed in the evaluation of dynamic complexity, since the business analyst, contrary to the project manager, perceived the project as influenced by the business environment external to the project scope (Fig. 13.9).

The stakeholder analysis mapped the presence of three types of stakeholders, based on their perceived interest, attitude, and influence: a savior, with a good level of interest toward the project and a positive attitude; a friend, with a high interest on the project and a positive attitude; and a time bomb, critical for the low level of interest, the occasional positive attitude, and the strong influence on the project (Fig. 13.10).

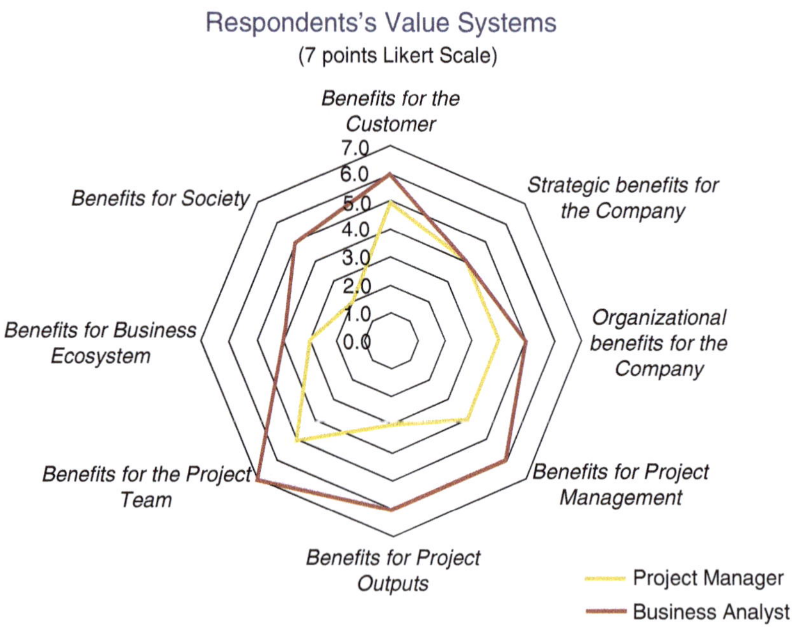

Fig. 13.8 Project *Alpha*-2 – Respondents' value systems

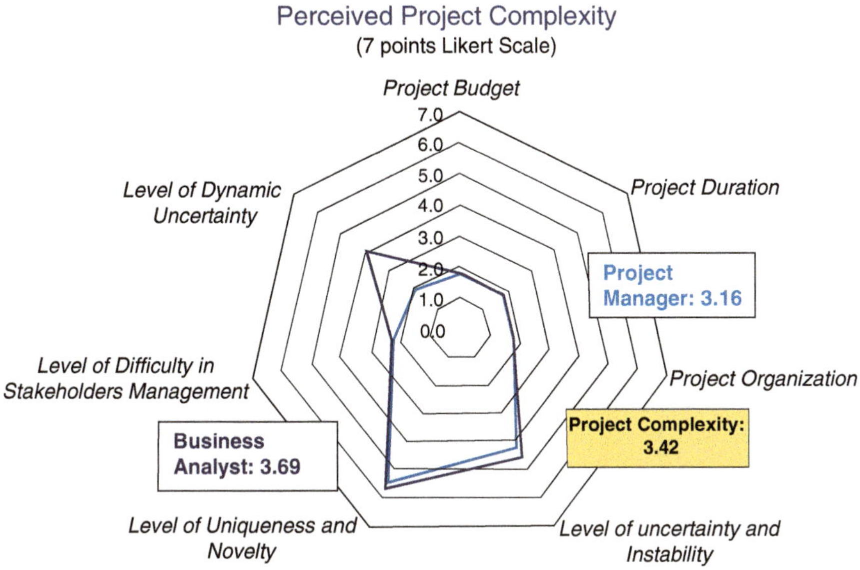

Fig. 13.9 Project *Alpha*-2 – Perceived project complexity

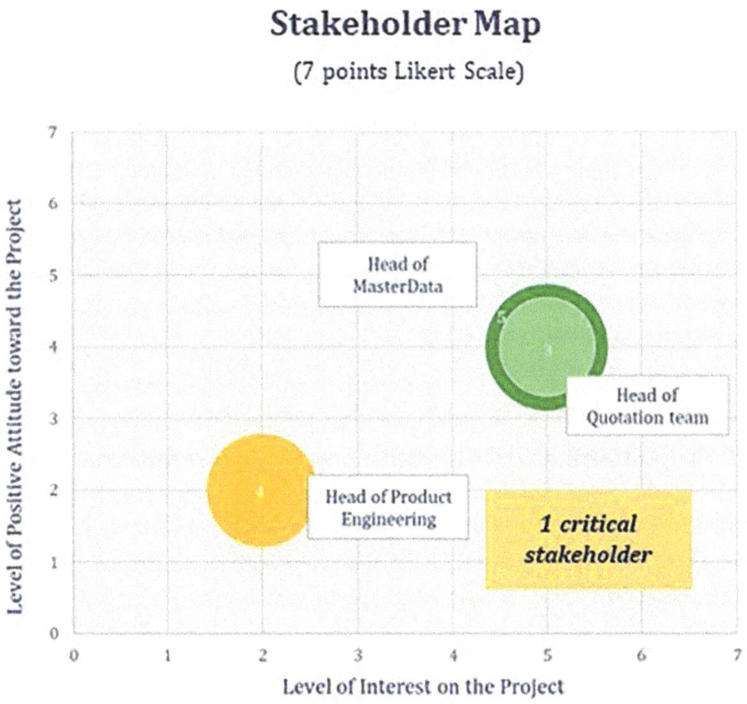

Fig. 13.10 Project *Alpha*-2 – Stakeholder map

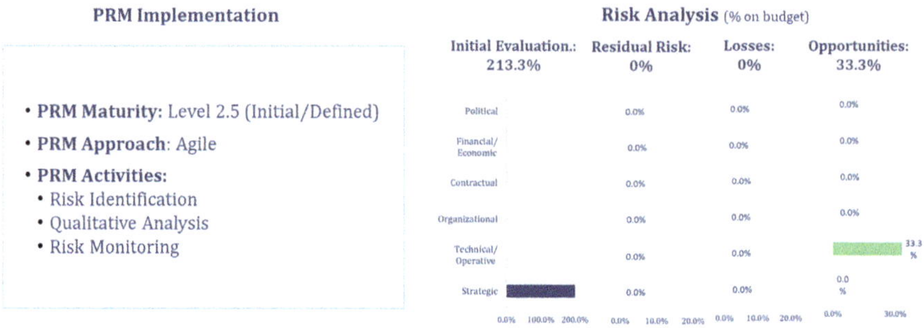

Fig. 13.11 Project *Alpha*-2 – PRM implementation and risk analysis

An agile approach to PRM has been adopted with a *maturity level* 2.5 labelled "Initial/Defined" (Yeo & Ren, 2009). As reported in Fig. 13.11, risk identification, qualitative risk analysis, and risk monitoring were the activities implemented as part of the PRM process.

Concerning the *risk analysis*, the interviews allowed to identify a strategic risk generated by the uncertainty about project requirements and scope, result of the insufficient stakeholders' awareness, and alignment about their own needs in the customer company. The strategic risk has been identified, mitigated, and encountered during the project. The project manager requested formal customer decisions at the critical decision points during the project life cycle, and *Alpha* was able to capture an opportunity through PRM, proposing a technical solution that led to saving 33.3% of the project budget.

The overall *PRM economic value*, generated through strategic risk mitigation, is equal to $PVI_{econ} = 5.61$, fully captured by *Alpha* (Fig. 13.12). Indeed, *Alpha* caught the business opportunity generated by the management of strategic risk, leading to relevant savings in costs. The cost of PRM implementation was paid by *Alpha* as part of the project management activities; *Alpha* invested approximately 44% of the budget in the reshaping of the project, including a scope change and the implementation of a different solution for the customer company.

The overall *PRM intangible benefit*, mainly generated for the customer company, the project team, and the project management, is equal to $U_{intang} = 4.92$ (Fig. 13.12).

13.4.3 Project Alpha-3: Order Date Confirmation Automation

The project manager, the business analyst, and a business consultant were interviewed. The investigation on the respondents' value system revealed the benefits generated for the customer company, for the project team, and for *Alpha*, as the most relevant for all the respondents (Fig. 13.13). In addition, the business analyst and the business consultant had similar perceptions about the relevance of the benefits produced for the project outputs, for the business ecosystem, and for the society; the business consultant considered important also the organizational benefits for *Alpha*, due to the specific professional background.

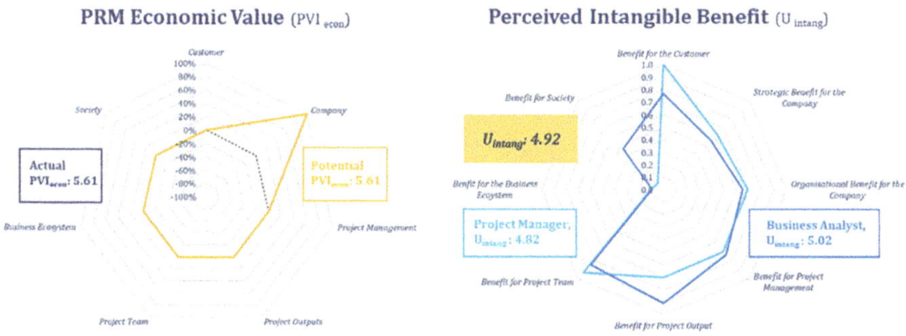

Fig. 13.12 Project *Alpha*-1 – PRM economic value and intangible benefit

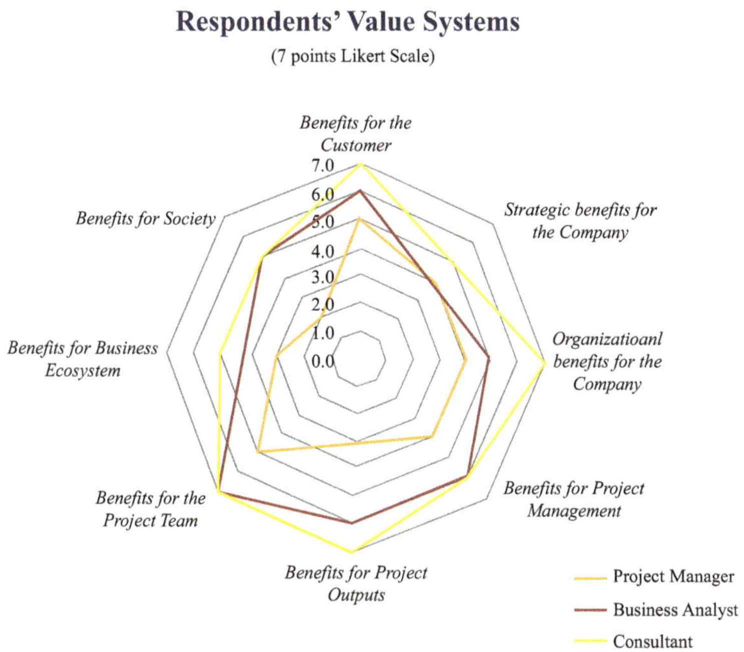

Fig. 13.13 Project *Alpha*-3 – Respondents' value systems

Respondents demonstrated very different perceptions about the level of *project complexity*, considered averagely medium (3.40, on a scale from 1, very low, to 7, very high). Specifically, the project manager considered the project as not complex (2.90), the business consultant assigned a medium complexity (3.20), while the business analyst perceived the project to be quite complex (4.10), in relation to the level of uncertainty and instability, difficulty in stakeholder management, and dynamic uncertainty. Moreover, they mutually agreed that the level of project uniqueness and novelty was the main source of complexity, due to the project innovativeness and a certain instability of the project requirements (Fig. 13.14).

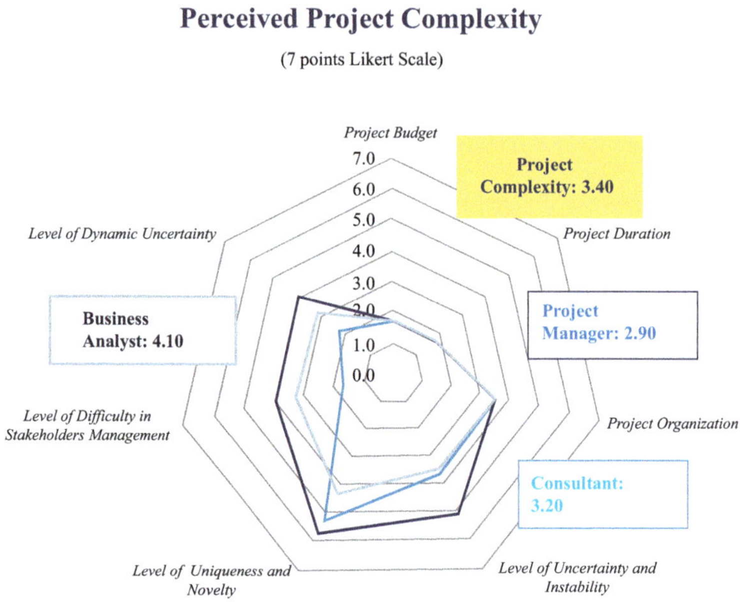

Fig. 13.14 Project *Alpha*-3 – Perceived project complexity

Two types of *stakeholders* were detected by the respondents, namely, a savior and an acquaintance, characterized by a low level of interest in the project, a passive attitude, and a weak influence in the project. However, the stakeholders map in Fig. 13.15 shows the absence of critical stakeholders.

An agile approach to PRM has been adopted with a *maturity level* 2.5 labelled "Initial/Defined" (Yeo & Ren, 2009). As reported in Fig. 13.16, risk identification, qualitative risk analysis, and risk monitoring were the activities implemented as part of the PRM process.

The *risk analysis* allowed to identify a technical/operative risk as the main one. The source of this risk resides in the level of uncertainty generated by gap between the required technology innovativeness and the ability to effectively develop those functionalities. Technical risk has been identified, mitigated, and encountered during the project. In particular, *Alpha* hired and involved in the project a new employee (software developer) with specific skills and knowledge on the latest technology, leading to a reduction of the number of sprints (from five to three), and generating an estimated saving of 46.2% of the project budget (Fig. 13.16).

The *PRM economic value generated* was obtained by mitigating the technical/operational risk and capturing a business opportunity that led to relevant cost savings. The cost of PRM implementation was paid by *Alpha* as part of the project management activities (1.5% of the project budget). Thanks to the high value of the captured opportunity, the *PRM economic value* is equal to $PVI_{econ} = 41.25$ (Fig. 13.17).

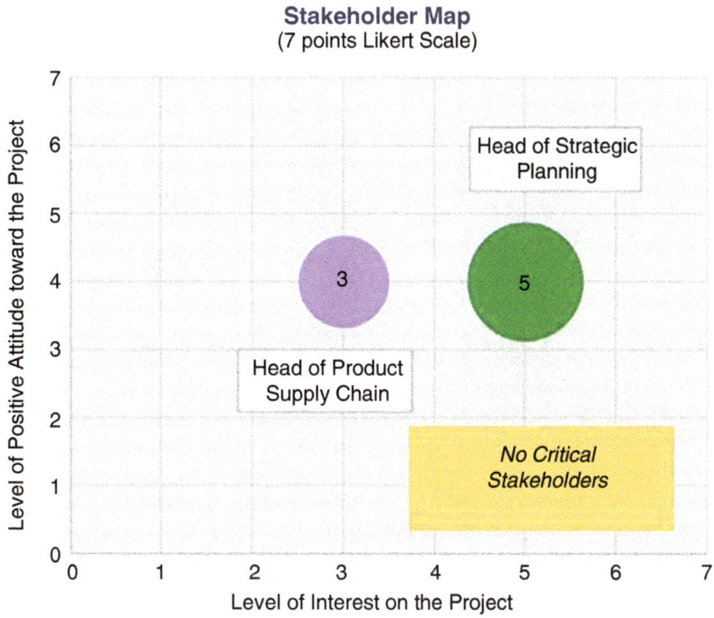

Fig. 13.15 Project *Alpha*-3 –Stakeholder map

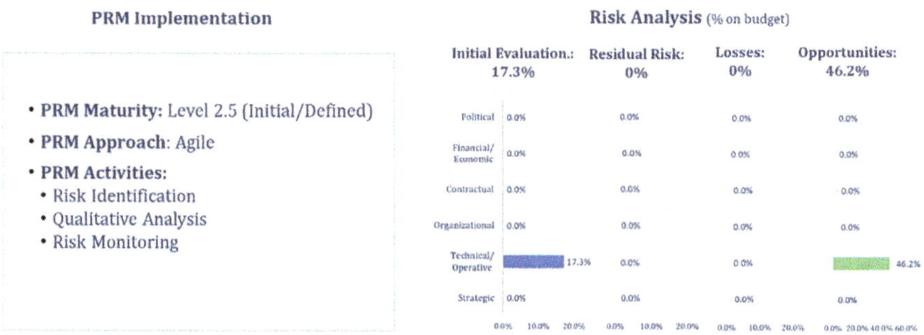

Fig. 13.16 Project *Alpha*-3 – PRM implementation and risk analysis

The respondents' perceptions show a high PRM *intangible benefit* generated (5.05), with effects mainly on the customer company, the project team, and the project management in terms of complying delivery times and budget, improved complexity management, problem-solving, and decision-making. Moreover, the intangible benefit also affected the project outputs' quality and innovativeness (Fig. 13.17).

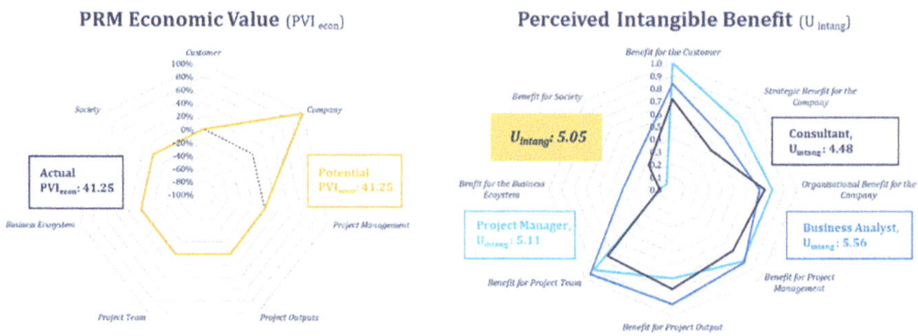

Fig. 13.17 Project *Alpha*-3 – PRM economic value and intangible benefit

13.5 Discussion

The information collected allowed to analyze the three *Alpha* projects, according to the project complexity, the stakeholders' criticality, the PRM maturity level, the risk analysis, the generated economic value, and the intangible benefit produced. In particular, to answer to RQ1 and RQ2 (What economic value and intangible (not monetary) benefit are generated through PRM for stakeholders? How can the economic value and the intangible benefit generated through PRM be measured?), the value generated through PRM was investigated, including the economic and intangible (not monetary) components, and a value measurement instrument that adopts a multistakeholder perspective was defined (PVI_{econ}, U_{intang}).

In each project, the PRM system was able to foster the business opportunities created by the uncertainty, instability, innovativeness, and novelty of the project context, generating, and capturing an economic value for *Alpha*. This led to new activities, project extensions, and scope enlargements. The PRM system also generated an economic value for the customer company, through the reduction of negative risk. The PRM economic value ranged from $PVI_{econ} = 5.50$ in *Alpha*-1 to $PVI_{econ} = 41.25$ in *Alpha*-3. Also, intangible benefit was produced by the PRM system, ranging from $U_{intang} = 3.74$ in the project *Alpha*-1 to $U_{intang} = 5.05$ in the project *Alpha*-3. The PRM intangible benefit impacted primarily the customer company, increasing the customer satisfaction and trust; the project management, aligning the project with the overall business strategy and improving planning and forecasting, problem-solving, and decision-making; the project output, in terms of quality and innovation; the project team, enhancing the performance, skills, and capabilities in PRM but also the satisfaction and morale.

In response to RQ3 (How do contextual factors influence PRM value generation?), the effects of the context on the process of value generation through PRM were evaluated. The results highlighted the importance of three contextual factors on the value generated: the number of critical stakeholders, the project complexity, and the delta project complexity perceived by the stakeholders. These three factors together define the project context criticality: projects with a higher level of

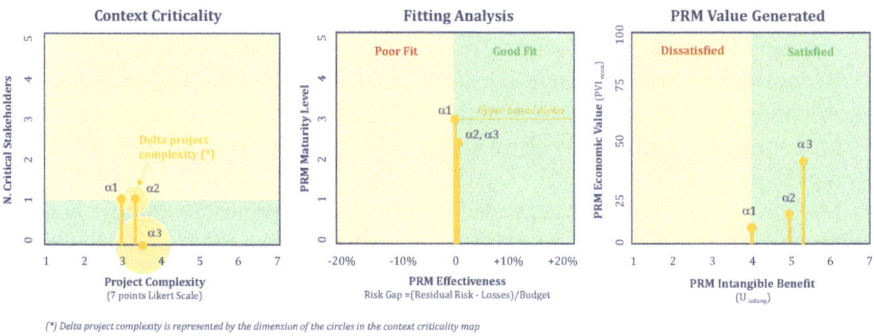

Fig. 13.18 Context criticality, fitting analysis, and PRM value generated

innovation and novelty were perceived as more complex but with greater differences in the perceived project complexity by stakeholders. For instance, *Alpha*-3 is characterized by a high delta perceived complexity (17.1%) (Fig. 13.18).

In addition, the PRM value depended on the fit between the maturity level of the PRM system and the project context criticality: Projects with higher context criticality required a higher level of maturity of the PRM implementation, and this level must be implementable by the company's RM system. However, the decision about the PRM system is influenced by stakeholders' perceptions and awareness of the context complexity and risks, especially the project complexity and the number of critical stakeholders. As shown in the fitting analysis in Fig. 13.18, projects context was perceived as not particularly critical, characterized by a low perceived complexity and a limited number of critical stakeholders. The maturity levels of the PRM systems implemented in the three projects were fully adequate for the contexts in which the projects were developed, resulting in relevant PRM economic value and PRM intangible benefit. In particular, the PRM system in *Alpha*-1 was implemented with the highest level of maturity despite the lowest level of context criticality. This high level of maturity rose the stakeholders' expectations about PRM, resulting in a lower value generated (economic and intangible).

Addressing RQ4 (How can PRM be improved to increase the value generated?), the PRM value could be improved by maximizing the fit between the PRM maturity level and the context criticality. The results emerging from *Alpha* show that despite the small investment in PRM, almost the full PRM value generation potential has been exploited.

Based on these results, some hallmarks useful to foster and improve value generation and resilience in projects through PRM have been grasped:

- Considering the diverse respondents' value systems.
- Mapping all the relevant stakeholders and defining the most appropriate strategy to manage them.
- Evaluating the context criticality (number of critical stakeholders and project complexity) and aligning stakeholders' perceptions.

- Adapting the PRM maturity level to the context criticality and ensuring that the company RM system can actually express the required level of maturity.
- Recovering the level of fitting enhances the creation of value and resilience.
- Adopting a multilevel approach in the assessment of the value generated.
- Monitoring the impact of positive and negative risks on project stakeholders during the project life cycle.
- Measuring the PRM value generated at the end of the project to improve both the company RM system and the PRM system to be implemented in future projects.

13.6 Conclusion

This work presents an overview of a case study in the IT consulting sector, providing considerable insights on how to improve the value generated and resilience through PRM for multiple stakeholders and contributing to address the literature gaps and contradictions. Indeed, some preliminary indications of general validity on how to foster value generation through PRM emerged: (1) adopting a multilevel approach in the analysis of the value generated; (2) considering the scope of PRM, and in particular which project stakeholders should be involved in PRM; (3) mapping all relevant stakeholders groups at the beginning of the PRM process and defining the most appropriate strategies to manage them; (4) considering the diverse respondents' value systems in the assessment of the intangible benefit generated; and (5) adapting the PRM maturity level to the context criticalities with the aim of enhancing value and resilience.

The research offers innovative contributions from both an academic and a managerial perspective. From an academic point of view, it enriches the current knowledge with a framework for the analysis of the relationships between the characteristics of the context, the PRM implementation, and the value generated. The results contribute to enrich the PRM literature, offering a deeper understanding of PRM value generation while providing indications about future directions.

From a practical point of view, it provides a new measurement system for the value generated through PRM. The analysis allowed to formulate new guidelines for the assessment of the adequacy of the PRM system and of any potential improvements, and for increasing the value generated in future projects. Therefore, the results will support companies in enhancing value generated and resilience in projects, improving both their economic value and the intangible benefits for stakeholders.

The multistakeholder approach proposed in the research facilitates the study of the value generated at different levels of analysis, particularly individual, project, organizational, business ecosystem, and society levels, with the aim of guaranteeing a shared value (economic and intangible) among the project stakeholders. With particular reference to social implications, the results assure that risks at the societal level (e.g., environmental, social, occupational, or health risks) are adequately considered and managed while including society at large among the targets of PRM value generation.

This analysis has also some limitations since empirical research has been limited to one single embedded case belonging to the IT consulting sector. Consequently, extending the empirical analysis to other cases in this sector could confirm the validity of the first indications emerging from the current study. Moreover, other business industries could be considered, particularly those in which companies are process oriented rather than project oriented, providing additional value to the research.

13.7 PROValue©: A Tool to Assess and Improve the PRIM SYSTEM

All the analyses proposed in this chapter have been performed with PROValue© (Project Risk and Opportunities Management for Value Generation), a software tool specifically developed by the authors of this research to support data analysis (Fig. 13.19).

PROValue© allows managers to analyze and optimize the PRM system to project complexity, in order to maximize the economic and intangible value generated for project stakeholders through the management of project risks.

PROValue© requires specific competence to be used and is protected by copyright. However, readers interested in performing an assessment of their own PRM system can contact the authors of the chapter for support, thus also making a valuable contribution toward the development of the scientific research in this field.

Acknowledgments The authors gratefully acknowledge the Grant VERB_SID19_01 funded by the University of Padova.

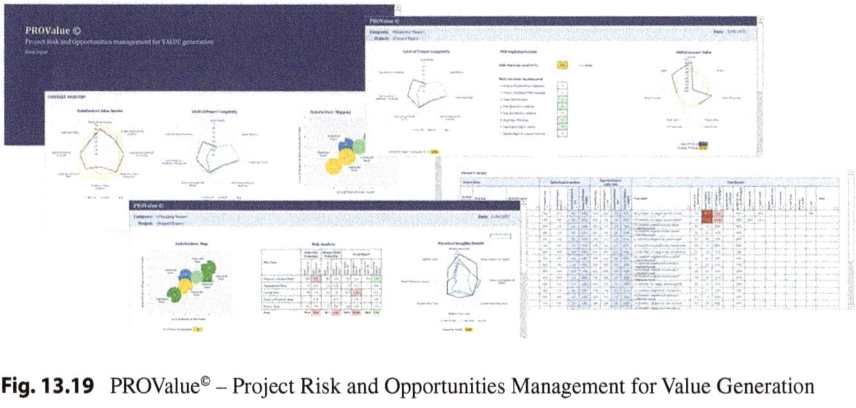

Fig. 13.19 PROValue© – Project Risk and Opportunities Management for Value Generation

References

Ahmadi-Javid, A., Fateminia, S. H., & Gemünden, H. G. (2020). A method for risk response planning in project portfolio management. *Project Management Journal, 51*, 77–95. https://doi.org/10.1177/8756972819866577

Andersen, E. S. (2014). Value creation using the mission breakdown structure. *International Journal of Project Management, 32*, 885–892. https://doi.org/10.1016/j.ijproman.2013.11.003

Andersen, E. S. (2016). Do project managers have different perspectives on project management? *International Journal of Project Management, 34*, 58–65. https://doi.org/10.1016/j.ijproman.2015.09.007

Bakker, R. M. (2010). Taking stock of temporary organizational forms: A systematic review and research agenda. *International Journal of Management Reviews, 12*, 466–486. https://doi.org/10.1111/j.1468-2370.2010.00281.x

Besner, C., & Hobbs, B. (2012). The paradox of risk management: A project management practice perspective. *International Journal of Managing Projects in Business, 5*. https://doi.org/10.1108/17538371211214923

Borge, D. (2002). *The book of risk*. Wiley.

Branzei, O., & Abdelnour, S. (2010). Another day, another dollar: Enterprise resilience under terrorism in developing countries. *Journal of International Business Studies, 41*(5), 804–825. https://doi.org/10.1057/jibs.2010.6

Buganová, K., & Šimíčková, J. (2019). Risk management in traditional and agile project management. *Transportation Research Procedia, 40*, 986–993. https://doi.org/10.1016/j.trpro.2019.07.138

Chroust, G., & Aumayr, G. (2017). Resilience 2.0: Computer-aided disaster management. *Journal of Systems Science and Systems Engineering, 26*, 321–335. https://doi.org/10.1007/s11518-017-5335-7

Conroy, G., & Soltan, H. (1998). ConSERV, a project specific risk management concept. *International Journal of Project Management, 16*, 353–366. https://doi.org/10.1016/S0263-7863(98)00012-X

Crispim, J., Silva, L. H., & Rego, N. (2019). Project risk management practices: The organizational maturity influence. *IJMPB, 12*, 187–210. https://doi.org/10.1108/IJMPB-10-2017-0122

Dahlberg, R. (2015). Resilience and complexity: Conjoining the discourses of two contested concepts. *Culture Unbound: Journal of Current Cultural Research, 7*, 541–557. https://doi.org/10.3384/cu.2000.1525.1572541

de Bakker, K., Boonstra, A., & Wortmann, H. (2010). Does risk management contribute to IT project success? A meta-analysis of empirical evidence. *International Journal of Project Management*. Elsevier Ltd and IPMA, *28*(5), 493–503. https://doi.org/10.1016/j.ijproman.2009.07.002

de Camprieu, R., Desbiens, J., & Feixue, Y. (2007). "Cultural" differences in project risk perception: An empirical comparison of China and Canada. *International Journal of Project Management, 25*, 683–693. https://doi.org/10.1016/j.ijproman.2007.07.005

de Carvalho, M. M., & Rabechini Junior, R. (2015). Impact of risk management on project performance: The importance of soft skills. *International Journal of Production Research, 53*(2), 321–340. https://doi.org/10.1080/00207543.2014.919423

Dey, P. K. (2012). Project risk management using multiple criteria decision-making technique and decision tree analysis: A case study of Indian oil refinery. *Production Planning and Control, 23*, 903–921. https://doi.org/10.1080/09537287.2011.586379

Durst, S., Bruns, G., & Henschel, T. (2018). The management of knowledge risks: What do we really know? In *Global business expansion: Concepts, methodologies, tools, and applications* (pp. 258–269). IGI Global.

Elkington, P., & Smallman, C. (2002). Managing project risks: A case study from the utilities sector. *International Journal of Project Management, 20*, 49–57. https://doi.org/10.1016/S0263-7863(00)00034-X

European Standard 12973. (2000). Value management.

European Standards 12973. (2000). EN 12973.

Fitsilis, P. (2008). Comparing PMBOK and agile project management software development processes. *Advances in Computer and Information Sciences and Engineering*, 378–383. https://doi.org/10.1007/978-1-4020-8741-7_68

Geraldi, J. G., Lee-Kelley, L., & Kutsch, E. (2010). The Titanic sunk, so what? Project manager response to unexpected events. *International Journal of Project Management, 28*, 547–558. https://doi.org/10.1016/j.ijproman.2009.10.008

Henschel, T., & Durst, S. (2016). Risk management in Scottish, Chinese and German small and medium-sized enterprises: A country comparison. *International Journal of Entrepreneurship and Small Business, 29*(1), 112–132.

Henschel, T., & Lantzsch, A. D. (2022). The relationship between ERM and performance revisited: Empirical evidence from SMEs. In *Risk management: Insights from different settings* (pp. 95–113). Springer.

ISO 31000. (2018). International Organization for Standardization: Geneva, Switzerland.

Javani, B., & Rwelamila, P. M. D. (2016). Risk management in IT projects – A case of the South African public sector. *International Journal of Managing Projects in Business, 9*, 389–413. https://doi.org/10.1108/IJMPB-07-2015-0055

Jiang, J. J., & Klein, G. (2001). Software project risks and development focus. *Project Management Journal, 32*, 4–9. https://doi.org/10.1177/875697280103200102

Jun, L., Qiuzhen, W., & Qingguo, M. (2011). The effects of project uncertainty and risk management on IS development project performance: A vendor perspective. *International Journal of Project Management, 29*, 923–933. https://doi.org/10.1016/j.ijproman.2010.11.002

Keeney, R. L., & Raiffa, H. (1993). *Decisions with multiple objectives – Preferences and value tradeoffs*. Cambridge University Press.

Kutsch, E. (2008). The effect of intervening conditions on the management of project risk. *International Journal of Managing Projects in Business, 1*(4), 602–610. https://doi.org/10.1108/17538370810906282

Laursen, M., & Svejvig, P. (2016). Taking stock of project value creation: A structured literature review with future directions for research and practice. *International Journal of Project Management, 34*, 736–747. https://doi.org/10.1016/j.ijproman.2015.06.007

Lepak, D. P., Smith, K. G., & Taylor, M. S. (2007). Value creation and value capture: A multilevel perspective. *Academy of Management Review, 32*, 180–194. https://doi.org/10.5465/AMR.2007.23464011

Linnenluecke, M. K. (2017). Resilience in business and management research: A review of influential publications and a research agenda. *International Journal of Management Reviews, 19*(1), 4–30. https://doi.org/10.1111/ijmr.12076

Marle, F. (2020). An assistance to project risk management based on complex systems theory and agile project management. *Complexity*. https://doi.org/10.1155/2020/3739129

Mendelow, A. (1991). Stakeholder mapping. In *Proceedings of the 2nd international conference on information systems*.

Mitchell, R. K., Agle, B. R., & Wood, D. J. (1997). Toward a theory of stakeholder identification and salience: Defining the principle of who and what really counts. *The Academy of Management Review, 22*, 853–886. https://doi.org/10.2307/259247

Morris, P. (2013). *Reconstructing project management*. Wiley Blackwell.

Muhammedamin, H., Hagelaar, G., van der Velde, G., & Omta, S. W. F. (2021). Conceptualization of SMEs' business resilience: A systematic literature review. *Cogent Business & Management, 8*(1). https://doi.org/10.1080/23311975.2021.1938347

Murray-Webster, R., & Simon, P. (2006). *Making sense of stakeholder mapping*. PM World Today Tips and Techniques.

PMI. (2013). *A guide to the project management body of knowledge (PMBOK guide)* (5th ed.). PMI.

PMI. (2017). *A guide to the project management body of knowledge (PMBOK guide)* (6th ed.). PMI.

Qazi, A., Quigley, J., Dickson, A., & Kirytopoulos, K. A. (2016). Project Complexity and Risk Management (ProCRiM): Towards modelling project complexity driven risk paths in construction projects. *International Journal of Project Management, 34*, 1183–1198. https://doi.org/10.1016/j.ijproman.2016.05.008

Quartermain, M. (2002). Value engineering. In Management A.f.P (Ed.), *Project management pathways*. Association for Project Management.

Radner, R., & Shepp, L. (1996). Risk vs. profit potential: A model for corporate strategy. *Journal of Economic Dynamics and Control, 20*, 1373–1393. https://doi.org/10.1016/0165-1889(95)00904-3

Raz, T., & Michael, E. (2001). Use and benefits of tools for project risk management. *International Journal of Project Management, 19*, 9–17. https://doi.org/10.1016/S0263-7863(99)00036-8

Sanchez, H., Robert, B., Bourgault, M., & Pellerin, R. (2009). Risk management applied to projects, programs, and portfolios. *International Journal of Managing Projects in Business, 2*, 14–35. https://doi.org/10.1108/17538370910930491

Scholz, R. W., & Tietje, T. O. (2002). *Embedded case study methods: Integrating quantitative and qualitative knowledge*. SAGE.

Serpell, A. F., Ferrada, X., & Rubio, L. (2019). Measuring the performance of project risk management: A preliminary model. *Organization, Technology and Management in Construction: an International Journal, 11*, 1984–1991. https://doi.org/10.2478/otmcj-2019-0005

Serra, C. E. M., & Kunc, M. (2015). Benefits realisation management and its influence on project success and on the execution of business strategies. *International Journal of Project Management, 33*, 53–66. https://doi.org/10.1016/j.ijproman.2014.03.011

Shenhar, A., Dvir, D., Levy, O., & Maltz, A. (2001). Project success: A multidimensional strategic concept. *Long Range Planning, 34*, 699–725. https://doi.org/10.1016/S0024-6301(01)00097-8

Shimizu, T., Won Park, Y., & Hong, P. (2012). Project managers for risk management: Case for Japan. *Benchmarking: An International Journal, 19*(4/5), 532–547. https://doi.org/10.1108/14635771211257990

Sommer, S., & Loch, C. (2003). Incomplete incentive contracts under ambiguity and complexity. *SSRN Electronic Journal*. https://doi.org/10.2139/ssrn.452521

Taleb, N. N. (2012). *Antifragile: Things that gain from disorder*. Random House Publishing Group.

Tavares, B. G., da Silva, C. E. S., & de Souza, A. D. (2019). Risk management analysis in Scrum software projects. *International Transactions in Operational Research, 26*, 1884–1905. https://doi.org/10.1111/itor.12401

Testorelli, R., & Verbano, C. (2020). Value creation with project risk management: A systematic literature review. In *Business theory and practice across industries and markets, EuroMed academy of business conference book of proceedings* (pp. 1399–1404).

Testorelli, R., & Verbano, C. (2022). An empirical framework to sustain value generation with project risk management: A case study in the IT consulting sector. *Sustainability, 14*, 12117.

Tognazzo, A., Gubitta, P., & Favaron, S. D. (2016). Does slack always affect resilience? A study of quasi-medium-sized Italian firms. *Entrepreneurship and Regional Development, 28*(9–10), 768–790. https://doi.org/10.1080/08985626.2016.1250820

Turner, R., Ledwith, A., & Kelly, J. (2010). Project management in small to medium-sized enterprises: Matching processes to the nature of the firm. *International Journal of Project Management, 28*, 744–755. https://doi.org/10.1016/j.ijproman.2010.06.005

Voss, C., Tsikriktsis, N., & Frohlich, M. (2002). Case research in operations management. *International Journal of Operations & Production Management, 22*, 195–219. https://doi.org/10.1108/01443570210414329

Wallace, L., Keil, M., & Rai, A. (2004). Understanding software project risk: A cluster analysis. *Information & Management, 42*, 115–125. https://doi.org/10.1016/j.im.2003.12.007

Williams, N., Vorley, T., & Ketikidis, P. H. (2013). Economic resilience and entrepreneurship: A case study of the Thessaloniki City Region. *Local Economy, 28*(4), 399–415.

Willumsen, P., Oehmen, J., Stingl, V., & Geraldi, J. (2019). Value creation through project risk management. *International Journal of Project Management, 37*, 731–749. https://doi.org/10.1016/j.ijproman.2019.01.007

Winter, M., Smith, C., Morris, P., & Cicmil, S. (2006). Directions for future research in project management: The main findings of a UK government-funded research network. *International Journal of Project Management, 24*, 638–649. https://doi.org/10.1016/j.ijproman.2006.08.009

Yeo, K. T., & Ren, Y. (2009). Risk management capability maturity model for complex product systems (CoPS) projects. *Systems Engineering, 12*, 275–294. https://doi.org/10.1002/sys.20123

Yin, R. K. (2013). *Case study research: Design and methods* (5th ed.). SAGE.

14 Unlocking Resource Efficiency: Pathways for Microenterprises in Estonia to Offer Green Products and Services

Samuel Foli

14.1 Introduction

In recent years, there has been a growing recognition of the paramount importance for businesses to adopt resource-efficient and environmentally sustainable practices (Schanes et al., 2019; Borel-Saladin & Turok, 2013). This awareness is particularly evident in Europe, where initiatives like the European Green Deal[1] underscore the urgency of addressing environmental challenges and transitioning towards sustainable business practices. As part of this larger endeavour, the implementation of the Non-Financial Reporting Directive (NFRD), later replaced by the Corporate Sustainability Reporting Directive (CSRD), aims to modernise and strengthen the rules for companies' reporting of social and environmental information, though it offers exemptions for microenterprises.[2] While the focus of attention has been primarily on large enterprises (e.g., Amendolagine et al., 2021; Papetti et al., 2019; Burritt et al., 2020), it is increasingly crucial to recognise the significant potential of microenterprises in driving sustainable development through their efficient use of resources (Lawrence et al., 2006). This recognition is especially critical in countries

[1] The European Great Deal. Available at https://commission.europa.eu/strategy-and-policy/priorities-2019-2024/european-green-deal_en

[2] European Union Corporate sustainability reporting. Available at https://finance.ec.europa.eu/capital-markets-union-and-financial-markets/company-reporting-and-auditing/company-reporting/corporate-sustainability-reporting_en

S. Foli (✉)
Tallinn, Estonia

Reykjavik, Iceland
e-mail: folisamuel11@gmail.com

S. Durst, T. Henschel (eds.), *Small and Medium-Sized Enterprise (SME) Resilience*, Management for Professionals, https://doi.org/10.1007/978-3-031-50836-3_14

like Estonia, where microenterprises constitute over 91.9% of all enterprises (OECD, 2022), highlighting their capacity to collectively contribute substantially to sustainable development efforts.

However, this important area of sustainable development has been relatively understudied, leading to a scarcity of research on resource efficiency in microenterprises (Alves & Dumke de Medeiros, 2015; Pardo Martínez & Cotte Poveda, 2022). While some studies (e.g., Özbuğday et al., 2020; Bodas-Freitas & Corrocher, 2019) have explored the link between resource efficiency and firm performance, there is a notable gap in understanding the specific relationship between resource efficiency and the production of green products and services in the context of microenterprises. This knowledge gap is significant as the ability to provide environmentally friendly products and services can be a crucial factor in attracting environmentally conscious consumers (Waldron, 2021) and enhancing the resilience of microenterprises against market turbulence or crises (Zulkiffli et al., 2022).

Furthermore, addressing the link between resource efficiency and the production of green products and services requires a more nuanced approach, such as configuration analysis, to help identify the various combinations of enablers that can serve as pathways for microenterprises to offer green products and services. None of the previous studies – to the best of the author's knowledge – have applied this approach to understand the unique context of microenterprises in this regard. Additionally, there is a geographical gap in research on Eastern European countries (Prokop et al., 2022; Gallego-Schmid et al., 2020), despite their recent efforts towards green transition (Estonian Investment Agency, 2023), particularly in the case of Estonia. Thus, this chapter aims to address these gaps by focusing on the enablers of resource efficiency and leveraging them as conditions that can serve as pathways for microenterprises in Estonia to offer green products and services.

This chapter is structured into five sections. Section 14.2 provides a theoretical background. The research method is explained in Sect. 14.3. Section 14.4 presents the results and discussion. Finally, Sect. 14.5 concludes and highlights the managerial implications of the study.

14.2 Theoretical Background

This section provides a brief overview of microenterprises in Estonia, how resource efficiency is conceptualised in this context, and the various enablers of resource efficiency that are related to the offering of green products and services.

14.2.1 Microenterprises in Estonia

In this chapter, microenterprises are characterised in accordance with the SMEs classification,[3] denoting businesses with less than 10 employees and an annual

[3] European Commission (2021). SME definition. https://single-market-economy.ec.europa.eu/smes/sme-definition_en. Accessed.

turnover or balance sheet total of less than €2 million. These enterprises are known for their flexibility (Ávila-Rosales et al., 2023), a crucial characteristic that allows them to adapt to changes in market conditions and customer needs (Durst et al., 2023b). This is especially advantageous in industries that are subject to rapid change or disruption, such as technology or renewable energy. In fact, microenterprises are a critical component of modern economies (Sandberg, 2003), contributing significantly to employment and overall economic growth (Peters & Brijlal, 2011). Estonia serves as an excellent example of the positive impact microenterprises can have on an economy. In 2019, microenterprises in Estonia employed a third of the workforce and accounted for nearly a third of the country's total value added (OECD, 2022). This highlights the significant role these businesses play in supporting job creation and driving economic development.

Over the past decade, there has been a consistent growth in the proportion of microenterprises in Estonia, as shown in Fig. 14.1. This increase has led to a greater overall representation of microenterprises in the country's total number of enterprises, including small and medium-sized ones. Consequently, these microenterprises collectively exert significant numerical power and influence. This increase in the proportion of microenterprises in Estonia can be attributed to the government's efforts to create a favourable business environment (Estonian Investment Agency, 2023). This includes an easy online registration system, low administrative costs,

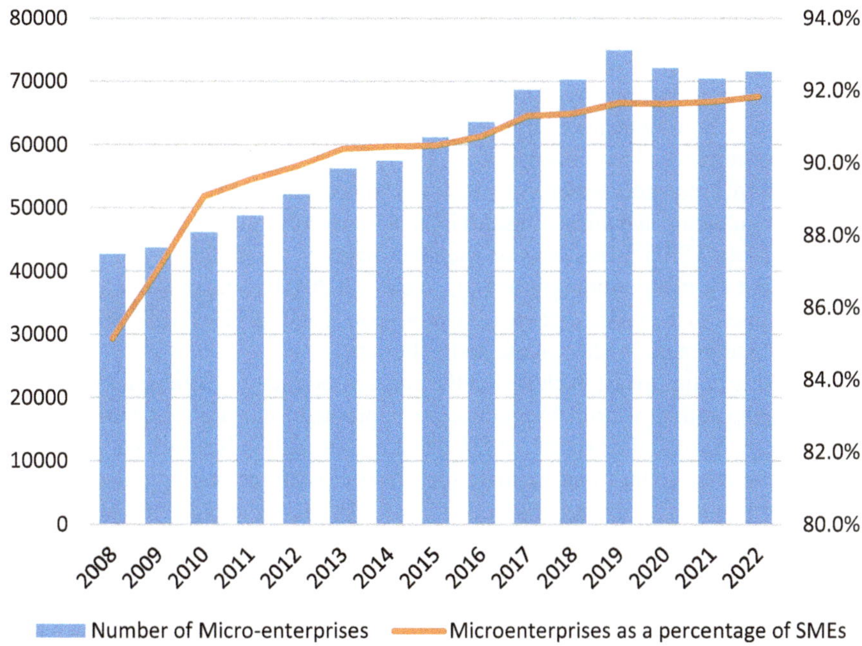

Fig. 14.1 Progressive growth of microenterprises in Estonia. (Source: Authors' compilation based on Source (Statistics Research Department (2023). Available at https://www.statista.com/statistics/879041/number-of-smes-in-estonia/))

and a flat tax system, all of which are crucial for the survival and success of microenterprises given their limited resources such as finance and expertise (Durst et al., 2022). Such policies have made entrepreneurship more accessible, even for individuals with limited financial resources or those who want to start a business part-time. Moreover, Estonia's investment in digital infrastructure has provided microenterprises with an advantage. They can easily access government services online, which saves them time and money. Additionally, Estonia's robust start-up ecosystem fosters innovation and entrepreneurship, providing microenterprises with the support they need to grow and succeed. Despite the Estonia government's efforts to create a favourable business environment, obstacles still exist for these enterprises, in particular, in implementing resource-efficient strategies (Marino & Pariso, 2020; Melece, 2016). For instance, they may lack access to necessary capital for energy efficiency measures, personnel and time, organisational responsibility, and detailed knowledge of such measures. These challenges have been highlighted in previous studies (Sorrell et al., 2000; Thollander, 2008; Thiede et al., 2013), emphasising the need to understand the combinations of resource-efficient conditions in relation to the enterprises' quest to offer green products and services.

14.2.2 Resource Efficiency

In recent years, there has been a growing interest in resource efficiency within green literature. Resource efficiency is a concept that combines the terms "resource" and "efficiency". To define resource efficiency, it is important to understand these units separately. First, the term "resource" can be classified in several ways, including as financial and non-financial (Barney, 1991), tangible and intangible (Khan et al., 2023), and human and natural (Barnabas, 1977), among others. In this context, however, the term "resource" specifically refers to "objects of nature which are extracted by man from nature and taken as useful input to man-controlled processes" (Tecchio et al., 2017, p. 1535). Efficiency, on the other hand, is the ability to achieve maximum output by using minimum input (Li et al., 2020). Hence, resource efficiency can be defined as the process of creating more goods and services while using fewer resources and generating less waste and pollution.

From this definition, it is clear that the concept of resource efficiency is closely related to the ability of firms to produce green products and services. Furthermore, studies (e.g., Yurdakul & Kazan, 2020; Corsini et al., 2019) have shown that firms can achieve cost savings and improve their overall performance by reducing their resource consumption during production. This is because the reduction in resource usage leads to less waste generation and lower energy consumption, resulting in improved efficiency. Additionally, producing green products and services can create new opportunities for growth and expansion as consumers increasingly prioritise environmentally friendly options. Firms that prioritise resource efficiency and adopt green production practices can benefit from improved reputation (Gupta & Kumar, 2013) and brand recognition (Tsai et al., 2020).

Resource efficiency actions have been empirically examined to uncover enablers or factors associated with adoption (e.g., Ghadimi et al., 2021; Sindhwani et al., 2022). These factors can be either internal to the firm or the result of external factors (Moreno-Mondéjar & Cuerva, 2020). In a combinatorial approach, the author of this study focuses on four specific enablers or conditions that can lead to the production of green products and services through resource efficiency. Each of these four conditions will be discussed in the next subsections.

14.2.2.1 Grants and Subsidies

Grants and subsidies play a critical role in promoting resource efficiency (İncekara, 2022; Hoogendoorn et al., 2015), especially for microenterprises (Bodas-Freitas & Corrocher, 2019), as they often lack the financial resources to implement resource-efficient practices on their own. In addition to reducing the cost of investment in resource efficiency measures and technologies, financial incentives like grants and subsidies can also encourage microenterprises to adopt these practices. For instance, the Estonian government provides several forms of financial support to microenterprises, including a 0% income tax rate on retained and reinvested profits (Estonian Investment Agency, 2023), as well as grants dedicated to various areas such as digital transformation, climate, energy, bio economy, and natural resources (Ahmadov et al., 2022). As a result of these initiatives, microenterprises in Estonia have seen significant success (Lahtvee, 2012), especially as consumer demand for environmentally friendly products increases and competition intensifies.

Moreover, tax breaks can also be granted to businesses that invest in resource efficiency innovations, thereby creating additional incentives for such investments (Ashton et al., 2018; Jordan et al., 2014). Research and development funding can also be provided to firms through grants and subsidies to encourage innovation and the development of new resource-efficient technologies and practices. This can lead to the creation of green products, processes, and services that not only improve environmental performance but also enhance the competitiveness of firms. As such, it is reasonable to theorise that grants and subsidies offered to microenterprises can encourage them to adopt resource-efficient practices. This establishes a connection between the financial support provided by grants and subsidies and offering of green products and services.

14.2.2.2 Demonstration of New Technologies or Processes

The act of demonstrating new technologies or processes to improve resource efficiency (Becken & Dolnicar, 2016) involves showcasing and illustrating the benefits and effectiveness of innovative approaches aimed at enhancing the efficient use of resources. This differs from investing in or leveraging new technologies or processes, which involves allocating financial resources towards acquiring, developing, or implementing such innovations (Himanshu Gupta et al., 2020). However, both approaches share a common objective of driving green initiatives particularly in the context of resource efficiency.

Previous studies (e.g., Shrivastava, 1995; Jun et al., 2021; Muñoz-Pascual et al., 2021) have established the impact of utilising new technologies or processes on green initiatives, which is not surprising. As exemplified in Kuo and Smith's (2018) review paper, companies that integrate technological advancements into their production processes are able to develop a range of ecological products. However, the investigation into the demonstration of new technologies or processes for enhancing resource efficiency has received limited scholarly attention. Based on the existing literature, this study finds it pertinent to incorporate the examination of such demonstrations as a crucial aspect in improving resource efficiency.

Given the recognised significance of investments in new technologies or processes in advancing green initiatives, alongside the relatively under-explored aspect of demonstrating new technologies or processes to enhance resource efficiency, it is theoretically reasonable to suggest that the former relationship can, in turn, promote the development and provision of green products and services.

14.2.2.3 Better Cooperation Between Companies

Cooperation between companies is essential for advancing the green policy agenda and achieving sustainability (Kundurpi et al., 2021; Pedersen, 2017; Walker & Preuss, 2008), particularly for microenterprises. While larger firms may have greater access to resources and specialised knowledge (Arora & Gambardella, 1990), microenterprises tend to face challenges even just to recruit and retain individuals with expertise in this area, i.e., sustainability, let alone the ability to conduct in-house research and development necessary for the development and implementation of resource-efficient strategies. In light of these challenges, microenterprises often depend on collaboration and partnerships with other organisations to keep up with their sustainability efforts (Brinkmann et al., 2014).

While business sustainability and its related concepts have gained significant attention in academic literature (Khan & Haleem, 2021; Prashar & Sunder, 2020) and become familiar to many organisations (microenterprises inclusive), successful implementation goes beyond mere buzzwords; it requires technical knowledge and skills (Biondi et al., 2002). Collaborative initiatives could provide microenterprises with valuable opportunities to learn from larger established companies that have successfully implemented resource-efficient practices. Through these partnerships, microenterprises can exchange insights, methodologies, and lessons learned, benefiting from the expertise and practical knowledge of their collaborative counterparts. By tapping into this shared pool of resources, microenterprises can overcome barriers and acquire the technical know-how (Biondi et al., 2002) needed to navigate the complexities of resource efficiency. This resource sharing ultimately enables microenterprises to enhance their overall resource management and improve their ability to offer green products and services.

14.2.2.4 Clearer Rules on the Use of Secondary Raw Materials

Clearer rules on the use of secondary raw materials have the potential to enhance resource efficiency (Ratner et al., 2021) and stimulate firms to offer green products and services. Secondary raw materials are materials obtained through recycling, reclamation, or recovery processes from waste or by-products (Smol et al., 2021). Transparent and well-defined rules regarding the utilisation of secondary raw materials align with the principles of a circular economy; instead of discarding used materials as waste, they are recycled, reused, and repurposed (Kowalski & Makara, 2021; Peleg Mizrachi & Tal, 2022). This reduces the dependence on primary resources and minimises waste generation.

Furthermore, clear rules on secondary raw materials create market transparency and present various opportunities for microenterprises (Gupta & Kumar, 2013). Stakeholders, including consumers, businesses, and investors, develop confidence in the sustainability and quality of products made from secondary raw materials. This increased market demand for green products and services gives microenterprises that comply with environmental standards a competitive advantage (Tsai et al., 2020). Clarity in rules allows these enterprises to distinguish themselves and attract environmentally conscious consumers, thereby enhancing their market competitiveness.

Based on these arguments, it is reasonable to state that the establishment of clearer rules regarding the use of secondary raw materials has significant implications for resource efficiency and serves as an incentive for microenterprises to offer environmentally friendly products.

14.3 Research Method

14.3.1 Data and Sample

This study utilised data extracted from the Flash Eurobarometer 456 (Small and Medium Enterprises, Resource Efficiency and Green Markets, wave 4) dataset.[4] The Flash Eurobarometer 456 dataset was produced by TNS Political & Social and co-ordinated by the European Commission's Directorate-General for Communication to investigate the actions taken by small and medium-sized enterprises (SMEs) to achieve resource efficiency, as well as to explore their potential for producing green products and services. The dataset's credibility is unquestionable, as it has been used in several published scientific papers (e.g., Darmandieu et al., 2022; Özbuğday et al., 2020).

Given that the dataset includes responses from companies in various countries, including the 28-member states of the European Union (EU) and others such as Albania, Iceland, Macedonia, Moldavia, Montenegro, Norway, Serbia, Turkey, and the United States, the author specifically selected companies from Estonia for this study. After screening the sample, it was observed that some companies had 250 or more employees, which is not surprising given the lack of consensus on what number of employees constitutes an SME across different countries (Foli et al., 2023). To address this, the European Commission's criteria for SMEs were applied to filter out only companies with less than 10 employees (microenterprise). Additionally,

[4] European Commission, B. (2018) 'Flash Eurobarometer 456 (Small and Medium Enterprises, Resource Efficiency and Green Markets, wave 4)'. GESIS Datenarchiv, Köln. ZA6917 Datenfile Version 1.0.0, https://doi.org/10.4232/1.12966

incomplete responses were removed, resulting in a final sample size of 188 usable responses for analysis. Among the 188 microenterprises included in the analysis, the services sector accounted for 28.2%, retail comprised 29.3%, industry represented approximately 26.6%, and manufacturing accounted for approximately 15.9%.

14.3.2 Measures

The measures used for the variables in this study were not developed or adapted by the author but rather by TNS Political & Social (co-ordinated by the European Commission). This organisation is known for its strict standards and protocols in data collection, which ensure the validity and reliability of the research instrument. Therefore, the measures employed in this study can be considered to follow a scientific approach and adhere to high standards in data collection.

The outcome variable, *offer green products and services (OGPS)*, is measured using a 4-point scale (1, yes; 2, no but you are planning to do so in the next 2 years; 3, no and you are not planning to do so; 4, don't know), which requires respondents to indicate whether they offer green products or services. The condition variables are measured on a binary scale (0, 1) through a general question asking: "Which of the following would help your company the most to be more resource efficient?" The options provided were:

- 0 – not mentioned; 1 – grants or subsidies (GS)
- 0 – not mentioned; 1 – demonstration of new technologies or processes (DNT)
- 0 – not mentioned; 1 – better cooperation between companies (BC); 0 – not mentioned; 1 – clearer rules on the use of secondary raw materials (CR)

14.3.3 fsQCA Analysis

The study employed the fuzzy-set qualitative comparative analysis (fsQCA) technique to analyse the data. This technique is widely used in social science research (e.g., Durst et al., 2023a, b; Kraus et al., 2018) to test theories and assumptions, particularly when dealing with small sample sizes (Ragin, 2008). FsQCA utilises Boolean algebra logic to examine the relationships between an outcome and all combinations of independent variables. To conduct the analysis, the extracted data – which include microenterprises in Estonia – was re-processed using Excel to create cases based on the NACE enterprise classification. The data was then uploaded to the fsQCA software,[5] and the 3-step process of data calibration, truth table building, and minimisation using Boolean algebra logic was followed. In the data calibration step, the maximum number of each variable was used for full membership, the

[5] Ragin, Charles C. and Sean Davey. 2022. Fuzzy-Set/Qualitative Comparative Analysis 4.0. Irvine, California: Department of Sociology, University of California.

average for cross-over, and the minimum for non-members, following Durst et al.'s (2021) recommendation. Next, the truth table building command was executed to generate all possible combinations of causal variables with the outcome variable. The truth table minimisation was then conducted to reduce the number of necessary and sufficient conditions needed to achieve the outcome of interest. During the generation of solutions, some prime implicants were found to be tied. However, given the exploratory nature of the study, which sought to identify a wide range of possible combinations of causal variables associated with the outcome, it was deemed appropriate to include all prime implicants in the analysis.

14.4 Results and Discussion

Table 14.1 displays the intermediate solution, which is the preferred choice when interpreting fsQCA results (Rihoux & Ragin, 2008), compared to the parsimonious and complex solutions. In this table, solid black circles indicate the presence of a variable (condition), white circles denote the absence or negation of a variable, and blank cells represent the irrelevance/do not care variable to the offer of green products and services.

To assess the robustness of the overall solution/model, the solution consistency and coverage statistics are analysed. First, the solution consistency surpasses the minimum threshold of 0.75, recording a value of 0.916. This indicates that the configurations established are indeed sufficient conditions that lead to the offer of green products and services (Ragin, 2008). The high consistency value suggests a strong correspondence between the model and the observed data, implying that the model can account for 96.1% of the variation in the outcome variable by considering the selected conditions or causal factors.

Second, the solution coverage is reported as 0.641, indicating that the selected causal conditions or factors in the analysis cover approximately 64.1% of the observed cases in the dataset. In other words, the model is capable of explaining a

Table 14.1 Fuzzy-set qualitative comparative analysis (fsQCA) analysis of the configurational combinations of micro firms

	Path	GS	DNT	BC	CR	Raw coverage	Unique coverage	Consistency	Solution coverage	Solution consistency
Micro firms (n = 188) [α]	A1	●	O	O		0.519	0.148	0.968	0.641	0.916
	A2		O	O	●	0.407	0.036	1.000		
	A3	●		O	●	0.400	0.029	0.906		
	A4	●	O		●	0.428	0.057	1.000		

Notes: "●" represents presence of causal conditions; "O" represents absence or negation of causal conditions; blank "..." represents "don't care" conditions; cases for α = 10, coded according to the NACE classification. *GS* grants or subsidies, *DNT* demonstration of new technologies or processes, *BC* better cooperation between companies, *CR* clearer rules on the use of secondary raw materials significant proportion (64.1%) of the cases based on the chosen conditions or factors.

Turning to the main results, it is shown that a combination of conditions such as grants and subsidies, demonstration of new technologies or processes, better cooperation between companies, and clearer rules on the use of secondary raw materials does not necessarily lead to the offering of green products and services. Instead, the results highlight that there are four distinct pathways through which resource efficiency can stimulate the provision of green products and services for microenterprises. In line with the research aim, the following paragraphs will discuss and interpret each of these pathways.

Pathway A1, which meets the minimum consistency requirement (>0.75) (Ragin, 2008), demonstrates that grants and subsidies alone can be a sufficient condition for microenterprises to offer green products and services. This suggests that in the absence of demonstrating new technologies or processes and weaker cooperation between companies, grants and subsidies can still play a significant role in motivating microenterprises to provide green offerings. Given the specific context of these enterprises, it is understandable why the government of Estonia is committed to providing necessary incentives in the form of grants and subsidies (Estonian Investment Agency, 2023), as they take a prominent role in this pathway.

Pathway A2, which also meets the minimum consistency requirement (>0.75) (Ragin, 2008), demonstrates that having clearer rules on the use of secondary raw materials alone can yield a similar outcome, even in the absence of demonstrating new technologies or processes and weaker cooperation between companies. This finding strongly supports the principles of the circular economy (Kowalski & Makara, 2021; Peleg Mizrachi & Tal, 2022). It suggests that the ability of microenterprises to provide green products and services heavily relies on the existence of well-defined regulations regarding the use of secondary raw materials. This not only creates a demand for such enterprises but also encourages them to start offering green products and services in order to generate profits while also fostering a positive perception among stakeholders, including the public (Gupta & Kumar, 2013).

Pathways A3 and *A4*, which meet the minimum consistency requirement (>0.75) (Ragin, 2008), demonstrate that the combination of grants and subsidies with clearer rules on the use of secondary raw materials leads to the offering of green products and services, even in cases of lower cooperation between companies or the absence of demonstrating new technologies or processes. This finding aligns with the underlying assumptions of grants and subsidies (Ashton et al., 2018; Jordan et al., 2014), as well as the importance of well-defined regulations regarding the use of secondary raw materials (Ratner et al., 2021), in driving microenterprises towards the realisation of offering green products and services. The combination of grants and subsidies with clearer rules, as evident in both *Pathways A3* and *A4*, reinforces the earlier findings of *Pathways A1* and *A2*, thereby emphasising the significant role played by grants, subsidies, and clearer rules on the use of secondary raw materials in motivating microenterprises to offer green products and services. Notably, across all four pathways, the absence of demonstrating new technologies or processes or weaker cooperation between companies suggests that these factors do not have a significant influence on the decision of microenterprises, particularly in Estonia, to provide green products or services.

14.5 Conclusion and Management Implications

The aim of this chapter was to explore factors that enable resource efficiency and use them as pathways for microenterprises in Estonia to offer green products and services. By using the fsQCA technique, this study revealed four distinct pathways, highlighting that grants and subsidies, along with clearer rules on the use of secondary raw materials, are sufficient conditions to motivate Estonian microenterprises to initiate the provision of green products and services. These findings hold great significance for various stakeholders, including the microenterprises themselves, the Estonian government, the European Union, and the global community.

Specifically, the identified pathways offer valuable practical insights for policymakers and industry stakeholders, highlighting the necessary steps to establish an environment that facilitates the adoption of sustainable practices by microenterprises. One effective measure is the provision of grants and subsidies, which can serve as incentives for microenterprises to embrace sustainable practices. While it is recognised that such measures may already be in place in Estonia (Estonian Investment Agency, 2023), the government agency should make a deliberate effort to increase awareness and ensure that microenterprises are adequately informed about these opportunities. By doing so, policymakers can encourage more microenterprises to take advantage of these incentives and transition towards sustainable business models.

In addition to grants and subsidies, policymakers can play a crucial role by establishing clearer guidelines on resource utilisation (Ratner et al., 2021). This involves providing microenterprises with a solid framework that outlines the best practices for incorporating sustainable measures into their operations. By offering specific guidelines and regulations, policymakers can eliminate uncertainties and ambiguities, providing microenterprises with the necessary guidance to effectively implement and integrate sustainable practices into their business processes.

By combining targeted measures such as grants and subsidies with clearer guidelines on resource utilisation, policymakers can create an environment that actively supports and encourages microenterprises in Estonia to adopt sustainable practices. This holistic approach ensures that microenterprises not only have access to financial incentives but also have the necessary knowledge and guidance to navigate the implementation of sustainable initiatives successfully. As a result, microenterprises are more likely to embrace and integrate green practices into their operations, contributing to a more sustainable and environmentally conscious business landscape in Estonia.

Given that the implications of this study extend to both policymakers and microenterprises, it is important to provide a concise summary of recommendations for each group. The following list offers practical guidance for both microenterprises and policymakers.

14.5.1 Recommendations for Policymakers

1. Develop and implement targeted policies and initiatives that specifically support and incentivise microenterprises to adopt green practices and offer environmentally friendly products and services.
2. Establish funding programs, grants, and subsidies dedicated to assisting microenterprises in implementing sustainable practices, such as energy efficiency improvements or eco-friendly product development.
3. Streamline and clarify regulations related to green practices and sustainable resource utilisation, providing clear guidelines for microenterprises to navigate and comply with.
4. Create capacity-building programs and training opportunities for microenterprises to enhance their understanding and implementation of green technologies and sustainable business practices.
5. Foster collaboration and knowledge-sharing platforms between government agencies, industry associations, and microenterprises to exchange best practices, facilitate networking, and support the development of green initiatives.

14.5.2 Recommendations for Microenterprises

1. Seek out and take advantage of available grants, subsidies, and financial incentives provided by the government to support the adoption of green practices and the development of eco-friendly products and services.
2. Stay informed about and comply with regulations and guidelines related to resource utilisation, recycling, and waste management to ensure sustainable operations.
3. Invest in training and skill development programs to enhance knowledge and expertise in green technologies, sustainable manufacturing processes, and eco-design principles.
4. Collaborate with research institutions, larger organisations, and industry partners to leverage resources, expertise, and opportunities for joint innovation and product development.
5. Explore financing options and support mechanisms available for microenterprises interested in investing in sustainable infrastructure, equipment upgrades, or renewable energy solutions.
6. Participate in networking events, trade fairs, and industry conferences to showcase your eco-friendly offerings and connect with potential buyers, suppliers, and partners.
7. Educate and engage consumers about the environmental benefits of choosing green products and services, highlighting your microenterprise's commitment to sustainability.
8. Seek guidance and support from government agencies, industry associations, and business development centres to access mentoring, advisory services, and shared facilities or resources.

Continuously monitor and evaluate the environmental impact of your operations and products, striving for continuous improvement and innovation in sustainability practices.

References

Ahmadov, T., Gerstlberger, W., & Prause, G. K. (2022). Fiscal incentives for circular economy: Insights from the Baltic States. In V. Prokop, J. Stejskal, J. Horbach, & W. Gerstlberger (Eds.), *Business models for the circular economy: A European perspective* (pp. 219–239). Springer. https://doi.org/10.1007/978-3-031-08313-6_9

Alves, J. L. S., & Dumke de Medeiros, D. (2015). Eco-efficiency in micro-enterprises and small firms: A case study in the automotive services sector. *Journal of Cleaner Production, 108*, 595–602. https://doi.org/10.1016/j.jclepro.2015.07.063

Amendolagine, V., Lema, R., & Rabellotti, R. (2021). Green foreign direct investments and the deepening of capabilities for sustainable innovation in multinationals: Insights from renewable energy. *Journal of Cleaner Production, 310*, 127381. https://doi.org/10.1016/j.jclepro.2021.127381

Arora, A., & Gambardella, A. (1990). Complementarity and external linkages: The strategies of the large firms in biotechnology. *The Journal of Industrial Economics, 38*(4), 361–379. https://doi.org/10.2307/2098345

Ashton, W. S., Panero, M. A., Izquierdo Cruz, C., & Hurtado Martin, M. (2018). Financing resource efficiency and cleaner production in Central America. *Clean Technologies and Environmental Policy, 20*(1), 53–63. https://doi.org/10.1007/s10098-017-1452-8

Ávila-Rosales, F. M., Zambrano-Alcívar, K. G., Mendoza-García, K. A., & Párraga-Zambrano, L. A. (2023). Administrative management, importance for the microenterprise. *Journal of Pharmaceutical Negative Results*, 1401–1411. https://doi.org/10.47750/pnr.2023.14.S02.170

Barnabas, A. P. (1977). Concepts and strategies for integrated development of human and natural resources. *Indian Journal of Public Administration, 23*(2), 340–348. https://doi.org/10.1177/0019556119770209

Barney, J. (1991). Firm resources and sustained competitive advantage. *Journal of Management, 17*(1), 99–120. https://doi.org/10.1177/014920639101700108

Becken, S., & Dolnicar, S. (2016). Uptake of resource efficiency measures among European small and medium-sized accommodation and food service providers. *Journal of Hospitality and Tourism Management, 26*, 45–49. https://doi.org/10.1016/j.jhtm.2015.11.001

Biondi, V., Iraldo, F., & Meredith, S. (2002). Achieving sustainability through environmental innovation: The role of SMEs. *International Journal of Technology Management, 24*(5–6), 612–626.

Bodas-Freitas, I.-M., & Corrocher, N. (2019). The use of external support and the benefits of the adoption of resource efficiency practices: An empirical analysis of European SMEs. *Energy Policy, 132*, 75–82. https://doi.org/10.1016/j.enpol.2019.05.019

Borel-Saladin, J. M., & Turok, I. N. (2013). The green economy: Incremental change or transformation? *Environmental Policy and Governance, 23*(4), 209–220. https://doi.org/10.1002/eet.1614

Brinkmann, P., Håkansson, A., Būtienė, I., Kjærsgard, H., Mortensen, B. K., Martens, J., et al. (2014). The use of networks as a strategic approach of micro-enterprises in the agri-food sector. *The International Journal of Entrepreneurship and Innovation, 15*(3), 169–178. https://doi.org/10.5367/ijei.2014.0156

Burritt, R. L., Christ, K. L., Rammal, H. G., & Schaltegger, S. (2020). Multinational enterprise strategies for addressing sustainability: The need for consolidation. *Journal of Business Ethics, 164*(2), 389–410. https://doi.org/10.1007/s10551-018-4066-0

Corsini, F., Appio, F. P., & Frey, M. (2019). Exploring the antecedents and consequences of environmental performance in micro-enterprises: The case of the Italian craft beer industry. *Technological Forecasting and Social Change, 138*, 340–350. https://doi.org/10.1016/j.techfore.2018.10.018

Darmandieu, A., Garcés-Ayerbe, C., Renucci, A., & Rivera-Torres, P. (2022). How does it pay to be circular in production processes? Eco-innovativeness and green jobs as moderators of a cost-efficiency advantage in European small and medium enterprises. *Business Strategy and the Environment, 31*(3), 1184–1203. https://doi.org/10.1002/bse.2949

Durst, S., Chowdhury, F., Davila, A., Kraus, S., & Cheng, C.-F. (2021). Employees' psychological characteristics and sustainable leadership in firms with high and low entrepreneurial orientation. *Journal of Small Business Strategy (Archive Only), 31*(3), 59–71. https://libjournals.mtsu.edu/index.php/jsbs/article/view/1987

Durst, S., Henschel, T., & Salzmann, J. (2022). Crisis management practices in small- and medium-sized firms. In S. Durst & T. Henschel (Eds.), *Crisis management for small and medium-sized enterprises (SMEs): Strategies for external crises* (pp. 15–27). Springer. https://doi.org/10.1007/978-3-030-91727-2_3

Durst, S., Davila, A., Foli, S., Kraus, S., & Cheng, C.-F. (2023a). Antecedents of technological readiness in times of crises: A comparison between before and during COVID-19. *Technology in Society, 72*, 102195. https://doi.org/10.1016/j.techsoc.2022.102195

Durst, S., Edvardsson, I. R., & Foli, S. (2023b). Knowledge management in SMEs: A follow-up literature review. *Journal of Knowledge Management, 27*(11), 25–58. https://doi.org/10.1108/JKM-04-2022-0325

Estonian Investment Agency. (2023). *The Green Transition Action Plan 2023–2025 received a lot of feedback and attention*. https://www.riigikantselei.ee/en/news/green-transition-action-plan-2023-2025-received-lot-feedback-and-attention. Accessed on August 5, 2023.

Foli, S., Durst, S., & Romero, E. D. (2023). Evaluation of operational knowledge risks in SMEs – Using a Grey-DEMATEL technique. *Journal of Information and Knowledge Management*.

Gallego-Schmid, A., Chen, H.-M., Sharmina, M., & Mendoza, J. M. F. (2020). Links between circular economy and climate change mitigation in the built environment. *Journal of Cleaner Production, 260*, 121115. https://doi.org/10.1016/j.jclepro.2020.121115

Ghadimi, P., O'Neill, S., Wang, C., & Sutherland, J. W. (2021). Analysis of enablers on the successful implementation of green manufacturing for Irish SMEs. *Journal of Manufacturing Technology Management, 32*(1), 85–109. https://doi.org/10.1108/JMTM-10-2019-0382

Gupta, S., & Kumar, V. (2013). Sustainability as corporate culture of a brand for superior performance. *Journal of World Business, 48*(3), 311–320. https://doi.org/10.1016/j.jwb.2012.07.015

Gupta, H., Kusi-Sarpong, S., & Rezaei, J. (2020). Barriers and overcoming strategies to supply chain sustainability innovation. *Resources, Conservation and Recycling, 161*, 104819. https://doi.org/10.1016/j.resconrec.2020.104819

Hoogendoorn, B., Guerra, D., & van der Zwan, P. (2015). What drives environmental practices of SMEs? *Small Business Economics, 44*(4), 759–781. https://doi.org/10.1007/s11187-014-9618-9

İncekara, M. (2022). Determinants of process reengineering and waste management as resource efficiency practices and their impact on production cost performance of small and medium enterprises in the manufacturing sector. *Journal of Cleaner Production, 356*, 131712. https://doi.org/10.1016/j.jclepro.2022.131712

Jordan, N. D., Lemken, T., & Liedtke, C. (2014). Barriers to resource efficiency innovations and opportunities for smart regulations – The case of Germany. *Environmental Policy and Governance, 24*(5), 307–323. https://doi.org/10.1002/eet.1632

Jun, W., Ali, W., Bhutto, M. Y., Hussain, H., & Khan, N. A. (2021). Examining the determinants of green innovation adoption in SMEs: A PLS-SEM approach. *European Journal of Innovation Management, 24*(1), 67–87. https://doi.org/10.1108/EJIM-05-2019-0113

Khan, S., & Haleem, A. (2021). Investigation of circular economy practices in the context of emerging economies: A CoCoSo approach. *International Journal of Sustainable Engineering, 14*(3), 357–367. https://doi.org/10.1080/19397038.2020.1871442

Khan, M., Ajmal, M. M., Jabeen, F., Talwar, S., & Dhir, A. (2023). Green supply chain management in manufacturing firms: A resource-based viewpoint. *Business Strategy and the Environment, 32*(4), 1603–1618. https://doi.org/10.1002/bse.3207

Kowalski, Z., & Makara, A. (2021). The circular economy model used in the polish agro-food consortium: A case study. *Journal of Cleaner Production, 284*, 124751. https://doi.org/10.1016/j.jclepro.2020.124751

Kraus, S., Ribeiro-Soriano, D., & Schüssler, M. (2018). Fuzzy-set qualitative comparative analysis (fsQCA) in entrepreneurship and innovation research – The rise of a method. *International Entrepreneurship and Management Journal, 14*(1), 15–33. https://doi.org/10.1007/s11365-017-0461-8

Kundurpi, A., Westman, L., Luederitz, C., Burch, S., & Mercado, A. (2021). Navigating between adaptation and transformation: How intermediaries support businesses in sustainability transitions. *Journal of Cleaner Production, 283*, 125366. https://doi.org/10.1016/j.jclepro.2020.125366

Kuo, T.-C., & Smith, S. (2018). A systematic review of technologies involving eco-innovation for enterprises moving towards sustainability. *Journal of Cleaner Production, 192*, 207–220. https://doi.org/10.1016/j.jclepro.2018.04.212

Lahtvee, V. (2012). *Resource efficiency gains and green growth perspectives in Estonia*. Friedrich-Ebert-Stiftung, Central and Eastern Europe.

Lawrence, S. R., Collins, E., Pavlovich, K., & Arunachalam, M. (2006). Sustainability practices of SMEs: The case of NZ. *Business Strategy and the Environment, 15*(4), 242–257. https://doi.org/10.1002/bse.533

Li, G., Luo, Z., Anwar, M., Lu, Y., Wang, X., & Liu, X. (2020). Intellectual capital and the efficiency of SMEs in the transition economy China: Do financial resources strengthen the routes? *PLoS One, 15*(7), e0235462. https://doi.org/10.1371/journal.pone.0235462

Marino, A., & Pariso, P. (2020). Comparing European countries' performances in the transition towards the circular economy. *Science of the Total Environment, 729*, 138142. https://doi.org/10.1016/j.scitotenv.2020.138142

Melece, L. (2016). Challenges and opportunities of circular economy and green economy. *Engineering for Rural Development, 25*, 1162–1169.

Moreno-Mondéjar, L., & Cuerva, M. C. (2020). Fostering investment in resource efficiency actions: The case of European SMEs. *Energy Efficiency, 13*(7), 1329–1351. https://doi.org/10.1007/s12053-020-09888-y

Muñoz-Pascual, L., Curado, C., & Galende, J. (2021). How does the use of information technologies affect the adoption of environmental practices in SMEs? A mixed-methods approach. *Review of Managerial Science, 15*(1), 75–102. https://doi.org/10.1007/s11846-019-00371-2

OECD. (2022). *Financing SMEs and entrepreneurs 2022*.

Özbuğday, F. C., Fındık, D., Metin Özcan, K., & Başçı, S. (2020). Resource efficiency investments and firm performance: Evidence from European SMEs. *Journal of Cleaner Production, 252*, 119824. https://doi.org/10.1016/j.jclepro.2019.119824

Papetti, A., Menghi, R., Di Domizio, G., Germani, M., & Marconi, M. (2019). Resources value mapping: A method to assess the resource efficiency of manufacturing systems. *Applied Energy, 249*, 326–342. https://doi.org/10.1016/j.apenergy.2019.04.158

Pardo Martínez, C. I., & Cotte Poveda, A. (2022). Strategies to improve sustainability: An analysis of 120 microenterprises in an emerging economy. *Global Sustainability, 5*, e3. https://doi.org/10.1017/sus.2022.3

Pedersen, C. (2017). Local authorities in dialogue with small and medium-sized enterprises. In *Small and medium-sized enterprises and the environment* (pp. 203–218). Routledge.

Peleg Mizrachi, M., & Tal, A. (2022). Regulation for promoting sustainable, fair and circular fashion. *Sustainability, 14*(1), 502. https://www.mdpi.com/2071-1050/14/1/502

Peters, R. M., & Brijlal, P. (2011). The relationship between levels of education of entrepreneurs and their business success: A study of the Province of Kwazulu-Natal, South Africa. *Industry and Higher Education, 25*(4), 265–275. https://doi.org/10.5367/ihe.2011.0048

Prashar, A., & Sunder, M. V. (2020). A bibliometric and content analysis of sustainable development in small and medium-sized enterprises. *Journal of Cleaner Production, 245*, 118665. https://doi.org/10.1016/j.jclepro.2019.118665

Prokop, V., Gerstlberger, W., Zapletal, D., & Striteska, M. K. (2022). The double-edged role of firm environmental behaviour in the creation of product innovation in Central and Eastern European countries. *Journal of Cleaner Production, 331*, 129989. https://doi.org/10.1016/j.jclepro.2021.129989

Ragin, C. (2008). *Redesigning social inquiry: Fuzzy sets and beyond*. University of Chicago Press.

Ratner, S., Gomonov, K., Lazanyuk, I., & Revinova, S. (2021). Barriers and drivers for circular economy 2.0 on the firm level: Russian case. *Sustainability, 13*(19), 11080. https://www.mdpi.com/2071-1050/13/19/11080

Rihoux, B., & Ragin, C. C. (2008). *Configurational comparative methods: Qualitative comparative analysis (QCA) and related techniques*. Sage.

Sandberg, K. W. (2003). An exploratory study of women in micro enterprises: Gender-related differences. *Journal of Small Business and Enterprise Development, 10*(4), 408–417. https://doi.org/10.1108/14626000310504710

Schanes, K., Jäger, J., & Drummond, P. (2019). Three scenario narratives for a resource-efficient and low-carbon Europe in 2050. *Ecological Economics, 155*, 70–79. https://doi.org/10.1016/j.ecolecon.2018.02.009

Shrivastava, P. (1995). Environmental technologies and competitive advantage. *Strategic Management Journal, 16*(S1), 183–200. https://doi.org/10.1002/smj.4250160923

Sindhwani, R., Kumar, R., Behl, A., Singh, P. L., Kumar, A., & Gupta, T. (2022). Modelling enablers of efficiency and sustainability of healthcare: A m-TISM approach. *Benchmarking: An International Journal, 29*(3), 767–792. https://doi.org/10.1108/BIJ-03-2021-0132

Smol, M., Marcinek, P., & Koda, E. (2021). Drivers and barriers for a circular economy (CE) implementation in Poland – A case study of raw materials recovery sector. *Energies, 14*(8), 2219. https://www.mdpi.com/1996-1073/14/8/2219

Sorrell, S., Schleich, J., Scott, S., O'Malley, E., Trace, F., Boede, U., et al. (2000). *Barriers to energy efficiency in public and private organisations: Final report to the European Commission*. University of Sussex, SPRU Environment and Energy.

Tecchio, P., McAlister, C., Mathieux, F., & Ardente, F. (2017). In search of standards to support circularity in product policies: A systematic approach. *Journal of Cleaner Production, 168*, 1533–1546. https://doi.org/10.1016/j.jclepro.2017.05.198

Thiede, S., Posselt, G., & Herrmann, C. (2013). SME appropriate concept for continuously improving the energy and resource efficiency in manufacturing companies. *CIRP Journal of Manufacturing Science and Technology, 6*(3), 204–211. https://doi.org/10.1016/j.cirpj.2013.02.006

Thollander, P. (2008). *Towards increased energy efficiency in Swedish industry: Barriers, driving forces & policies*. Linköping University Electronic Press.

Tsai, P.-H., Lin, G.-Y., Zheng, Y.-L., Chen, Y.-C., Chen, P.-Z., & Su, Z.-C. (2020). Exploring the effect of Starbucks' green marketing on consumers' purchase decisions from consumers' perspective. *Journal of Retailing and Consumer Services, 56*, 102162. https://doi.org/10.1016/j.jretconser.2020.102162

Waldron, S. (2021). *Corporate social responsibility is not public relations: How to put CSR at the heart of your company and maximize the business benefits*. LID Publishing.

Walker, H., & Preuss, L. (2008). Fostering sustainability through sourcing from small businesses: Public sector perspectives. *Journal of Cleaner Production, 16*(15), 1600–1609. https://doi.org/10.1016/j.jclepro.2008.04.014

Yurdakul, M., & Kazan, H. (2020). Effects of eco-innovation on economic and environmental performance: Evidence from Turkey's manufacturing companies. *Sustainability, 12*(8), 3167. https://www.mdpi.com/2071-1050/12/8/3167

Zulkiffli, S. N. A., Zaidi, N. F. Z., Padlee, S. F., & Sukri, N. K. A. (2022). Eco-innovation capabilities and sustainable business performance during the COVID-19 pandemic. *Sustainability, 14*(13), 7525. https://www.mdpi.com/2071-1050/14/13/7525

Position Paper: Resilience in SMEs—What Philosophy and Ethics Got to Do with It?

15

Aive Pevkur

15.1 The Value of Philosophy in Thinking of Resilience

In the broadest sense, resilience is the power of recovery. More specifically, resilience is defined as the, ability of something or someone to recover and return to normality after confronting an abnormal, alarming and often unexpected threat" (McAslan 2010), p 1). In his paper, McAslan gives an overview of the concept starting from the introduction of the term into the English language in the early 17th century until nowadays, its areas of application and characteristics. He identifies the application of the notion of resilience to organizations comparatively recent development, following its usage in reference to materials, ecosystems, and individuals, respectively—a trajectory that mirrors the historical path of resilience research.

To understand the role and function of resilience in small and medium enterprises, it needs not just the historical or linguistic understanding of the term, but also to think about the meaning (philosophical endeavor) and value (ethical exercise) of resilience in the context of SMEs. The subsequent discussion offers a brief overview of the benefits of examining resilience from these perspectives. Over the last decade, the number of research on organization resilience has grown rapidly, particularly in years of COVID-19, 2020–2022, as evidenced by a Scopus database search for *resilience and *organization.[1] However, within this same timeframe, only 112 papers addressed the topic of organizational resilience in SMEs, with the highest volume of papers (35) being published in 2023 (Table 15.1).

[1] Accessed on 18.01.2024

A. Pevkur (✉)
Tallinn University of Technology, Tallinn, Estonia
e-mail: aive.pevkur@taltech.ee

S. Durst, T. Henschel (eds.), *Small and Medium-Sized Enterprise (SME) Resilience*, Management for Professionals, https://doi.org/10.1007/978-3-031-50836-3_15

Table 15.1 The number of articles in Scopus database for *resilience and *organization and *SMEs

Year	2014	2015	2016	2017	2018	2019	2020	2021	2022	2023	In total
Resilience AND organization	491	563	656	734	914	1,095	1,387	1,751	1,801	2110	11502
Resilience AND organization AND SMEs	2	3	4	4	5	8	7	12	32	35	112

Organization management studies of the resilience predominantly focus on conceptualization and measurement of organizational resilience (Hillmann & Guenther, 2021). Most of the studies, looking at the small and medium enterprise resilience, look at building or modelling organizational resilience (Ciasullo et al., 2022; Sánchez-García et al., 2023), enhancing resilience (Zutshi et al., 2021), improving resilience (Radic et al., 2022), or on business resilience (Brown et al., 2022) or business model resilience (Radic et al., 2022).

Despite the focus on fortifying resilience in SMEs, many studies pay less heed to the concept itself. As Hillmann and Guenther admit, researchers criticize the concept for being fuzzy and, therefore, lacking a consistent definition, which reduces the significance of the concept for practice and research (Hillmann & Guenther, 2021). Vogus and Sutcliffe propose a definition of resilience as "the maintenance of positive adjustment under challenging conditions such that the organization emerges from those conditions strengthened and more resourceful" (p. 3418). They continue, "resiling from ongoing strain and discrete jolts implies the presence of latent resources that can be activated, combined, and recombined in new situations as challenges arise. As such, resilience implies more than a specific adaptation. This doesn't mean that competence in one period wholly predicts later competence in a linear deterministic way; rather competence in one period increases the probability of competence in the next" (ibid). That means resilience is not just one competence the organization can acquire and implement but rather that to be resilient, it needs a complex amalgamation of qualities that endow an organization with resilience, often recognized only post hoc. A good organizational crisis or risk or safety management does not safeguard or prepare organizations for small internal or external interruptions which might threat the enterprise. Vogus and Sutcliffe (2007) call that "the inherent fallibility of any organizational system." Resilience could, thus, be viewed as a mindset which expects not just knowing the nature of business but also acknowledging the indefinite and turbulent environment.

In entrepreneurship, resilience is conceptualized as the ability to react and positively adapt a venture within the context of adversity and uncertainty (Santos et al., 2023). It is the ability to withstand and anticipate adversity and make changes that ensure the survival of the company, even in challenging circumstances. This can open opportunities for new growth through quick adaptation to changing situations. However, the question remains: Is it feasible to prepare for all possible challenges?

According to McAslan, organizational resilience aims to bring tasks and activities like strategic and operational plans and programs which address risk, business continuity, security, emergencies, and crises, together as a single process—one that sits at the very center of an organization's management ethos and way of operating (McAslan, 2010, p. 7). Underlying the studies on resilience seems to be a hidden assumption that having more information and knowledge enables to foresee problems and foster resilience.

The Enlightenment era heralded the maxim that knowledge is power. The belief that knowing more and having more management systems can prevent collapse represents the linear, deterministic view to the situation. Paradoxically, despite the rapid increase of organizational resilience studies in years 2020–2021, the number of bankruptcies in SMEs increased significantly (OECD, 2021).

Resilience seems to be a distinct concept in organizational studies; it does not offer a specific structure or guideline for organizations but rather resembles organizational culture, embodying intangible aspects. Vogus and Sutcliffe point out that resilience inheres in beliefs as well as affective, behavioral, and cognitive processes (Vogus & Sutcliffe, 2007). Thus, it reminds us that not all features influencing the entrepreneurship can be controlled. Embracing a resilience mindset alerts entrepreneurs to the impossibility of controlling all the aspects of business sustainability. Successful organizations acknowledge that. Vogus and Sutcliffe describe that attitude as the carefulness for the unexpected and admitting the imperfection (ibid). It can be inferred, therefore, that resilient organizations must embrace a degree of fatalism, acknowledging that not everything occurring in business can be controlled. This acceptance necessitates a certain philosophical-metaphysical perspective on conducting business.

The subsequent question is, how can a mindset conducive to resilience be cultivated? An intriguing approach is provided by Jeyansingam by introducing the study on tutorial intervention to encourage resilience among medical students (Jeyasingam, 2022). He posits that by asking and contemplating philosophical questions such as "What is medicine?" or "Why medicine is difficult?" promotes an approach to address uncertainty, thereby encouraging students to develop mature defense mechanisms for problem-solving. By analogy, asking questions such as "What is entrepreneurship?" or "Why doing business is difficult?" might lead to develop a more metaphysical approach to conducting business, thereby fostering resilience in SMEs. As mentioned above, resilience is linked more to organizational culture, its intangible aspects than to measurable criteria or statistics. Kampmann and Pedell convincingly demonstrate in their study that "individuals will invest more in a resilience-promoting activity when they receive information about a risk factor in story rather than in statistical form" (Kampmann & Pedell, 2022, pp. 714–715). That leads to the Socratic endeavor that to be resilient, to act in a way to increase resilience in SMEs, one should think about the concept and the value of resilience. This consideration leads us to the realm of ethics, especially to organizational ethos as a set of grounding values, moral beliefs, and attitudes in companies, as McAslan (2010) put resilience at the very center of an organization's management ethos and way of operating.

15.2 Ethics and Resilience: Unveiling the Connection

Resilience, when considered in conjunction with ethics, is primarily discussed from a personal perspective as moral resilience (Lachman, 2016; Schroeter, 2017), defined as the ability and willingness to speak and take right and good action in the face of an adversity that is moral/ethical in nature.

In organizational contexts, ethics revolves around the management of certain values, which are integrated into the organizational culture. In SMEs, the role of ethics and values often exists in a latent state. The set of values might be implicit or explicit and could include resilience as a core value.

Studies on resilience in SMEs have been ongoing for more than a decade (Sullivan-Taylor & Branicki, 2011; Branicki et al., 2018). However, these studies primarily involve analyzing data collected within organizations and then interpreting it from a theoretical perspective. Depending on the researcher's framework, the focus could be on identifying and understanding the indicators used to evaluate organizational resilience (Rahi, 2018) or exploring the role of a "Culture of Excellence" in cultivating resilience within the organization (Joseph et al., 2022). Kotsios provides an overview of recent studies conducted at both micro and macro levels, delving into business resilience (Kotsios, 2023).

A common pattern observed in these studies is that the researcher assesses the state of resilience within the enterprise, but there appears to be a lack of emphasis on an internal approach from the perspective of the SME itself, its values or culture. In other words, the studies tend to focus more on external evaluations of resilience rather than examining how SMEs understand, perceive, and cultivate resilience as a core value within their own organizational culture. Regrettably, the author was unable to locate any studies that specifically address the core values of SMEs, which would provide insights into whether resilience is considered a core value or if there is evidence of managerial or organizational discussions about resilience within SMEs.

To investigate how resilience as a value manifests in practice, using Socratic method and asking philosophical questions might be considered as one of the possible strategies. This hypothesis was tested in an episodic interview with the CEO of an SME. The CEO was discovered through personal contacts, and the selection criteria focused on finding someone whose company had recently experienced unpredictable changes. The method was chosen as "the starting point for the episodic interview is the assumption that subjects' experiences of a certain domain are stored and remembered in forms of narrative-episodic and semantic knowledge. Whereas episodic knowledge is organized closer to experiences and linked to concrete situations and circumstances, semantic knowledge is based on concepts, assumptions and relations which are abstracted from these and generalized. …The episodic interview yields context-related presentations in the form of a narrative, because these are closer to experiences and their generative context than other presentational forms" (Flick, 2014, pp. 273–274). The interviewee was encouraged to tell a story of his company (background information) and the current situation, and concerning his understanding of resilience, concrete pointed questions ("What does 'resilience' mean for you?" "How your company can be resilient?") were asked. In

April 2023, the author conducted an in-person interview where the respondent's answers were recorded in writing, and then the respondent was asked to review and confirm the text.

The company with approximately 50 employees operates in the technology sector and the international market. The CEO has more than 15 years of experience in the field. The CEO recently had to lay off 15 employees due to unpredictable changes in the economic environment and required cost reduction in order to maintain viability.

When asked, "What does 'resilience' mean for you?" the CEO replied:

> It is the ability to make changes that ensure the survival of the company, even when times are tough. This can open opportunities for new growth and quick adaptation to changing circumstances.

To the question how to be resilient, he explained:

> The starting point is to have an understanding of what might happen, such as predicting sales results. If the situation is difficult to predict, various scenarios can be played out—good, very good, bad, very bad—to determine how the company will survive. On one hand, surviving in adverse circumstances often necessitates cutting costs and, regrettably, laying off employees. On the other hand, reducing the workforce below a critical level can be dangerous for the company, as processes may no longer function properly. It is necessary to consider how to redesign or change processes, such as reviewing customer segments. The emotional aspect of employees is also important, as their resilience affects those who remain. Motivation may decline in the short term due to an increase in workload and the inability to reorganize the work effectively.

> Employees want to be successful and contribute to a successful company. Layoffs are perceived as a sign that the company is struggling and in danger, which may cause employees to consider leaving. Motivation declines. Cost reduction was necessary to ensure the survival of the company, and the company's position has improved as a result. The primary risk is that costs are too high, which creates secondary risks such as processes, employees, and communication. Resilience is necessary for employees to assess and cope with the situation. At the same time, the company experienced its most successful quarter of the year, although it was clear that the business environment would remain unstable for the rest of the year. For employees, to whom everything seemed fine, it was a big shock.

The CEO's responses reveal that even though the company and its leadership have not explicitly engaged with the concept of resilience (in his own words), by posing these questions, characteristics of a resilient organization, such as readiness for the unexpected and acknowledgment of imperfection, surfaced.

Resilience is not an intrinsic value, but rather a result of preparedness. It depends on the readiness to make swift decisions and adapt to new circumstances. This readiness ensures resilience, but it must be considered beforehand. In a crisis, action takes precedence over deliberation. The readiness of leaders in SMEs for quick responses and decisions that increase resilience expects preparedness. Are the companies resilient enough to endure difficult times, or are they simply mercenaries? Companies with vision, who acknowledge changing circumstances, are resilient.

15.3 Concluding Remarks

In conclusion, the concept of resilience in Small and Medium-sized Enterprises (SMEs) is a multifaceted one, necessitating a philosophical and ethical exploration to enrich our understanding and application of it in practice. The study demonstrated that resilience extends beyond mere crisis management, serving as a complex set of organizational qualities that form an intangible cultural mindset. This mindset embraces the inherent fallibility of any organizational system and acknowledges the unpredictable nature of the business environment. A resilient organization, therefore, is not only prepared for unexpected challenges but also embodies a degree of fatalism. The investigation further highlighted the significance of ethics in resilience, advocating for the integration of resilience into an organization's ethos. In light of the dynamic and volatile global business landscape, there is a pressing need for more theoretical-ethical and philosophical studies to broaden the discourse on resilience. This study was a modest attempt in that direction, underscoring the importance of asking the right philosophical questions and fostering a resilience-oriented ethos in SMEs. However, much more research is required to fully understand the philosophical and ethical dimensions of resilience in SMEs. Future research should continue to delve into these aspects and contribute to developing robust, resilient enterprises capable of navigating an ever-evolving and turbulent business world.

References

Branicki, L. J., et al. (2018). How entrepreneurial resilience generates resilient SMEs. *International Journal of Entrepreneurial Behavior & Research, 24*(7), 1244–1263. https://doi.org/10.1108/IJEBR-11-2016-0396

Brown, K., et al. (2022). Factors impacting SME business resilience post-COVID-19. *Sustainability, 14*(22), 14850. https://doi.org/10.3390/su142214850

Ciasullo, M. V., et al. (2022). Building SMEs' resilience in times of uncertainty: The role of big data analytics capability and co-innovation. *Transforming Government: People, Process and Policy, 16*(2), 203–217. https://doi.org/10.1108/tg-07-2021-0120

Flick, U. (2014). *An introduction to qualitative research* (Edition 5). Sage.

Hillmann, J., & Guenther, E. (2021). Organizational resilience: A valuable construct for management research? *International Journal of Management Reviews, 23*(1), 7–44. https://doi.org/10.1111/ijmr.12239

Jeyasingam, N. (2022). Philosophy for resilience: A meaningful intervention for medical students. *Journal of Academic Ethics, 20*(1), 67–72. https://doi.org/10.1007/s10805-021-09394-5

Joseph, N., et al. (2022). Fostering resilience through the culture of excellence (CoE) practices: Explorative insights from a talent management SME. *Measuring Business Excellence, 26*(2), 163–179. https://doi.org/10.1108/MBE-06-2021-0082

Kampmann, A., & Pedell, B. (2022). Using storytelling to promote organizational resilience: An experimental study of different forms of risk communication. *Schmalenbach Journal of Business Research, 74*(4), 695–725. https://doi.org/10.1007/s41471-022-00143-x

Kotsios, P. (2023). Business resilience skills for SMEs. *Journal of Innovation and Entrepreneurship, 12*(1), 37. https://doi.org/10.1186/s13731-023-00304-0

Lachman, V. D. (2016). Moral resilience: Managing and preventing moral distress and moral residue. *Medsurg Nursing, 25*(2), 121–124.

McAslan, A. (2010). *The concept of resilience: Understanding its origins, meaning and utility* (p. 1). Torrens Resilience Institute.

OECD. (2021). *Bankruptcies in 2020 and 2021 vs. 2019*. https://doi.org/10.1787/e0fb3c2c-en

Radic, M., et al. (2022). Development of a business model resilience framework for managers and strategic decision-makers. *Schmalenbach Journal of Business Research, 74*(4), 575–601. https://doi.org/10.1007/s41471-022-00135-x

Rahi, K. (2018). Indicators to assess organizational resilience—A review of empirical literature. *International Journal of Disaster Resilience in the Built Environment, 10*(2/3), 85–98. https://doi.org/10.1108/IJDRBE-11-2018-0046

Sánchez-García, J. Y., et al. (2023). Modeling organizational resilience in SMEs: A system dynamics approach. *Global Journal of Flexible Systems Management, 24*(1), 29–50. https://doi.org/10.1007/s40171-022-00322-z

Santos, S. C., et al. (2023). How digitalization reinvented entrepreneurial resilience during COVID-19. *Technological Forecasting and Social Change, 189*, 122398. https://doi.org/10.1016/j.techfore.2023.122398

Schroeter, K. (2017). Ethics in practice: From moral distress to moral resilience. *Journal of Trauma Nursing, 24*(5), 290–291. https://doi.org/10.1097/JTN.0000000000000317

Sullivan-Taylor, B., & Branicki, L. (2011). Creating resilient SMEs: Why one size might not fit all. *International Journal of Production Research, 49*(18), 5565–5579. https://doi.org/10.1080/00207543.2011.563837

Vogus, T. J., & Sutcliffe, K. M. (2007). Organizational resilience: Towards a theory and research agenda. In *2007 IEEE international conference on systems, man and cybernetics*. https://doi.org/10.1109/ICSMC.2007.4414160

Zutshi, A., et al. (2021). From challenges to creativity: Enhancing SMEs' resilience in the context of COVID-19. *Sustainability, 13*(12), 6542. https://doi.org/10.3390/su13126542

Part III

Conclusions & Outlook

Conclusions and Outlook 16

Susanne Durst and Thomas Henschel

16.1 Avenues for Further Research

As has been shown throughout this book and in previous research, the rigorous study of resilience in and for SMEs is of a recent nature and our body of knowledge can be viewed as fragmented at most. Despite recent developments pushed by the pandemic and the war in Ukraine, there is still little in the existing literature on the practice of resilience. This refers to the use of methods, approaches, and solutions. Thus, the content presented in this book can be considered as relevant and timely contributions to address this situation by providing some new insights in the field/related fields which in turn can help in both enlarging and deepening our extant knowledge base.

With this in mind, the main idea of this concluding chapter is to identify further research opportunities for people (e.g., established academics, early career researchers, but also practitioners) interested in researching and advancing the topic of resilience in general and resilience in and for SMEs in particular, thus contributing to the further development of the field.

Table 16.1 presents a number of proposals that are divided into different broad topics which are followed by (1) research areas that could be addressed and (2) proposals of concrete research questions. The proposed topics/themes are further

S. Durst (✉)
Reykjavik University, Reykjavik, Iceland
e-mail: susanned@ru.is

T. Henschel (✉)
Hochschule für Technik und Wirtschaft Berlin, University of Applied Sciences, Berlin, Germany
e-mail: henschel@htw-berlin.de

S. Durst, T. Henschel (eds.), *Small and Medium-Sized Enterprise (SME) Resilience*, Management for Professionals, https://doi.org/10.1007/978-3-031-50836-3_16

Table 16.1 List of resilience research avenues

Topic	Suggestions	Research questions
General		
Operationalization of the term(s)	Researchers in the field should provide their understanding of the resilience concept to demonstrate definitional rigor which in turn would facilitate a comparison among studies and their findings.	Is a phase model useful for addressing resilience in SMEs? If not, what would be alternative models to study resilience in SMEs? What are the relationships between different resilience concepts (internal and external ones)? And what does that mean for resilience in SMEs?
Methodology	Development/test of frameworks/models/taxonomies by applying alternative and different research approaches (i.e., different designs, different/alternative data collection methods/different datasets). For example, Delphi rounds among actors from SMEs, government, and academia to understand the perception of resilience concepts and its elements.	What are suitable research methods for studying resilience in different environments/overtime/types of SMEs? What are suitable units of analysis? How to combine these units of analysis in the best way?
Level of analysis	Utilization of multilevel perspective to uncover the underlying factors associated with the effective achievement of resilience in SMEs	What are suitable levels of analysis for studying resilience in SMEs? What are suitable research methods for studying resilience from different levels of analysis? What are the consequences of missing resilience at different levels (individual/group/organization/society)?
Location and composition of research teams	Research would benefit from a broader variety of researchers coming from different parts of the world. Research teams should involve researchers from different countries and disciplines.	What role does the culture play in carrying out SME resilience research projects? How and in what way can resilience research benefit from cross-cultural and interdisciplinary research teams?

(continued)

Table 16.1 (continued)

Topic	Suggestions	Research questions
Specific		
Awareness-raising	Awareness about the need for managing different resilience strategies in all types of SMEs	How to disseminate the awareness about risks, crises, and their management among all organization members? How to develop a resilience-aware mindset in different types of SMEs? How to develop a resilience-aware culture in different types of SMEs? How to develop and execute resilience related training programs in SMEs? Who should be in charge of running these programs?
Resilience and performance	Cross-country perspective Cross-culture perspective Cross-sector perspective Different types of performance	How can the performance of resilience in SMEs be measured? What measures might be useful and applicable? What are trade-offs between resilience practices and performance? How do resilience efforts lead to performance?
Resilience and leadership	The strategic view of resilience in SMEs Leadership approaches to resilience in different types of small firms/cultures/sectors	Are there different types of resilience strategies in organizations? If yes, what are they? Do/does the resilience strategies/strategy vary between different types of organizations/countries? What makes a leader a resilient leader? How to develop this type of leaders? In which situations do these leaders excel the most?

(continued)

Table 16.1 (continued)

Topic	Suggestions	Research questions
Resilience and culture	Cross-country perspective Cross-culture perspective Cross-sector perspective	How do different countries vary in their approaches to resilience? What business cultures are beneficial for the implementation of resilience concepts? How to develop resilience-related cultures? How to update these resilience-related cultures continuously to meet changing environments?
Resilience and governance	Structures Mechanisms Processes Decision-making	How and in what way can the resilience concept be integrated into small firms' governance framework? How to govern for present and future risks and crises in the best possible way?
Resilience and digitalization/digital transformation	Resilience systems in organizations for digitalization/digital transformation	What resilience frameworks support the digital transformation of organizations? What digital solutions/techniques support resilience, its effectiveness in particular? What supports/hampers the realization of these resilience systems?
Resilience and gamification	Use of gamification to enhance the effectiveness and efficiency of resilience strategies in SMES	Can selected game mechanics be used to solve the issue of lacking motivation in resilience? Can selected game mechanisms be implemented in order to provide organizations with a clearly structured resilience process, allowing for revelation of tacit knowledge and its free exchange? Can selected game mechanics facilitate a setting in which cognitive biases are reduced?

(continued)

Table 16.1 (continued)

Topic	Suggestions	Research questions
Resilience and Human Resource Management (HRM)	Resilience as an early warning system for skills shortage, skills at risk, or need for reskilling/upskilling	How to design a resilience solution that help smaller firms address present and future skills needs? How to integrate resilience in a small firm's HRM in general and its activities regarding skills identification, skills development, and skills retention in particular? Does succession planning/people replacement benefit from resilience approaches and vice versa?
Resilience and communication	Resilience communication (internally and externally)	How to communicate about risks and crises to different stakeholders? What channels should be used? What communication elements work best for reaching the different stakeholders? Who in smaller firms should be in charge of resilience communication? How to align the different communication activities in SMEs?
Resilience and sustainability/circular economy	Resilience as an essential function to become a sustainable organization Resilience as an essential function to address the opportunities and challenges related to sustainability Resilience as an antecedent for sustainability/transition to circular economy	Can resilience efforts support SMEs reach their sustainability-related aims? Can resilience help in getting insights into the benefits of the organizations' sustainability activities? Can the resilience concept support organizations in complying with sustainability-related laws and regulations? How does resilience contribute to sustainability/transformation to circular economy and vice versa?
Resilience and Artificial Intelligence (AI)	AI to integrate the risk management and crisis management activities into a holistic resilience system for the entire organization	How can generative AI tools and frameworks support the integration of risk and crisis management into holistic resilience system in SMEs? How can generative AI tool improve the resilience efforts of SMEs?

divided into general topics which highlight ideas for the field's theoretical (further) development and specific topics that address areas of application.

The content of Table 16.1 has been compiled as an outcome of the content presented in this book and the book editors' own past and ongoing research activities in the area under investigation as well as related ones.

The content of Table 16.1 clarifies that the study of resilience has much to offer and would highly benefit from interdisciplinary research teams or research efforts, respectively, as resilience is an interface topic that should be solidly anchored in any smaller organization's governance and business model(s).

As shown throughout the book, research on resilience should (and can) be conducted in all types of SMEs, i.e., micro-, small-, and medium-sized enterprises, as well as start-ups and mature companies. Overall, each of the chapters included in this book provides a unique perspective on resilience and offers valuable insights for organizations seeking to build their resilience concept. However, there is tension between the need for a comprehensive and more nuanced understanding of resilience and practical and actionable frameworks that can be applied in real-world SME contexts. SME decision-makers must balance these competing needs to manage risks and respond to adversity effectively and proactively.

Given the importance of resilience in SMEs, there is a need for further research to examine the factors that contribute to resilience, as well as the impact of external shocks on the resilience of SMEs. More research could support practitioners, policymakers, and SME consultants to develop strategies to support the resilience of SMEs, which is critical for economic development and growth. We hope that the readers of this book agree with us on this need and are (even) willing and prepared to go on from here.

Index

S. Durst, T. Henschel (eds.), *Small and Medium-Sized Enterprise (SME) Resilience*, Management for Professionals, https://doi.org/10.1007/978-3-031-50836-3

GPSR Compliance
The European Union's (EU) General Product Safety Regulation (GPSR) is a set of rules that requires consumer products to be safe and our obligations to ensure this.

If you have any concerns about our products, you can contact us on

ProductSafety@springernature.com

In case Publisher is established outside the EU, the EU authorized representative is:

Springer Nature Customer Service Center GmbH
Europaplatz 3
69115 Heidelberg, Germany

www.ingramcontent.com/pod-product-compliance
Ingram Content Group UK Ltd.
Pitfield, Milton Keynes, MK11 3LW, UK
UKHW022215051026
15624UKWH00001B/169
* 9 7 8 3 0 3 1 5 0 8 3 5 6 *